ÉCRITS

A Selection

BY JACQUES LACAN

Television

Feminine Sexuality

The Seminar of Jacques Lacan, edited by Jacques-Alain Miller

JACQUES LACAN
ÉCRITS
A SELECTION

TRANSLATED BY
BRUCE FINK

IN COLLABORATION WITH
HÉLOÏSE FINK
AND
RUSSELL GRIGG

W. W. Norton & Company
New York • London

For information about permission to reproduce selections from this book, write to
Permissions, W. W. Norton & Company, Inc., 500 Fifth Avenue, New York, NY 10110

Manufacturing by Quebecor Fairfield

Library of Congress Cataloging-in-Publication Data

Lacan, Jacques, 1901–
[Ecritis. English. Selections.]
Ecritis : a selection / Jacques Lacan ; translated by Bruce Fink in collaboration with
Héloïse Fink and Russell Grigg.
p. cm.
Includes bibliographical references and indexes.
ISBN 0-393-05058-0
1. Psychoanalysis. I. Fink, Bruce, 1956– II. Title.

BF173.L14213 2002
150.19'5—dc21   2002026372

ISBN 0-393-32528-8 pbk.

W. W. Norton & Company, Inc., 500 Fifth Avenue, New York, N.Y. 10110
www.wwnorton.com

W. W. Norton & Company Ltd., Castle House, 75/76 Wells Street, London W1T 3QT

1 2 3 4 5 6 7 8 9 0

Table of Contents

Acknowledgments

My work on this translation received support from several quarters: from Jacques-Alain Miller, the general editor of Lacan's work in France and head of the École de la Cause Freudienne, who approved the project back in 1994; from the National Endowment for the Humanities, which committed $90,000 over the course of three years to prepare this new translation; from the Society for the Humanities at Cornell University, where I was a fellow during the 1997–1998 academic year and released from my usual teaching and administrative responsibilities; and last but far from least, from Duquesne University, where I teach, which generously reduced my teaching load and provided financial backing throughout much of the project. At Duquesne I would especially like to thank Drs. Constance Ramirez, Andrea Lex, William Fischer, Russell Walsh, and the late Michael Weber for their unfailing efforts on my behalf.

Translator's Note

The translation provided here is entirely new. It originated as part of a larger project, that of preparing a complete English version of the twenty-nine major texts and six introductions and appendices included in *Écrits* (Paris: Éditions du Seuil, 1966), only nine of which were included in the original *Écrits: A Selection* (New York: Norton, 1977). This new *Selection* is the first fruit of this more encompassing endeavor.

Given the degree to which Lacan's texts have been—and will continue to be, I suspect—subjected to close readings, I have been careful to respect his terminology as much as possible. I have translated here with the notion that the repetition of terms from one sentence to the next, from one paragraph to the next, and from one text to the next, may be springboards for future interpretations and have attempted to either repeat them identically in the translation or at least provide the French in brackets or endnotes so that the repetition is not lost.

All paragraph breaks here correspond to Lacan's, and the original French pagination is included in the margins to facilitate comparison with the French text, referred to throughout as "*Écrits* 1966." The footnotes included at the end of each text are Lacan's, several of which were added in the smaller, two-volume edition published in the Points collection by Seuil in 1970 and 1971 as *Écrits I* and *Écrits II*, referred to throughout simply as "Points." Words or phrases followed by an asterisk (*) are given by Lacan

in English in the French original. Translator's interpolations are placed in
square brackets and translator's notes are included at the back of the book,
keyed to the marginal French pagination. Although the texts are placed in
chronological order, they were written for very different occasions and
audiences and need not be read in any specific order (indeed, I'd recom-
mend starting with "Function and Field").

Collaborators

Héloïse Fink was a constant collaborator throughout this project, hashing
out difficult formulations and constructions with me day in and day out,
comparing the French and English line by line, and researching obscure
terms and expressions. She helped me avoid myriad pitfalls, and together we
explored the ways in which two languages encounter and miss each other.

Russell Grigg, Psychoanalyst and Professor of Philosophy at Deakin
University in Australia, provided innumerable corrections, alternative readings, and recommendations concerning style on the basis of his close comparison of the French and English texts in their entirety. He made a very
substantial contribution to the finished product.

A number of other people helped me struggle with Lacan's texts on a more
occasional basis. Jacques-Alain Miller graciously devoted a couple of after-
noons to assisting me with some of Lacan's more difficult formulations;
Slavoj Zizek advised me on a number of Hegelian references; Richard Klein
(Cornell University) supplied insight into several passages; Henry Sullivan
(University of Missouri-Columbia) provided useful comments on "The
Mirror Stage"; Marc Silver made valuable suggestions regarding "Function
and Field"; Mario Beira gave helpful feedback on "Direction of the
Treatment"; Yael Goldman and Thomas Svolos provided a number of ref-
erences; and Anette Schwarz and Suzanne Stewart assisted me with several
Latin phrases. Margot Backas at the National Endowment for the
Humanities and Susan Buck-Morss at Cornell University supported this
project in more ways than one.
     I have also looked to several published sources for help with refer-
ences, including Anthony Wilden's early translation of Lacan's "The
Function and Field of Speech and Language in Psychoanalysis" in *The
Language of the Self* (Baltimore: Johns Hopkins University Press, 1975),
William Richardson and John Muller's *Lacan and Language* (New York:

International Universities Press, 1982), and Alan Sheridan's 1977 version of *Écrits: A Selection*. The first two provide far more notes than I could include here and readers may find their additional notes useful. I have checked the notes I have borrowed for further corroboration and my judgment will sometimes be seen to differ from theirs.

Despite input from several collaborators and consultation of varied sources (my favorites being the recent *Robert: Dictionnaire historique de la langue française* and the voluminous *Trésor de la langue française*), numerous errors no doubt remain. Lacan's incredibly broad background and in-depth knowledge of psychiatry, psychoanalysis, philosophy, mathematics, and literature are such that I have surely misunderstood specialized terminology, overlooked references to specific authors, and just generally misinterpreted the French—Lord knows it's easy enough to do given Lacan's singular style! Readers who believe they have found mistakes of whatever kind are encouraged to send comments to me via the publisher. I consider this translation a work in progress, and hope to improve on the texts here in the complete edition.

Bruce Fink

Abbreviations Used in the Text

GW   *Gesammelte Werke* (Sigmund Freud)
IJP   *International Journal of Psycho-Analysis*
IPA   International Psycho-Analytical Association
PQ   *Psychoanalytic Quarterly*
PUF   Presses Universitaires de France
SE   *Standard Edition of the Complete Psychological Works of Sigmund Freud*

Bibliographical References in
Chronological Order

The Mirror Stage as Formative of the I *Function*
An early version of this paper was delivered at the Fourteenth International Congress of Psychoanalysis in Marienbad on August 2–8, 1936, with Ernest Jones presiding. It was part of the second scientific session held on August 3 at 3:40 P.M., and was listed under the title "The Looking-glass Phase" in *IJP* XVIII, 1 (1937): 78. The present version was delivered on July 17, 1949, in Zurich at the Sixteenth International Congress of Psychoanalysis, and was published in *Revue Française de Psychanalyse* 4 (1949): 449–55.

Aggressiveness in Psychoanalysis
Theoretical paper presented in Brussels in mid-May 1948 at the Eleventh Congress of French-Speaking Psychoanalysts. It was published in *Revue Française de Psychanalyse* 3 (1948): 367–88.

The Function and Field of Speech and Language in Psychoanalysis
Paper presented at the Rome Congress held at the Institute of Psychology at the University of Rome on September 26 and 27, 1953. It was published in *La Psychanalyse* 1 (1956): 81–166.

The Freudian Thing, or the Meaning of the Return to Freud in Psychoanalysis
An expanded version of a lecture given at the Vienna Neuropsychiatric Clinic on November 7, 1955. It came out in *L'Évolution Psychiatrique* 1 (1956): 225–52.

The Instance of the Letter in the Unconscious, or Reason Since Freud
Lecture given on May 9, 1957, in the Descartes Amphitheater at the Sorbonne, at the request of the philosophy group of the Fédération des étudiants ès Lettres. The paper was written up May 14–16, 1957, and published in *La Psychanalyse* 3 (1957): 47–81, the theme of the volume being "Psychoanalysis and the Sciences of Man."

On a Question Prior to Any Possible Treatment of Psychosis
This article contains the most important material from the first two terms of the 1955–1956 seminar, *The Psychoses*. It was written up in December 1957 and January 1958, and came out in *La Psychanalyse* 4 (1959): 1–50.

*The Signification of the Phallus (*Die Bedeutung des Phallus*)*
Lecture given in German on May 9, 1958, at the Max Planck Society in Munich, at the invitation of Professor Paul Matussek.

The Direction of the Treatment and the Principles of Its Power
This is the first of two papers Lacan presented at the Royaumont International Colloquium held July 10–13, 1958, at the invitation of the Société Française de Psychanalyse. It was published in *La Psychanalyse* 6 (1961): 149–206.

The Subversion of the Subject and the Dialectic of Desire in the Freudian Unconscious
Contribution to a conference on "La Dialectique," held in Royaumont September 19–23, 1960, at the invitation of Jean Wahl. The conference was organized by the "Colloques philosophiques internationaux."

ÉCRITS

A Selection

The Mirror Stage as Formative of the *I* Function

as Revealed in Psychoanalytic Experience

Delivered on July 17, 1949, in Zurich at the Sixteenth International
Congress of Psychoanalysis

The conception of the mirror stage I introduced at our last congress thirteen years ago, having since been more or less adopted by the French group, seems worth bringing to your attention once again—especially today, given the light it sheds on the *I* function in the experience psychoanalysis provides us of it. It should be noted that this experience sets us at odds with any philosophy directly stemming from the *cogito*.

Some of you may recall the behavioral characteristic I begin with that is explained by a fact of comparative psychology: the human child, at an age when he is for a short while, but for a while nevertheless, outdone by the chimpanzee in instrumental intelligence, can already recognize his own image as such in a mirror. This recognition is indicated by the illuminative mimicry of the *Aha-Erlebnis*, which Köhler considers to express situational apperception, an essential moment in the act of intelligence.

Indeed, this act, far from exhausting itself, as in the case of a monkey, in eventually acquired control over the uselessness of the image, immediately gives rise in a child to a series of gestures in which he playfully experiences the relationship between the movements made in the image and the reflected environment, and between this virtual complex and the reality it duplicates—namely, the child's own body, and the persons and even things around him.

This event can take place, as we know from Baldwin's work, from the age

94   of six months on; its repetition has often given me pause to reflect upon the striking spectacle of a nursling in front of a mirror who has not yet mastered walking, or even standing, but who—though held tightly by some prop, human or artificial (what, in France, we call a *trotte-bébé* [a sort of walker])—overcomes, in a flutter of jubilant activity, the constraints of his prop in order to adopt a slightly leaning-forward position and take in an instantaneous view of the image in order to fix it in his mind.

In my view, this activity has a specific meaning up to the age of eighteen months, and reveals both a libidinal dynamism that has hitherto remained problematic and an ontological structure of the human world that fits in with my reflections on paranoiac knowledge.

It suffices to understand the mirror stage in this context *as an identification*, in the full sense analysis gives to the term: namely, the transformation that takes place in the subject when he assumes [*assume*] an image—an image that is seemingly predestined to have an effect at this phase, as witnessed by the use in analytic theory of antiquity's term, "imago."

The jubilant assumption [*assomption*] of his specular image by the kind of being—still trapped in his motor impotence and nursling dependence—the little man is at the *infans* stage thus seems to me to manifest in an exemplary situation the symbolic matrix in which the *I* is precipitated in a primordial form, prior to being objectified in the dialectic of identification with the other, and before language restores to it, in the universal, its function as subject.

This form would, moreover, have to be called the "ideal-I"[1]—if we wanted to translate it into a familiar register—in the sense that it will also be the rootstock of secondary identifications, this latter term subsuming the libidinal normalization functions. But the important point is that this form situates the agency known as the ego, prior to its social determination, in a fictional direction that will forever remain irreducible for any single individual or, rather, that will only asymptotically approach the subject's becoming, no matter how successful the dialectical syntheses by which he must resolve, as *I*, his discordance with his own reality.

95   For the total form of his body, by which the subject anticipates the maturation of his power in a mirage, is given to him only as a gestalt, that is, in an exteriority in which, to be sure, this form is more constitutive than constituted, but in which, above all, it appears to him as the contour of his stature that freezes it and in a symmetry that reverses it, in opposition to the turbulent movements with which the subject feels he animates it. Through these two aspects of its appearance, this gestalt—whose power [*prégnance*] should be considered linked to the species, though its motor style is as yet

unrecognizable—symbolizes the *I*'s mental permanence, at the same time as it prefigures its alienating destination. This gestalt is also replete with the correspondences that unite the *I* with the statue onto which man projects himself, the phantoms that dominate him, and the automaton with which the world of his own making tends to achieve fruition in an ambiguous relation.

Indeed, for imagos—whose veiled faces we analysts see emerge in our daily experience and in the penumbra of symbolic effectiveness[2]—the specular image seems to be the threshold of the visible world, if we take into account the mirrored disposition of the *imago of one's own body* in hallucinations and dreams, whether it involves one's individual features, or even one's infirmities or object projections; or if we take note of the role of the mirror apparatus in the appearance of *doubles*, in which psychical realities manifest themselves that are, moreover, heterogeneous.

The fact that a gestalt may have formative effects on an organism is attested to by a biological experiment that is so far removed from the idea of psychical causality that it cannot bring itself to formulate itself in such terms. The experiment nevertheless acknowledges that it is a necessary condition for the maturation of the female pigeon's gonad that the pigeon see another member of its species, regardless of its sex; this condition is so utterly sufficient that the same effect may be obtained by merely placing a mirror's reflective field near the individual. Similarly, in the case of the migratory locust, the shift within a family line from the solitary to the gregarious form can be brought about by exposing an individual, at a certain stage of its development, to the exclusively visual action of an image akin to its own, provided the movements of this image sufficiently resemble those characteristic of its species. Such facts fall within a realm of homeomorphic identification that is itself subsumed within the question of the meaning of beauty as formative and erogenous.

But mimetic facts, understood as heteromorphic identification, are of just as much interest to us insofar as they raise the question of the signification of space for living organisms—psychological concepts hardly seeming less appropriate for shedding light here than the ridiculous attempts made to reduce these facts to the supposedly supreme law of adaptation. We need but recall how Roger Caillois (still young and fresh from his break with the sociological school at which he trained) illuminated the subject when, with the term "legendary psychasthenia," he subsumed morphological mimicry within the derealizing effect of an obsession with space.

As I myself have shown, human knowledge is more independent than animal knowledge from the force field of desire because of the social dialectic that structures human knowledge as paranoiac;[3] but what limits it is the "scant reality" surrealistic unsatisfaction denounces therein. These reflections lead me to recognize in the spatial capture manifested by the mirror stage, the effect in man, even prior to this social dialectic, of an organic inadequacy of his natural reality—assuming we can give some meaning to the word "nature."

The function of the mirror stage thus turns out, in my view, to be a particular case of the function of imagos, which is to establish a relationship between an organism and its reality—or, as they say, between the *Innenwelt* and the *Umwelt*.

In man, however, this relationship to nature is altered by a certain dehiscence at the very heart of the organism, a primordial Discord betrayed by the signs of malaise and motor uncoordination of the neonatal months. The objective notions of the anatomical incompleteness of the pyramidal tracts and of certain humoral residues of the maternal organism in the newborn confirm my view that we find in man a veritable *specific prematurity of birth*.

Let us note in passing that this fact is recognized as such by embryologists, under the heading "fetalization," as determining the superiority of the so-called higher centers of the central nervous system, and especially of the cerebral cortex which psychosurgical operations will lead us to regard as the intra-organic mirror.

This development is experienced as a temporal dialectic that decisively projects the individual's formation into history: the mirror stage is a drama whose internal pressure pushes precipitously from insufficiency to anticipation—and, for the subject caught up in the lure of spatial identification, turns out fantasies that proceed from a fragmented image of the body to what I will call an "orthopedic" form of its totality—and to the finally donned armor of an alienating identity that will mark his entire mental development with its rigid structure. Thus, the shattering of the *Innenwelt* to *Umwelt* circle gives rise to an inexhaustible squaring of the ego's audits.

This fragmented body—another expression I have gotten accepted into the French school's system of theoretical references—is regularly manifested in dreams when the movement of an analysis reaches a certain level of aggressive disintegration of the individual. It then appears in the form of disconnected limbs or of organs exoscopically represented, growing wings and taking up arms for internal persecutions that the visionary Hieronymus Bosch fixed for all time in painting, in their ascent in the fifteenth century to the imaginary zenith of modern man. But this form turns out to be tangible even at the organic level, in the lines of "fragilization" that define the hysteric's fantasmatic anatomy, which is manifested in schizoid and spasmodic symptoms.

Correlatively, the *I* formation is symbolized in dreams by a fortified camp, or even a stadium—distributing, between the arena within its walls and its outer border of gravel-pits and marshes, two opposed fields of battle where the subject bogs down in his quest for the proud, remote inner castle whose form (sometimes juxtaposed in the same scenario) strikingly symbolizes the id. Similarly, though here in the mental sphere, we find fortified structures constructed, the metaphors for which arise spontaneously, as if deriving from the subject's very symptoms, to designate the mechanisms of obsessive neurosis: inversion, isolation, reduplication, undoing   98
what has been done, and displacement.

But were I to build on these subjective data alone—were I to so much as free them from the experiential condition that makes me view them as based on a language technique—my theoretical efforts would remain exposed to the charge of lapsing into the unthinkable, that of an absolute subject. This is why I have sought, in the present hypothesis grounded in a confluence of objective data, a *method of symbolic reduction* as my guiding grid.

It establishes a genetic order in *ego defenses*, in accordance with the wish formulated by Anna Freud in the first part of her major book, and situates (as against a frequently expressed prejudice) hysterical repression and its returns at a more archaic stage than obsessive inversion and its isolating processes, situating the latter as prior to the paranoiac alienation that dates back to the time at which the specular *I* turns into the social *I*.

This moment at which the mirror stage comes to an end inaugurates, through identification with the imago of one's semblable and the drama of primordial jealousy (so well brought out by the Charlotte Bühler school in cases of transitivism in children), the dialectic that will henceforth link the *I* to socially elaborated situations.

It is this moment that decisively tips the whole of human knowledge [*savoir*] into being mediated by the other's desire, constitutes its objects in an abstract equivalence due to competition from other people, and turns the *I* into an apparatus to which every instinctual pressure constitutes a danger, even if it corresponds to a natural maturation process. The very normalization of this maturation is henceforth dependent in man on cultural intervention, as is exemplified by the fact that sexual object choice is dependent upon the Oedipus complex.

In light of my conception, the term "primary narcissism," by which analytic doctrine designates the libidinal investment characteristic of this moment, reveals in those who invented it a profound awareness of semantic latencies. But it also sheds light on the dynamic opposition between this libido and sexual libido, an opposition they tried to define when they invoked destructive and even death instincts in order to explain the obvious relationship between narcissistic libido and the alienating *I* function, and the aggressiveness deriving therefrom in all relations with others, even in relations involving aid of the most good-Samaritan variety.

99   The fact is that they encountered that existential negativity whose reality is so vigorously proclaimed by the contemporary philosophy of being and nothingness.

Unfortunately, this philosophy grasps that negativity only within the limits of a self*-sufficiency of consciousness, which, being one of its premises, ties the illusion of autonomy in which it puts its faith to the ego's constitutive misrecognitions. While it draws considerably on borrowings from psychoanalytic experience, this intellectual exercise culminates in the pretense of grounding an existential psychoanalysis.

At the end of a society's historical enterprise to no longer recognize that it has any but a utilitarian function, and given the individual's anxiety faced with the concentration-camp form of the social link whose appearance seems to crown this effort, existentialism can be judged on the basis of the justifications it provides for the subjective impasses that do, indeed, result therefrom: a freedom that is never so authentically affirmed as when it is within the walls of a prison; a demand for commitment that expresses the inability of pure consciousness to overcome any situation; a voyeuristic-sadistic idealization of sexual relationships; a personality that achieves self-realization only in suicide; and a consciousness of the other that can only be satisfied by Hegelian murder.

These notions are opposed by the whole of analytic experience, insofar as it teaches us not to regard the ego as centered on the *perception-consciousness system* or as organized by the "reality principle"—the expression of a scientific bias most hostile to the dialectic of knowledge—but, rather, to take as our point of departure the *function of misrecognition* that characterizes the ego in all the defensive structures so forcefully articulated by Anna Freud. For, while *Verneinung* [negation] represents the blatant form of that function, its effects remain largely latent as long as they are not illuminated by some reflected light at the level of fate where the id manifests itself.

The inertia characteristic of the *I* formations can thus be understood as providing the broadest definition of neurosis, just as the subject's capture by his situation gives us the most general formulation of madness—the kind found within the asylum walls as well as the kind that deafens the world with its sound and fury.

The sufferings of neurosis and psychosis provide us schooling in the passions of the soul, just as the balance arm of the psychoanalytic scales—when we calculate the angle of its threat to entire communities—provides us with an amortization rate for the passions of the city.

At this intersection of nature and culture, so obstinately scrutinized by the anthropology of our times, psychoanalysis alone recognizes the knot of imaginary servitude that love must always untie anew or sever.

For such a task we can find no promise in altruistic feeling, we who lay bare the aggressiveness that underlies the activities of the philanthropist, the idealist, the pedagogue, and even the reformer.

In the subject to subject recourse we preserve, psychoanalysis can accompany the patient to the ecstatic limit of the "*Thou art that,*" where the cipher of his mortal destiny is revealed to him, but it is not in our sole power as practitioners to bring him to the point where the true journey begins.

Notes

1. I have let stand the peculiar translation I adopted in this article for Freud's *Ideal Ich* [*je-idéal*], without further comment except to say that I have not maintained it since.

2. See Claude Lévi-Strauss' essay, entitled "L'efficacité symbolique," in *Revue de l'histoire des religions* CXXXV, 1 (1949): 5–27.

3. See, on this point, the texts that follow, pages 111 and 180 [*Écrits* 1966].

Aggressiveness in Psychoanalysis

Theoretical Paper Presented in Brussels in mid-May 1948 at the
Eleventh Congress of French-Speaking Psychoanalysts

The preceding paper presented to you the use I make of the notion of aggressiveness in clinical work and therapy.[1] That notion must now be put to the test before you to determine whether or not we can wrest a concept from it that may lay claim to scientific usefulness—in other words, a concept that can objectify facts that are of a comparable order in reality or, more categorically, that can establish a dimension of analytic experience in which these objectified facts may be regarded as variables.

All of us here at this gathering share an experience based on a technique and a system of concepts to which we are faithful, as much because the system was developed by the man who opened up all of that experience's pathways to us, as because it bears the living mark of its stages of development. In other words, contrary to the dogmatism with which we are taxed, we know that this system remains open as regards both its completion and a number of its articulations.

These hiatuses seem to come together in the enigmatic signification Freud expressed with the term "death instinct"—attesting, rather like the figure of the Sphinx, to the aporia this great mind encountered in the most profound attempt to date to formulate one of man's experiences in the biological register.

This aporia lies at the heart of the notion of aggressiveness, whose role in the psychical economy we appreciate better every day.

That is why the question of the metapsychological nature of the deadly tendencies is constantly being raised by our theoretically-inclined colleagues, not without contradiction, and often, it must be admitted, in a rather formalistic way.

I would simply like to proffer a few remarks or theses inspired by my   102
years of reflection upon this veritable aporia in psychoanalytic doctrine, and by the sense I have—after reading numerous works—of our responsibility for the current evolution of laboratory psychology and psychotherapy. I am referring, on the one hand, to so-called "behaviorist" research that seems to me to owe its best results (insignificant as they sometimes appear compared to the sizable theoretical apparatus with which they are framed) to the often implicit use it makes of categories psychoanalysis has contributed to psychology; and, on the other hand, to the kind of treatment, given to both adults and children, that might be placed under the heading of "psychodrama," which looks to abreaction for its therapeutic power—trying to exhaust it at the level of role playing—and to which classical psychoanalysis has, once again, contributed the actual guiding notions.

Thesis I: *Aggressiveness manifests itself in an experience that is subjective in its very constitution.*

It is, in fact, useful to reconsider the phenomenon of psychoanalytic experience. In trying to get at the basics, reflection upon this is often omitted.

It can be said that psychoanalytic action develops in and through verbal communication, that is, in a dialectical grasping of meaning. Thus it presupposes a subject who manifests himself verbally in addressing another subject.

It cannot be objected to us that this latter subjectivity must be null and void, according to the ideal physics lives up to—eliminating it by using recording devices, though it cannot avoid responsibility for human error in reading the results.

Only a subject can understand a meaning; conversely, every meaning phenomenon implies a subject. In analysis, a subject presents himself as capable of being understood and is, in effect; introspection and supposedly projective intuition are not the *a priori* vitiations that psychology, taking its first steps along the path of science, believed to be irreducible. This would be to create an impasse out of moments that are abstractly isolated from a dialogue, whereas one should instead trust in its movement: it was to   103
Freud's credit that he assumed the risks involved before overcoming them by means of a rigorous technique.

Can his results ground a positive science? Yes, if the experience can be verified by everyone. Now this experience, constituted between two subjects, one of whom plays in the dialogue the role of ideal impersonality (a point that will require explanation later), may, once completed—its only conditions having to do with the capability of this subject, which is something that may be required in all specialized research—be begun anew by the second subject with a third. This apparently initiatory path is simply transmission by recurrence, which should surprise no one since it stems from the very bipolar structure of all subjectivity. Only the speed at which the experience spreads is affected thereby; and while it may be debated whether the experience is restricted to the region in which a specific culture reigns—although no sound anthropology can raise objections on that score—all the indicators suggest that its results can be relativized sufficiently to become generalizable, thus satisfying the humanitarian postulate inseparable from the spirit of science.

Thesis II: *Aggressiveness presents itself in analysis as an aggressive intention and as an image of corporal dislocation, and it is in such forms that it proves to be effective.*

Analytic experience allows us to experience intentional pressure. We read it in the symbolic meaning of symptoms—once the subject sheds the defenses by which he disconnects them from their relations with his everyday life and history—in the implicit finality of his behavior and his refusals, in his bungled actions, in the avowal of his favorite fantasies, and in the rebuses of his dream life.

We can almost measure it in the demanding tone that sometimes permeates his whole discourse, in his pauses, hesitations, inflections, and slips of the tongue, in the inaccuracies of his narrative, irregularities in his application of the fundamental rule, late arrivals at sessions, calculated absences, and often in his recriminations, reproaches, fantasmatic fears, angry emotional reactions, and displays designed to intimidate. Actual acts of violence are as rare as might be expected given the predicament that led the patient to the doctor, and its transformation, accepted by the patient, into a convention of dialogue.

104

The specific effect of this aggressive intention is plain to see. We regularly observe it in the formative action of an individual on those who are dependent upon him: intentional aggressiveness gnaws away, undermines, and disintegrates; it castrates; it leads to death. "And I thought you were impotent!" growled a mother with a tiger's cry, to her son, who, not without great difficulty, had confessed to her his homosexual tendencies. One could see that her permanent aggressiveness as a virile woman had taken its toll. It has always been impossible, in such cases, for us to divert the blows of the analytic enterprise itself.

This aggressiveness is, of course, exercised within real constraints. But we know from experience that it is no less effective when conveyed by one's mien [*expressivité*]: a harsh parent intimidates by his mere presence, and the image of the Punisher scarcely needs to be brandished for the child to form such an image. Its effects are more far-reaching than any physical punishment.

After the repeated failures encountered by classical psychology in its attempts to account for the mental phenomena known as "images"—a term whose expressive value is confirmed by all its semantic acceptations—psychoanalysis proved itself capable of accounting for the concrete reality they represent. That was because it began with their formative function in the subject, and revealed that if common images make for certain individual differences in tendencies, they do so as variations of the matrices that other specific images—which in my vocabulary correspond to antiquity's term "imago"—constitute for the "instincts" themselves.

Among the latter images are some that represent the elective vectors of aggressive intentions, which they provide with an efficacy that might be called magical. These are the images of castration, emasculation, mutilation, dismemberment, dislocation, evisceration, devouring, and bursting open of the body—in short, the imagos that I personally have grouped together under the heading "imagos of the fragmented body," a heading that certainly seems to be structural.

There is a specific relationship here between man and his own body that is also more generally manifested in a series of social practices: from tattooing, incision, and circumcision rituals in primitive societies to what might be called the procrustean arbitrariness of fashion, in that it contradicts, in advanced societies, respect for the natural forms of the human body, the idea of which is a latecomer to culture.

One need but listen to the stories and games made up by two to five year olds, alone or together, to know that pulling off heads and cutting open bellies are spontaneous themes of their imagination, which the experience of a busted-up doll merely fulfills.

One must leaf through a book of Hieronymus Bosch's work, including views of whole works as well as details, to see an atlas of all the aggressive images that torment mankind. The prevalence that psychoanalysis has discovered among them of images based on a primitive autoscopy of the oral organs and organs derived from the cloaca is what gives rise to the shapes of the demons in Bosch's work. Even the ogee of the *angustiae* of birth can be found in the gates to the abyss through which they thrust the damned; and even narcissistic structure may be glimpsed in the glass spheres in which the exhausted partners of the "Garden of Earthly Delights" are held captive.

These phantasmagorias crop up constantly in dreams, especially when an analysis appears to reflect off the backdrop of the most archaic fixations. I will mention here a dream recounted by one of my patients, whose aggressive drives manifested themselves in obsessive fantasies. In the dream he saw himself in a car, with the woman with whom he was having a rather difficult love-affair, being pursued by a flying fish whose balloon-like body was so transparent that one could see the horizontal level of liquid it contained: an image of vesical persecution of great anatomical clarity.

These are all basic aspects of a gestalt that is characteristic of aggression in man and that is tied to both the symbolic character and cruel refinement of the weapons he builds, at least at the artisanal stage of his industry. The imaginary function of this gestalt will be clarified in what follows.

Let us note here that to attempt a behaviorist reduction of the analytic process—to which a concern with rigor, quite unjustified in my view, might impel some of us—is to deprive the imaginary function of its most important subjective facts, to which favorite fantasies bear witness in consciousness and which have enabled us to conceptualize the imago, which plays a formative role in identification.

106

Thesis III: *The mainsprings of aggressiveness determine
the rationale for analytic technique.*

Dialogue in itself seems to involve a renunciation of aggressiveness; from Socrates onward, philosophy has always placed its hope in dialogue to make reason triumph. And yet ever since Thrasymachus made his mad outburst at the beginning of that great dialogue, *The Republic*, verbal dialectic has all too often proved a failure.

I have emphasized that the analyst cures through dialogue, curing cases of madness that are just as serious. What virtue, then, did Freud add to dialogue?

The rule proposed to the patient in analysis allows him to advance in an intentionality that is blind to any other purpose than that of freeing him from suffering or ignorance of whose very limits he is unaware.

His voice alone will be heard for a period of time whose duration depends on the analyst's discretion. In particular, it will soon become apparent to him, indeed confirmed, that the analyst refrains from responding at the level of giving advice or making plans. This constraint seems to run counter to the desired end and so must be justified by some profound motive.

What, then, lies behind the analyst's attitude, sitting there as he does across from him? The concern to provide the dialogue with a participant who is as devoid as possible of individual characteristics. We efface ourselves, we leave the field in which the interest, sympathy, and reactions a speaker seeks to find on his interlocutor's face might be seen, we avoid all manifestations of our personal tastes, we conceal whatever might betray them, we depersonalize ourselves and strive to represent to the other an ideal of impassability.

We are not simply expressing thereby the apathy we have had to bring about in ourselves to be equal to the task of understanding our subject, nor are we striving to make our interpretative interventions take on the oracular quality they must possess against this backdrop of inertia.

We wish to avoid the trap hidden in the appeal, marked by faith's eternal pathos, the patient addresses to us. It harbors a secret within itself: "Take upon yourself," he tells us, "the suffering that weighs so heavily on my shoulders; but I can see that you are far too content, composed, and comfortable to be worthy of bearing it." 107

What appears here as the arrogant affirmation of one's suffering will show its face—and sometimes at a moment decisive enough to give rise to the kind of "negative therapeutic reaction" that attracted Freud's attention—in the form of the resistance of *amour-propre*, to use the term in all the depth given it by La Rochefoucauld, which is often expressed thus: "I can't bear the thought of being freed by anyone but myself."

Of course, due to a more unfathomable heartfelt exigency, the patient expects us to share in his pain. But we take our cue from his hostile reaction, which already made Freud wary of any temptation to play the prophet. Only saints are sufficiently detached from the deepest of our shared passions to avoid the aggressive repercussions of charity.

As for presenting our own virtues and merits as examples, the only person I have ever known to resort to that was some big boss, thoroughly imbued with the idea, as austere as it was innocent, of his own apostolic value; I still recall the fury he unleashed.

In any case, such reactions should hardly surprise us analysts, we who expose the aggressive motives behind all so-called philanthropic activity.

We must, nevertheless, bring out the subject's aggressiveness toward us, because, as we know, aggressive intentions form the negative transference that is the inaugural knot of the analytic drama.

This phenomenon represents the patient's imaginary transference onto us of one of the more or less archaic imagos, which degrades, diverts, or inhibits the cycle of a certain behavior by an effect of symbolic subduction, which has excluded a certain function or body part from the ego's control by an accident of repression, and which has given its form to this or that agency of the personality through an act of identification.

108 It can be seen that the most incidental pretext is enough to arouse an aggressive intention that reactualizes the imago—which has remained permanent at the level of symbolic overdetermination that we call the subject's unconscious—along with its intentional correlate.

Such a mechanism often proves to be extremely simple in hysteria: in the case of a girl afflicted with astasia-abasia, which for months had resisted the most varied forms of therapeutic suggestion, I was immediately identified with a constellation of the most unpleasant features that the object of a passion formed for her, a passion marked, moreover, by a fairly strong delusional tone. The underlying imago was that of her father, and it was enough for me to remark that she had not had his support (a lack which I knew had dominated her biography in a highly fanciful manner) for her to be cured of her symptom, without, it might be said, her having understood anything or her morbid passion having in any way been affected.

Such knots are, as we know, more difficult to untie in obsessive neurosis, precisely because of the well-known fact that its structure is particularly designed to camouflage, displace, deny, divide, and muffle aggressive intentions; it does so by a defensive decomposition that is so similar in its principles to that illustrated by the stepping and staggering technique that a number of my patients have themselves employed military fortification metaphors to describe themselves.

As to the role of aggressive intention in phobia, it is, as it were, manifest.

Thus it is not inadvisable to reactivate such an intention in psychoanalysis.

What we try to avoid in our technique is to allow the patient's aggressive intention to find support in a current idea about us that is well enough developed for it to become organized in such reactions as opposition, negation, ostentation, and lying that our experience has shown to be characteristic modes of the agency known as the ego in dialogue.

I am characterizing this agency here, not by the theoretical construction Freud gives of it in his metapsychology—that is, as the "perception-

consciousness" system—but by what he recognized as the ego's most constant phenomenological essence in analytic experience, namely, *Verneinung*   109
[negation], urging us to detect its presence in the most general index of an
inversion owing to a prior judgment.

In short, by "ego" I designate [1] the nucleus given to consciousness—
though it is opaque to reflection—that is marked by all the ambiguities
which, from self-indulgence to bad faith, structure the human subject's lived
experience of the passions; [2] the "I" that, while exposing its facticity to
existential criticism, opposes its irreducible inertia of pretenses and misrecognition to the concrete problematic of the subject's realization.

Far from attacking it head on, the analytic maieutic takes a detour that
amounts, in the end, to inducing in the subject a guided paranoia. Indeed,
one aspect of analytic action is to bring about the projection of what
Melanie Klein calls "bad internal objects," which is a paranoiac mechanism
certainly, but in this context it is highly systematized, in some sense filtered,
and properly checked.

This is the aspect of our praxis that corresponds to the category of space,
provided we include in it the imaginary space in which the dimension of
symptoms develops, which structures them like excluded islets, inert scotomas, or parasitic autonomisms in the person's functioning.

Corresponding to the other dimension, the temporal, is anxiety and its
impact, whether patent as in the phenomenon of flight or inhibition, or
latent as when it only appears with the imago that arouses it.

Again, let me repeat, this imago reveals itself only to the extent that our
attitude offers the subject the pure mirror of a smooth surface.

To understand what I'm saying here, imagine what would happen if a patient
saw in his analyst an exact replica of himself. Everyone senses that the patient's
excess of aggressive tension would prove such an obstacle to the manifestation
of transference that its useful effect could only be brought about very slowly—
and this is what happens in certain training analyses. If we imagine it, in the
extreme case, experienced in the uncanny form characteristic of the apprehensions of one's *double*, the situation would trigger uncontrollable anxiety.

Thesis IV: *Aggressiveness is the tendency correlated with a mode of*   110
identification I call narcissistic, which determines the formal structure
of man's ego and of the register of entities characteristic of his world.

The subjective experience of analysis immediately inscribes its results in
concrete psychology. Let me simply indicate here what it contributes to the

psychology of the emotions when it demonstrates the meaning common to states as diverse as fantasmatic fear, anger, active sorrow, and psychasthenic fatigue.

To shift now from the subjectivity of intention to the notion of a tendency to aggress is to make a leap from the phenomenology of our experience to metapsychology.

But this leap manifests nothing more than a requirement of our thought which, in order now to objectify the register of aggressive reactions, and given our inability to seriate it according to its quantitative variations, must include it in a formula of equivalence. That is what we do with the notion of "libido."

The aggressive tendency proves to be fundamental in a certain series of significant personality states, namely, the paranoid and paranoiac psychoses.

In my work I have emphasized that there is a correlation—due to their strictly parallel seriation—between the quality of aggressive reaction to be expected from a particular form of paranoia and the stage of mental genesis represented by the delusion that is symptomatic of that form. The correlation appears even more profound when the aggressive act dissolves the delusional construction; I have shown this in the case of a curable form, self-punishing paranoia.

Thus aggressive reactions form a continuous series, from the violent, unmotivated outburst of the act, through the whole range of belligerent forms, to the cold war of interpretative demonstrations. This series parallels another, that of imputations of harm, the explanations for which—without mentioning the obscure *kakon* to which the paranoiac attributes his discordance with all living things—run the gamut from poison (borrowed from the register of a highly primitive organicism), to evil spells (magic), influence (telepathy), physical intrusion (lesions), diversion of intent (abuse), theft of secrets (dispossession), violation of privacy (profanation), injury (legal action), spying and intimidation (persecution), defamation and character assassination (prestige), and damages and exploitation (claims).

I have shown that in each case this series—in which we find all the successive envelopes of the person's biological and social status—is based on an original organization of ego and object forms that are also structurally affected thereby, even down to the spatial and temporal categories in which the ego and the object are constituted. The latter are experienced as events in a perspective of mirages, as affections with something stereotypical about them that suspends their dialectical movement.

Janet, who so admirably demonstrated the signification of feelings of persecution as phenomenological moments of social behaviors, did not explore their common characteristic, which is precisely that they are constituted by stagnation in one of these moments, similar in strangeness to the faces of actors when a film is suddenly stopped in mid-frame.

Now, this formal stagnation is akin to the most general structure of human knowledge, which constitutes the ego and objects as having the attributes of permanence, identity, and substance—in short, as entities or "things" that are very different from the gestalts that experience enables us to isolate in the mobility of the field constructed according to the lines of animal desire.

Indeed, this formal fixation, which introduces a certain difference of level, a certain discordance between man as organism and his *Umwelt*, is the very condition that indefinitely extends his world and his power, by giving his objects their instrumental polyvalence and symbolic polyphony, as well as their potential as weaponry.

What I have called paranoiac knowledge is therefore shown to correspond in its more or less archaic forms to certain critical moments that punctuate the history of man's mental genesis, each representing a stage of objectifying identification.

We can glimpse its stages in children by simple observation, in which Charlotte Bühler, Elsa Köhler, and, following in their footsteps, the Chicago School have revealed several levels of significant manifestations, though only analytic experience can give them their exact value by making it possible to reintegrate subjective relations in them. 112

The first level shows us that the very young child's experience of itself— insofar as it is related to the child's semblable—develops on the basis of a situation that is experienced as undifferentiated. Thus, around the age of eight months, in confrontations between children—which, if they are to be fruitful, must be between children whose difference in age is no more than two and a half months—we see gestures of fictitious actions by which one subject renews the other's imperfect gesture by confusing their distinct application, and synchronies of spectacular capture that are all the more remarkable as they precede the complete coordination of the motor systems they involve.

Thus the aggressiveness that is manifested in the retaliations of slaps and blows cannot be regarded solely as a playful manifestation of the exercise of strength and their employment in getting to know the body. It must be understood within a broader realm of coordination: one that will subordinate the functions of tonic postures and vegetative tension to a social relativity, whose prevalence in the expressive constitution of human emotions has been remarkably well emphasized by Wallon.

Furthermore, I believed I myself could highlight the fact that, on such occasions, the child anticipates at the mental level the conquest of his own body's functional unity, which is still incomplete at the level of volitional motricity at that point in time.

What we have here is a first capture by the image in which the first moment of the dialectic of identifications is sketched out. It is linked to a gestalt phenomenon, the child's very early perception of the human form, a form which, as we know, holds the child's interest right from the first months of life and, in the case of the human face, right from the tenth day. But what demonstrates the phenomenon of recognition, implying subjectivity, are the signs of triumphant jubilation and the playful self-discovery that characterize the child's encounter with his mirror image starting in the sixth month. This behavior contrasts sharply with the indifference shown by the

very animals that perceive this image—the chimpanzee, for example—once they have tested its vanity as an object; and it is even more noteworthy as it occurs at an age when the child lags behind the chimpanzee in instrumental intelligence, only catching up with the latter at eleven months of age.

What I have called the "mirror stage" is of interest because it manifests the affective dynamism by which the subject primordially identifies with the visual gestalt of his own body. In comparison with the still very profound lack of coordination in his own motor functioning, that gestalt is an ideal unity, a salutary imago. Its value is heightened by all the early distress resulting from the child's intra-organic and relational discordance during the first six months of life, when he bears the neurological and humoral signs of a physiological prematurity at birth.

It is this capture by the imago of the human form—rather than *Einfühlung*, the absence of which is abundantly clear in early childhood—that dominates the whole dialectic of the child's behavior in the presence of his semblable between six months and two and a half years of age. Throughout this period, one finds emotional reactions and articulated evidence of a normal transitivism. A child who beats another child says that he himself was beaten; a child who sees another child fall, cries. Similarly, it is by identifying with the other that he experiences the whole range of bearing and display reactions—whose structural ambivalence is clearly revealed in his behaviors, the slave identifying with the despot, the actor with the spectator, the seduced with the seducer.

There is a sort of structural crossroads here to which we must accommodate our thinking if we are to understand the nature of aggressiveness in man and its relation to the formalism of his ego and objects. It is in this erotic relationship, in which the human individual fixates on an image that alienates him from himself, that we find the energy and the form from which the organization of the passions that he will call his ego originates.

Indeed, this form crystallizes in the subject's inner conflictual tension, which leads to the awakening of his desire for the object of the other's desire: here the primordial confluence precipitates into aggressive competition, from which develops the triad of other people, ego, and object. Spangling the space of spectacular communion, this triad is inscribed there according to its own formalism, and it so completely dominates the affect of *Einfühlung* that a child at that age may not recognize the people he knows   114
best if they appear in completely different surroundings.

But if the ego seems to be marked, right from the outset, by this aggressive relativity—which minds starved for objectivity might equate with an animal's emotional erections when it is distracted by a desire in the course of its experimental conditioning—how can we escape the conclusion that each great instinctual metamorphosis, punctuating the individual's life, throws its delimitation back into question, composed as it is of the conjunction of the subject's history with the unthinkable innateness of his desire?

This is why man's ego is never reducible to his lived identity, except at a limit that even the greatest geniuses have never been able to approach; and why, in the depressive disruptions constituted by reversals experienced due to a sense of inferiority, the ego essentially engenders deadly negations that freeze it in its formalism. "What happens to me has nothing to do with what I am. There's nothing about you that is worthwhile."

Thus the two moments, when the subject negates himself and when he accuses the other, become indistinguishable; and we see here the paranoiac structure of the ego that finds its analog in the fundamental negations highlighted by Freud in the three delusions: jealousy, erotomania, and interpretation. It is the very delusion of the misanthropic beautiful soul, casting out onto the world the disorder that constitutes his being.

Subjective experience must be fully accredited if we are to recognize the central knot of ambivalent aggressiveness, which at the present stage of our culture is given to us in the dominant form of *resentment*, including even its most archaic aspects in the child. Thus, Saint Augustine, because he lived at a similar time, without having to suffer from a "behaviorist" resistance—in the sense in which I use the term—foreshadowed psychoanalysis by giving us an exemplary image of such behavior in the following terms: "*Vidi ego et expertus sum zelantem parvulum: nondum loquebatur et intuebatur pallidus amaro aspectu conlactaneum suum"* ("I myself have seen and known an infant to be jealous even though it could not speak. It became pale, and cast bitter looks on its foster-brother"). Thus Augustine forever ties the situation of spectacular absorption (the child observed), the emotional reaction (pale), and the reactivation of images of primordial frustration (with an envenomed look)—which are the psychical and somatic coordinates of the earliest aggressiveness—to the infant (preverbal) stage of early childhood.

Only Melanie Klein, studying children on the verge of language, dared to project subjective experience into that earlier period; observation, nevertheless, enables us to affirm its role there in the simple fact, for example, that a child who does not yet speak reacts differently to punishment than to brutality.

Through Klein we have become aware of the function of the imaginary primordial enclosure formed by the imago of the mother's body; through her we have the mapping, drawn by children's own hands, of the mother's inner empire, and the historical atlas of the internal divisions in which the imagos of the father and siblings—whether real or virtual—and the subject's own voracious aggression dispute their deleterious hold over her sacred regions. We have also become aware of the persistence in the subject of the shadow of "bad internal objects," related to some accidental "association" (to use a term concerning which we should emphasize the organic meaning analytic experience gives it, as opposed to the abstract meaning it retains from Humean ideology). Hence we can understand by what structural means re-evoking certain imaginary *personae* and reproducing certain situational inferiorities may *disconcert* the adult's voluntary functions in the most rigorously predictable way—namely, by their fragmenting impact on the imago involved in the earliest identification.

By showing us the primordial nature of the "depressive position," the extremely archaic subjectivization of a *kakon*, Melanie Klein pushes back the limits within which we can see the subjective function of identification at work, and she especially enables us to situate the first superego formation as extremely early.

But it is important to delimit the orbit within which the following relations, some of which have yet to be elucidated, are situated in our theoretical work—guilt tension, oral harmfulness, hypochondriacal fixation, not to mention primordial masochism which I am excluding from my remarks here—in order to isolate the notion of an aggressiveness linked to the narcissistic relationship and to the structures of systematic misrecognition and objectification that characterize ego formation.

A specific satisfaction, based on the integration of an original organic chaos [*désarroi*], corresponds to the *Urbild* of this formation, alienating as it may be due to its function of rendering foreign. This satisfaction must be conceived of in the dimension of a vital dehiscence constitutive of man and makes unthinkable the idea of an environment that is preformed for him; it is a "negative" libido that enables the Heraclitean notion of Discord— which the Ephesian held to be prior to harmony—to shine once more.

Thus, there is no need to look any further to find the source of the energy the ego borrows to put in the service of the "reality principle," a question Freud raises regarding repression.

This energy indubitably comes from "narcissistic passion" provided one conceives of the ego according to the subjective notion I am proposing here as consonant with the register of analytic experience. The theoretical difficulties encountered by Freud seem, in fact, to stem from the mirage of objectification, inherited from classical psychology, constituted by the idea of the "perception-consciousness" system, in which the existence of every-thing the ego neglects, scotomizes, and misrecognizes in the sensations that make it react to reality, and of everything it doesn't know, exhausts, and ties down in the meanings it receives from language, suddenly seems to be over-looked—a surprising oversight on the part of the man who succeeded in forcing open the borders of the unconscious with the power of his dialectic.

Just as the superego's insane oppression lies at the root of the well-founded imperatives of moral conscience, mad passion—specific to man, stamping his image on reality—is the obscure foundation of the will's rational mediations.

The notion of aggressiveness as a tension correlated with narcissistic structure in the subject's becoming allows us to encompass in a very simply formu-lated function all sorts of accidents and atypicalities in that becoming.

I shall indicate here how I conceive of its dialectical link with the function of the Oedipus complex. In its normal form, its function is that of sublima-tion, which precisely designates an identificatory reshaping of the subject and—as Freud wrote when he felt the need for a "topographical" coordina-tion of psychical dynamisms—a *secondary identification* by introjection of the imago of the parent of the same sex.

The energy for that identification is provided by the first biological surge of genital libido. But it is clear that the structural effect of identification with a rival is not self-evident, except at the level of fable, and can only be con-ceptualized if the way is paved for it by a primary identification that struc-

117

tures the subject as rivaling with himself. In fact, a note of biological impotence is met with again here—as is the effect of anticipation characteristic of
the human psyche's genesis—in the fixation of an imaginary "ideal,"
which, as analysis has shown, determines whether or not the "instinct" conforms to the individual's physiological sex. A point, let it be said in passing,
whose anthropological import cannot be too highly stressed. But what interests me here is what I shall refer to as the "pacifying" function of the ego-
ideal: the connection between its libidinal normativeness and a cultural
normativeness, bound up since the dawn of history with the imago of the
father. Here, obviously, lies the import that Freud's work, *Totem and Taboo*,
still has, despite the mythical circularity that vitiates it, insofar as from a
mythological event—the killing of the father—it derives the subjective
dimension that gives this event its meaning: guilt.

Indeed, Freud shows us that the need for a form of participation, which
neutralizes the conflict inscribed after killing him in the situation of rivalry
among the brothers, is the basis for identification with the paternal totem.
Oedipal identification is thus the identification by which the subject transcends the aggressiveness constitutive of the first subjective individuation. I
have stressed elsewhere that it constitutes a step in the establishment of the
distance by which, with feelings akin to respect, a whole affective assumption of one's fellow man is brought about.

Only the anti-dialectical mentality of a culture which, dominated as it is
by objectifying ends, tends to reduce all subjective activity to the ego's being,
can justify Von den Steinen's astonishment when confronted by a Bororo
who said, "I'm an ara." All the "primitive mind" sociologists scurry about
118   trying to fathom this profession of identity, which is no more surprising
upon reflection than declaring, "I'm a doctor" or "I'm a citizen of the French
Republic," and certainly presents fewer logical difficulties than claiming,
"I'm a man," which at most can mean no more than, "I'm like the person
who, in recognizing him to be a man, I constitute as someone who can recognize me as a man." In the final analysis, these various formulations can be
understood only in reference to the truth of "I is an other," less dazzling to
the poet's intuition than it is obvious from the psychoanalyst's viewpoint.

Who, if not us, will call back into question the objective status of this "I,"
which a historical evolution peculiar to our culture tends to confuse with the
subject? The specific impact of this anomaly on every level of language
deserves to be displayed, and first and foremost as regards the first person
as grammatical subject in our languages [*langues*]—the "I love" that
hypostasizes a tendency in a subject who denies it. An impossible mirage in

linguistic forms, among which the most ancient are to be found, and in which the subject appears fundamentally in the position of a determinative or instrumental of the action.

Let us not pursue here the critique of all the abuses of the *cogito ergo sum*, recalling instead that, in analytic experience, the ego represents the center of all resistances to the treatment of symptoms.

It was inevitable that analysis, after emphasizing the reintegration of tendencies excluded by the ego—those tendencies underlying the symptoms it tackled at first, most of which were related to *failed* Oedipal identification—should eventually discover the "moral" dimension of the problem.

Parallel to that, what came to the fore were, on the one hand, the role played by the aggressive tendencies in the structure of symptoms and personality and, on the other, all sorts of "uplifting" conceptions of the liberated libido, one of the first of which can be attributed to French psychoanalysts under the heading of "oblativity."

It is, in fact, clear that genital libido operates by blindly going beyond the individual for the sake of the species and that its sublimating effects in the Oedipal crisis are at the root of the whole process of man's cultural subordination. Nevertheless, one cannot overemphasize the irreducible character of narcissistic structure and the ambiguity of a notion that tends to misrecognize the constancy of aggressive tension in all moral life that involves subjection to this structure: for no amount of oblativity could free altruism from it. This is why La Rochefoucauld could formulate his maxim, in which his rigor concurs with the fundamental theme of his thought, on the incompatibility between marriage and delight.

We would be allowing the cutting edge of analytic experience to become dull if we deluded ourselves, if not our patients, into believing in some sort of preestablished harmony that would free social conformity—made possible by the reduction of symptoms—of its tendency to induce aggressiveness in the subject.

Theoreticians in the Middle Ages showed a rather different kind of penetration when they debated whether love could be understood in terms of a "physical" theory or an "ecstatic" theory, both of which involved the reabsorption of man's ego, the one by its reintegration into a universal good, the other by the subject's effusion toward an object devoid of alterity.

In all of an individual's genetic phases and at every degree of a person's human accomplishment, we find this narcissistic moment in the subject in a before in which he must come to terms with a libidinal frustration and in an after in which he transcends himself in a normative sublimation.

This conception allows us to understand the aggressiveness involved in the effects of all the subject's regressions, aborted undertakings, and refusals of typical development, especially at the level of sexual realization—and more precisely within each of the great phases that the libidinal metamorphoses bring about in human life, whose major function analysis has demonstrated: weaning, the Oedipal stage, puberty, maturity, and motherhood, not to mention the involutional climacteric. I have often said that the emphasis initially placed in psychoanalytic doctrine on the Oedipal conflict's aggressive retortions in the subject corresponded to the fact that the effects of the complex were first glimpsed in *failed attempts* to resolve it.

There is no need to emphasize that a coherent theory of the narcissistic phase clarifies the ambivalence peculiar to the "partial drives" of scotophilia, sadomasochism, and homosexuality, as well as the stereotypical, ceremonial formalism of the aggressiveness that is manifested in them. I am talking here about the often barely "realized" apprehension of other people in the practice of certain of these perversions, their subjective value actually being very different from that ascribed to them in the otherwise very striking existential reconstructions Sartre provided.

I should also like to mention in passing that the decisive function I ascribe to the imago of one's own body in the determination of the narcissistic phase enables us to understand the clinical relation between congenital anomalies of functional lateralization (left-handedness) and all forms of inversion of sexual and cultural normalization. This reminds us of the role attributed to gymnastics in the "beautiful and good" ideal of education among the Ancient Greeks and leads us to the social thesis with which I will conclude.

Thesis V: *This notion of aggressiveness as one of the intentional coordinates of the human ego, especially as regards the category of space, allows us to conceive of its role in modern neurosis and in the malaise in civilization.*

Here I want to merely sketch out a perspective regarding the verdicts analytic experience allows us to come to in the present social order. The preeminence of aggressiveness in our civilization would already be sufficiently demonstrated by the fact that it is usually confused in everyday morality with the virtue of strength. Quite rightly understood as indicative of ego development, aggressiveness is regarded as indispensable in social practice and is so widely accepted in our mores that, in order to appreciate its cultural peculiarity, one must become imbued with the meaning and efficient virtues of a practice like that of *yang* in the public and private morality of the Chinese.

Were it not superfluous, the prestige of the idea of the struggle for life would be sufficiently attested to by the success of a theory that was able to make us endorse a notion of selection based solely on the animal's conquest of space as a valid explanation for the developments of life. Indeed, Darwin's success seems to derive from the fact that he projected the predations of Victorian society and the economic euphoria that sanctioned for that society the social devastation it initiated on a planetary scale, and that he justified its predations with the image of a laissez-faire system in which the strongest predators compete for their natural prey.

Before Darwin, however, Hegel had provided the definitive theory of the specific function of aggressiveness in human ontology, seeming to prophesy the iron law of our own time. From the conflict between Master and Slave, he deduced the entire subjective and objective progress of our history, revealing in its crises the syntheses represented by the highest forms of the status of the person in the West, from the Stoic to the Christian, and even to the future citizen of the Universal State.

Here the natural individual is regarded as nil, since the human subject is nothing, in effect, before the absolute Master that death is for him. The satisfaction of human desire is possible only when mediated by the other's desire and labor. While it is the recognition of man by man that is at stake in the conflict between Master and Slave, this recognition is based on a radical negation of natural values, whether expressed in the master's sterile tyranny or in work's productive tyranny.

The support this profound doctrine lent to the slave's constructive Spartacism, recreated by the barbarity of the Darwinian century, is well known.

The relativization of our sociology by the scientific collection of the cultural forms we are destroying in the world—and the analyses, bearing truly psychoanalytic marks, in which Plato's wisdom shows us the dialectic common to the passions of the soul and of the city—can enlighten us as to the reason for this barbarity. Namely, to employ the jargon that corresponds to our approaches to man's subjective needs, the increasing absence of all the saturations of the superego and ego-ideal that occur in all kinds of organic forms in traditional societies, forms that extend from the rituals of everyday intimacy to the periodical festivals in which the community manifests itself. We no longer know them except in their most obviously degraded guises. Furthermore, in abolishing the cosmic polarity of the

male and female principles, our society is experiencing the full psychological impact of the modern phenomenon known as the "battle of the sexes."
Ours is an immense community, midway between a "democratic" anarchy
of the passions and their hopeless leveling out by the "great winged hornet" of narcissistic tyranny; it is clear that the promotion of the ego in our
existence is leading, in conformity with the utilitarian conception of man
that reinforces it, to an ever greater realization of man as an individual, in
other words, in an isolation of the soul that is ever more akin to its original
dereliction.

Correlatively, it seems—I mean for reasons whose historical contingency
is based on a necessity that certain of my considerations make it possible to
perceive—we are engaged in a technological enterprise on the scale of the
entire species. The question is whether the conflict between Master and
Slave will find its solution in the service of the machine, for which a psy-
chotechnics, that is already yielding a rich harvest of ever more precise
applications, will strive to provide race-car drivers and guards for regulating power stations.

The notion of the role of spatial symmetry in man's narcissistic structure is essential in laying the groundwork for a psychological analysis of
space, whose place I can merely indicate here. Animal psychology has
shown us that the individual's relation to a particular spatial field is socially
mapped in certain species, in a way that raises it to the category of subjective membership. I would say that it is the subjective possibility of the mirror projection of such a field into the other's field that gives human space
its originally "geometrical" structure, a structure I would willingly characterize as *kaleidoscopic*.

Such, at least, is the space in which the imagery of the ego develops, and
which intersects the objective space of reality. But does it provide us a secure
basis? Already in the *Lebensraum* ("living space") in which human competition grows ever keener, an observer of our species from outer space would
conclude we possess needs to escape with very odd results. But doesn't conceptual extension, to which we believed we had reduced reality [*réel*], later
seem to refuse to lend its support to the physicist's thinking? Having
extended our grasp to the farthest reaches of matter, won't this "realized"
space—which makes the great imaginary spaces in which the free games of
the ancient sages roamed seem illusory to us—thus vanish in turn in a roar
of the universal ground?

Whatever the case may be, we know how our adaptation to these exi-
gencies proceeds, and that war is increasingly proving to be the inevitable

and necessary midwife of all our organizational progress. The adaptation of adversaries, opposed in their social systems, certainly seems to be progressing toward a confluence of forms, but one may well wonder whether it is motivated by agreement as to their necessity, or by the kind of identification Dante, in the *Inferno*, depicts in the image of a deadly kiss.

Moreover, it doesn't seem that the human individual, as the material for such a struggle, is absolutely flawless. And the detection of "bad internal objects," responsible for reactions (that may prove extremely costly in terms of equipment) of inhibition and headlong flight—which we have recently learned to use in the selection of shock, fighter, parachute, and commando troops—proves that war, after having taught us a great deal about the genesis of the neuroses, is perhaps proving too demanding in its need for ever more neutral subjects to serve an aggression in which feeling is undesirable.

Nevertheless, we have a few psychological truths to contribute here too: namely, the extent to which the ego's supposed "instinct of self-preservation" willingly gives way before the temptation to dominate space, and above all the extent to which the fear of death, the "absolute Master"—presumed to exist in consciousness by a whole philosophical tradition from Hegel onward—is psychologically subordinate to the narcissistic fear of harm to one's own body.

I do not think it was futile to have highlighted the relation between the spatial dimension and a subjective tension, which—in the malaise of civilization—intersects with the tension of anxiety, approached so humanely by Freud, and which develops in the temporal dimension. I would willingly shed light on the latter, too, using the contemporary significations of two philosophies that would seem to correspond to the philosophies I just mentioned: that of Bergson, owing to its naturalistic inadequacy, and that of Kierkegaard owing to its dialectical signification.

Only at the intersection of these two tensions should one envisage the assumption by man of his original fracturing, by which it might be said that at every instant he constitutes his world by committing suicide, and the psychological experience of which Freud had the audacity to formulate as the "death instinct," however paradoxical its expression in biological terms may be.

In the "emancipated" man of modern society, this fracturing reveals that his formidable crack goes right to the very depths of his being. It is a self-punishing neurosis, with hysterical/hypochondriacal symptoms of its functional inhibitions, psychasthenic forms of its derealizations of other people and of the world, and its social consequences of failure and crime. It is this touching victim, this innocent escapee who has thrown off the shackles that condemn modern man to the most formidable social hell, whom we take in when he comes to us; it is this being of nothingness for whom, in our daily task, we clear anew the path to his meaning in a discreet fraternity—a fraternity to which we never measure up.

Note

1. Apart from the first line, this text is reproduced here in its original form.

The Function and Field of Speech and Language in Psychoanalysis

Paper delivered at the Rome Congress held at the Institute of
Psychology at the University of Rome on September 26 and 27, 1953

Preface

In particular, it should not be forgotten that the division into embryology, anatomy, physiology, psychology, sociology, and clinical work does not exist in nature and that there is only one discipline: a *neurobiology* to which observation obliges us to add the epithet *human* when it concerns us.
—Quotation chosen as an inscription for a psychoanalytic institute in 1952

The talk included here warrants an introduction that provides some context, since it was marked by its context.

The theme of this talk was proposed to me and my contribution was intended to constitute the customary theoretical paper given at the annual meeting that the association representing psychoanalysis in France at that time had held for eighteen years, a venerable tradition known as the "Congress of French-Speaking Psychoanalysts," though for the past two years it had been extended to Romance-language-speaking psychoanalysts (Holland being included out of linguistic tolerance). The Congress was to take place in Rome in September of 1953.

In the meantime, serious disagreements led to a secession within the French group. These disagreements came out on the occasion of the founding of a "psychoanalytic institute." The team that succeeded in imposing its statutes and program on the new institute was then heard to proclaim that it would prevent the person who, along with others, had tried to introduce a different conception of analysis from speaking in Rome, and it employed every means in its power to do so.

238   Yet it did not seem to those who thus founded the new Société Française de Psychanalyse that they had to deprive the majority of the students, who had rallied to their teaching, of the forthcoming event, or even to hold it elsewhere than in the eminent place in which it had been planned to be held.

The generous fellow feeling that had been shown them by the Italian group meant that they could hardly be regarded as unwelcome guests in the Universal City.

For my part, I considered myself assisted—however unequal I might prove to be to the task of speaking about speech—by a certain complicity inscribed in the place itself.

Indeed, I recalled that, well before the glory of the world's loftiest throne had been established, Aulus Gellius, in his *Noctes Atticae*, attributed to the place called *Mons Vaticanus* the etymology *vagire*, which designates the first stammerings of speech.

If, then, my talk was to be nothing more than a newborn's cry, at least it would seize the auspicious moment to revamp the foundations our discipline derives from language.

Moreover, this revamping derived too much meaning from history for me not to break with the traditional style—that places a "paper" somewhere between a compilation and a synthesis—in order to adopt an ironic style suitable to a radical questioning of the foundations of our discipline.

Since my audience was to be the students who expected me to speak, it was above all with them in mind that I composed this talk, and for their sake that I dispensed with the rules, observed by our high priests, requiring one to mime rigor with meticulousness and confuse rule with certainty.

Indeed, in the conflict that led to the present outcome, people had shown such an exorbitant degree of misrecognition regarding the students' autonomy as subjects that the first requirement was to counteract the constant tone that had permitted this excess.

The fact is that a vice came to light that went well beyond the local circumstances that led to the conflict. The very fact that one could claim to regulate the training of psychoanalysts in so authoritarian a fashion raised the question whether the established modes of such training did not paradoxically result in perpetual minimization.

239   The initiatory and highly organized forms which Freud considered to be

a guarantee of his doctrine's transmission are certainly justified by the situation of a discipline that can only perpetuate itself by remaining at the level of a complete experience.

But haven't these forms led to a disappointing formalism that discourages initiative by penalizing risk, and turns the reign of the opinion of the learned into a principle of docile prudence in which the authenticity of research is blunted even before it finally dries up?

The extreme complexity of the notions brought into play in our field is such that in no other area does a mind run a greater risk, in laying bare its judgment, of discovering its true measure.

But this ought to result in making it our first, if not only, concern to emancipate theses by elucidating principles.

The severe selection that is, indeed, required cannot be left to the endless postponements of a fastidious co-optation, but should be based on the fecundity of concrete production and the dialectical testing of contradictory claims.

This does not imply that I particularly value divergence. On the contrary, I was surprised to hear, at the London International Congress—where, because we had failed to follow the prescribed forms, we had come as appellants—a personality well disposed toward us deplore the fact that we could not justify our secession on the grounds of some doctrinal disagreement. Does this mean that an association that is supposed to be international has some other goal than that of maintaining the principle of the collective nature of our experience?

It is probably no big secret that it has been eons since this was the case, and it was without creating the slightest scandal that, to the impenetrable Mr. Zilboorg—who, making ours a special case, insisted that no secession should be accepted unless it is based on a scientific dispute—the penetrating Mr. Wälder could reply that, if we were to challenge the principles in which each of us believes his experience is grounded, our walls would very quickly dissolve into the confusion of Babel.

To my way of thinking, if I innovate, I prefer not to make a virtue of it.

In a discipline that owes its scientific value solely to the theoretical concepts Freud hammered out as his experience progressed—concepts which, because they continue to be poorly examined and nevertheless retain the ambiguity of everyday language, benefit from the latter's resonances while incurring misunderstanding—it would seem to me to be premature to break with the traditional terminology.

But it seems to me that these terms can only be made clearer if we estab-

240

lish their equivalence to the current language of anthropology, or even to the latest problems in philosophy, fields where psychoanalysis often need but take back its own property.

In any case, I consider it to be an urgent task to isolate, in concepts that are being deadened by routine use, the meaning they recover when we reexamine their history and reflect on their subjective foundations.

That, no doubt, is the teacher's function—the function on which all the others depend—and the one in which the value of experience figures best.

If this function is neglected, the meaning of an action whose effects derive solely from meaning is obliterated, and the rules of analytic technique, being reduced to mere recipes, rob analytic experience of any status as knowledge [connaissance] and even of any criterion of reality.

For no one is less demanding than a psychoanalyst when it comes to what gives his actions their status, which he himself is not far from regarding as magical because he doesn't know where to situate them in a conception of his field that he hardly dreams of reconciling with his practice.

The epigraph with which I have adorned this preface is a rather fine example of this.

Doesn't his conception of his field correspond to a conception of analytic training that is like that of a driving school which, not content to claim the unique privilege of issuing drivers' licenses, also imagines that it is in a position to supervise car construction?

Whatever this comparison may be worth, it is just as valid as those which are bandied about in our most serious conventicles and which, because they originated in our discourse to idiots, do not even have the savor of inside jokes, but seem to gain currency nevertheless due to their pompous ineptitude.

They begin with the well-known comparison between the candidate who allows himself to be prematurely dragged into practicing analysis and the surgeon who operates without sterilizing his instruments, and they go on to the comparison that brings tears to one's eyes for those unfortunate students 241 who are torn by their masters' conflicts just like children torn by their parents' divorce.

This late-born comparison seems to me to be inspired by the respect due to those who have, in effect, been subjected to what, toning down my thought, I will call a pressure to teach, which has put them sorely to the test; but on hearing the quavering tones of the masters, one may also wonder whether the limits of childishness have not, without warning, been stretched to the point of foolishness.

Yet the truths contained in these clichés are worthy of more serious examination.

As a method based on truth and demystification of subjective camouflage, does psychoanalysis display an incommensurate ambition to apply its principles to its own corporation—that is, to psychoanalysts' conception of their role in relation to the patient, their place in intellectual society, their relations with their peers, and their educational mission?

Perhaps, by reopening a few windows to the broad daylight of Freud's thought, my paper will allay the anguish some people feel when a symbolic action becomes lost in its own opacity.

Whatever the case may be, in referring to the context of my talk, I am not trying to blame its all too obvious shortcomings on the haste with which it was written, since both its meaning and its form derive from that same haste.

Moreover, in an exemplary sophism involving intersubjective time, I have shown the function of haste in logical precipitation, where truth finds its unsurpassable condition.[1]

Nothing created appears without urgency, nothing in urgency fails to surpass itself in speech.

Nor is there anything that does not become contingent here when the time comes when a man can identify in a single reason the side he takes and the disorder he denounces, in order to understand their coherence in reality [*réel*] and anticipate by his certainty the action that weighs them against each other.

Introduction   242

> We shall determine this while we are still at the aphelion of our matter, for,
> when we arrive at the perihelion, the heat is liable to make us forget it.
>   —Lichtenberg

> "Flesh composed of suns. How can such be?" exclaim the simple ones.
>   —R. Browning, *Parleying with Certain People*

Such is the fright that seizes man when he discovers the true face of his power that he turns away from it in the very act—which is his act—of laying it bare. This is true in psychoanalysis. Freud's Promethean discovery was such an act, as his work attests; but that act is no less present in each psychoanalytic experience humbly conducted by any one of the workers trained in his school.

One can trace over the years a growing aversion regarding the functions of speech and the field of language. It is responsible for the "changes in aim and technique" that are acknowledged within the psychoanalytic movement, and whose relation to the general decline in therapeutic effectiveness is nevertheless ambiguous. Indeed, the emphasis on the object's resistance in current psychoanalytic theory and technique must itself be subjected to the dialectic of analysis, which can but recognize in this emphasis the attempt to provide the subject with an alibi.

Let me try to outline the topography of this movement. If we examine the literature that we call our "scientific activity," the current problems of psychoanalysis clearly fall into three categories:

(A) The function of the imaginary, as I shall call it, or, to put it more directly, of fantasies in the technique of psychoanalytic experience and in the constitution of the object at the different stages of psychical development. The impetus in this area has come from the analysis of children and from the favorable field offered to researchers' efforts and temptations by the preverbal structurations approach. This is also where its culmination is now inducing a return by raising the question of what symbolic sanction is to be attributed to fantasies in their interpretation.

243 (B) The concept of libidinal object relations which, by renewing the idea of treatment progress, is quietly altering the way treatment is conducted. The new perspective began here with the extension of psychoanalytic method to the psychoses and with the momentary receptiveness of psychoanalytic technique to data based on a different principle. Psychoanalysis leads here to an existential phenomenology—indeed, to an activism motivated by charity. Here, too, a clear-cut reaction is working in favor of a return to symbolization as the crux of technique.

(C) The importance of countertransference and, correlatively, of analytic training. Here the emphasis has resulted from the difficulties related to the termination of analytic treatment that intersect the difficulties related to the moment at which training analysis ends with the candidate beginning to practice. The same oscillation can be observed here: On the one hand, the analyst's being is said, not without audacity, to be a non-negligible factor in the effects of an analysis and even a factor whose conduct should be brought out into the open at the end of the game; on the other hand, it is put forward no less energetically that a solution can come only from an ever deeper exploration of the unconscious mainspring.

Apart from the pioneering activity these three problems manifest on three different fronts, they have one thing in common with the vitality of the psychoanalytic experience that sustains them. It is the temptation that presents itself to the analyst to abandon the foundation of speech, and this precisely in areas where its use, verging on the ineffable, would seem to require examination more than ever: namely, the child's education by its mother, Samaritan-type aid, and dialectical mastery. The danger becomes great indeed if the analyst also abandons his own language, preferring established languages about whose compensations for ignorance he knows very little.

In truth, we would like to know more about the effects of symbolization in the child, and the officiating mothers in psychoanalysis—even those who give our top committees a matriarchal air—are not exempt from the confusion of tongues by which Ferenczi designated the law of the child/adult relationship.[2]

Our wise men's ideas about the perfect object-relation are based on a rather uncertain conception and, when exposed, they reveal a mediocrity that hardly does credit to the profession.

244

There can be no doubt that these effects—where the psychoanalyst resembles the type of modern hero represented by ridiculous feats in situations of confusion—could be corrected by an appropriate return to the study of the functions of speech, a field the analyst ought by now to have mastered.

But it seems that this central field of our domain has been left fallow since Freud. Note how he himself refrained from venturing too far into its periphery: He discovered children's libidinal stages by analyzing adults and intervened in little Hans' case only through the mediation of his parents; he deciphered a whole section of the language of the unconscious in paranoid delusion, but used for this purpose only the key text Schreber left behind in the volcanic debris of his spiritual catastrophe. Freud rose, however, to a position of total mastery regarding the dialectic of the work and the tradition of its meaning.

Does this mean that if the place of the master remains empty, it is not so much due to his disappearance as to an increasing obliteration of the meaning of his work? To convince ourselves of this, isn't it enough for us to note what is happening in that place?

A technique is being transmitted there, one that is gloomy in style— indeed, it is reticent in its opacity—and that any attempt to let in critical fresh air seems to upset. It has, in truth, assumed the appearance of a formalism that is taken to such ceremonial lengths that one might well suspect that it bears the same similarity to obsessive neurosis as Freud found so convincingly in the practice, if not the genesis, of religious rites.

When we consider the literature that this activity produces for its own nourishment, the analogy becomes even more marked: the impression is often that of a curious closed circuit in which ignorance of the origin of terms generates problems in reconciling them, and in which the effort to solve these problems reinforces the original ignorance.

In order to home in on the causes of this deterioration of analytic discourse, one may legitimately apply psychoanalytic method to the collectivity that sustains it.

Indeed, to speak of a loss of the meaning of psychoanalytic action is as true and futile as it is to explain a symptom by its meaning as long as the latter is not recognized. But we know that, in the absence of such recognition, analytic action can only be experienced as aggressive at the level at which it is situated; and that, in the absence of the social "resistances" which the psychoanalytic group used to find reassuring, the limits of its tolerance toward its own activity—now "accepted," if not actually approved of—no longer depend upon anything but the numerical percentage by which its presence in society is measured.

These principles suffice to separate out the symbolic, imaginary, and real conditions that determine the defenses we can recognize in the doctrine—isolation, undoing what has been done, denial, and, in general, misrecognition.

Thus, if the importance of the American group to the psychoanalytic movement is measured by its mass, we can evaluate the conditions one finds there by their weight.

In the symbolic order, first of all, one cannot neglect the importance of the *c* factor which, as I noted at the Congress of Psychiatry in 1950, is a constant that is characteristic of a given cultural milieu: the condition, in this case, of ahistoricism, which is widely recognized as the major feature of "communication" in the United States, and which in my view is diametrically opposed to analytic experience. To this must be added a native mindset, known as behaviorism, which so dominates psychological notions in America that it clearly has now altogether topped Freud's inspiration in psychoanalysis.

As for the other two orders, I leave to those concerned the task of assessing what the mechanisms that manifest themselves in the life of psychoanalytic associations owe to relations of standing within the group and to the effects of their free enterprise felt by the whole of the social body, respectively. I

245

also leave to them the task of determining the credence to be lent to a notion emphasized by one of their most lucid representatives—namely, the convergence that occurs between the alien status of a group dominated by immigrants and the distance it is lured into taking from its roots by the function called for by the aforementioned cultural conditions.

In any case, it seems indisputable that the conception of psychoanalysis in the United States has been inflected toward the adaptation of the individual to the social environment, the search for behavior patterns, and all the objectification implied in the notion of "human relations."* And the indigenous term, "human engineering,"* strongly implies a privileged position of exclusion with respect to the human object.

246

Indeed, the eclipse in psychoanalysis of the liveliest terms of its experience—the unconscious and sexuality, which will apparently cease before long to even be mentioned—may be attributed to the distance necessary to sustain such a position.

We need not take sides concerning the formalism and small-time shop mentality, both of which have been noted and decried in the analytic group's own official documents. Pharisees and shopkeepers interest us only because of their common essence, which is the source of the difficulties both have with speech, particularly when it comes to "talking shop."*

The fact is that while incommunicability of motives may sustain a "grand master," it does not go hand in hand with true mastery—at least not with the mastery teaching requires. This was realized in the past when, in order to sustain one's preeminence, it was necessary, for form's sake, to give at least one class.

This is why the attachment to traditional technique—which is unfailingly reaffirmed by the same camp—after a consideration of the results of the tests carried out in the frontier fields enumerated above, is not unequivocal; the equivocation can be gauged on the basis of the substitution of the term "classic" for "orthodox" that is used to qualify it. One remains true to propriety because one has nothing to say about the doctrine itself.

For my part, I would assert that the technique cannot be understood, nor therefore correctly applied, if one misunderstands the concepts on which it is based. My task shall be to demonstrate that these concepts take on their full meaning only when oriented in a field of language and ordered in relation to the function of speech.

A point regarding which I should note that in order to handle any Freudian concept, reading Freud cannot be considered superfluous, even for those concepts that go by the same name as everyday notions. This is demonstrated, as I am reminded by the season, by the misadventure of Freud's theory of the instincts when revised by an author somewhat less than alert to what Freud explicitly stated to be its mythical content. Obviously, the author could hardly be aware of it, since he approaches the theory through Marie Bonaparte's work, which he repeatedly cites as if it were equivalent to Freud's text—without the reader being in any way alerted to the fact—relying perhaps, not without reason, on the reader's good taste not to confuse the two, but proving nonetheless that he hasn't the slightest inkling of the secondary text's true level. The upshot being that—moving from reductions to deductions and from inductions to hypotheses—the author, by way of the strict tautology of his false premises, comes to the conclusion that the instincts in question are reducible to the reflex arc. Like the classic image of the pile of plates—whose collapse leaves nothing in the hands of the comedian but two ill-matched fragments—the complex construction that moves from the discovery of the migrations of the libido in the erogenous zones to the metapsychological passage from a generalized pleasure principle to the death instinct becomes the binomial of a passive erotic instinct, modeled on the activity of the lice seekers so dear to the poet, and a destructive instinct, identified simply with motor functioning. A result that merits an honorable mention for the art, intentional or otherwise, of taking the consequences of a misunderstanding to their most rigorous conclusions.

I. Empty Speech and Full Speech in the Psychoanalytic Realization of the Subject

> "Put true and stable speech into my mouth
> and make of me a cautious tongue"
> —*The Internal Consolation*, Chapter XLV:
> That one should not believe everyone
> and of slight stumbling over words.

> *Cause toujours.*
> —Motto of "causalist" thought

Whether it wishes to be an agent of healing, training, or sounding the depths, psychoanalysis has but one medium: the patient's speech. The obviousness of this fact is no excuse for ignoring it. Now all speech calls for a response.

I will show that there is no speech without a response, even if speech meets only with silence, provided it has an auditor, and this is the heart of its function in analysis.

But if the psychoanalyst is not aware that this is how speech functions, he will experience its call [*appel*] all the more strongly; and if emptiness is the first thing to make itself heard in analysis, he will feel it in himself and he will seek a reality beyond speech to fill the emptiness.   248

This leads the analyst to analyze the subject's behavior in order to find in it what the subject is not saying. Yet for him to get the subject to admit to the latter, he obviously has to talk about it. He thus speaks now, but his speech has become suspicious because it is merely a response to the failure of his silence, when faced with the perceived echo of his own nothingness.

But what, in fact, was the appeal the subject was making beyond the emptiness of his words [*dire*]? It was an appeal to truth at its very core, through which the calls of humbler needs vacillate. But first and from the outset it was the call of emptiness itself, in the ambiguous gap of an attempted seduction of the other by means in which the subject manifests indulgence, and on which he stakes the monument of his narcissism.

"That's introspection all right!" exclaims the bombastic, smug fellow who knows its dangers only too well. He is certainly not the last, he admits, to have tasted its charms, even if he has exhausted its benefits. Too bad he has no more time to waste. For you would hear some fine profundities from him were he to come and lie on your couch!

It is strange that analysts who encounter this sort of person early on in their experience still consider introspection to be of importance in psychoanalysis. For the minute you accept his wager, all the fine things he thought he had been saving up slip his mind. If he forces himself to recount a few, they don't amount to much; but others come to him so unexpectedly that they strike him as idiotic and silence him for quite a while. That's what usually happens.[3]

He then grasps the difference between the mirage of the monologue whose accommodating fancies once animated his bombast, and the forced labor of a discourse that leaves one no way out, on which psychologists (not without humor) and therapists (not without cunning) have bestowed the name "free association."

For it really is work—so much so that some have said it requires an apprenticeship, and have even considered this apprenticeship to constitute its true formative value. But if viewed in this way, what does it train but a skilled worker?

Then what of this work? Let us examine its conditions and fruit in the hope of shedding more light on its aim and benefits.   249

The aptness of the German word *Durcharbeiten*—equivalent to the English "working through"*—has been recognized in passing. It has been the despair of French translators, despite what the immortal words of a master of French style offered them by way of an exhaustive exercise: "Cent fois sur le métier, remettez . . ."—but how does the work [*l'ouvrage*] progress here?

The theory reminds us of the triad: frustration, aggressiveness, regression. This explanation seems so comprehensible that it may well spare us the effort to comprehend. Intuition is prompt, but we should be all the more suspicious of something obvious when it has become a received idea. Should analysis ever expose its weakness, it would be advisable not to rest content with recourse to "affectivity." This taboo-word of dialectical incapacity will, along with the verb "to intellectualize" (whose pejorative acceptation makes this incapacity meritorious), remain, in the history of the language, the stigmata of our obtuseness regarding the subject.[4]

Let us ask ourselves instead where this frustration comes from. Is it from the analyst's silence? Responding to the subject's empty speech—even and especially in an approving manner—often proves, by its effects, to be far more frustrating than silence. Isn't it, rather, a frustration that is inherent in the subject's very discourse? Doesn't the subject become involved here in an ever greater dispossession of himself as a being, concerning which—by dint of sincere portraits which leave the idea of his being no less incoherent, of rectifications that do not succeed in isolating its essence, of stays and defenses that do not prevent his statue from tottering, of narcissistic embraces that become like a puff of air in animating it—he ends up recognizing that this being has never been anything more than his own construction [*oeuvre*] in the imaginary and that this construction undercuts all certainty in him? For in the work he does to reconstruct it *for another*, he encounters anew the fundamental alienation that made him construct it *like another*, and that has always destined it to be taken away from him *by another*.[5]

This ego,* whose strength our theorists now define by its capacity to bear
frustration, is frustration in its very essence.[6] Not frustration of one of the subject's desires, but frustration of an object in which his desire is alienated; and the more developed this object becomes, the more profoundly the subject becomes alienated from his jouissance. It is thus a frustration at one remove, a frustration that the subject—even were he to reduce its form in his discourse to the passivating image by which the subject makes himself an object by displaying himself before the mirror—could not be satisfied with,

since even if he achieved the most perfect resemblance to that image, it would still be the other's jouissance that he would have gotten recognized there. Which is why there is no adequate response to this discourse, for the subject regards as contemptuous [*mépris*] any speech that buys into his mistake [*méprise*].

The subject's aggressiveness here has nothing to do with animals' aggressiveness when their desires are frustrated. This explanation, which most seem happy with, masks another that is less agreeable to each and every one of us: the aggressiveness of a slave who responds to being frustrated in his labor with a death wish.

Thus we can see how this aggressiveness may respond to any intervention which, by exposing the imaginary intentions of the subject's discourse, dismantles the object the subject has constructed to satisfy them. This is, in effect, what is referred to as the analysis of resistances, and we can immediately see the danger that lies therein. It is already indicated by the existence of the naive analyst who has never seen any manifestations of aggressiveness except for the aggressive signification of his subjects' fantasies.[7]

He is the same one who, not hesitating to plead for a "causalist" analysis that would aim to transform the subject in the present by learned explanations of his past, betrays well enough, even in his very tone, the anxiety he wishes to spare himself—the anxiety of having to think that his patient's freedom may depend on that of his own intervention. If the expedient he seizes upon is beneficial at some point to the subject, it is no more beneficial than a stimulating joke and will not detain me any longer.

Let us focus instead on the *hic et nunc* [here and now] to which some analysts feel we should confine the handling of the analysis. It may indeed be useful, provided the analyst does not detach the imaginary intention he uncovers in it from the symbolic relation in which it is expressed. Nothing must be read into it concerning the subject's ego that cannot be assumed anew by him in the form of the "*I*," that is, in the first person.

"I was this only in order to become what I can be": if this were not the constant culmination of the subject's assumption [*assomption*] of his own mirages, where could we find progress here?

Thus the analyst cannot without danger track down the subject in the intimacy of his gestures, or even in that of his stationary state, unless he reintegrates them as silent parties into the subject's narcissistic discourse— and this has been very clearly noted, even by young practitioners.

The danger here is not of a negative reaction on the subject's part, but rather of his being captured in an objectification—no less imaginary than before—of his stationary state, indeed, of his statue, in a renewed status of his alienation.

The analyst's art must, on the contrary, involve suspending the subject's certainties until their final mirages have been consumed. And it is in the subject's discourse that their dissolution must be punctuated.

Indeed, however empty his discourse may seem, it is so only if taken at face value—the value that justifies Mallarmé's remark, in which he compares the common use of language to the exchange of a coin whose obverse and reverse no longer bear but eroded faces, and which people pass from hand to hand "in silence." This metaphor suffices to remind us that speech, even when almost completely worn out, retains its value as a *tessera*.

Even if it communicates nothing, discourse represents the existence of communication; even if it denies the obvious, it affirms that speech consti-
252   tutes truth; even if it is destined to deceive, it relies on faith in testimony.

—Thus the psychoanalyst knows better than anyone else that the point is to figure out [*entendre*] to which "part" of this discourse the significant term is relegated, and this is how he proceeds in the best of cases: he takes the description of an everyday event as a fable addressed as a word to the wise, a long prosopopeia as a direct interjection, and, contrariwise, a simple slip of the tongue as a highly complex statement, and even the rest of a silence as the whole lyrical development it stands in for.

It is, therefore, a propitious punctuation that gives meaning to the subject's discourse. This is why the ending of the session—which current technique makes into an interruption that is determined purely by the clock and, as such, takes no account of the thread of the subject's discourse—plays the part of a scansion which has the full value of an intervention by the analyst that is designed to precipitate concluding moments. Thus we must free the ending from its routine framework and employ it for all the useful aims of analytic technique.

This is how regression can occur, regression being but the bringing into the present in the subject's discourse of the fantasmatic relations discharged by an ego* at each stage in the decomposition of its structure. After all, the regression is not real; even in language it manifests itself only by inflections, turns of phrase, and "stumblings so slight" that even in the extreme case they cannot go beyond the artifice of "baby talk" engaged in by adults. Imputing to regression the reality of a current relation to the object amounts to projecting the subject into an alienating illusion that merely echoes one of the analyst's own alibis.

This is why nothing could be more misleading for the analyst than to seek to guide himself by some supposed "contact" he experiences with the subject's reality. This vacuous buzzword of intuitionist and even phenomenological psychology has become extended in contemporary usage in a way that is thoroughly symptomatic of the ever scarcer effects of speech in the present social context. But its obsessive value becomes flagrant when it is recommended in a relationship which, according to its very rules, excludes all real contact.

Young analysts, who might nevertheless allow themselves to be impressed by the impenetrable gifts such recourse implies, will find no better way of dispelling their illusions than to consider the success of the supervision they themselves receive. The very possibility of that supervision would become problematic from the perspective of contact with the patient's reality [*réel*]. On the contrary, the supervisor manifests a second sight—that's the word for it!—which makes the experience at least as instructive for him as for his supervisee. And the less the supervisee demonstrates such gifts—which are considered by some to be all the more incommunicable the bigger the to-do they themselves make about their secrets regarding technique—the truer this almost becomes.

The reason for this enigma is that the supervisee serves as a filter, or even as a refractor, of the subject's discourse, and in this way a ready-made stereography is presented to the supervisor, bringing out from the start the three or four registers on which the musical score constituted by the subject's discourse can be read.

If the supervisee could be put by the supervisor into a subjective position different from that implied by the sinister term *contrôle* (advantageously replaced, but only in English, by "supervision"*), the greatest benefit he would derive from this exercise would be to learn to put himself in the position of that second subjectivity into which the situation automatically puts the supervisor.

There he would find the authentic path by which to reach what is expressed only very approximately by the classic formulation of the analyst's diffuse, or even absentminded, attention. For it is essential to know what that attention aims at; as all my work shows, it certainly does not aim at an object beyond the subject's speech the way it does for certain analysts who force themselves to never lose sight of that object. If this had to be the path of analysis, then it would surely have recourse to other means—otherwise it would provide the only example of a method that forbade itself the means to its own ends.

The only object that is within the analyst's reach is the imaginary relation

253

that links him to the subject qua ego; and although he cannot eliminate it, he can use it to adjust the receptivity of his ears, which is, according to both physiology and the Gospels, the normal use made of them: having ears *in order not to hear* [*entendre*], in other words, in order to detect what is to be understood [*entendu*]. For he has no other ears, no third or fourth ear designed for what some have tried to describe as a direct transaudition of the unconscious by the unconscious. I shall say what we are to make of this supposed mode of communication later.

254

I have, thus far, approached the function of speech in analysis from its least rewarding angle, that of "empty" speech in which the subject seems to speak in vain about someone who—even if he were such a dead ringer for him that you might confuse them—will never join him in the assumption of his desire. I have pointed out the source of the growing devaluation of speech in both analytic theory and technique, and have had to lift incrementally, as if a heavy mill wheel had fallen on speech, what can only serve as the sails that drive the movement of analysis: namely, individual psychophysiological factors that are, in reality, excluded from its dialectic. To regard the goal of psychoanalysis as to modify their characteristic inertia is to condemn oneself to the fiction of movement, with which a certain trend in psychoanalytic technique seems to be satisfied.

If we turn now to the other end of the spectrum of psychoanalytic experience—its history, casuistry, and treatment process—we shall learn to oppose the value of anamnesis as the index and mainspring of therapeutic progress to the analysis of the *hic et nunc*, hysterical intersubjectivity to obsessive intrasubjectivity, and symbolic interpretation to the analysis of resistance. The realization of full speech begins here.

Let us examine the relation it constitutes.

Let us recall that, shortly after its birth, the method introduced by Breuer and Freud was baptized the "talking cure"* by one of Breuer's patients, Anna O. Let us keep in mind that it was the experience inaugurated with this hysteric that led them to the discovery of the pathogenic event dubbed traumatic.

If this event was recognized as the cause of the symptom, it was because putting the event into words (in the patient's "stories"*) led to the removal of the symptom. Here the term "*prise de conscience*" (conscious realization), borrowed from the psychological theory that was immediately constructed to explain the fact, retains a prestige that merits the healthy distrust I believe is called for when it comes to explanations that parade as self-evident. The

psychological prejudices of Freud's day were opposed to seeing in verbalization as such any other reality than its *flatus vocis*. The fact remains that,   255
in the hypnotic state, verbalization is dissociated from conscious realization, and this alone is enough to require a revision of such a conception of its effects.

But why don't the valiant defenders of the behaviorist *Aufhebung* set an example here, making their point that they do not need to know whether the subject remembers anything whatsoever? She simply recounts the event. For my part, I would say that she verbalizes it, or—to further exploit this term whose resonances in French call to mind a Pandora figure other than the one with the box (in which the term should probably be locked up)— that she forces the event into the Word [*le verbe*] or, more precisely, into the *epos* by which she relates in the present the origins of her person. And she does this in a language that allows her discourse to be understood by her contemporaries and that also presupposes their present discourse. Thus it happens that the recitation of the *epos* may include a discourse of earlier days in its own archaic, even foreign tongue, or may even be carried out in the present with all the vivacity of an actor; but it is like indirect speech, isolated in quotation marks in the thread of the narrative, and, if the speech is performed, it is on a stage implying the presence not only of a chorus, but of spectators as well.

Hypnotic remembering is, no doubt, a reproduction of the past, but it is above all a spoken representation and, as such, implies all sorts of presences. It stands in the same relation to the remembering while awake of what in analysis is curiously called "the material," as drama—in which the original myths of the City State are produced before its assembly of citizens—stands in relation to history, which may well be made up of materials, but in which a nation today learns to read the symbols of a destiny on the march. In Heideggerian language one could say that both types of remembering constitute the subject as *gewesend*—that is, as being the one who has thus been. But in the internal unity of this temporalization, entities [*l'étant*] mark the convergence of the having-beens [*des ayant été*]. In other words, if other encounters are assumed to have occurred since any one of these moments having been, another entity would have issued from it that would cause him to have been altogether differently.

The reason for the ambiguity of hysterical revelation of the past is not so much the vacillation of its content between the imaginary and reality [*réel*], for it is situated in both. Nor is it the fact that it is made up of lies. It is that it presents us with the birth of truth in speech, and thereby brings us up   256 against the reality of what is neither true nor false. At least, that is the most disturbing aspect of the problem.

For it is present speech that bears witness to the truth of this revelation in current reality and grounds it in the name of this reality. Now only speech bears witness in this reality to that portion of the powers of the past that has been thrust aside at each crossroads where an event has chosen.

This is why the condition of continuity in the anamnesis, by which Freud measures the completeness of the cure, has nothing to do with the Bergsonian myth of a restoration of duration in which the authenticity of each instant would be destroyed if it did not recapitulate the modulation of all the preceding instants. To Freud's mind, it is not a question of biological memory, nor of its intuitionist mystification, nor of the paramnesia of the symptom, but of remembering, that is, of history; he rests the scales—in which conjectures about the past make promises about the future oscillate—on the knife-edge of chronological certainties alone. Let's be categorical: in psychoanalytic anamnesis, what is at stake is not reality, but truth, because the effect of full speech is to reorder past contingencies by conferring on them the sense of necessities to come, such as they are constituted by the scant freedom through which the subject makes them present.

The meanders of the research pursued by Freud in his account of the case of the Wolf Man confirm these remarks by deriving their full meaning from them.

Freud demands a total objectification of proof when it comes to dating the primal scene, but he simply presupposes all the resubjectivizations of the event that seem necessary to him to explain its effects at each turning point at which the subject restructures himself—that is, as many restructurings of the event as take place, as he puts it, *nachträglich*, after the fact.[8] What's more, with an audacity bordering on impudence, he declares that he considers it legitimate, in analyzing the processes, to elide the time intervals during which the event remains latent in the subject.[9] That is to say, he annuls the *times for understanding* in favor of the *moments of concluding* which precipitate the subject's meditation toward deciding the meaning to be attached to the early event.

Let it be noted that *time for understanding* and *moment of concluding* are functions I have defined in a purely logical theorem,[10] and are familiar to my students as having proven extremely helpful in the dialectical analysis through which I guide them in the process of a psychoanalysis.

This assumption by the subject of his history, insofar as it is constituted by speech addressed to another, is clearly the basis of the new method Freud called psychoanalysis, not in 1904—as was taught until recently by an authority who, when he finally threw off the cloak of prudent silence, appeared on that day to know nothing of Freud except the titles of his works—but in 1895.[11]

In this analysis of the meaning of his method, I do not deny, any more than Freud himself did, the psychophysiological discontinuity manifested by the states in which hysterical symptoms appear, nor do I deny that these symptoms may be treated by methods—hypnosis or even narcosis—that reproduce the discontinuity of these states. It is simply that I repudiate any reliance on these states—as expressly as Freud forbade himself recourse to them after a certain moment in time—to either explain symptoms or cure them.

For if the originality of the method derives from the means it foregoes, it is because the means that it reserves for itself suffice to constitute a domain whose limits define the relativity of its operations.

Its means are those of speech, insofar as speech confers a meaning on the functions of the individual; its domain is that of concrete discourse qua field of the subject's transindividual reality; and its operations are those of history, insofar as history constitutes the emergence of truth in reality [*réel*].

First, in fact, when a subject begins an analysis, he accepts a position that is more constitutive in itself than all the orders by which he allows himself to be more or less taken in—the position of interlocution—and I see no disadvantage in the fact that this remark may leave the listener dumbfounded [*interloqué*]. For I shall take this opportunity to stress that the subject's act of addressing [*allocution*] brings with it an addressee [*allocutaire*][12]   in other words, that the speaker [*locuteur*][13] is constituted in it as intersubjectivity.

Second, it is on the basis of this interlocution, insofar as it includes the interlocutor's response, that it becomes clear to us why Freud requires restoration of continuity in the subject's motivations. An operational examination of this objective shows us, in effect, that it can only be satisfied in the intersubjective continuity of the discourse in which the subject's history is constituted.

Thus, while the subject may vaticinate about his history under the influence of one or other of those drugs that put consciousness to sleep and have been christened in our day "truth serums"—where the sureness of the misnomer betrays the characteristic irony of language—the simple retransmission of his own recorded discourse, even if pronounced by his doctor, cannot have the same effects as psychoanalytic interlocution because it comes to the subject in an alienated form.

The true basis of the Freudian discovery of the unconscious becomes clear in its position as a third term. This may be simply formulated in the following terms:

The unconscious is that part of concrete discourse qua transindividual, which is not at the subject's disposal in reestablishing the continuity of his conscious discourse.

This disposes of the paradox presented by the concept of the unconscious when it is related to an individual reality. For to reduce this concept to unconscious tendencies is to resolve the paradox only by avoiding analytic experience, which clearly shows that the unconscious is of the same nature as ideational functions, and even of thought. Freud plainly stressed this when, unable to avoid a conjunction of opposing terms in the expression "unconscious thought," he gave it the necessary support with the invocation: *sit venia verbo*. Thus we obey him by casting the blame, in effect, onto the Word, but onto the Word realized in discourse that darts from mouth to mouth, conferring on the act of the subject who receives its message the meaning that makes this act an act of his history and gives it its truth.

Hence the objection that the notion of unconscious thought is a contradiction in terms, which is raised by a psychology poorly grounded in its logic, collapses when confronted by the very distinctiveness of the psychoanalytic domain, insofar as this domain reveals the reality of discourse in its autonomy. And the psychoanalyst's *eppur si muove!* has the same impact as Galileo's, which is not that of a fact-based experiment but of an *experimentum mentis*.

The unconscious is the chapter of my history that is marked by a blank or occupied by a lie: it is the censored chapter. But the truth can be refound; most often it has already been written elsewhere. Namely,

- in monuments: this is my body, in other words, the hysterical core of neurosis in which the hysterical symptom manifests the structure of a language, and is deciphered like an inscription which, once recovered, can be destroyed without serious loss;
- in archival documents too: these are my childhood memories, just as impenetrable as such documents are when I do not know their provenance;
- in semantic evolution: this corresponds to the stock of words and acceptations of my own particular vocabulary, as it does to my style of life and my character;
- in traditions, too, and even in the legends which, in a heroicized form, convey my history;

- and, lastly, in its traces that are inevitably preserved in the distortions necessitated by the insertion of the adulterated chapter into the chapters surrounding it, and whose meaning will be reestablished by my exegesis.

Students who believe that, in order to understand Freud, reading Freud is preferable to reading Fenichel—and this belief is so rare that I try to foster it in my teaching—will realize, once they set about it, that what I have just said is hardly original, even in its verve; indeed, I have not used a single metaphor that Freud's works do not repeat with the frequency of a *leitmotif*, revealing the very fabric of his work.

At every instant of their practice from then on, they will more easily grasp the fact that these metaphors—like negation, whose doubling undoes it—lose their metaphorical dimension, and they will recognize that this is so because they are operating in metaphor's own realm, metaphor being but a synonym for the symbolic displacement brought into play in the symptom.

After that it will be easier for them to evaluate the imaginary displacement that motivates Fenichel's work, by gauging the difference in the solidity and efficacy of technique generated by referring to the supposedly organic stages of individual development and by searching for the particular events of a subject's history. It is precisely the difference that separates authentic historical research from the supposed laws of history, of which it can be said that every age finds its own philosopher to propagate them according to the values prevalent at the time.

This is not to say that there is nothing worth keeping in the different meanings uncovered in the general march of history along the path which runs from Bossuet (Jacques-Bénigne) to Toynbee (Arnold), and which is punctuated by the edifices of Auguste Comte and Karl Marx. Everyone knows, of course, that the laws of history are worth as little for directing research into the recent past as they are for making any reasonable presumptions about tomorrow's events. Besides, they are modest enough to postpone their certainties until the day after tomorrow, and not too prudish either to allow for the adjustments that permit predictions to be made about what happened yesterday.

If, therefore, their role in scientific progress is rather slight, their interest nevertheless lies elsewhere: in their considerable role as ideals. For it leads us to distinguish between what might be called the primary and secondary functions of historicization.

For to say of psychoanalysis and of history that, qua sciences, they are both sciences of the particular, does not mean that the facts they deal with

260

261

are purely accidental or even factitious, or that their ultimate value comes
down to the brute aspect of trauma.

Events are engendered in a primal historicization—in other words, history is already being made on the stage where it will be played out once it
has been written down, both in one's heart of hearts and outside.

At one moment in time, a certain riot in the Faubourg Saint-Antoine is
experienced by its actors as a victory or defeat of the Parliament or the
Court; at another moment, as a victory or defeat of the proletariat or the
bourgeoisie. And although it is "the common people," to use Cardinal de
Retz's expression, who always pay the price, it is not at all the same historical event—I mean that they do not leave behind the same sort of memory
in men's minds.

This is because, with the disappearance of the reality of the Parliament
and the Court, the first event will return to its traumatic value, allowing for
a progressive and authentic effacement, unless its meaning is expressly
revived. Whereas the memory of the second event will remain very much
alive even under censorship—just as the amnesia brought on by repression
is one of the liveliest forms of memory—as long as there are men who enlist
their revolt in the struggle for the proletariat's political ascension, that is,
men for whom the keywords of dialectical materialism have meaning.

Thus it would be going too far to say that I am about to carry these
remarks over into the field of psychoanalysis, since they are already there,
and since the clear distinction they establish between two things that were
formerly confused—the technique of deciphering the unconscious and the
theory of instincts, or even drives—goes without saying.

What we teach the subject to recognize as his unconscious is his history—in other words, we help him complete the current historicization of
the facts that have already determined a certain number of the historical
"turning points" in his existence. But if they have played this role, it is
already as historical facts, that is, as recognized in a certain sense or censored
in a certain order.

Thus, every fixation at a supposed instinctual stage is above all a historical stigma: a page of shame that one forgets or undoes, or a page of glory
that obliges. But what is forgotten is recalled in acts, and the undoing of
what has been done contradicts what is said elsewhere, just as obligation perpetuates in symbols the very mirage in which the subject found himself
trapped.

To put it succinctly, the instinctual stages are already organized in subjectivity when they are being lived. And to put it clearly, the subjectivity of

the child who registers as victories and defeats the epic of the training of his sphincters—enjoying in the process the imaginary sexualization of his cloacal orifices, turning his excremental expulsions into aggressions, his retentions into seductions, and his movements of release into symbols—*is not fundamentally different* from the subjectivity of the psychoanalyst who strives to restore the forms of love that he calls "pregenital" in order to understand them.

In other words, the anal stage is no less purely historical when it is actually experienced than when it is reconceptualized, nor is it less purely grounded in intersubjectivity. But officially recognizing it as a stage in some supposed instinctual maturation immediately leads even the best minds off track, to the point of seeing in it the reproduction in ontogenesis of a stage of the animal phylum that should be sought in ascaris, even in jellyfish—a speculation which, ingenious as it may be when penned by Balint, leads others to the most incoherent musings, or even to the folly that goes looking in protista for the imaginary schema of breaking and entering the body, fear of which is supposed to govern feminine sexuality. Why not look for the image of the ego in shrimp, under the pretext that both acquire a new shell after every molting?

In the 1910s and 1920s, a certain Jaworski constructed a very pretty system in which the "biological level" could be found right up to the very confines of culture, and which actually provided shellfish their historical counterpart at some period of the late Middle Ages, if I remember rightly, due to a flourishing of armor in both; indeed, it left no animal form without some human correspondent, excepting neither mollusks nor vermin.

Analogy is not the same thing as metaphor, and the use that the philosophers of nature have made of it requires the genius of Goethe, but even his example is not encouraging. No course is more repugnant to the spirit of our discipline, and it was by deliberately avoiding analogy that Freud   263
opened up the path appropriate to the interpretation of dreams and, along with it, to the notion of analytic symbolism. Analytic symbolism, I insist, is strictly opposed to analogical thinking—a dubious tradition that still leads some people, even in our own ranks, to consider the latter to go hand in hand with the former.

This is why excessive excursions into the ridiculous must be used for their eye-opening value, since, by opening our eyes to the absurdity of a theory, they direct our attention back to dangers that have nothing theoretical about them.

This mythology of instinctual maturation, built out of bits and pieces selected from Freud's work, actually engenders intellectual problems whose vapor, condensing into nebulous ideals, in return irrigates the original myth with its showers. The best writers spill their ink positing equations that satisfy the requirements of that mysterious "genital love"* (there are notions whose strangeness is better placed in the parenthesis of a borrowed term, and they initial their attempt with an admission of a *non liquet*). No one, however, appears to be shaken up by the malaise this results in; and people see it, rather, as a reason to encourage all the Münchhausens of psychoanalytic normalization to raise themselves up by the hair on their head in the hope of attaining the paradise of full realization of the genital object, indeed of the object itself.

The fact that we analysts are in a good position to know the power of words is no reason to emphasize the insoluble character of their power, or to "bind heavy burdens, hard to bear, and lay them on men's shoulders," as Christ's malediction is expressed to the Pharisees in the text of Saint Matthew.

The poverty of the terms within which we try to contain a subjective problem may thus leave a great deal to be desired to particularly exacting minds, should they compare these terms to those that structured, in their very confusion, the ancient quarrels over Nature and Grace.[14] This poverty may thus leave them apprehensive as to the quality of the psychological and sociological effects they can expect from the use of these terms. And it is to be hoped that a better appreciation of the functions of the Logos will dissipate the mysteries of our fantastic charismata.

To confine ourselves to a more lucid tradition, perhaps we can understand the celebrated maxim by La Rochefoucauld—"There are people who would never have fallen in love but for hearing love discussed"—not in the romantic sense of a thoroughly imaginary "realization" of love that would make this remark into a bitter objection, but as an authentic recognition of what love owes to the symbol and of what speech brings with it by way of love.

In any case, one need but consult Freud's work to realize to what a secondary and hypothetical rank he relegates the theory of the instincts. The theory cannot in his eyes stand up for a single instant to the least important particular fact of a history, he insists, and the *genital narcissism* he invokes when summarizing the case of the Wolf Man clearly shows how much he scorns the constituted order of the libidinal stages. Moreover, he evokes instinctual conflict there only to immediately distance himself from it and recognize in the symbolic isolation of the "I am not castrated," in which the subject asserts himself, the compulsive form to which his heterosexual object choice remains riveted, in opposition to the effect of homosexualizing capture undergone by the ego when it was brought back to the imaginary matrix of the primal scene. This is, in truth, the subjective conflict—in which it is only a question of the vicissitudes of subjectivity, so much so that the "I" wins and loses against the "ego" at the whim of religious catechization or indoctrinating *Aufklärung*—a conflict whose effects Freud brought the subject to realize through his help before explaining them to us in the dialectic of the Oedipus complex.

It is in the analysis of such a case that one clearly sees that the realization of perfect love is the fruit not of nature but of grace—that is, the fruit of an intersubjective agreement imposing its harmony on the rent nature on which it is based.

"But what, then, is this subject that you keep drumming into our ears?" some impatient auditor finally exclaims. "Haven't we already learned the lesson from Monsieur de La Palice that everything experienced by the individual is subjective?"

Naive mouth—whose eulogy I shall spend my final days preparing—   265
open up again to hear me. No need to close your eyes. The subject goes far beyond what is experienced "subjectively" by the individual; he goes exactly as far as the truth he is able to attain—which will perhaps come out of the mouth you have already closed again. Yes, this truth of his history is not all contained in his script, and yet the place is marked there in the painful conflicts he experiences because he knows only his own lines, and even in the pages whose disarray gives him little comfort.

The fact that the subject's unconscious is the other's discourse appears more clearly than anywhere else in the studies Freud devoted to what he called telepathy, as it is manifested in the context of an analytic experience. This is the coincidence between the subject's remarks and facts he cannot have known about, but which are still at work in the connections to another analysis in which the analyst is an interlocutor—a coincidence which is, moreover, most often constituted by an entirely verbal, even homonymic, convergence, or which, if it includes an act, involves an "acting out"* by one of the analyst's other patients or by the patient's child who is also in analysis. It is a case of resonance in the communicating networks of discourse, an exhaustive study of which would shed light on similar facts of everyday life.

The omnipresence of human discourse will perhaps one day be embraced under the open sky of an omnicommunication of its text. This is not to say that human discourse will be any more in tune with it than it is now. But this is the field that our experience polarizes in a relation that is only apparently a two-person relation, for any positioning of its structure in merely dyadic terms is as inadequate to it in theory as it is damaging to its technique.

266   *II. Symbol and Language as Structure and Limit of the Psychoanalytic Field*

Τὴν ἀρχήν ὅ τι χάι λαλῶ ὑμῖν
—Gospel according to Saint John, 8.25

Do crossword puzzles.
—Advice to a young psychoanalyst

To take up the thread of my argument again, let me repeat that it is by a reduction of a particular subject's history that psychoanalysis touches on relational gestalts, which analysis extrapolates into regular development; but that neither genetic psychology nor differential psychology, on both of which analysis may shed light, is within its scope, because both require experimental and observational conditions that are related to those of analysis in name alone.

To go even further: What separates out from common experience (which is confused with sense experience only by professional thinkers) as psychology in its crudest form—namely, the wonder that wells up, during some momentary suspension of daily cares, at what pairs off human beings in a disparity that goes beyond that of the grotesques of Leonardo or Goya, or surprise at the resistance of the thickness characteristic of a person's skin to the caress of a hand still moved by the thrill of discovery without yet being blunted by desire—this, one might say, is abolished in an experience that is averse to such caprices and recalcitrant to such mysteries.

A psychoanalysis normally proceeds to its end without revealing to us very much of what is particular to our patient as regards his sensitivity to blows or colors, how quickly he grasps things with his hands or which parts of his body are sensitive, or his ability to retain things or invent, not to mention the vivacity of his tastes.

This paradox is only an apparent one and is not due to any personal failing; if it can be justified by the negative conditions of analytic experience, it simply presses us a little harder to examine that experience in terms of what is positive in it.

267   For this paradox is not resolved by the efforts of certain people who—like the philosophers Plato mocked for being so driven by their appetite for reality [*réel*] that they went about embracing trees—go so far as to take every

episode in which this reality, that slips away, rears its head for the lived reaction of which they prove so fond. For these are the very people who, making their objective what lies beyond language, react to analysis' "Don't touch" rule by a sort of obsession. If they keep going in that direction, I dare say the last word in transference reaction will be sniffing each other. I am not exaggerating in the least: nowadays, a young analyst-in-training, after two or three years of fruitless analysis, can actually hail the long-awaited advent of the object-relation in being smelled by his subject, and can reap as a result of it the *dignus est intrare* of our votes, the guarantors of his abilities.

If psychoanalysis can become a science (for it is not yet one) and if it is not to degenerate in its technique (and perhaps this has already happened), we must rediscover the meaning of its experience.

To this end, we can do no better than return to Freud's work. Claiming to be an expert practitioner does not give an analyst the right to challenge Freud III, because he does not understand him, in the name of a Freud II whom he thinks he understands. And his very ignorance of Freud I is no excuse for considering the five great psychoanalyses as a series of case studies as badly chosen as they are written up, however marvelous he thinks it that the grain of truth hidden within them managed to escape.[15]

We must thus take up Freud's work again starting with the *Traumdeutung* [*The Interpretation of Dreams*] to remind ourselves that a dream has the structure of a sentence or, rather, to keep to the letter of the work, of a rebus—that is, of a form of writing, of which children's dreams are supposed to represent the primordial ideography, and which reproduces, in adults' dreams, the simultaneously phonetic and symbolic use of signifying elements found in the hieroglyphs of ancient Egypt and in the characters still used in China.

But even this is no more than the deciphering of the instrument. What is important is the version of the text, and that, Freud tells us, is given in the telling of the dream—that is, in its rhetoric. Ellipsis and pleonasm, hyperbaton or syllepsis, regression, repetition, apposition—these are the syntactical displacements; metaphor, catachresis, antonomasia, allegory, metonymy, and synecdoche—these are the semantic condensations; Freud teaches us to read in them the intentions—whether ostentatious or demonstrative, dissimulating or persuasive, retaliatory or seductive—with which the subject modulates his oneiric discourse.

We know that he laid it down as a rule that the expression of a desire must always be sought in a dream. But let us be sure we understand what he meant by this. If Freud accepts, as the reason for a dream that seems to run counter to his thesis, the very desire to contradict him on the part of a subject whom he had tried to convince of his theory,[16] how could he fail to accept the same reason for himself when the law he arrived at is supposed to have come to him from other people?

In short, nowhere does it appear more clearly that man's desire finds its meaning in the other's desire, not so much because the other holds the keys to the desired object, as because his first object(ive) is to be recognized by the other.

Indeed, we all know from experience that from the moment an analysis becomes engaged in the path of transference—and this is what indicates to us that it has become so engaged—each of the patient's dreams is to be interpreted as a provocation, a latent avowal or diversion, by its relation to the analytic discourse, and that as the analysis progresses, his dreams become ever more reduced to the function of elements in the dialogue taking place in the analysis.

In the case of the psychopathology of everyday life, another field consecrated by another text by Freud, it is clear that every bungled action is a successful, even "well phrased," discourse, and that in slips of the tongue it is the gag that turns against speech, and from just the right quadrant for its word to the wise to be sufficient.

But let us go straight to the part of the book where Freud deals with chance and the beliefs it gives rise to, and especially to the facts regarding which he applies himself to showing the subjective efficacy of associations to numbers that are left to the fate of an unmotivated choice, or even of a random selection. Nowhere do the dominant structures of the psychoanalytic field reveal themselves better than in such a success. Freud's appeal, in passing, to unknown thought processes is nothing more in this case than his last-ditch excuse for the total confidence he placed in symbols, a confidence that wavers as the result of being fulfilled beyond his wildest dreams.

If, for a symptom, whether neurotic or not, to be considered to come under psychoanalytic psychopathology, Freud insists on the minimum of overdetermination constituted by a double meaning—symbol of a defunct conflict beyond its function in a *no less symbolic* present conflict—and if he teaches us to follow the ascending ramification of the symbolic lineage in the text of the patient's free associations, in order to detect the nodal points [*noeuds*] of its structure at the places where its verbal forms intersect, then it is already quite clear that symptoms can be entirely resolved in an analysis of language, because a symptom is itself structured like a language: a symptom is language from which speech must be delivered.

To those who have not studied the nature of language in any depth, the experience of numerical association will immediately show what must be grasped here—namely, the combinatory power that orders its equivocations—and they will recognize in this the very mainspring of the unconscious.

Indeed, if—from the numbers obtained by breaking up the series of digits [*chiffres*] in the chosen number, from their combination by all the operations of arithmetic, and even from the repeated division of the original number by one of the numbers split off from it—the resulting numbers[17] prove symbolic among all the numbers in the subject's own history, it is because they were already latent in the initial choice. And thus if the idea that these very numbers [*chiffres*] determined the subject's fate is refuted as superstitious, we must nevertheless admit that everything analysis reveals to the subject as his unconscious lies in the existing order of their combinations—that is, in the concrete language they represent.

We shall see that philologists and ethnographers reveal enough to us about the combinatory sureness found in the completely unconscious systems with which they deal for them to find nothing surprising in the proposition I am putting forward here.

But should anyone still have reservations about what I am saying, I would appeal once more to the testimony of the man who, having discovered the unconscious, warrants credence when he designates its place; he will not fail us.

For, however little interest has been taken in it—and for good reason— *Jokes and Their Relation to the Unconscious* remains the most unchallengeable of his works because it is the most transparent; in it, the effect of the unconscious is demonstrated in all its subtlety. And the visage it reveals to us is that of wit [*l'esprit*] in the ambiguity conferred on it by language, where the other face of its regalian power is the witticism [*pointe*], by which the whole of its order is annihilated in an instant—the witticism, indeed, in which language's creative activity unveils its absolute gratuitousness, in which its domination of reality [*réel*] is expressed in the challenge of nonmeaning, and in which the humor, in the malicious grace of the free spirit [*esprit libre*], symbolizes a truth that does not say its last word.

We must follow Freud, along the book's admirably compelling detours, on the walk on which he leads us in this chosen garden of bitterest love.

Here everything is substantial, everything is a real gem. The mind [*esprit*] that lives as an exile in the creation whose invisible support he is, knows that he is at every instant the master capable of annihilating it. No matter how disdained the forms of this hidden royalty—haughty or perfidious, dandy-

270

like or debonair—Freud can make their secret luster shine. Stories of the marriage-broker on his rounds in the ghettos of Moravia—that derided Eros figure, like him born of penury and pain—discreetly guiding the avidity of his ill-mannered client, and suddenly ridiculing him with the illuminating nonsense of his reply. "He who lets the truth escape like that," comments Freud, "is in reality happy to throw off the mask."

It is truth, in fact, that throws off the mask in coming out of his mouth, but only so that the joke might take on another and more deceptive mask: the sophistry that is merely a stratagem, the logic that is merely a lure, even comedy that tends merely to dazzle. The joke is always about something else. "A joke [*esprit*] in fact entails such a subjective conditionality [. . .]: a joke is only what I accept as such," continues Freud, who knows what he is talking about.

Nowhere is the individual's intent more evidently surpassed by the subject's find—nowhere is the distinction I make between the individual and the subject so palpable—since not only must there have been something foreign to me in my find for me to take pleasure in it, but some of it must remain foreign for this find to hit home. This takes on its importance due to the necessity, so clearly indicated by Freud, of a joke's third person, who is always presupposed, and to the fact that a joke does not lose its power when told in the form of indirect speech. In short, this points, in the Other's locus, to the amboceptor that is illuminated by the artifice of the joke [*mot*] erupting in its supreme alacrity.

There is only one reason for a joke to fall flat: the platitude of any explanation given of its truth.

Now this relates directly to our problem. The current disdain for studies on the language of symbols—which can be seen simply by glancing at the table of contents of our publications before and after the 1920s—corresponds in our discipline to nothing less than a change of object, whose tendency to align itself with the most undifferentiated level of communication, in order to accommodate the new objectives proposed for psychoanalytic technique, is perhaps responsible for the rather gloomy balance sheet that the most lucid analysts have drawn up of its results.[18]

How, indeed, could speech exhaust the meaning of speech—or, to put it better with the Oxford logical positivists, the meaning of meaning*—if not in the act that engenders it? Thus Goethe's reversal of its presence at the origin, "In the beginning was the act," is itself reversed in its turn: it was certainly the Word that was [*était*] in the beginning, and we live in its creation, but it is our mental [*esprit*] action that continues this creation by constantly renewing it. And we can only think back to this action by allowing ourselves to be driven ever further ahead by it.

I shall try it myself only in the knowledge that this is its pathway . . .

No one is supposed to be ignorant of the law; this formulation, provided by   272
the humor in our Code of Laws, nevertheless expresses the truth in which our experience is grounded, and which our experience confirms. No man is actually ignorant of it, because the law of man has been the law of language since the first words of recognition presided over the first gifts—it having taken the detestable Danai, who came and fled by sea, for men to learn to fear deceptive words accompanying faithless gifts. Up until then, these gifts, the act of giving them and the objects given, their transmutation into signs, and even their fabrication, were so closely intertwined with speech for the pacific Argonauts—uniting the islets of their community with the bonds [*noeuds*] of a symbolic commerce—that they were designated by its name.[19]

Is it with these gifts, or with the passwords that give them their salutary nonmeaning, that language begins along with law? For these gifts are already symbols, in the sense that symbol means pact, and they are first and foremost signifiers of the pact they constitute as the signified; this is plainly seen in the fact that the objects of symbolic exchange—vases made to remain empty, shields too heavy to be carried, sheaves that will dry out, lances that are thrust into the ground—are all destined to be useless, if not superfluous by their very abundance.

Is this neutralization by means of the signifier the whole of the nature of language? Were this the case, one would find a first approximation of language among sea swallows, for instance, during display, materialized in the fish they pass each other from beak to beak; ethologists—if we must agree with them in seeing in this the instrument of a stirring into action of the group that is tantamount to a party—would then be altogether justified in recognizing a symbol in this activity.

It can be seen that I do not shrink from seeking the origins of symbolic behavior outside the human sphere. But it is certainly not by the pathway of an elaboration of signs, the pathway Jules H. Masserman,[20] following in the footsteps of so many others, has taken. I shall dwell on it for an instant here, not only because of the savvy tone with which he outlines his approach, but   273
also because his work has been well received by the editors of our official journal, who—following a tradition borrowed from employment agencies—never neglect anything that might provide our discipline with "good references."

Think of it—we have here a man who has reproduced neurosis ex-per-i-men-tal-ly in a dog tied down on a table, and by what ingenious methods: a bell, the plate of meat that it announces, and the plate of apples that arrives instead; I'll spare you the rest. He will certainly not be one, at least so he assures us, to let himself be taken in by the "extensive ruminations," as he puts it, that philosophers have devoted to the problem of language. Not him, he's going to grab it by the throat.

Can you imagine?—a raccoon can be taught, by a judicious conditioning of his reflexes, to go to his food box when he is presented with a card on which the meal he is to be served is printed. We are not told whether it lists the various prices, but the convincing detail is added that if the service disappoints him, he comes back and tears up the card that promised too much, just as a furious woman might do with the letters of a faithless lover (*sic*).

This is one of the arches supporting the road by which the author leads us from the signal to the symbol. It is a two-way street, and the way back is illustrated by no less imposing structures.

For if, in a human subject, you associate the ringing of a bell with the projection of a bright light into his eyes and then the ringing alone to the order, "contract,"* you will succeed in getting the subject to make his pupils contract just by pronouncing the order himself, then by whispering it, and eventually just by thinking it—in other words, you will obtain a reaction of the nervous system that is called autonomic because it is usually inaccessible to intentional effects. Thus, if we are to believe Masserman, a certain Hudgkins "had created in a group of people a highly individualized configuration of cognate and visceral reactions to the idea-symbol 'contract'—a response which could be traced through their special experiences to an apparently remote but actually basic physiologic source: in this instance, simply the protection of the retina from excessive light." And Masserman concludes: "The significance of such experiments for psycho-somatic and linguistic research hardly needs further elaboration."

For my part, I would have been curious to know whether subjects trained in this way also react to the enunciation of the same term in the expressions "marriage contract,"* "contract bridge,"* and "breach of contract,"* and even when the term is progressively shortened to the articulation of its first syllable alone: contract, contrac, contra, contr . . . The control test required by strict scientific method would then be supplied all by itself as the French reader muttered this syllable under his breath, even though he would have been subjected to no other conditioning than that of the bright light projected on the problem by Masserman himself. I would then ask this author whether the effects thus observed among conditioned subjects still appeared to so easily do without further elaboration. For either the effects would no longer be produced, thus revealing that they do not even conditionally depend on the semanteme, or they would continue to be produced, raising the question of the semanteme's limits.

In other words, they would cause the distinction between the signifier and the signified, so blithely confounded by the author in the English term "idea-symbol,"* to appear in the very word as instrument. And without needing to examine the reactions of subjects conditioned to react to the command "don't contract," or even to the complete conjugation of the verb "to contract," I could remark to the author that what defines any element whatsoever of a language [langue] as belonging to language is that, for all the users of the language [langue], this element is distinguished as such in the supposedly constituted set of homologous elements.

Thus, the particular effects of this element of language are linked to the existence of this set, prior to any possible link with any of the subject's particular experiences. And to consider this last link independently of any reference to the first is simply to deny the characteristic function of language to this element.

This reminder of first principles might perhaps save our author from discovering, with an unequaled naïveté, the verbatim correspondence of the grammatical categories of his childhood to relations found in reality.

This monument of naïveté—of a kind which is, moreover, common enough in these matters—would not be worth so much attention if it had not been erected by a psychoanalyst, or rather by someone who, as if by chance, relates everything to it which is produced by a certain tendency in psychoanalysis—under the heading of the theory of the ego or technique of the analysis of defenses—that is diametrically opposed to Freudian experience; he thereby manifests a contrario that a sound conception of language is coherent with the preservation of Freudian experience. For Freud's discovery was that of the field of the effects, in man's nature, of his relations to the symbolic order and the fact that their meaning goes all the way back to the most radical instances of symbolization in being. To ignore the symbolic order is to condemn Freud's discovery to forgetting and analytic experience to ruin.

I declare—and this is a declaration that cannot be divorced from the serious intent of my present remarks—that I would prefer to have the raccoon I mentioned earlier sitting in the armchair to which, according to our author, Freud's shyness confined the analyst by placing him behind the couch, rather than a scientist who discourses on language and speech as Masserman does.

For—thanks to Jacques Prévert ("A stone, two houses, three ruins, four ditch diggers, a garden, some flowers, a raccoon")—the raccoon, at least, has definitively entered the poetic bestiary and partakes as such, in its essence, of the symbol's eminent function. But that being resembling us who professes, as Masserman does, a systematic misrecognition of that function, forever banishes himself from everything that can be called into existence by it. Thus, the question of the place to be assigned the said semblable in the classification of natural beings would seem to me to smack of a misplaced humanism, if his discourse, crossed with a technique of speech of which we are the guardians, were not in fact too fertile, even in engendering sterile monsters within it. Let it be known therefore, since he also credits himself with braving the reproach of anthropomorphism, that this is the last term I would employ in saying that he makes his own being the measure of all things.

Let us return to our symbolic object, which is itself extremely substantial [*consistant*] in its matter, even if it has lost the weight of use, but whose imponderable meaning will produce displacements of some weight. Is that, then, law and language? Perhaps not yet.

276   For even if there appeared among the sea swallows some kaid of the colony who, by gulping down the symbolic fish from the others' gaping beaks, were to inaugurate the exploitation of swallow by swallow—a fanciful notion I enjoyed developing one day—this would not in any way suffice to reproduce among them that fabulous history, the image of our own, whose winged epic kept us captive on *Penguin Island*; something else would still be needed to create a "swallowized" universe.

This "something else" completes the symbol, making language of it. In order for the symbolic object freed from its usage to become the word freed from the *hic et nunc*, the difference resides not in the sonorous quality of its matter, but in its vanishing being in which the symbol finds the permanence of the concept.

Through the word—which is already a presence made of absence—absence itself comes to be named in an original moment whose perpetual re-creation Freud's genius detected in a child's game. And from this articulated couple of presence and absence—also sufficiently constituted by the drawing in the sand of a simple line and a broken line of the *koua* mantics of China—a language's [*langue*] world of meaning is born, in which the world of things will situate itself.

Through what becomes embodied only by being the trace of a nothingness and whose medium thus cannot be altered, concepts, in preserving the duration of what passes away, engender things.

For it is still not saying enough to say that the concept is the thing itself, which a child can demonstrate against the Scholastics. It is the world of words that creates the world of things—things which at first run together in the *hic et nunc* of the all in the process of becoming—by giving its concrete being to their essence, and its ubiquity to what has always been: κτῆμα ἐς ἀεὶ.

Man thus speaks, but it is because the symbol has made him man. Even if, in fact, overabundant gifts welcome a stranger who has made himself known to a group, the life of natural groups that constitute a community is subject to the rules of matrimonial alliance—determining the direction in which the exchange of women takes place—and to the mutual services determined by marriage: as the ŠiRonga proverb says, "A relative by marriage is an elephant's hip." Marriage ties are governed by an order of preference whose law concerning kinship names is, like language, imperative for the group in its forms, but unconscious in its structure. Now, in this structure, whose harmony or conflicts govern the restricted or generalized exchange discerned in it by ethnologists, the startled theoretician refinds the whole logic of combinations; thus the laws of number—that is, of the most highly purified of all symbols—prove to be immanent in the original symbolism. At least, it is the richness of the forms—in which what are known as the elementary structures of kinship develop—that makes those laws legible in the original symbolism. And this suggests that it is perhaps only our unawareness of their permanence that allows us to believe in freedom of choice in the so-called complex structures of marriage ties under whose law we live. If statistics has already allowed us to glimpse that this freedom is not exercised randomly, it is because a subjective logic seems to orient its effects.

This is precisely where the Oedipus complex—insofar as we still acknowledge that it covers the whole field of our experience with its signification—will be said, in my remarks here, to mark the limits our discipline assigns to subjectivity: namely, what the subject can know of his unconscious participation in the movement of the complex structures of marriage ties, by verifying the symbolic effects in his individual existence of the tangential movement toward incest that has manifested itself ever since the advent of a universal community.

The primordial Law is therefore the Law which, in regulating marriage

277

ties, superimposes the reign of culture over the reign of nature, the latter being subject to the law of mating. The prohibition of incest is merely the subjective pivot of that Law, laid bare by the modern tendency to reduce the objects the subject is forbidden to choose to the mother and sisters, full license, moreover, not yet being entirely granted beyond them.

This law, then, reveals itself clearly enough as identical to a language order. For without names for kinship relations, no power can institute the order of preferences and taboos that knot and braid the thread of lineage through the generations. And it is the confusion of generations which, in the Bible as in all traditional laws, is cursed as being the abomination of the Word and the desolation of the sinner.

Indeed, we know the damage a falsified filiation can do, going as far as dissociation of the subject's personality, when those around him conspire to sustain the lie. It may be no less when, as a result of a man marrying the mother of the woman with whom he has had a son, the son's brother will be his biological mother's half-brother. But if the son is later adopted— and I have not invented this example—by the sympathizing couple formed by a daughter of his father's previous marriage and her husband, he will find himself once again a half-brother, this time of his foster mother; and one can imagine the complex feelings he will have while awaiting the birth of a child who, in this recurring situation, will be his brother and nephew simultaneously.

So too, the mere time-lag produced in the order of generations by a late-born child of a second marriage, where a young mother finds herself the same age as an older brother from the first marriage, can produce similar effects; as we know, this was true in Freud's own family.

This same function of symbolic identification—allowing primitive man to believe he is the reincarnation of an ancestor with the same name, and even determining an alternating recurrence of characteristics in modern man—thus brings about a dissociation of the Oedipus complex in subjects exposed to such discordances in the paternal relation, in which the constant source of its pathogenic effects must be seen. Indeed, even when it is represented by a single person, the paternal function concentrates in itself both imaginary and real relations that always more or less fail to correspond to the symbolic relation that essentially constitutes it.

It is in the *name of the father* that we must recognize the basis of the symbolic function which, since the dawn of historical time, has identified his person with the figure of the law. This conception allows us to clearly distinguish, in the analysis of a case, the unconscious effects of this function from the narcissistic relations, or even real relations, that the subject has with the image and actions of the person who embodies this function; this results in a mode of comprehension that has repercussions on the very way in which interventions are made by the analyst. Practice has confirmed the fecundity of this conception to me, as well as to the students whom I have introduced to this method. And, both in supervision and case discussions, I have often had occasion to stress the harmful confusion produced by neglecting it.

Thus it is the virtue of the Word that perpetuates the movement of the Great Debt whose economy Rabelais, in a famous metaphor, extended to the stars themselves. And we shall not be surprised that the chapter in which he anticipates ethnographic discoveries with the macaronic inversion of kinship names, reveals in the Word the substantific divination of the human mystery that I am trying to elucidate here.

279

Identified with sacred *hau* or omnipresent *mana*, the inviolable Debt is the guarantee that the voyage on which women and goods are sent will bring back to their point of departure, in a never-failing cycle, other women and other goods, all bearing an identical entity: what Lévi-Strauss calls a "zero-symbol," thus reducing the power of Speech to the form of an algebraic sign.

Symbols in fact envelop the life of man with a network so total that they join together those who are going to engender him "by bone and flesh" before he comes into the world; so total that they bring to his birth, along with the gifts of the stars, if not with the gifts of the fairies, the shape of his destiny; so total that they provide the words that will make him faithful or renegade, the law of the acts that will follow him right to the very place where he is not yet and beyond his very death; and so total that through them his end finds its meaning in the last judgment, where the Word absolves his being or condemns it—unless he reaches the subjective realization of being-toward-death.

Servitude and grandeur in which the living being would be annihilated, if desire did not preserve his part in the interferences and pulsations that the cycles of language cause to converge on him, when the confusion of tongues intervenes and the orders thwart each other in the tearing asunder of the universal undertaking.

But for this desire itself to be satisfied in man requires that it be recognized, through the accord of speech or the struggle for prestige, in the symbol or the imaginary.

What is at stake in an analysis is the advent in the subject of the scant reality that this desire sustains in him, with respect to symbolic conflicts and imaginary fixations, as the means of their accord, and our path is the inter-subjective experience by which this desire gains recognition.

Thus we see that the problem is that of the relations between speech and language in the subject.

Three paradoxes in these relations present themselves in our domain.

In madness, of whatever nature, we must recognize on the one hand the negative freedom of a kind of speech that has given up trying to gain recognition, which is what we call an obstacle to transference; and, on the other, the singular formation of a delusion which—whether fabular, fantastical, or cosmological, or rather interpretative, demanding, or idealist—objectifies the subject in a language devoid of dialectic.[21]

The absence of speech is manifested in madness by the stereotypes of a discourse in which the subject, one might say, is spoken instead of speaking; we recognize here the symbols of the unconscious in petrified forms that find their place in a natural history of these symbols alongside the embalmed forms in which myths are presented in our collections of them. But it would be wrong to say that the subject assumes these symbols: the resistance to their recognition is no less strong in psychosis than in the neuroses, when the subject is led to recognize them by an attempt at treatment.

Let it be said in passing that it would be worthwhile noting the places in social space that our culture has assigned these subjects, especially as regards their relegation to the social services relating to language, for it is not unlikely that we find here one of the factors that consign such subjects to the effects of the breakdown produced by the symbolic discordances character-istic of the complex structures of civilization.

The second case is represented by the privileged field of psychoanalytic discovery—namely, symptoms, inhibition, and anxiety in the constitutive economy of the different neuroses.

Here speech is driven out of the concrete discourse that orders conscious-ness, but it finds its medium either in the subject's natural functions—provided a painful organic sensation wedges open the gap between his individual being and his essence, which makes illness what institutes the existence of the sub-ject in the living being[22]—or in the images that, at the border between the *Umwelt* and the *Innenwelt*, organize their relational structuring.

A symptom here is the signifier of a signified that has been repressed from the subject's consciousness. A symbol written in the sand of the flesh and on the veil of Maia, it partakes of language by the semantic ambiguity that I have already highlighted in its constitution.

But it is fully functioning speech, for it includes the other's discourse in the secret of its cipher [*chiffre*].

It was by deciphering this speech that Freud rediscovered the first language of symbols,[23] still alive in the sufferings of civilized man (*Das Unbehagen in der Kultur* [*Civilization and Its Discontents*]).

Hieroglyphics of hysteria, blazons of phobia, and labyrinths of *Zwangsneurose* [obsessive neurosis]; charms of impotence, enigmas of inhibition, and oracles of anxiety; talking arms of character,[24] seals of self-punishment, and disguises of perversion: these are the hermetic elements that our exegesis resolves, the equivocations that our invocation dissolves, and the artifices that our dialectic absolves, by delivering the imprisoned meaning in ways that run the gamut from revealing the palimpsest to providing the solution [*mot*] of the mystery and to pardoning speech.

The third paradox of the relation of language to speech is that of the subject who loses his meaning in the objectifications of discourse. However metaphysical its definition may seem, we cannot ignore its presence in the foreground of our experience. For this is the most profound alienation of the subject in our scientific civilization, and it is this alienation that we encounter first when the subject begins to talk to us about himself. In order to eliminate it entirely, analysis should thus be conducted until it has reached the endpoint of wisdom.

To provide an exemplary formulation of this, I can find no more relevant terrain than the usage of everyday speech, pointing out that the expression *"ce suis-je"* ["it is I"] of Villon's era has become inverted in the expression *"c'est moi"* ["it's me"] of modern man.

The me [*moi*] of modern man, as I have indicated elsewhere, has taken on its form in the dialectical impasse of the beautiful soul who does not recognize his very reason for being in the disorder he denounces in the world.

But a way out of this impasse is offered to the subject where his discourse rants and raves. Communication can be validly established for him in science's collective undertaking and in the tasks science ordains in our universal civilization; this communication will be effective within the enormous objectification constituted by this science, and it will allow him to forget his subjectivity. He will make an effective contribution to the collective undertaking in his daily work and will be able to occupy his leisure time with all the pleasures of a profuse culture which—providing everything from detective novels to historical memoirs and from educational lectures to the orthopedics of group relations—will give him the wherewithal to forget his own

282

existence and his death, as well as to misrecognize the particular meaning of his life in false communication.

If the subject did not rediscover through regression—often taken as far back as the mirror stage [*stade*]—the inside of a stadium [*stade*] in which his ego contains his imaginary exploits, there would hardly be any assignable limits to the credulity to which he would have to succumb in this situation. Which is what makes our responsibility so formidable when, with the mythical manipulations of our doctrine, we bring him yet another opportunity to become alienated, in the decomposed trinity of the ego,* the superego,* and the id,* for example.

Here it is a wall of language that blocks speech, and the precautions against verbalism that are a theme of the discourse of "normal" men in our culture merely serve to increase its thickness.

There might be some point in measuring its thickness by the statistically determined total pounds of printed paper, miles of record grooves, and hours of radio broadcasts that the said culture produces per capita in sectors A, B, and C of its domain. This would be a fine research topic for our cultural organizations, and it would be seen that the question of language does not remain entirely within the region of the brain in which its use is reflected in the individual.

> *We are the hollow men*
> *We are the stuffed men*
> *Leaning together*
> *Headpiece filled with straw. Alas!*
> *(and so on.)*

283   The resemblance between this situation and the alienation of madness—insofar as the formulation given above is authentic, namely, that the mad subject is spoken rather than speaking—is obviously related to the requirement, presupposed by psychoanalysis, of true speech. If this consequence, which takes the paradoxes that are constitutive of what I am saying here as far as they can go, were to be turned against the common sense of the psychoanalytic perspective, I would readily grant the pertinence of this objection, but only to find my own position confirmed in it—by a dialectical reversal for which there would be no shortage of authorized patrons, beginning with Hegel's critique of "the philosophy of the skull," and stopping only at Pascal's resounding warning, at the dawn of the historical era of the "me" ["*moi*"], formulated in the following terms: "Men

are so necessarily mad that it would be another twist of madness not to be mad."

This is not to say, however, that our culture pursues its course in the shadows outside of creative subjectivity. On the contrary, creative subjectivity has not ceased in its struggle to renew here the never-exhausted power of symbols in the human exchange that brings them to light.

To emphasize the small number of subjects who prop up this creation would be to give in to a romantic perspective by comparing things that are not equivalent. The fact is that this subjectivity, regardless of the domain in which it appears—mathematics, politics, religion, or even advertising—continues to animate the movement of humanity as a whole. Looking at it from another, probably no less illusory, angle would lead us to emphasize the opposite trait: the fact that its symbolic character has never been more manifest. The irony of revolutions is that they engender a power that is all the more absolute in its exercise, not because it is more anonymous, as people say, but because it is reduced more completely to the words that signify it. The strength of churches lies more than ever in the language they have been able to maintain: an instance, it should be noted, that Freud left aside in the article in which he sketches out for us what I call the "collective subjectivities" of the Church and the Army.

Psychoanalysis has played a role in the direction of modern subjectivity, and it cannot sustain this role without aligning it with the movement in modern science that elucidates it.

This is the problem of the foundations that must assure our discipline its place among the sciences: a problem of formalization, which, it must be admitted, has gotten off to a very bad start.

For it seems that, possessed anew by the very shortcoming in the medical mind in opposition to which psychoanalysis had to constitute itself, we were trying to jump back on the bandwagon of science—being half a century behind the movement of the sciences—by following medicine's example.

This leads to abstract objectification of our experience on the basis of fictitious, or even simulated, principles of experimental method—in which we find the effect of biases that must first be swept from our field if we wish to cultivate it according to its authentic structure.

As practitioners of the symbolic function, it is surprising that we shy away from delving deeper into it, going so far as to neglect the fact that this function situates us at the heart of the movement that is establishing a new order of the sciences, with a rethinking of anthropology.

This new order simply signifies a return to a notion of true science whose

284

credentials are already inscribed in a tradition that begins with Plato's *Theaetetus*. This notion has degenerated, as we know, in the positivist reversal which, by making the human sciences the crowning glory of the experimental sciences, in fact subordinates them to the latter. This conception results from an erroneous view of the history of science founded on the prestige of a specialized development of experimentation.

Today, however, the conjectural sciences are discovering once again the age-old notion of science, forcing us to revise the classification of the sciences we have inherited from the nineteenth century in a direction clearly indicated by the most lucid thinkers.

One need but follow the concrete evolution of the various disciplines in order to become aware of this.

Linguistics can serve us as a guide here, since that is the vanguard role it is given by contemporary anthropology, and we cannot remain indifferent to it.

The form of mathematicization in which the discovery of the *phoneme* is inscribed, as a function of pairs of oppositions formed by the smallest graspable discriminative semantic elements, leads us to the very foundations that Freud's final doctrine designates as the subjective sources of the symbolic function in a vocalic connotation of presence and absence.

285   And the reduction of any language [*langue*] to a group comprised of a very small number of such phonemic oppositions, initiating an equally rigorous formalization of its highest-level morphemes, puts within our reach a strict approach to our own field.

It is up to us to adopt this approach to discover how it intersects with our own field, just as ethnography, which follows a course parallel to our own, is already doing by deciphering myths according to the synchrony of mythemes.

Isn't it striking that Lévi-Strauss—in suggesting the involvement in myths of language structures and of those social laws that regulate marriage ties and kinship—is already conquering the very terrain in which Freud situates the unconscious?[25]

It is thus impossible not to make a general theory of the symbol the axis of a new classification of the sciences where the sciences of man will reassume their central position as sciences of subjectivity. Let me indicate its core principle, which, of course, does not obviate the need for further elaboration.

The symbolic function presents itself as a twofold movement in the subject: man makes his own action into an object, but only to return its foundational place to it in due time. In this equivocation, operating at every instant, lies the whole progress of a function in which action and knowledge [*connaissance*] alternate.[26]

Here are two examples, one borrowed from the classroom, the other from the very pulse of our time:

- The first is mathematical: in phase one, man objectifies two collections he has counted in the form of two cardinal numbers; in phase two, he manages to add the two collections using these numbers (see the example cited by Kant in the introduction to the transcendental aesthetic, section IV, in the second edition of the *Critique of Pure Reason*);
- The second is historical: in phase one, a man who works at the level of production in our society considers himself to belong to the ranks of the proletariat; in phase two, in the name of belonging to it, he joins in a general strike.

If these two examples come from areas which, for us, are the most highly contrasted in the domain of the concrete—the first involving the ever freer play of mathematical law, the second, the brazen face of capitalist exploitation—it is because, although they seem to come from radically different realms, their effects come to constitute our subsistence, precisely by intersecting there in a double reversal: the most subjective science having forged a new reality, and the shadow of the social divide arming itself with a symbol in action.

Here the distinction people make between the exact sciences and those for which there is no reason to refuse the appellation "conjectural" no longer seems to be acceptable—for lack of any grounds for that distinction.[27]

For exactness must be distinguished from truth, and conjecture does not exclude rigor. If experimental science derives its exactness from mathematics, its relation to nature is nonetheless problematic.

Indeed, if our link to nature incites us to wonder poetically whether it is not nature's own movement that we refind in our science, in

> . . . *cette voix*
> *Qui se connaît quand elle sonne*
> *N'être plus la voix de personne*
> *Tant que des ondes et des bois,*

it is clear that our physics is but a mental fabrication in which mathematical symbols serve as instruments.

For experimental science is not so much defined by the quantity to which it is in fact applied, as by the measurement it introduces into reality [*réel*].

This can be seen in relation to the measurement of time without which experimental science would be impossible. Huyghens' clock, which alone gave experimental science its precision, is merely the organ that fulfills Galileo's hypothesis concerning the equal gravitational pull on all bodies—that is, the hypothesis of uniform acceleration that confers its law, since it is the same, on every instance of falling.

287   It is amusing to point out that the instrument was completed before the hypothesis could be verified by observation, and that the clock thereby rendered the hypothesis useless at the same time as it offered it the instrument it needed to be rigorous.[28]

But mathematics can symbolize another kind of time, notably the intersubjective time that structures human action, whose formulas are beginning to be provided by game theory, still called strategy, but which it would be better to call "stochastics."

The author of these lines has attempted to demonstrate in the logic of a sophism the temporal mainsprings through which human action, insofar as it is coordinated with the other's action, finds in the scansion of its hesitations the advent of its certainty; and, in the decision that concludes it, gives the other's action—which it now includes—its direction [*sens*] to come, along with its sanction regarding the past.

I demonstrate there that it is the certainty anticipated by the subject in the "time for understanding" which—through the haste that precipitates the "moment of concluding"—determines the other's decision that makes the subject's own movement an error or truth.

This example indicates how the mathematical formalization that inspired Boolean logic, and even set theory, can bring to the science of human action the structure of intersubjective time that psychoanalytic conjecture needs to ensure its own rigor.

If, moreover, the history of the historian's technique shows that its progress is defined in the ideal of an identification of the historian's subjectivity with the constitutive subjectivity of the primal historicization in which events are humanized, it is clear that psychoanalysis finds its precise scope here: that is, in knowledge [*connaissance*], as realizing this ideal, and in efficacy, as finding its justification here. The example of history also dissipates like a mirage the recourse to the "lived reaction" that obsesses both our technique and our theory, for the fundamental historicity of the events we

are concerned with suffices to conceive the possibility of a subjective reproduction of the past in the present.

Furthermore, this example makes us realize how psychoanalytic regres-
sion implies the progressive dimension of the subject's history—which   288
Freud rightly considered to be lacking in the Jungian concept of neurotic
regression—and we see how analytic experience itself renews this progression by assuring its continuation.

Finally, the reference to linguistics will introduce us to the method which,
by distinguishing synchronic from diachronic structurings in language, will
enable us to better understand the different value our language takes on in
the interpretation of resistances and of transference, and to differentiate the
effects characteristic of repression and the structure of the individual myth
in obsessive neurosis.

The list of disciplines Freud considered important sister sciences for an
ideal Department of Psychoanalysis is well known. Alongside psychiatry
and sexology we find "the history of civilization, mythology, the psychology of religions, literary history, and literary criticism."

This whole group of subjects, determining the curriculum for instruction
in technique, can be easily accommodated in the epistemological triangle I
have described, and would provide an advanced level of instruction in analytic theory and technique with its primer.

For my part, I would be inclined to add: rhetoric, dialectic (in the technical sense this term takes on in Aristotle's *Topics*), grammar, and poetics—
the supreme pinnacle of the aesthetics of language—which would include
the neglected technique of witticisms.

While these subject headings may sound somewhat old-fashioned to certain people, I would not hesitate to endorse them as a return to our sources.

For psychoanalysis in its early development, intimately linked to the
discovery and study of symbols, went so far as to partake in the structure
of what was called "the liberal arts" in the Middle Ages. Deprived,
like them, of a true formalization, psychoanalysis became organized, like
them, into a body of privileged problems, each one promoted by some
felicitous relation of man to his own measure, taking on a charm and a
humanity owing to this particularity that in our eyes might well make up
for their somewhat recreational appearance. But let us not disdain this
appearance in the early developments of psychoanalysis; indeed, it   289
expresses nothing less than the re-creation of human meaning in an arid
era of scientism.

These early developments should be all the less disdained since psycho-

analysis has hardly raised the bar by setting off along the false pathways of
a theorization that runs counter to its dialectical structure.

Psychoanalysis can provide scientific foundations for its theory and
technique only by adequately formalizing the essential dimensions of its
experience, which—along with the historical theory of the symbol—are
intersubjective logic and the temporality of the subject.

III. The Resonances of Interpretation and the Time
of the Subject in Psychoanalytic Technique

> Between man and love,
> There is woman.
> Between man and woman,
> There is a world.
> Between man and the world,
> There is a wall.
> —Antoine Tudal, *Paris in the Year 2000*

> *Nam Sibyllam quidem Cumis ego ipse oculis meis vidi in ampulla pendere, et
> cum illi pueri dicerent:* Σιβύλλα τι θέλεις, *respondebat illa:* ἀποθανεῖν
> θέλω.
> —Petronius, *Satyricon*, XLVIII

Bringing psychoanalytic experience back to speech and language as its foundations is of direct concern to its technique. While it is not situated in the
ineffable, we see the one-way slippage that has occurred, distancing interpretation from its core. We are thus justified in suspecting that this deviation
in psychoanalytic practice explains the new aims to which psychoanalytic
theory has become receptive.

If we look at the situation a little more closely, we see that the problems
of symbolic interpretation began by intimidating our little group before
becoming embarrassing to it. The successes obtained by Freud now aston-
ish people because of the unseemly indoctrination they appear to involve,
and the display thereof—so evident in the cases of Dora, the Rat Man, and
the Wolf Man—strikes us as nothing short of scandalous. Indeed, our clever
colleagues do not shrink from doubting whether the technique employed in
these cases was actually any good.

This disaffection in the psychoanalytic movement stems, in truth, from a
confusion of tongues, about which the most representative personality of its
present hierarchy made no secret in a recent conversation with me.

It is well worth noting that this confusion grows when each analyst

290

believes he has been assigned the job of discovering in our experience the conditions of a complete objectification, and when the enthusiasm that greets his theoretical attempts is greater the more detached from reality they prove to be.

It is clear that the principles of the analysis of the resistances, as well-founded as they may be, have in practice occasioned an ever greater misrecognition of the subject, because they have not been understood in relation to the intersubjectivity of speech.

If we follow the proceedings of Freud's first seven sessions with the Rat Man, which are reported to us in full, it seems highly improbable that Freud did not recognize the resistances as they arose arising precisely in the places where our modern practitioners tell us he overlooked them—since it is Freud's own text, after all, that enables the practitioners to pinpoint them. Once again Freud's texts manifest an exhaustion of the subject that amazes us, and no interpretation has thus far exploited all of its resources.

I mean that Freud not only let himself be duped into encouraging his subject to go beyond his initial reticence, but also understood perfectly well the seductive scope of this game in the imaginary. To convince oneself of this, one need but read the description he gives us of the expression on his patient's face during the patient's painful narrative of the purported torture that supplied the theme of his obsession, that of the rat forced into the victim's anus: "His face," Freud tells us, "reflected horror at a jouissance of which he was unaware." The effect in the present of his repeating this narrative did not escape Freud, no more than did the fact that he identified his analyst with the "cruel captain" who forced this narrative to become etched in the subject's memory, nor therefore the import of the theoretical clarifications the subject required as security before going on with what he was saying.

291

Far from interpreting the resistance here, however, Freud astonishes us by granting the patient's request, to such an extent that he seems to let himself be roped into the subject's game.

But the extremely approximate character of the explanations with which Freud gratifies him, so approximate as to appear crude, is sufficiently instructive: it is clearly not so much a question here of doctrine or indoctrination as of a symbolic gift of speech—ripe with a secret pact, in the context of the imaginary participation which includes it—whose import will be revealed later in the symbolic equivalence the subject establishes in his mind between rats and the florins with which he remunerates the analyst.

We can see therefore that Freud, far from misrecognizing the resistance, uses it as a propitious predisposition for setting in motion the resonances of speech, and he conducts himself, as far as possible, in accordance with the first definition he gave of resistance, by employing it to involve the subject in his message. He later changes tack abruptly when he sees that, as a result of being handled delicately, the resistance is serving to keep the dialogue at the level of a conversation in which the subject tries to continue seducing the analyst by slipping beyond his reach.

But we learn that analysis consists in playing on the multiple staves of the score that speech constitutes in the registers of language—which is where overdetermination comes in, the latter having no meaning except in this order.

And we have simultaneously isolated here the mainspring of Freud's success. In order for the analyst's message to respond to the subject's profound questioning, the subject must understand it as a response that concerns him alone; and the privilege Freud's patients enjoyed, in receiving its good word from the lips of the very man who was its herald, satisfied this demand of theirs.

Let us note in passing that the Rat Man had had a prior taste of it, since he had thumbed through *The Psychopathology of Everyday Life*, which had just come out.

Which doesn't imply that the book is very much better known today, even among analysts, but the popularization of Freud's concepts and their resorption into what I call the wall of language, would deaden the effect of our speech were we to give it the style of Freud's remarks to the Rat Man.

The point here is not to imitate him. In order to rediscover the effect of Freud's speech, I won't resort to its terms but rather to the principles that govern it.

These principles are nothing but the dialectic of self-consciousness, as it is realized from Socrates to Hegel, beginning with the ironic assumption that all that is rational is real, only to precipitate into the scientific judgment that all that is real is rational. But Freud's discovery was to demonstrate that this verifying process authentically reaches the subject only by decentering him from self-consciousness, to which he was confined by Hegel's reconstruction of the phenomenology of mind. In other words, this discovery renders still flimsier any search for "conscious realization" which, apart from being a psychological phenomenon, is not inscribed within the conjuncture of the particular moment that alone gives body to the universal, and failing which the latter dissipates into generality.

These remarks define the limits within which it is impossible for our technique to ignore the structuring moments of Hegel's phenomenology: first and foremost, the master/slave dialectic, the dialectic of the beautiful soul and the law of the heart, and generally everything that allows us to understand how the constitution of the object is subordinate to the realization of the subject.

But if there is still something prophetic in Hegel's insistence on the fundamental identity of the particular and the universal, an insistence that reveals the extent of his genius, it is certainly psychoanalysis that provides it with its paradigm by revealing the structure in which this identity is realized as disjunctive of the subject, and without appealing to the future.

Let me simply say that this, in my view, constitutes an objection to any reference to totality in the individual, since the subject introduces division therein, as well as in the collectivity that is the equivalent of the individual. Psychoanalysis is what clearly relegates both the one and the other to the status of mirages.

This would seem to be something that could no longer be forgotten, were it not precisely psychoanalysis that teaches us that it is forgettable—confirmation of which turns out, by a reversal [*retour*] that is more legitimate than one might think, to come from psychoanalysts themselves, their "new tendencies" representing this forgetting.

Now while Hegel's work is also precisely what we need to confer a meaning on so-called analytic neutrality other than that the analyst is simply in a stupor, this does not mean that we have nothing to learn from the elasticity of the Socratic method or even from the fascinating proceedings of the technique by which Plato presents it to us, were it only by our sensing in Socrates and his desire the unresolved enigma of the psychoanalyst, and by situating in relation to Platonic vision our own relation to truth—in this case, however, in a way that respects the distance separating the reminiscence Plato was led to presume to exist in any advent of the ideas, from the exhaustion of being consummated in Kierkegaardian repetition.[29]

But there is also a historical difference between Socrates' interlocutor and ours that is worth weighing. When Socrates relies on an artisanal form of reason that he can extract just as well from a slave's discourse, it is in order to impress upon authentic masters the necessity of an order that turns their power into justice and the city's magic words [*maîtres-mots*] into truth. But we analysts deal with slaves who think they are masters, and who find in a language—whose mission is universal—support for their servitude in the bonds of its ambiguity. So much so that one might humorously say that our goal is to restore in them the sovereign freedom displayed by Humpty

Dumpty when he reminds Alice that he is, after all, master of the signifier, even if he is not master of the signified from which his being derived its shape.

We always come back, then, to our twofold reference to speech and language. In order to free the subject's speech, we introduce him to the language of his desire, that is, to the *primary language* in which—beyond what he tells us of himself—he is already speaking to us unbeknown to himself, first and foremost, in the symbols of his symptom.

It is certainly a language that is at stake in the symbolism brought to light in analysis. This language, corresponding to the playful wish found in one of Lichtenberg's aphorisms, has the universal character of a tongue that would be understood in all other tongues, but at the same time—since it is the language that grabs hold of desire at the very moment it becomes humanized by gaining recognition—it is absolutely particular to the subject.

It is thus a *primary language*, by which I do not mean a primitive language, since Freud—whose merit for having made this total discovery warrants comparison with Champollion's—deciphered it in its entirety in the dreams of our contemporaries. The essential field of this language was rather authoritatively defined by one of the earliest assistants associated with Freud's work, and one of the few to have brought anything new to it: I mean Ernest Jones, the last survivor of those to whom the seven rings of the master were passed and who attests by his presence in the honorary positions of an international association that they are not reserved solely for relic bearers.

In a fundamental article on symbolism,[30] Jones points out on page 102 that, although there are thousands of symbols in the sense in which the term is understood in analysis, all of them refer to one's own body, blood relatives, birth, life, and death.

This truth, recognized *de facto* by Jones, enables us to understand that although the symbol, psychoanalytically speaking, is repressed in the unconscious, it bears in itself no mark of regression or even of immaturity. For it to have its effects in the subject, it is thus enough that it make itself heard, since these effects operate unbeknown to him—as we admit in our everyday experience, when we explain many reactions by normal and neurotic subjects as their response to the symbolic meaning of an act, a relation, or an object.

It is thus indisputable that the analyst can play on the power of symbols by evoking them in a calculated fashion in the semantic resonances of his remarks.

This is surely the path by which a return to the use of symbolic effects can proceed in a renewed technique of interpretation.

We could adopt as a reference here what the Hindu tradition teaches about *dhvani*,[31] defining it as the property of speech by which it conveys what it does not say. This is illustrated by a little tale whose naïveté, which appears to be required in such examples, proves funny enough to induce us to penetrate to the truth it conceals.   295

A girl, it is said, is awaiting her lover on the bank of a river when she sees a Brahmin coming along. She approaches him and exclaims in the most amiable tones: "What a lucky day this is for you! The dog whose barking used to frighten you will not be on this river bank again, for it was just devoured by a lion that roams around here . . ."

The absence of the lion may thus have as many effects as his spring—which, were he present, would only come once, according to the proverb relished by Freud.

The *primary* character of symbols in fact makes them similar to those numbers out of which all other numbers are composed; and if they therefore underlie all the semantemes of a language, we shall be able to restore to speech its full evocative value by a discreet search for their interferences, following the course of a metaphor whose symbolic displacement neutralizes the secondary meanings of the terms it associates.

To be taught and to be learned, this technique would require a profound assimilation of the resources of a language [*langue*], especially those that are concretely realized in its poetic texts. It is well known that Freud was steeped in German literature, which, by virtue of an incomparable translation, can be said to include Shakespeare's plays. Every one of his works bears witness to this, and to the continual recourse he had to it, no less in his technique than in his discovery. Not to mention his broad background in the classics, his familiarity with the modern study of folklore, and his keeping abreast of contemporary humanism's conquests in the area of ethnography.

Analytic practitioners should be asked not to consider it futile to follow Freud along this path.

But the tide is against us. It can be gauged by the condescending attention paid to the "wording,"* as if to some novelty; and the English morphology here provides a notion that is still difficult to define with a prop that is sufficiently subtle for people to make a big to-do about it.

What this notion covers, however, is hardly encouraging when we see an author[32] amazed at having achieved an entirely different success in the interpretation of one and the same resistance by the use, "without conscious pre-   296 meditation," he emphasizes, of the term "need for love"* instead of and in the place of "demand for love,"* which he had first put forward, without seeing anything in it (as he himself tells us). While the anecdote is supposed to confirm the interpretation's reference to the "ego psychology"* in the title of the article, it refers instead, it seems, to the analyst's ego psychology,* insofar as this interpretation makes do with such a weak use of English that he can extend his practice of analysis right to the very brink of gibberish.[33]

The fact is that need* and demand* have diametrically opposed meanings for the subject, and to maintain that they can be used interchangeably for even an instant amounts to a radical ignorance of the *summoning* characteristic of speech.

For in its symbolizing function, speech tends toward nothing less than a transformation of the subject to whom it is addressed by means of the link it establishes with the speaker—namely, by bringing about a signifying effect.

This is why we must return once more to the structure of communication in language and definitively dispel the mistaken notion of "language as signs," a source in this realm of confusions about discourse and of errors about speech.

If communication based on language is conceived as a signal by which the sender informs the receiver of something by means of a certain code, there is no reason why we should not lend as much credence and even more to every other kind of sign when the "something" in question concerns the individual: indeed, we are quite right to prefer every mode of expression that verges on natural signs.

It is in this way that the technique of speech has been discredited among us and we find ourselves in search of a gesture, a grimace, a posture adopted, a face made, a movement, a shudder—nay, a stopping of usual movement—for we are subtle and nothing will stop us from setting our bloodhounds on the scent.

I shall show the inadequacy of the conception of language as signs by the very manifestation that best illustrates it in the animal kingdom, a manifestation which, had it not recently been the object of an authentic discovery, would have to have been invented for this purpose.

It is now generally recognized that, when a bee returns to its hive after gathering nectar, it transmits an indication of the existence of nectar near or far away from the hive to its companions by two sorts of dances. The second is the most remarkable, for the plane in which the bee traces out a figure eight—a shape that gave it the name "wagging dance"*—and the frequency of the figures executed within a given time, designate, on the one hand, the exact direction to be followed, determined in relation to the sun's inclination (by which bees are able to orient themselves in all kinds of weather, thanks to their sensitivity to polarized light), and, on the other hand, the distance at which the nectar is to be found up to several miles away. The other bees respond to this message by immediately setting off for the place thus designated.

It took some ten years of patient observation for Karl von Frisch to decode this kind of message, for it is certainly a code or signaling system, whose generic character alone forbids us to qualify it as conventional.

But is it a language, for all that? We can say that it is distinguished from language precisely by the fixed correlation between its signs and the reality they signify. For, in a language, signs take on their value from their relations to each other in the lexical distribution of semantemes as much as in the positional, or even flectional, use of morphemes—in sharp contrast to the fixity of the coding used by bees. The diversity of human languages takes on its full value viewed in this light.

Furthermore, while a message of the kind described here determines the action of the "socius," it is never retransmitted by the socius. This means that the message remains frozen in its function as a relay of action, from which no subject detaches it as a symbol of communication itself.[14]   298

The form in which language expresses itself in and of itself defines subjectivity. Language says: "You will go here, and when you see this, you will turn off there." In other words, it refers to discourse about the other [*discours de l'autre*]. It is enveloped as such in the highest function of speech, inasmuch as speech commits its author by investing its addressee with a new reality, as for example, when a subject seals his fate as a married man by saying "You are my wife."

Indeed, this is the essential form from which all human speech derives more than the form at which it arrives.

Hence the paradox that one of my most acute auditors believed to be an objection to my position when I first began to make my views known on analysis as dialectic; he formulated it as follows: "Human language would then constitute a kind of communication in which the sender receives his own message back from the receiver in an inverted form." I could but adopt this objector's formulation, recognizing in it the stamp of my own thinking; for I maintain that speech always subjectively includes its own reply, that "Thou wouldst not seek Me, if thou hadst not found Me" simply validates the same truth, and that this is why, in the paranoiac refusal of recognition, it is in the form of a negative verbalization that the unavowable feeling eventually emerges in a persecutory "interpretation."

Thus when you congratulate yourself for having met someone who speaks the same language as you, you do not mean that you encounter each other in the discourse of everyman, but that you are united to that person by a particular way of speaking.

The antinomy immanent in the relations between speech and language thus becomes clear. The more functional language becomes, the less suited it is to speech, and when it becomes overly characteristic of me alone, it loses its function as language.

We are aware of the use made in primitive traditions of secret names, with which the subject identifies his own person or his gods so closely that to reveal these names is to lose himself or betray these gods; and what our patients confide in us, as well as our own recollections, teach us that it is not at all rare for children to spontaneously rediscover the virtues of that use.

Finally, the speech value of a language is gauged by the intersubjectivity of the "we" it takes on.

By an inverse antinomy, it can be observed that the more language's role is neutralized as language becomes more like information, the more *redundancies* are attributed to it. This notion of redundancy originated in research that was all the more precise because a vested interest was involved, having been prompted by the economics of long-distance communication and, in particular, by the possibility of transmitting several conversations on a single telephone line simultaneously. It was observed that a substantial portion of the phonetic medium is superfluous for the communication actually sought to be achieved.

This is highly instructive to us,[35] for what is redundant as far as information is concerned is precisely what plays the part of resonance in speech.

For the function of language in speech is not to inform but to evoke.

What I seek in speech is a response from the other. What constitutes me as a subject is my question. In order to be recognized by the other, I proffer what was only in view of what will be. In order to find him, I call him by a name that he must assume or refuse in order to answer me.

I identify myself in language, but only by losing myself in it as an object. What is realized in my history is neither the past definite as what was, since it is no more, nor even the perfect as what has been in what I am, but the future anterior as what I will have been, given what I am in the process of becoming.

If I now face someone to question him, there is no cybernetic device imaginable that can turn his response into a reaction. The definition of "response" as the second term in the "stimulus-response" circuit is simply a metaphor sustained by the subjectivity attributed to animals, only to be elided thereafter in the physical schema to which the metaphor reduces it. This is what I have called putting a rabbit into a hat so as to pull it out again later. But a reaction is not a response.

If I press an electric button and a light goes on, there is a response only to *my* desire. If in order to obtain the same result I must try a whole system of relays whose correct position is unknown to me, there is a question only in relation to my expectation, and there will not be a question any more once I have learned enough about the system to operate it flawlessly.

But if I call the person to whom I am speaking by whatever name I like, I notify him of the subjective function he must take up in order to reply to me, even if it is to repudiate this function.

The decisive function of my own response thus appears, and this function is not, as people maintain, simply to be received by the subject as approval or rejection of what he is saying, but truly to recognize or abolish him as a subject. Such is the nature of the analyst's *responsibility* every time he intervenes by means of speech.

The problem of the therapeutic effects of inexact interpretation, raised by Edward Glover in a remarkable paper,[36] thus led him to conclusions where the question of exactness fades into the background. For not only is every spoken intervention received by the subject as a function of his structure, but the intervention itself takes on a structuring function due to its form. Indeed, nonanalytic psychotherapies, and even utterly ordinary medical "prescriptions," have the precise impact of interventions that could be qualified as obsessive systems of suggestion, as hysterical suggestions of a phobic nature, and even as persecutory supports, each psychotherapy deriving its particular character from the way it sanctions the subject's misrecognition of his own reality.   301

Speech is in fact a gift of language, and language is not immaterial. It is a subtle body, but body it is. Words are caught up in all the body images that captivate the subject; they may "knock up" the hysteric, be identified with the object of *Penisneid*, represent the urinary flow of urethral ambition, or represent the feces retained in avaricious jouissance.

Furthermore, words themselves can suffer symbolic lesions and accomplish imaginary acts whose victim is the subject. Recall the *Wespe* (wasp), castrated of its initial W to become the S.P. of the Wolf Man's initials, at the moment he carried out the symbolic punishment to which he himself was subjected by Grusha, the wasp.

Recall too the S that constitutes the residue of the hermetic formula into which the Rat Man's conjuratory invocations became condensed after Freud had extracted the anagram of his beloved's name from its cipher, and that, tacked onto the beginning of the final "amen" of his jaculatory prayer, eternally inundated the lady's name with the symbolic ejecta of his impotent desire.

Similarly, an article by Robert Fliess,[37] inspired by Abraham's inaugural remarks, shows us that one's discourse as a whole may become eroticized, following the displacements of erogeneity in the body image, momentarily determined by the analytic relationship.

Discourse then takes on a urethral-phallic, anal-erotic, or even oral-sadistic function. It is noteworthy, moreover, that the author grasps its effect above all in the silences that mark inhibition of the satisfaction the subject derives from it.

In this way speech may become an imaginary or even real object in the subject and, as such, debase in more than one respect the function of language. I shall thus relegate such speech to the parenthesis of the resistance it manifests.

302 But not in order to exclude it from the analytic relationship, for the latter would then lose everything, including its *raison d'être*.

Analysis can have as its goal only the advent of true speech and the subject's realization of his history in its relation to a future.

Maintaining this dialectic is directly opposed to any objectifying orientation of analysis, and highlighting this necessity is of capital importance if we are to see through the aberrations of the new trends in psychoanalysis.

I shall illustrate my point here by once again returning to Freud, and, since I have already begun to make use of it, to the case of the Rat Man.

Freud goes so far as to take liberties with the exactness of the facts when it is a question of getting at the subject's truth. At one point, Freud glimpses the determinant role played by the mother's proposal that he marry her cousin's daughter at the origin of the present phase of his neurosis. Indeed, as I have shown in my seminar, this flashes through Freud's mind owing to his own personal experience. But he does not hesitate to interpret its effect to the subject as that of a prohibition by his dead father against his liaison with his lady-love.

This interpretation is not only factually, but also psychologically, inexact, for the father's castrating activity—which Freud affirms here with an insistence that might be believed systematic—played only a secondary role in this case. But Freud's apperception of the dialectical relationship is so apt that the interpretation he makes at that moment triggers the decisive destruction of the lethal symbols that narcissistically bind the subject both to his dead father and to his idealized lady, their two images being sustained, in an equivalence characteristic of the obsessive, one by the fantasmatic aggressiveness that perpetuates it, the other by the mortifying cult that transforms it into an idol.

Similarly, it is by recognizing the forced subjectivization of the obsessive debt[38]—in the scenario of futile attempts at restitution, a scenario that too perfectly expresses its imaginary terms for the subject to even try to enact it, the pressure to repay the debt being exploited by the subject to the point of delusion—that Freud achieves his goal. This is the goal of bringing the subject to rediscover—in the story of his father's lack of delicacy, his marriage to the subject's mother, the "pretty but penniless girl," his wounded love-life, and his ungrateful forgetting of his beneficent friend—to rediscover in this story, along with the fateful constellation that presided over the subject's very birth, the unfillable gap constituted by the symbolic debt against which his neurosis is a protest.

303

There is no trace here at all of recourse to the ignoble specter of some sort of early "fear," or even to a masochism that it would be easy enough to brandish, much less to that obsessive buttressing propagated by some analysts in the name of the analysis of the defenses. The resistances themselves, as I have shown elsewhere, are used as long as possible in the direction [*sens*] of the progress of the discourse. And when it is time to put an end to them, we manage to do so by giving in to them.

For this is how the Rat Man is able to insert into his subjectivity its true mediation in a transferential form: the imaginary daughter he gives Freud in order to receive her hand in marriage from him, and who unveils her true face to him in a key dream—that of death gazing at him with its bituminous eyes.

And although it was with this symbolic pact that the ruses of the subject's servitude came to an end, reality did not fail him, it seems, in granting him these nuptial wishes. The footnote added to the case in 1923—which Freud dedicated as an epitaph to this young man who had found in the risks of war "the end that awaited so many worthy young men on whom so many hopes had been founded," thus concluding the case with all the rigor of destiny—elevates it to the beauty of tragedy.

In order to know how to respond to the subject in analysis, the method is to first determine where his ego* is situated—the ego* that Freud himself defined as formed by a verbal nucleus—in other words, to figure out through whom and for whom the subject asks *his question*. As long as this is not known, we risk misconstruing the desire that must be recognized there and the object to whom this desire is addressed.

The hysteric captivates this object in a subtle intrigue and her ego* is in the third person by means of whom the subject enjoys the object who incarnates her question. The obsessive drags into the cage of his narcissism the objects in which his question reverberates in the multiplied alibi of deadly figures and, mastering their high-wire act, addresses his ambiguous homage toward the box in which he himself has his seat, that of the master who cannot be seen [*se voir*].

Trahit sua quemque voluptas; one identifies with the spectacle and the other puts on a show [*donne à voir*].

In the case of the hysterical subject, for whom the term "acting out"* takes on its literal meaning since he acts outside himself, you have to get him to recognize where his action is situated. In the case of the obsessive, you have to get yourself recognized in the spectator, who is invisible from the stage, to whom he is united by the mediation of death.

It is therefore always in the relation between the subject's *ego* and his discourse's *I* that you must understand the meaning of the discourse if you are to unalienate the subject.

But you cannot possibly achieve this if you cleave to the idea that the subject's ego is identical to the presence that is speaking to you.

This error is fostered by the terminology of the topography that is all too tempting to an objectifying cast of mind, allowing it to slide from the ego defined as the perception-consciousness system—that is, as the system of the subject's objectifications—to the ego conceived of as the correlate of an absolute reality and thus, in a singular return of the repressed in psychologistic thought, to once again take the ego as the "reality function" in relation to which Pierre Janet organizes his psychological conceptions.

Such slippage occurred only because it was not realized that, in Freud's work, the ego,* id,* superego* topography is subordinate to the metapsychology whose terms he was propounding at the same time and without which the topography loses its meaning. Analysts thus became involved in a sort of psychological orthopedics that will continue to bear fruit for a long time to come.

Michael Balint has provided a thoroughly penetrating analysis of the interaction between theory and technique in the genesis of a new conception of analysis, and he finds no better term to indicate its result than the watchword he borrows from Rickman: the advent of a "two-body psychology."*

Indeed, it couldn't be better put. Analysis is becoming the relation of two bodies between which a fantasmatic communication is established in which the analyst teaches the subject to apprehend himself as an object. Subjectivity is admitted into analysis only as long as it is bracketed as an illusion, and speech is excluded from a search for lived experience that becomes its supreme aim; but its dialectically necessary result appears in the fact that, since the analyst's subjectivity is freed [*délivrée*] from all restraint, this leaves the subject at the mercy [*livré*] of every summons of the analyst's speech.

305

Once the intrasubjective topography has become entified, it is in fact realized in the division of labor between the subjects present. This deviant use of Freud's formulation that all that is id* must become ego* appears in a demystified form: the subject, transformed into an *it*, has to conform to an ego* which the analyst has no trouble recognizing as his ally, since it is, in fact, the analyst's own ego.*

It is precisely this process that is expressed in many a theoretical formulation of the splitting* of the ego* in analysis. Half of the subject's ego* crosses over to the other side of the wall that separates the analysand from the analyst, then half of the remaining half, and so on, in an asymptotic progression that never succeeds—regardless of how great the inroads it makes into the opinion the subject will have formed of himself—in crushing his every possibility of reversing the aberrant effects of his analysis.

But how could a subject, who undergoes a type of analysis based on the principle that all his formulations are systems of defense, defend himself against the total disorientation to which this principle consigns the analyst's dialectic?

Freud's interpretation, the dialectical method of which appears so clearly in the case of Dora, does not present these dangers, for when the analyst's biases (that is, his countertransference, a term whose correct use, in my view, cannot be extended beyond the dialectical reasons for his error) have misled him in his intervention, he immediately pays a price for it in the form of a negative transference. For the latter manifests itself with a force that is all the greater the further such an analysis has already led the subject toward an authentic recognition, and what usually results is the breaking off of the analysis.

This is exactly what happened in Dora's case, because of Freud's relentless attempts to make her think Herr K. was the hidden object of her desire; the constitutive biases of Freud's countertransference led him to see in Herr K. the promise of Dora's happiness.

Dora herself was undoubtedly mistaken [*feintée*] about her relationship

306   with Herr K., but she did not feel any the less that Freud was too. Yet when she comes back to see him, after a lapse of fifteen months—in which the fateful cipher of her "time for understanding" is inscribed—we can sense that she begins to feign to have been feigning. The convergence of this feint, raised to the second power, with the aggressive intent Freud attributes to it—not inaccurately, of course, but without recognizing its true mainspring—presents us with a rough idea of the intersubjective complicity that an "analysis of resistances," sure of being within its rights, might have perpetuated between them. There can be little doubt that, with the means now available to us due to the "progress" that has been made in our technique, this human error could have been extended well beyond the point at which it would have become diabolical.

   None of this is my own invention, for Freud himself recognized after the fact the preliminary source of his failure in his own misrecognition at that time of the homosexual position of the object aimed at by the hysteric's desire.

   The whole process that led to this current trend in psychoanalysis no doubt goes back, first of all, to the analyst's guilty conscience about the miracle his speech performs. He interprets the symbol and, lo and behold, the symptom—which inscribes the symbol in letters of suffering in the subject's flesh—disappears. This thaumaturgy is unbecoming to us. For, after all, we are scientists and magic is not a justifiable practice. So we disclaim responsibility by accusing the patient of magical thinking. Before long we'll be preaching the Gospel according to Lévy-Bruhl to him. But in the meantime—behold—we have become thinkers again, and have reestablished the proper distance between ourselves and our patients; for we had, no doubt, a little too quickly abandoned the tradition of respecting that distance, a tradition expressed so nobly in the lines by Pierre Janet in which he spoke of the feeble abilities of the hysteric compared to our own lofty ones. "She understands nothing about science," he confides to us regarding the poor little thing, "and doesn't even imagine how anybody could be interested in it . . . If we consider the absence of control that characterizes hysterics' thinking, rather than allowing ourselves to be scandalized by their lies, which, in any case, are very naive, we should instead be astonished that there are so many honest ones . . ."

   Since these lines represent the feelings to which many of those present-day analysts who condescend to speak to the patient "in his own language" have reverted, they may help us understand what has happened in the mean-
307   time. For had Freud been capable of endorsing such lines, how could he

have heard as he did the truth contained in the little stories told by his first patients, or deciphered a dark delusion like Schreber's to such a great extent as to broaden it to encompass man eternally bound to his symbols?

Is our reason so weak that it cannot see that it is the same in the meditations of scientific discourse and in the first exchange of symbolic objects, and cannot find here the identical measure of its original cunning?

Need I point out what the yardstick of "thought" is worth to practitioners of an experience that associates the job of thought more closely with a mental eroticism than with an equivalent of action?

Must the person who is speaking to you attest that he need not resort to "thought" to understand that, if he is speaking to you at this moment about speech, it is insofar as we have in common a technique of speech which enables you to understand him when he speaks to you about it, and which inclines him to address those who understand nothing of it through you?

Of course, we must be attentive to the unsaid that dwells in the holes in discourse, but the unsaid is not to be understood like knocking coming from the other side of the wall.

If we are to concern ourselves from now on with nothing but such noises, as some analysts pride themselves on doing, it must be admitted that we have not placed ourselves in the most favorable of conditions to decipher their meaning—for how, without jumping to conclusions about their meaning, are we to translate what is not in and of itself language? Led then to call upon the subject, since it is after all to his account that we must transfer this understanding, we shall involve him with us in a wager, a wager that we understand their meaning, and then wait for a return that makes us both winners. As a result, in continuing to perform this shuttling back and forth, he will learn quite simply to beat time himself; it is a form of suggestion which is no worse than any other—in other words, one in which, as in every other form of suggestion, one does not know who starts the ball rolling. The procedure is recognized as being sound enough when it is a question of going to prison.[39]

Halfway to this extreme the question arises: does psychoanalysis remain a dialectical relation in which the analyst's nonaction guides the subject's discourse toward the realization of his truth, or is it to be reduced to a fantasmatic relation in which "two abysses brush up against each other" without touching, until the whole range of imaginary regressions is exhausted—reduced, that is, to a sort of "bundling"*[40] taken to the extreme as a psychological test?

In fact, this illusion—which impels us to seek the subject's reality beyond

the wall of language—is the same one that leads the subject to believe that
his truth is already there in us, that we know it in advance. This is also why
he is so open to our objectifying interventions.

He, of course, does not have to answer for this subjective error which,
whether it is avowed or not in his discourse, is immanent in the fact that he
entered analysis and concluded the original pact involved in it. And we can
still less neglect the subjectivity of this moment because it reveals the reason
for what may be called the constitutive effects of transference, insofar as
they are distinguished by an indication of reality from the constituted effects
that follow them.[41]

Freud, let us recall, in discussing the feelings people relate to the transference, insisted on the need to discern in them a reality factor. He concluded that it would be taking undue advantage of the subject's docility to
try to persuade him in every case that these feelings are a mere transferential repetition of the neurosis. Now, since these real feelings manifest themselves as primary and since our own charm remains a matter of chance,
there might seem to be some mystery here.

But this mystery is solved when viewed from the vantage point of the
phenomenology of the subject, insofar as the subject is constituted in the
search for truth. We need but consider the traditional facts—which
Buddhists provide us with, although they are not the only ones—to recognize in this form of transference the characteristic error of existence, broken
down by Buddhists into the following three headings: love, hate, and ignorance. It is therefore as a counter to the analytic movement that we shall
understand their equivalence in what is called a positive transference at the
outset—each one being shed light on by the other two in this existential
aspect, as long as one does not except the third, which is usually omitted
because of its proximity to the subject.

I am alluding here to the invective with which someone called upon
me to witness the lack of discretion shown by a certain work (which I have
already cited too often) in its insane objectification of the play of the instincts
in analysis, someone whose debt to me can be recognized by his use of the
term "real" in conformity with mine. It was in the following words that
he "unburdened his heart," as they say: "It is high time we put an end to the
fraud that tends to perpetuate the belief that anything real whatsoever takes
place during treatment." Let us leave aside what has become of him, for alas,
if analysis has not cured the dog's oral vice mentioned in the Scriptures, its
state is worse than before: it is others' vomit that it laps up.

This sally was not ill directed, since it sought in fact to distinguish

309

between those elementary registers, whose foundations I have since laid, known as the symbolic, the imaginary, and the real—a distinction never previously made in psychoanalysis.

Reality in analytic experience often, in fact, remains veiled in negative forms, but it is not that difficult to situate.

Reality is encountered, for instance, in what we usually condemn as active interventions; but it would be an error to limit its definition in this way.

For it is clear that the analyst's abstention—his refusal to respond—is also an element of reality in analysis. More exactly, the junction between the symbolic and the real lies in this negativity, insofar as it is pure—that is, detached from any particular motive. This follows from the fact that the analyst's nonaction is founded on the knowledge affirmed in the principle that all that is real is rational, and on the resulting motive that it is up to the subject to find anew its measure.

310

The fact remains that this abstention is not maintained indefinitely; when the subject's question assumes the form of true speech, we sanction it with our response; but I have shown that true speech already contains its own response—thus we are simply doubling his antiphon with our lay. What can this mean except that we do no more than give the subject's speech its dialectical punctuation?

Thus we see the other moment—which I have already pointed out theoretically—in which the symbolic and the real come together: in the function of time. It is worth dwelling for a moment on time's impact on technique.

Time plays a role in analytic technique in several ways.

It presents itself first in the total length of an analysis, and concerns the meaning to be given to the term of the analysis, which is a question that must be addressed prior to examining that of the signs of its end. I shall touch on the problem of setting a time limit to an analysis. But it is already clear that its length can only be expected to be indefinite for the subject.

This is true for two reasons that can only be distinguished from a dialectical perspective:

- The first, which is based on the limits of our field, and which confirms my remarks on the definition of its confines: we cannot predict how long a subject's *time for understanding* will last, insofar as it includes a psychological factor that escapes us by its very nature.
- The second, which is a characteristic of the subject, owing to which setting a time limit to his analysis amounts to a spatializing projection in

which he already finds himself alienated from himself: from the moment his truth's due date can be predicted—whatever may become of it in the intervening intersubjectivity—the fact is that the truth is already there; that is, we reestablish in the subject his original mirage insofar as he situates his truth in us and, by sanctioning this mirage with the weight of our authority, we set the analysis off on an aberrant path whose results will be impossible to correct.

311   This is precisely what happened in the famous case of the Wolf Man, and Freud so well understood its exemplary importance that he used the case to support his argument in his article on analysis, finite or indefinite.[42]

Setting in advance a time limit to an analysis, the first form of active intervention, inaugurated (*pro pudor!*) by Freud himself—regardless of the divinatory (in the true sense of the term)[43] sureness the analyst may evince in following Freud's example—will invariably leave the subject alienated from his truth.

We find confirmation of this point in two facts from the Wolf Man case:

In the first place, despite the whole network of proofs demonstrating the historicity of the primal scene, and despite the conviction he displays concerning it—remaining imperturbable to the doubts Freud methodically cast on it in order to test him—the Wolf Man never managed to integrate his recollection of the primal scene into his history.

Secondly, the same patient later demonstrated his alienation in the most categorical way: in a paranoid form.

It is true that another factor comes in here, through which reality intervenes in the analysis—namely, the gift of money whose symbolic value I shall leave aside for another occasion, but whose import is already indicated in what I have said about the link between speech and the gift that constitutes primitive exchange. In this case, the gift of money is reversed by an initiative of Freud's in which—as in the frequency with which he returns to the case—we can recognize his unresolved subjectivization of the problems this case left in abeyance. And no one doubts but that this was a triggering
312   factor of the Wolf Man's psychosis, though without really being able to say why.

Don't we realize, nevertheless, that allowing a subject to be nourished at the expense of the analytic academy in return for the services he rendered to science as a case (for it was in fact through a group collection that the Wolf Man was supported) is also to decisively alienate him from his truth?

The material furnished in the supplementary analysis of the Wolf Man

entrusted to Ruth Mack Brunswick illustrates the responsibility of the previous treatment with Freud by demonstrating my remarks on the respective
places of speech and language in psychoanalytic mediation.

What's more, it is from the perspective of speech and language that one
can grasp how Mack Brunswick took her bearings not at all badly in her delicate position in relation to the transference. (The reader will be reminded
of the very "wall" in my metaphor, as it figures in one of the Wolf Man's
dreams, the wolves in the key dream displaying their eagerness to get
around it . . .) Those who attend my seminar know all this, and others can
try their hand at it.[44]

What I want to do is touch on another aspect of the function of time in
analytic technique that is currently a matter of much debate. I wish to say
something about the length of sessions.

Here again it is a question of an element that manifestly belongs to reality, since it represents our work time, and viewed from this angle it alls
within the purview of professional regulations that may be considered
predominant.

But its subjective impact is no less important—and, first of all, on the
analyst. The taboo surrounding recent discussion of this element is sufficient proof that the analytic group's subjectivity is hardly liberated on this
question; and the scrupulous, not to say obsessive, character that observing
a standard takes on for some if not most analysts—a standard whose historical and geographical variations nevertheless seem to bother no one—is a
clear sign of the existence of a problem that analysts are reluctant to broach
because they realize to what extent it would entail questioning the analyst's
function.

Secondly, no one can ignore its importance to the subject in analysis. The
unconscious, it is said—in a tone that is all the more knowing the less the
speaker is capable of justifying what he means—the unconscious needs time
to reveal itself. I quite agree. But I ask: how is this time to be measured? By
what Alexandre Koyré calls "the universe of precision"? We obviously live
in such a universe, but its advent for man is relatively recent, since it goes
back precisely to Huyghens' clock—in other words, to 1659—and the dis-
content of modern man precisely does not indicate that this precision serves
him as a liberating factor. Is this time—the time characteristic of the fall of
heavy bodies—in some way sacred in the sense that it corresponds to the
time of the stars as it was fixed for all eternity by God—who, as
Lichtenberg tells us, winds our sundials? Perhaps we could acquire a somewhat better idea of time by comparing the amount of time required for the

creation of a symbolic object with the moment of inattention in which we drop it.

Whatever the case may be, if it is problematic to characterize what we do during this time as work, I believe I have made it quite clear that we can characterize what the patient does during this time as work.

But the reality, whatever it may be, of this time consequently takes on a localized value: that of receiving the product of this labor.

We play a recording role by serving a function which is fundamental in any symbolic exchange—that of gathering what *do kamo*, man in his authenticity, calls "the lasting word."

A witness blamed for the subject's sincerity, trustee of the record of his discourse, reference attesting to its accuracy, guarantor of its honesty, keeper of its testament, scrivener of its codicils, the analyst is something of a scribe.

But he remains the master of the truth of which this discourse constitutes the progress. As I have said, it is the analyst above all who punctuates its dialectic. And here he is apprehended as the judge of the value of this discourse. This has two consequences.

The ending of a session cannot but be experienced by the subject as a punctuation of his progress. We know how he calculates the moment of its arrival in order to tie it to his own timetable, or even to his evasive maneuvers, and how he anticipates it by weighing it like a weapon and watching out for it as he would for a place of shelter.

It is a fact, which can be plainly seen in the study of manuscripts of symbolic writings, whether the Bible or the Chinese canonical texts, that the absence of punctuation in them is a source of ambiguity. Punctuation, once 314   inserted, establishes the meaning; changing the punctuation renews or upsets it; and incorrect punctuation distorts it.

The indifference with which ending a session after a fixed number of minutes has elapsed interrupts the subject's moments of haste can be fatal to the conclusion toward which his discourse was rushing headlong, and can even set a misunderstanding in stone, if not furnish a pretext for a retaliatory ruse.

Beginners seem more struck by the effects of this impact than others—which gives one the impression that for others it is just a routine.

The neutrality we manifest in strictly applying the rule that sessions be of a specified length obviously keeps us on the path of nonaction.

But this nonaction has a limit, otherwise we would never intervene at all—so why make intervening impossible at this point, thereby privileging it?

The danger that arises if this point takes on an obsessive value for the analyst lies simply in the fact that it lends itself to the subject's connivance, a connivance that is available not only to the obsessive, although it takes on a special force for him, owing precisely to his impression that he is working. The sense of forced labor that envelops everything for this subject, including even his leisure activities, is only too well known.

This sense is sustained by his subjective relation to the master insofar as it is the master's death that he awaits.

Indeed, the obsessive manifests one of the attitudes that Hegel did not develop in his master/slave dialectic. The slave slips away when faced with the risk of death, when the opportunity to acquire mastery is offered to him in a struggle for pure prestige. But since he knows he is mortal, he also knows that the master can die. Hence he can accept to work for the master and give up jouissance in the meantime; and, unsure as to when the master will die, he waits.

This is the intersubjective reason for both the doubt and procrastination that are obsessive character traits.

Meanwhile, all his work is governed by this intention and thus becomes doubly alienating. For not only is the subject's creation [*oeuvre*] taken away from him by another—the constitutive relation of all labor—but the subject's recognition of his own essence in his creation, in which this labor finds its justification, eludes him no less, for he himself "is not in it." He is in the anticipated moment of the master's death, at which time he will begin to live; but in the meantime he identifies with the master as dead and is thus already dead himself.

He nevertheless strives to fool the master by demonstrating his good intentions through hard work. This is what the dutiful children of the analytic catechism express in their crude language by saying that the subject's ego* is trying to seduce his superego.*

This intrasubjective formulation is immediately demystified if we understand it in the analytic relationship, where the subject's "working through" is in fact employed to seduce the analyst.

And it is no accident that, once the dialectical progress begins to approach the challenging of the ego's* intentions in our subjects, the fantasy of the analyst's death—often experienced in the form of fear or even of anxiety—never fails to be produced.

And the subject then sets off again in an even more demonstrative elaboration of his "good will."

Can there be any doubt, then, about what happens when the master manifests disdain for the product of such work? The subject's resistance may become completely disconcerted.

From then on, his alibi—hitherto unconscious—begins to unveil itself to him, and we see him passionately seek the why and wherefore of so much effort.

I would not say so much about it if I had not been convinced—in experimenting with what have been called my "short sessions," at a stage in my career that is now over—that I was able to bring to light in a certain male subject fantasies of anal pregnancy, as well as a dream of its resolution by Cesarean section, in a time frame in which I would normally still have been listening to his speculations on Dostoyevsky's artistry.

In any case, I am not here to defend this procedure, but to show that it has a precise dialectical meaning in analytic technique.[45]

And I am not the only one to have remarked that it bears a certain resemblance to the technique known as Zen, which is applied to bring about the subject's revelation in the traditional ascesis of certain Far Eastern schools.

316   Without going to the extremes to which this technique is taken, since they would be contrary to certain of the limitations imposed by our own, a discreet application of its basic principle in analysis seems much more acceptable to me than certain methods of the so-called analysis of the resistances, insofar as such an application does not in itself entail any danger of alienating the subject.

For it shatters discourse only in order to bring forth speech.

Here we are, then, up against the wall—up against the wall of language. We are in our place here, that is, on the same side of the wall as the patient, and it is off this wall—which is the same for him as for us—that we shall try to respond to the echo of his speech.

There is nothing that is anything but outer darkness to us beyond this wall. Does this mean that we thoroughly master the situation? Certainly not, and on this point Freud has bequeathed us his testament regarding the negative therapeutic reaction.

The key to this mystery, it is said, is in the insistence [*instance*] of a primary masochism—in other words, in a pure manifestation of the death instinct whose enigma Freud propounded for us at the height of his career.

We cannot discount it, any more than I can postpone examining it here.

For I note that two different groups join forces in refusing to accept this culminating point of Freud's doctrine: those whose approach to analysis revolves around a conception of the ego* which I have shown to be erroneous, and those who, like Reich, take the principle of seeking an ineffable organic expression beyond speech so far that, like him, in order to free it from its armor, they might symbolize, as he does, the orgasmic induction that, like him, they expect from analysis in the superimposition of the two vermicular forms whose stupefying schema is found in his book, *Character Analysis*.

Once I have demonstrated the profound relationship uniting the notion of the death instinct to problems of speech, we will see that a rigorous logic governing intellectual productions underlies this joining of forces.

As even a moment's reflection shows, the notion of the death instinct involves a basic irony, since its meaning has to be sought in the conjunction of two opposing terms: "instinct" which, in its broadest acceptation, is the law that regulates the successive stages of a behavioral cycle in order to accomplish a life function; and "death" which appears first of all as the destruction of life.

317

Nevertheless, the definition of life provided by Bichat at the dawn of biology as the set of forces that resist death, and the most modern conception of life—found in Cannon's notion of homeostasis—as the function of a system maintaining its own equilibrium, are there to remind us that life and death come together in a relation of polar opposites at the very heart of phenomena that people associate with life.

Hence the congruence of the contrasting terms of the death instinct with the phenomena of repetition, Freud in fact relating the former to the latter with the term "automatism," would not cause difficulty were it simply a question of a biological notion.

But, as we all know, it is not, which is what makes the problem a stumbling block to so many of us. The fact that numerous analysts balk at the apparent incompatibility of these terms might well be worth our attention, for it manifests a dialectical innocence that would probably be disconcerted by the classical problem posed to semantics in the determinative statement, "a hamlet on the Ganges," by which Hindu aesthetics illustrates the second form of the resonances of language.[46]

This notion of the death instinct must be broached through its resonances in what I will call the poetics of Freud's work—a first avenue for getting at its meaning, and a dimension that is essential for understanding the dialectical repercussion of its origins at the apogee marked by this notion. It should be recalled, for example, that Freud tells us his vocation for medicine came to him during a public reading of Goethe's famous "Hymn to Nature"—that is, in a text that was brought to light by one of Goethe's friends, which the poet, in the twilight of his life, agreed to recognize as a putative child of the most youthful effusions of his pen.

At the other end of Freud's life, we see in the article on analysis considered as finite or indefinite that he explicitly relates his new conception to the
318   conflict of the two principles governing the alternation of all life according
to Empedocles of Agrigentum in the fifth century B.C.—that is, in the pre-
Socratic era in which nature and mind were not distinguished.

These two facts are a sufficient indication to us that what is at stake here
is a myth of the dyad, whose exposition by Plato is, moreover, mentioned in
Beyond the Pleasure Principle, a myth that can only be understood in the subjectivity of modern man by raising it to the negativity of the judgment in
which it is inscribed.

This is to say that, just as the repetition automatism—which is just as
completely misunderstood by those who wish to separate its two terms—
aims at nothing but the historicizing temporality of the experience of transference, so the death instinct essentially expresses the limit of the subject's
historical function. This limit is death—not as the possible end date of the
individual's life, nor as the subject's empirical certainty, but, as Heidegger
puts it, as that "possibility which is the subject's ownmost, which is unconditional, unsurpassable, certain, and as such indeterminable"—the subject
being understood as defined by his historicity.

Indeed, this limit is present at every instant in what is finished in this history. It represents the past in its real form; it is not the physical past whose
existence is abolished, nor the epic past as it has become perfected in the
work of memory, nor the historical past in which man finds the guarantor
of his future, but rather the past which manifests itself in an inverted form
in repetition.[47]

This is the dead person [*le mort*] subjectivity takes as its partner in the
triad instituted by its mediation in the universal conflict of *Philia*, love, and
Neikos, strife.

Thus there is no further need to resort to the outdated notion of primary
masochism to explain repetitive games in which subjectivity simultaneously
masters its dereliction and gives birth to the symbol.

These are occultation games which Freud, in a flash of genius, presented
to us so that we might see in them that the moment at which desire is human-
319   ized is also that at which the child is born into language.

We can now see that the subject here does not simply master his deprivation by assuming it—he raises his desire to a second power. For his action
destroys the object that it causes to appear and disappear by *bringing about*
its absence and presence in advance. His action thus negativizes the force
field of desire in order to become its own object to itself. And this object,

being immediately embodied in the symbolic pair of two elementary exclamations, announces the subject's diachronic integration of the dichotomy of
phonemes, whose synchronic structure the existing language offers up for
him to assimilate; the child thus begins to become engaged in the system of
the concrete discourse of those around him by reproducing more or less
approximately in his *Fort!* and *Da!* the terms he receives from them.

Fort! Da! It is already when quite alone that the desire of the human child
becomes the desire of another, of an alter ego who dominates him and
whose object of desire is henceforth his own affliction.

Should the child now address an imaginary or real partner, he will see
that this partner too obeys the negativity of his discourse, and since his call
has the effect of making the partner slip away, he will seek to bring about
the reversal that brings the partner back to his desire through a banishing
summons.

Thus the symbol first manifests itself as the killing of the thing, and this
death results in the endless perpetuation of the subject's desire.

The first symbol in which we recognize humanity in its vestiges is the
burial, and death as a means can be recognized in every relation in which
man is born into the life of his history.

This is the only life that endures and is true, since it is transmitted without being lost in a tradition passed on from subject to subject. It is impossible not to see how loftily this life transcends that inherited by the animal, in
which the individual fades into the species, since no memorial distinguishes
its ephemeral appearance from the appearance that reproduces it in the
invariability of the type. Indeed, apart from the hypothetical mutations of
the phylum that must be integrated by a subjectivity that man is still only
approaching from the outside, nothing, except the experiments in which
man uses it, distinguishes a particular rat from rats in general, a horse from
horses, nothing except the amorphous passage from life to death—whereas
Empedocles, by throwing himself into Mount Etna, leaves forever present   320
in the memory of men the symbolic act of his being-toward-death.

Man's freedom is entirely circumscribed within the constitutive triangle
of the following: the renunciation he imposes on the other's desire by threat-
ening to kill the other in order to enjoy the fruits of the other's serfdom, the
sacrifice of his life that he agrees to for the reasons that give human life its
measure, and the suicidal abnegation of the vanquished party that deprives
the master of his victory and leaves him to his inhuman solitude.

Of these figures of death, the third is the supreme detour by which the
immediate particularity of desire, reconquering its ineffable form, refinds in

negation a final triumph. And we must recognize its meaning, for as analysts we deal with it. It is not, in fact, a perversion of instinct, but rather a desperate affirmation of life that is the purest form we can find of the death instinct.

The subject says "No!" to this darting game of intersubjectivity in which desire gains recognition for a moment only to lose itself in a will that is the other's will. The subject patiently withdraws his precarious life from the churning aggregations of the symbol's Eros in order to finally affirm life in a speechless curse.

When we want to get at what was before the serial games of speech in the subject and what is prior to the birth of symbols, we find it in death, from which his existence derives all the meaning it has. Indeed, he asserts himself with respect to others as a death wish; if he identifies with the other, it is by freezing him in the metamorphosis of his essential image, and no being is ever conjured up by him except among the shadows of death.

To say that this mortal meaning reveals in speech a center that is outside of language is more than a metaphor—it manifests a structure. This structure differs from the spatialization of the circumference or sphere with which some people like to schematize the limits of the living being and its environment: it corresponds rather to the relational group that symbolic logic designates topologically as a ring.

321   If I wanted to give an intuitive representation of it, it seems that I would have to resort not to the two-dimensionality of a zone, but rather to the three-dimensional form of a torus, insofar as a torus' peripheral exteriority and central exteriority constitute but one single region.[48]

This schema represents the endless circularity of the dialectical process that occurs when the subject achieves his solitude, whether in the vital ambiguity of immediate desire or in the full assumption of his being-toward-death.

But we can simultaneously see that the dialectic is not individual, and that the question of the termination of an analysis is that of the moment at which the subject's satisfaction is achievable in the satisfaction of all—that is, of all those it involves in a human undertaking. Of all the undertakings that have been proposed in this century, the psychoanalyst's is perhaps the loftiest, because it mediates in our time between the care-ridden man and the subject of absolute knowledge. This is also why it requires a long subjective ascesis, indeed one that never ends, since the end of training analysis itself is not separable from the subject's engagement in his practice.

Let whoever cannot meet at its horizon the subjectivity of his time give it up then. For how could he who knows nothing of the dialectic that engages him in a symbolic movement with so many lives possibly make his being the axis of those lives? Let him be well acquainted with the whorl into which his era draws him in the ongoing enterprise of Babel, and let him be aware of his function as an interpreter in the strife of languages. As for the darkness of the *mundus* around which the immense tower is coiled, let him leave to mystical vision the task of seeing the putrescent serpent of life rise up there on an everlasting rod.

Allow me to laugh if these remarks are accused of turning the meaning of Freud's work away from the biological foundations he would have wished for it toward the cultural references with which it is rife. I do not wish to preach to you the doctrine of the *b* factor, designating the first, nor of the *c* factor, designating the second. All I have tried to do is remind you of the neglected *a*, *b*, *c* structure of language, and to teach you to spell once again the forgotten ABC's of speech.

For what recipe would guide you in a technique that is composed of the first and derives its effects from the second, if you did not recognize the field of the one and the function of the other?

Psychoanalytic experience has rediscovered in man the imperative of the Word as the law that has shaped him in its image. It exploits the poetic function of language to give his desire its symbolic mediation. May this experience finally enable you to understand that the whole reality of its effects lies in the gift of speech[49]; for it is through this gift that all reality has come to man and through its ongoing action that he sustains reality.

If the domain defined by this gift of speech must be sufficient for both your action and your knowledge, it will also be sufficient for your devotion. For it offers the latter a privileged field.

When the Devas, the men, and the Asuras were finishing their novitiate with Prajapati, as we read in the first Brahmana of the fifth lesson of the Brihadaranyaka Upanishad, they begged him, "Speak to us."

"*Da*," said Prajapati, god of thunder. "Did you hear me?" And the Devas answered, saying: "Thou hast said to us: *Damyata*, master yourselves"—the sacred text meaning that the powers above are governed by the law of speech.

"*Da*," said Prajapati, god of thunder. "Did you hear me?" And the men answered, saying: "Thou hast said to us: *Datta*, give"—the sacred text meaning that men recognize each other by the gift of speech.

"*Da*," said Prajapati, god of thunder. "Did you hear me?" And the Asuras answered, saying: "Thou hast said to us: *Dayadhvam*, be merci-

322

ful"—the sacred text meaning that the powers below resound [*résonnent*][50] to the invocation of speech.

That, continues the text, is what the divine voice conveys in the thunder: Submission, gift, grace. *Da da da*.

For Prajapati replies to all: "You have heard me."

Notes

1. See "Logical Time," *Écrits* 1966, 197–213.

2. Ferenczi, "Confusion of Tongues between the Adult and the Child," *IJP* XXX, 4 (1949): 225–30.

3. (Added in 1966:) The preceding paragraph has been rewritten.

4. (Added in 1966:) Previously I had written: "in psychological matters."

5. (Added in 1966:) The preceding paragraph has been rewritten.

6. This is the crux of a deviation that concerns both practice and theory. For to identify the ego* with the subject's self-discipline is to confuse imaginary isolation with mastery of the instincts; here one is liable to make errors of judgment in the conduct of the treatment—such as trying to strengthen the ego* in many neuroses that are caused by its overly strong structure, which is a dead end. Hasn't my friend Michael Balint written that a strengthening of the ego* should be beneficial to a subject suffering from *ejaculatio praecox* because it would permit him to prolong the suspension of his desire? But how can we think this, when it is precisely to the fact that his desire depends on the imaginary function of the ego* that the subject owes the short-circuiting of the act—which psychoanalytic clinical experience clearly shows to be intimately related to narcissistic identification with the partner.

7. This in the same work I praised at the end of my introduction (added in 1966). It is clear in what follows that aggressiveness is only a side effect of analytic frustration, though it can be reinforced by a certain type of intervention; as such, it is not the reason for the frustration/regression pair.

8. *GW* XII, 71; *Cinq psychanalyses* (Paris: PUF, 1954), 356, a weak translation of the term.

9. *GW* XII, 72, fn1, the last few lines. The concept of *Nachträglichkeit* is underlined in the footnote. *Cinq psychanalyses*, 356, fn1.

10. See *Écrits* 1966, 204–10.

11. Freud uses the term in an article accessible to even the least demanding of French readers, since it came out in the *Revue Neurologique*, a journal generally found on bookshelves in hospital staff rooms. The blunder exposed here illustrates, among other things, how the said authority I saluted on page 246 [in *Écrits* 1966] measures up to his leadership.*

12. (Added in 1966:) Even if he is speaking to everyone in general and no one in particular [*à la cantonade*]. He addresses that Other (with a capital O) whose theoretical basis I have since consolidated, and which demands a certain *epoche* in returning to the term to which I limited myself at that time: that of "intersubjectivity."

13. I am borrowing these terms from the late and sorely missed Édouard Pichon who, both in the directions he gave for the advent of our discipline and in those that guided him in the murky shadows of persons, showed a divination that I can only attribute to his practice of semantics.

14. (Added in 1966:) This reference to the aporia of Christianity announced a more precise one at its Jansenist climax: a reference to Pascal whose wager, still intact, forced me to take up the whole question again in order to get at what it conceals that is inestimable to psychoanalysts—which is still, at this date (June 1966), unrevealed.

15. (Added in 1966:) This remark was made by one of the psychoanalysts most involved in the debate.

16. See *Gegenwunschträume* in the *Traumdeutung*, *GW* II, 156–57 and 163–64; *SE* IV, 151 and 157–58.

17. (Added in 1966:) In order to evaluate the results of these procedures the reader should become thoroughly acquainted with the notes found in Émile Borel's book *Le Hasard* (Paris: F. Alcan, 1914), which I recommended already at that time, on the triviality of the "remarkable" results obtained by beginning in this way with just any number.

18. See C. I. Oberndorf, "Unsatisfactory Results of Psychoanalytic Therapy," *PQ* XIX (1950): 393–407.

19. See, among others, *Do Kamo: Person and Myth in the Melanesian World*, by Maurice Leenhardt [trans. Basia Miller Gulati (Chicago: University of Chicago Press, 1979)], chapters IX and X.

20. Jules H. Masserman, "Language, Behaviour and Dynamic Psychiatry," *IJP* XXV, 1–2 (1944): 1–8.

21. Aphorism of Lichtenberg's: "A madman who imagines himself a prince differs from the prince who is in fact a prince only because the former is a negative prince, while the latter is a negative madman. Considered without their sign, they are alike."

22. To obtain an immediate subjective confirmation of this remark of Hegel's, it is enough to have seen in the recent epidemic a blind rabbit in the middle of a road, lifting the emptiness of its vision changed into a gaze toward the setting sun: it was human to the point of tragedy.

23. The lines before and after this term will show what I mean by it.

24. Reich's error, to which I shall return, caused him to mistake a coat of arms for armor.

25. See Claude Lévi-Strauss, "Language and the Analysis of Social Laws," *American Anthropologist* LIII, 2 (April–June 1951): 155–63.

26. (Added in 1966:) The last four paragraphs have been rewritten.

27. (Added in 1966:) The last two paragraphs have been rewritten.

28. On the Galilean hypothesis and Huyghens' clock, see Alexandre Koyré, "An Experiment in Measurement," *Proceedings of the American Philosophical Society* XCVII, 2 (April 1953): 222–37. (Added in 1966:) The last two paragraphs of my text have been rewritten.

29. (Added in 1966:) I have developed these indications as the opportunity presented itself. Four paragraphs rewritten.

30. "The Theory of Symbolism," *British Journal of Psychology* IX, 2. Reprinted in his *Papers on Psycho-Analysis* (Boston: Beacon, 1961) [the page number given in the text corresponds to this edition]. See [Lacan's article: "À la mémoire d'Ernest Jones: Sur sa théorie du symbolisme," *La Psychanalyse* V (1960): 1–20] *Écrits* 1966, 697–717.

31. I am referring here to the teaching of Abhinavagupta in the tenth century. See Dr. Kanti Chandra Pandey, "Indian Aesthetics," *Chowkamba Sanskrit Series*, Studies, II (Benares: 1950).

32. Ernst Kris, "Ego Psychology and Interpretation in Psychoanalytic Therapy," *PQ* XX, 1 (1951): 15–29; see the passage quoted on pages 27–28.

33. (Added in 1966:) Paragraph rewritten.

34. This for the use of whoever can still understand it after looking in the Littré for justification of a theory that makes speech into an "action beside," by the translation that it gives of the Greek *parabole* (why not "action toward" instead?)—without having noticed at the same time that, if this word nevertheless designates what it means, it is because of sermonizing usage that, since the tenth century, has reserved "Word" [*verbe*] for the Logos incarnate.

35. Each language has its own form of transmission, and since the legitimacy of such research is founded on its success, nothing stops us from drawing a moral from it. Consider, for example, the maxim I chose as an epigraph for the preface to this paper. [*En particulier, il ne faudra pas oublier que la séparation en embryologie, anatomie, physiologie,*

*psychologie, sociologie, clinique n'existe pas
dans la nature et qu'il n'y a qu'une discipline: la*
neurobiologie *à laquelle l'observation nous
oblige d'ajouter l'épithète d'*humaine *en ce qui
nous concerne.*] Since it is so laden with redundancies, its style may strike you as a bit lack-
luster. But lighten it of them and its audacity
will arouse the enthusiasm it deserves. Hear
ye: "Parfaupe ouclaspa nannanbryle anaphi
ologi psysocline ixispad anlana—égnia kune
n'rbiol' ô blijouter têtumaine ennouconç . . ."
Here the purity of its message is finally laid
bare. Its meaning raises its head here, the
owning of being [*l'aveu de l'être*] begins, and
our victorious intelligence bequeaths to the
future its immortal stamp.

36. "The Therapeutic Effect of Inexact
Interpretation: A Contribution to the Theory
of Suggestion," *IJP* XII, 4 (1931): 397–411.

37. "Silence and Verbalization: A
Supplement to the Theory of the 'Analytic
Rule,' " *IJP* XXX, 1 (1949): 21–30.

38. Here equivalent to my mind to the
term *Zwangsbefürchtung* [obsessive or compulsive fear or apprehension], which should
be broken down into its component elements
without losing any of the semantic resources
of the German language.

39. (Added in 1966:) Two paragraphs
rewritten.

40. This term refers to the custom, of
Celtic origin and still practiced by certain
Bible sects in America, of allowing a couple
engaged to be married, or even a passing
guest and the family's daughter, to spend the
night together in the same bed, provided that
they keep their clothes on. The word derives
its meaning from the fact that the girl is usually wrapped up in sheets. (Quincey speaks of
it. See also the book by Aurand le Jeune on
this practice among the Amish.) Thus the
myth of Tristan and Iseult, and even the complex that it represents, now underwrites the
analyst in his quest for the soul destined for
mystifying nuptials via the extenuation of its
instinctual fantasies.

41. (Added in 1966:) What I have since

designated as the basis of transference—
namely, the "subject-supposed-to-know"—is
thus already defined here.

42. This is the correct translation of the
two terms that have been rendered, with that
unfailing flair for mistranslation I mentioned
earlier, by "terminated analysis and interminable analysis."

43. See Aulus Gellius, *Attic Nights*, II, 4:
"In a trial, when it is a question of knowing
who shall be given the task of presenting the
accusation, and when two or more people
volunteer for this office, the judgment by
which the tribunal names the accuser is called
divination . . . This word comes from the fact
that since accuser and accused are two correlative terms that cannot continue to exist without each other, and since the type of judgment in question here presents an accused
without an accuser, it is necessary to resort to
divination in order to find what the trial does
not provide, what it leaves still unknown, that
is, the accuser."

44. (Added in 1966:) Two paragraphs
rewritten.

45. (Added in 1966:) Whether a chipped
stone or a cornerstone, my forte is that I
haven't given in on this point.

46. This is the form called Laksanalaksana.

47. (Added in 1966:) These four words
[*renversé dans la répétition*], in which my latest
formulation of repetition is found (1966),
have been substituted for an improper
recourse to the "eternal return" [*toujours
présent dans l'éternel retour*], which was all that
I could get across at that time.

48. (Added in 1966:) These are premises of
the topology I have been putting into practice
over the past five years.

49. It should be clear that it is not a question here of the "gifts" that novices are
always supposed not to have, but of a tone
that they are, indeed, missing more often than
they should be.

50. (Added in 1966:) Ponge writes it as follows: *réson.*

The Freudian Thing

or the Meaning of the Return
to Freud in Psychoanalysis

An expanded version of a lecture given at the
Vienna Neuropsychiatric Clinic on November 7, 1955[1]

To Sylvia

Situation in Time and Place of This Exercise

At a time when Vienna, in making itself heard again through the voice of its Opera, is reassuming, in a moving variation, its age-old mission at a crossroads of cultures from which she was able to create harmony, I have come here—not unfittingly, I think—to evoke the fact that this chosen city will remain, this time forever more, associated with a revolution in knowledge of Copernican proportions. I am referring to the fact that Vienna is the eternal site of Freud's discovery and that, owing to this discovery, the veritable center of human beings is no longer at the place ascribed to it by an entire humanist tradition.

Perhaps even prophets whose own countries were not entirely deaf to them must be eclipsed at some point in time, if only after their death. It is appropriate for a foreigner to exercise restraint in evaluating the forces at work in such a phase-effect.

The return to Freud, for which I am assuming here the role of herald, is thus situated elsewhere: where it is amply called for by the symbolic scandal which Dr. Alfred Winterstein, who is here with us today, rightly highlighted when it occurred during his tenure as president of the Vienna Psychoanalytic Society—namely, upon the inauguration of the commemorative plaque marking the house in which Freud pursued his heroic work—

the scandal being not that this monument was not dedicated to Freud by his fellow citizens, but that it was not commissioned by the international association of those who live off his patronage.

402   This failure is symptomatic, for it indicates that he was disowned, not by the land in which, by virtue of his tradition, he was merely a temporary guest, but by the very field he left in our care and by those to whom custody of that field was entrusted—that is, the psychoanalytic movement itself, where things have come to such a pass that to call for a return to Freud is seen as a reversal.

Since the time when the first sound of the Freudian message rang out from the Viennese bell to echo far and wide, many contingent factors have played a part in this story. Its reverberations seemed to be drowned out by the muffled collapses brought about by the first world conflict. Its propagation resumed with the immense human wrenching that fomented the second and was its most powerful vehicle. It was on the waves of hate's tocsin and discord's tumult—the panic-stricken breath of war—that Freud's voice reached us, as we witnessed the Diaspora of those who transmitted it, whose persecution was no coincidence. The shock waves were to reverberate to the very confines of our world, echoing on a continent where it would be untrue to say that history loses its meaning, since it is where history finds its limit. It would even be a mistake to think that history is absent there, since, already several centuries in duration, it weighs all the more heavily there due to the gulf traced out by its all-too-limited horizon. Rather it is where history is denied with a categorical will that gives enterprises their style, that of a cultural ahistoricism characteristic of the United States of North America.

This ahistoricism defines the assimilation required for one to be recognized there, in the society constituted by this culture. It was to its summons that a group of emigrants had to respond; in order to gain recognition, they could only stress their difference, but their function presupposed history at its very core, their discipline being the one that had reconstructed the bridge between modern man and ancient myths. The combination of circumstances was too strong and the opportunity too attractive for them not to give in to the temptation to abandon the core in order to base function on difference. Let us be clear about the nature of this temptation. It was neither that of ease nor that of profit. It is certainly easier to efface the principles of a doctrine than the stigmata of one's origins, and more profitable to subor-

403   dinate one's function to demand. But to reduce one's function to one's difference in this case is to give in to a mirage that is internal to the function itself, a mirage that grounds the function in this difference. It is to return to

the reactionary principle that covers over the duality of he who suffers and he who heals with the opposition between he who knows and he who does not. How could they avoid regarding this opposition as true when it is real and, on that basis, avoid slipping into becoming managers of souls in a social context that demands such offices? The most corrupting of comforts is intellectual comfort, just as the worst corruption is corruption of the best.

Thus Freud's comment to Jung (I have it from Jung's own mouth)—when, having been invited by Clark University, they arrived in view of New York Harbor and of the famous statue illuminating the universe, "They don't realize we're bringing them the plague"—was turned against him as punishment for the hubris whose antiphrasis and darkness do not extinguish its turbid brilliance. To catch its author in her trap, Nemesis had merely to take him at his word. We would be justified in fearing that Nemesis added a first-class ticket home.

Indeed, if something of the sort has happened, we have only ourselves to blame. For Europe seems rather to have faded from the concerns and style—if not the minds—of those who left, along with the repression of their bad memories.

I will not pity you for having been forgotten since it leaves me freer to present to you the project of a return to Freud, as some of us teaching at the Société Française de Psychanalyse conceive of it. We are not seeking to emphasize a return of the repressed here, but want to use the antithesis constituted by the phase that has passed in the psychoanalytic movement since Freud's death to show what psychoanalysis is not, and find with you a way to put back into force what has continued to sustain it, even in its very deviation—namely, the original meaning Freud preserved in it by his mere presence, which I should like to explain here.

How could this meaning escape us when it is attested to in a body of written work of the most lucid and organic kind? And how could it leave us hesitant when the study of this work shows us that its different stages and changes in direction are governed by Freud's inflexibly effective concern to maintain its original rigor?   404

His texts prove to be comparable to those that, in other times, human veneration has invested with the highest qualities, in that they withstand the test of the discipline of commentary, whose virtue one rediscovers in making use of it in the traditional way—not simply to situate what someone says in the context of his time, but to gauge whether the answer he gives to the questions he raises has or has not been superseded by the answer one finds in his work to current questions.

Will I be telling you anything new if I say that these texts—to which for the past four years I have devoted a two-hour seminar every Wednesday from November to July, without having taken up more than a quarter of them, although my commentary is based on the whole set of them—have surprised me and those who attend my seminars as only genuine discoveries can? These discoveries range from concepts that have remained unexploited to clinical details left to be unearthed by our exploration; they demonstrate how far the field investigated by Freud went beyond the avenues he left us by which to gain access to it, and how little his case studies, which sometimes give an impression of exhaustiveness, were subordinated to what he intended to demonstrate. Who, among the experts in disciplines other than psychoanalysis whom I have guided in reading these texts, has not been moved by this research in action—whether it is the research he has us follow in the *Traumdeutung* [*The Interpretation of Dreams*], the case study of the Wolf Man, or *Beyond the Pleasure Principle*? What an exercise for the training of minds, and what a message to lend one's voice to! And what better confirmation could there be of the methodical value of this training and the truth effect this message produces than the fact that the students to whom you transmit them bring you evidence of a transformation, occurring sometimes overnight, in their practice, which becomes simpler or more effective even before it becomes more transparent to them. I cannot provide you with a detailed account of this work in my talk here, for which I am indebted to the kindness of Professor Hoff for the opportunity to give it in this place of noble memory, to the convergence between my views and those of Dr. Arnold for the suggestion to give this talk here, and to my excellent and long-standing relations with Mr. Igor Caruso for knowing how it would be received in Vienna.

405

But I cannot forget that I owe part of my audience today to the indulgence of Mr. Susini, the director of the French Institute in Vienna. And this is why I must ask myself, coming now as I am to the meaning of the return to Freud that I am professing here, whether I am not running the risk of disappointing this part of my audience because it is less prepared than the specialists may be to understand me.

The Adversary

I am sure of my answer here—"Absolutely not"—assuming that what I am going to say is as it should be. The meaning of a return to Freud is a return to Freud's meaning. And the meaning of what Freud said may be conveyed to anyone because, while addressed to everyone, it concerns each person. One word suffices to make this point: Freud's discovery calls truth into question, and there is no one who is not personally concerned by truth.

It must seem rather odd that I should be flinging this word in your faces—a word of almost ill repute, a word banished from polite society. But isn't it inscribed in the very heart of analytic practice, since this practice is constantly rediscovering the power of truth in ourselves and in our very flesh?

Why, indeed, would the unconscious be more worthy of being recognized than the defenses that oppose it in the subject, so successfully that the defenses seem no less real than it? I am not reviving here the shoddy Nietzschean notion of the lie of life, nor am I marveling at the fact that one believes one believes, nor do I accept that to will something one need but want it badly enough. But I am asking where the peace that ensues in recognizing an unconscious tendency comes from if the latter is not truer than what restrained it in the conflict. For some time now this peace has, moreover, been quickly proving illusory, for psychoanalysts, not content to recognize as unconscious the defenses to be attributed to the ego, have increasingly identified the defense mechanisms—displacement of the   406 object, turning back against the subject, regression of form—with the very dynamic that Freud analyzed in the tendency, which thus seems to persist in the defenses with no more than a change of sign. Haven't people gone too far when they submit that the drive itself may be made conscious by the defense so that the subject won't recognize himself in it?

In order to try to explain these mysteries in a coherent discourse, I am, in spite of myself, using words that reestablish in that discourse the very duality that sustains them. But what I deplore is not that one cannot see the forest of the theory for the trees of the technique employed, but rather that it would take so little to believe that one is in the Bondy Forest, precisely because of the following notion, which is hiding behind each tree—namely, that there must be some trees that are truer than others, or, if you prefer, that not all trees are bandits. Without which, one might wind up asking where the bandits are who are not trees. Does this little, then, which can become everything on occasion, perhaps deserve an explanation? What is this truth without which there is no way of distinguishing the face from the mask, and apart from which there seems to be no other monster than the labyrinth itself? In other words, how are they to be distinguished, in truth, if they are all equally real?

Here the big clodhoppers come forward to slip onto the dove's feet—on which, as we know, truth is borne—and to swallow up the bird occasionally as well: "Our criterion," they cry, "is simply economic, you ideologist. Not all organizations of reality are equally economical." But at the point at which truth has already been brought to bear, the bird escapes unscathed when I ask, "Economical for whom?"

Things have gone too far this time. The adversary snickers: "We get the picture. Monsieur has a philosophical bent. Plato and Hegel will be showing up any minute now. Their stamp suffices. Whatever they endorse should be discarded and, anyway, if, as you said, this concerns everyone, it's of no interest to specialists like us. It can't even be classified in our documentation."

You think I'm joking here. But not at all: I subscribe to it.

If Freud contributed nothing more to the knowledge of man than the verity that there is something veritable, there is no Freudian discovery. 407 Freud simply belongs then to the line of moralists in whom a tradition of humanistic analysis is embodied, a milky way in the heavenly vault of European culture in which Balthazar Gracian and La Rochefoucauld are among the brightest stars, and Nietzsche is a nova as dazzling as it is short-lived. The latest to join them—and spurred on, like them, no doubt by a characteristically Christian concern for the authenticity of the stirrings of the soul—Freud was able to precipitate a whole casuistry into a map of Tendre, in which one couldn't care less about an orientation for the offices for which it was intended. Its objectivity is, in fact, strictly tied to the analytic situation, which, within the four walls that limit its field, can do very well without people knowing which way is north since they confuse north with the long axis of the couch, assumed to point in the direction of the analyst. Psychoanalysis is the science of the mirages that arise within this field. A unique experience, a rather abject one at that, but one that cannot be too highly recommended to those who wish to get to the crux of mankind's forms of madness, for, while revealing itself to be akin to a whole range of alienations, it sheds light on them.

This language is moderate enough—I am not the one who invented it. I have even heard a zealot of supposedly classical psychoanalysis define the latter as an experience whose privilege is strictly tied to the forms that regulate its practice, forms that cannot be altered one iota because, having been obtained by means of a miracle of chance, they provide access to a reality that transcends the phenomena of history, a reality in which a taste for order and a love of beauty, for example, find their permanent ground—namely, the objects of the preoedipal relation, shit and all that other crap.

This position cannot be refuted since its rules are justified by their outcomes, and the latter are taken as proof that the rules are well founded. Yet our questions proliferate anew: How did this prodigious miracle of chance occur? Whence stems this contradiction between the preoedipal mess, to which the analytic relationship can be reduced, according to our modern analysts, and the fact that Freud wasn't satisfied until he had reduced it to the Oedipal position? How can the sort of hothouse auscultation on which this "new-look"* of analytic experience borders be the final stage in a development that appeared at the outset to open up multiple paths among all the fields of creation? Or the same question put the other way round: If the objects discerned in this elective fermentation were thus discovered through some other pathway than that of experimental psychology, is experimental psychology qualified to rediscover them through its own procedures?

408

The replies we will receive from the interested parties leave no room for doubt. The motor force of analytic experience, even when explained in their terms, cannot simply be this mirage-like truth that can be reduced to the mirage of truth. It all began with a particular truth, an unveiling, the effect of which is that reality is no longer the same for us as it was before. This is what continues to attach the crazy cacophony of theory to the very heart of worldly things, and to prevent practice from degenerating to the level of the wretched who never manage to leave them behind (it should be understood that I am using the term to exclude cynics).

A truth, if it must be said, is not easy to recognize once it has become received. Not that there aren't any established truths, but they are so easily confused with the reality that surrounds them that no other artifice was for a long time found to distinguish them from it than to mark them with the sign of the spirit and, in order to pay them homage, to regard them as having come from another world. It is not the whole story to attribute to a sort of blindness on man's part the fact that truth is never to him a finer looking girl than when the light, held aloft by his arm as in the proverbial emblem, unexpectedly illuminates her nakedness. And one must play the fool [*la bête*] a bit to feign knowing nothing of what happens next. But stupidity remains characterized by bullheaded frankness when one wonders where one could have been looking for her before, the emblem scarcely helping to indicate the well, an unseemly and even malodorous place, rather than the jewelry box in which every precious form must be preserved intact.

The Thing Speaks of Itself

But now the truth in Freud's mouth takes the said bull [*bête*] by the horns: "To you I am thus the enigma of she who slips away as soon as she appears,

you men who try so hard to hide me under the tawdry finery of your pro-
prieties. Still, I admit your embarrassment is sincere, for even when you take
it upon yourselves to become my heralds, you acquire no greater worth by
wearing my colors than your own clothes, which are like you, phantoms that
you are. Where am I going, having passed into you? And where was I prior
to that? Will I perhaps tell you someday? But so that you will find me where
I am, I will teach you by what sign you can recognize me. Men, listen, I am
telling you the secret. I, truth, speak.

"Must I point out that you did not yet know this? Of course, some of you
who proclaimed yourselves my lovers, no doubt because of the principle
that one is never better served than by oneself in this kind of boasting, had
posited—in an ambiguous manner, and not without revealing the clumsiness brought on by the vanity that they were really concerned about—that
the errors of philosophy, that is, their own, could subsist only on my subsi-
dies. Yet having embraced these daughters of their thought, they eventually
found them as insipid as they were futile, and began associating anew with
opinions considered to be vulgar according to the moral standards of the
sages of old; the latter knew how to put such opinions—whether narrative,
litigious, guileful, or simply mendacious—in their place, but also to seek
them out in the home and in the forum, at the forge and at the fair. They
then realized that, by not being my parasites, these opinions seemed to be
serving me far better, and—who knows?—even to be acting as my militia,
the secret agents of my power. Several cases observed in certain games of
sudden transformations of error into truth, which seemed to be due only to
perseverance, set them on the path of this discovery. The discourse of
error—its articulation in action—could bear witness to the truth against the
apparent facts themselves. It was then that one of them tried to get the cunning of reason accepted into the rank of objects deemed worthy of study.
Unfortunately, he was a professor, and you were only too happy to listen to
his teachings with the dunce caps you were made to wear at school and
which have since served as ear-trumpets for those of you who are a bit deaf.
Remain content, then, with your vague sense of history and leave it to clever
people to found the world market in lies, the trade in all-out war, and the
new law of self-criticism on the guarantee of my future firm. If reason is as
cunning as Hegel said it was, it will do its job without your help.

"But for all that, you haven't rendered what you owe me obsolete or endlessly postponable. It falls due after yesterday and before tomorrow. And it
hardly matters whether you rush ahead to honor or evade it, since it will
grab you from behind in both cases. Whether you flee me in deceit or think

you can catch me in error, I will catch up with you in the mistake from which you cannot hide. Where the most cunning speech reveals a slight stumbling, it doesn't live up to its perfidy—I am now publicly announcing the fact— and it will be a bit harder after this to act as if nothing is happening, whether in good company or bad. But there is no need to wear yourselves out keeping a closer watch on yourselves. Even if the combined jurisdictions of politeness and politics declared that whatever claims to be associated with me is inadmissible when it presents itself in such an illicit manner, you would not get off so lightly, for the most innocent intention is disconcerted once it can no longer conceal the fact that one's bungled actions are the most successful and that one's failures fulfill one's most secret wishes. In any case, doesn't my escape—first from the dungeon of the fortress in which you think you are most sure to hold me by situating me not in yourselves, but in being itself—suffice to prove your defeat? I wander about in what you regard as least true by its very nature: in dreams, in the way the most far-fetched witticisms and the most grotesque nonsense* of jokes defy meaning, and in chance—not in its law, but rather in its contingency. And I never more surely proceed to change the face of the world than when I give it the profile of Cleopatra's nose.

"You can therefore reduce the traffic on the roads that you strove so hard to prove radiate from consciousness, and which were the ego's pride and joy, crowned by Fichte with the insignias of its transcendence. The long-term trade in truth no longer involves thought; strangely enough, it now seems to involve things: *rebus*, it is through you that I communicate, as Freud formulates it at the end of the first paragraph of the sixth chapter, devoted to the dreamwork, of his work on dreams and what dreams mean.

"But you must be careful here: the hard time Freud had becoming a professor will perhaps spare him your neglect, if not your deviation," the prosopopeia continues. "Listen carefully to what he says, and—as he said it of me, the truth that speaks—the best way to grasp it is to take it quite literally. Here, no doubt, things are my signs, but, I repeat, signs of my speech. If Cleopatra's nose changed the world's course, it was because it entered the world's discourse; for in order to change it for the longer or the shorter, it was sufficient, but it was also necessary, that it be a speaking nose.

"But it is your own nose that you must now use, albeit for more natural ends. Let a sense of smell surer than all your categories guide you in the race to which I challenge you. For if the cunning of reason, however disdainful it may have been of you, remained open to your faith, I, truth, will against you be the great Trickster, since I slip in not only via falsehood, but through

411

a crack too narrow to be found at feigning's weakest point and through the dream's inaccessible cloud, through the groundless fascination with mediocrity and the seductive impasse of absurdity. Seek, dogs that you become upon hearing me, bloodhounds that Sophocles preferred to put on the scent of the hermetic traces of Apollo's thief than on Oedipus' bleeding heels, certain as he was of finding the moment of truth with him at the sinister meeting at Colonus. Enter the lists at my call and howl at the sound of my voice. Now that you are already lost, I belie myself, I defy you, I slip away: you say that I am being defensive."

Parade

The return to darkness, which I think must be expected at this moment, is the signal for a "murder party"* that begins with an order forbidding everyone to leave, since anyone may now be hiding the truth under her dress, or even in her womb, as in the amorous fiction, *The Indiscreet Jewels*. The general question is: Who is speaking? And the question is not an irrelevant one. Unfortunately, the answers given are a bit hasty. First the libido is accused, which leads us in the direction of the jewels; but we must realize that the ego itself—although it fetters the libido, which pines for satisfaction—is sometimes the object of the libido's undertakings. One senses that the ego is about to collapse any minute, when the sound of broken glass informs everyone that it is the large drawing-room mirror that has sustained the accident, the golem of narcissism, hastily invoked to assist the ego, having thereby made its entrance. The ego is then generally regarded as the assassin, if not the victim, the upshot being that the divine rays of the good President Schreber begin to spread their net over the world, and the Sabbath of the instincts becomes truly complicated.

412

The comedy, which I shall interrupt here at the beginning of its second act, is less mean-spirited than is usually believed, since—attributing to a drama of knowledge a buffoonery that belongs only to those who act in this drama without understanding it—it restores to such people the authenticity from which they had fallen away ever further.

But if a more serious metaphor befits the protagonist, it is one that would show us in Freud an Actaeon perpetually set upon by dogs that are thrown off the scent right from the outset, dogs that he strives to get back on his tail, without being able to slow the race in which only his passion for the goddess leads him on. It leads him on so far that he cannot stop until he reaches the cave in which the chthonian Diana, in the damp shade that confounds the cave with the emblematic abode of truth, offers to his thirst, along with the smooth surface of death, the quasi-mystical limit of the most rational discourse the world has ever heard, so that we might recognize there the locus in which the symbol substitutes for death in order to take possession of the first budding of life.

As we know, this limit and this locus are still far from being reached by his disciples, when they don't simply refuse to follow him there altogether, and so the Actaeon who is dismembered here is not Freud, but every analyst in proportion to the passion that inflamed him and made him—according to the signification Giordano Bruno drew from this myth in his *Heroic Frenzies*—the prey of the dogs of his own thoughts.

To gauge the extent of this rending we must hear the irrepressible protests that arise from both the best and the worst, when one tries to bring them back to the beginning of the hunt, with the words that truth gave us as a viaticum—"I speak"—adding, "There is no speech without language." Their tumult drowns out what follows.

"Logomachia!" goes the strophe on one side. "What do you make of the preverbal, gestures and facial expressions, tone, melody, mood, and af-fec-tive con-tact?" To which others, no less vehement, give the antistrophe: "Everything is language: language when my heart beats faster as fear strikes and, if my patient faints at the roar of an airplane at its zenith, it is a way of *telling* me the memory she still has of the last bombing." Yes, eagle of thought, and when the plane's shape cuts out your semblance in the night-piercing beam of the searchlight, it is heaven's response.   413

Yet, in trying out these premises, people did not challenge the use of any of the forms of communication people might resort to in their exploits, neither signals nor images, content nor form, whether man or woman, even if this content were one of sympathy, the virtue of any proper form not being debated.

They began merely to repeat after Freud the key to his discovery: it [*ça*] speaks, precisely where it was least expected—namely, where it suffers. If there ever was a time when, to respond to it, it sufficed to listen to what it was saying (for the answer is already there in hearing it), let us assume that the great ones of the early days, the armchair giants, were struck by the curse that befalls titanic acts of daring, or that their chairs ceased to be conductors of the good word which they were vested to sit before. Be that as it may, since then, there have been more meetings between the psychoanalyst and psychoanalysis in the hope that the Athenian would reach his apex with Athena having emerged fully armed from Freud's head. Shall I tell you of the jealous fate, ever the same, that thwarted these meetings? Behind the mask where each of us was to meet his betrothed—alas! thrice alas! and a cry of horror at the thought of it, another woman having taken her place—he who was there was not him either.

Let us thus calmly return and spell out with the truth what it said of itself. The truth said, "I speak." In order for us to recognize this "I" on the basis of the fact that it speaks, perhaps we should not have jumped on the "I," but should have paused at the facets of the speaking. "There is no speech without language" reminds us that language is an order constituted by laws, about which we could at least learn what they exclude. For example, that language is different from natural expression and that it is not a code either; that language is not the same as information—take a close look at cybernetics and you'll see the difference; and that language is so far from being reducible to a superstructure that materialism itself was alarmed by this heresy—see Stalin's pronouncement on the question.

414

Should you like to know more about it, read Saussure, and since a bell tower can hide even the sun, let me make it clear that I am not referring to the Saussure of psychoanalytic repute, but to Ferdinand, who may be said to be the founder of modern linguistics.

The Thing's Order

A psychoanalyst should find it easy to grasp the fundamental distinction between signifier and signified, and to begin to familiarize himself with the two networks of nonoverlapping relations they organize.

The first network, that of the signifier, is the synchronic structure of the material of language insofar as each element takes on its precise usage therein by being different from the others; this is the principle of distribution that alone regulates the function of the elements of language [*langue*] at its different levels, from the phonemic pair of oppositions to compound expressions, the task of the most modern research being to isolate the stable forms of the latter.

The second network, that of the signified, is the diachronic set of concretely pronounced discourses, which historically affects the first network, just as the structure of the first governs the pathways of the second. What dominates here is the unity of signification, which turns out to never come down to a pure indication of reality [*réel*], but always refers to another signification. In other words, signification comes about only on the basis of taking things as a whole [*d'ensemble*].

Its mainspring cannot be grasped at the level at which signification usually secures its characteristic redundancy, for it always proves to exceed the things it leaves indeterminate within it.

The signifier alone guarantees the theoretical coherence of the whole as a whole. Its ability to do so is confirmed by the latest development in science, just as, upon reflection, we find it to be implicit in early linguistic experience.

These are the foundations that distinguish language from signs. Dialectic derives new strength from them.   415

For the remark on which Hegel bases his critique of the beautiful soul—according to which it is said to live (in every sense, even the economic sense of having something to live off of) precisely off the disorder it denounces—escapes being tautological only by maintaining the "tauto-ontic" of the beautiful soul as mediation, unrecognized by itself, of this disorder as primary in being.

However dialectical it may be, this remark cannot shake up the delusion of presumption to which Hegel applied it, remaining caught in the trap offered by the mirage of consciousness to the *I* infatuated with its own feeling, which Hegel turns into the law of the heart.

Of course this "I" in Hegel is defined as a legal being, making it more concrete than the real being from which people formerly thought it could be abstracted—as is clear from the fact that it implies both a civil status and an account status.

But it was left to Freud to make this legal being responsible for the disorder manifest in the most tightly closed field of the real being—namely, in the organism's pseudo-totality.

I explain this possibility by the congenital gap presented by man's real being in his natural relations, and by the reprising, in a sometimes ideographic, but also a phonetic and even grammatical usage, of the imaginary elements that appear to be fragmented in this gap.

But we have no need for this genesis to demonstrate the symptom's signifying structure. Once deciphered, it is plain to see and shows the omnipresence for human beings of the symbolic function stamped on the flesh.

What distinguishes a society grounded in language from an animal society, which even the ethnological standpoint allows us to see—namely, the fact that the exchange that characterizes such a society has other foundations than needs (even if it satisfies them), specifically, what has been called the gift "as total social fact"—can then be taken much further, so far as to constitute an objection to defining this society as a collection of individuals, since the immixing of subjects makes it a group with a very different structure.

This reintroduces the impact of truth as cause from a totally different angle, and requires a reappraisal of the process of causality—the first stage of which would seem to be to recognize the degree to which the heterogeneity of this impact is inherent.[2] It is strange that materialist thought seems to forget that it derived its impetus from this recourse to the heterogeneous. More interest might then be shown in a feature that is much more striking than the resistance to Freud mounted by the pedants—namely, the connivance this resistance encountered in collective consciousness.

If all causality evinces the subject's involvement, it will come as no surprise that every order conflict is attributed to him.

The terms in which I am posing the problem of psychoanalytic intervention make it sufficiently clear, I think, that its ethics are not individualistic.

But its practice in the American sphere has so summarily degenerated into a means of obtaining "success"* and into a mode of demanding "happiness"* that it must be pointed out that this constitutes a repudiation of psychoanalysis, a repudiation that occurs among too many of its adherents due to the pure and simple fact that they have never wanted to know anything about Freud's discovery, and that they will never know anything about it, even in the way implied by repression: for what is at work here is the mechanism of systematic misrecognition insofar as it simulates delusion, even in its group forms.

But had analytic experience been more rigorously linked to the general structure of semantics, in which it has its roots, it would have allowed us to convince [*convaincre*] them before having to vanquish [*vaincre*] them.

For the subject of whom I was just speaking as the legatee of recognized truth is definitely not the ego perceptible in the more or less immediate data of conscious jouissance or the alienation of labor. This de facto distinction is the same distinction found from the beginning to the end of Freud's work: from the Freudian unconscious, insofar as it is separated by a profound gulf from the preconscious functions, to Freud's last will and testament in lecture thirty-one of his *Neue Vorlesungen* [*New Introductory Lectures*], "Wo Es war, soll Ich werden."

A formulation in which signifying structuration clearly prevails.

Let us analyze it. Contrary to the form that the English translation— "Where the id was, there the ego shall be"*—cannot avoid, Freud said neither *das Es*, nor *das Ich*, as was his wont when designating the agencies he had used to organize his new topography for the previous ten years; and, considering the inflexible rigor of his style, this gives a particular emphasis to their use in this sentence. In any case—even without having to confirm, through a detailed examination of Freud's opus, that he in fact wrote *Das Ich und das Es* [*The Ego and the Id*] in order to maintain the fundamental distinction between the true subject of the unconscious and the ego as constituted in its nucleus by a series of alienating identifications—it seems here that it is in the locus *Wo* (Where) *Es* (the subject devoid of any *das* or other objectifying article) *war* (was [*était*]—it is a locus of being that is at stake, and that in this locus), *soll* (it is a duty in the moral sense that is announced here, as is confirmed by the single sentence that follows it, bringing the chapter to a close)[3] *Ich* (I, there must I—just as in French one announced "ce suis-je," "it is I," before saying "c'est moi," "it's me") *werden* (become [*devenir*]—not occur [*survenir*], or even happen [*advenir*], but be born [*venir au jour*] of this very locus insofar as it is a locus of being).

Even though it runs counter to the principles of economy of expression that must dominate a translation, I would thus agree to force the forms of the signifier a little in French in order to bring them into line with the weight of a still refractory signification, which the German tolerates better here; to do so I would play on the homophony between the German *Es* and the first letter of the word "subject." By the same token, I might feel more indulgent, at least momentarily, toward the first French translation that was provided of the word *Es*—namely, *le soi* (the self). The *ça* [the it or the id], which was eventually preferred, not groundlessly, does not seem to me to be much better, since it is rather to the German *das*, in the question, *Was ist das?*, that it corresponds in *das ist* (*c'est* [it is]). The elided *c'* that appears if we stick to the accepted equivalence thus suggests to me the production of a verb, *s'être*, which would express the mode of absolute subjectivity, insofar as Freud truly discovered it in its radical eccentricity: "Where it was" ["*Là où c'était*"], one might say, "Where (it) was itself" [*là où s'était*], as I would like it to be heard, "it is my duty that I come into being."[4]   418

You should realize that the point is not to analyze if and how the I [*le je*] and the ego [*le moi*] are distinct and overlap in each particular subject on the basis of a grammatical conception of their functions.

What a linguistic conception, which must shape the analytic worker in his basic initiation, will teach him is to expect the symptom to prove its signifying function, that is, that by which it differs from the natural index commonly designated by the term "symptom" in medicine. And in order to satisfy this methodological requirement, he will oblige himself to recognize its conventional use in the significations brought out by analytic dialogue (a dialogue whose structure I shall try to articulate). But he will maintain that these very significations can be grasped with certainty only in their context, that is, in the sequence constituted for each one of them by the signification that refers back to it and the signification to which it refers in the analytic discourse.

These basic principles can be easily applied in analytic technique and, in elucidating it, they dissipate many of the ambiguities which, being maintained even in the major concepts of transference and resistance, make the use that is made of them in practice exceedingly costly.

Resistance to the Resisters

To consider only resistance, whose use is increasingly confused with that of defense—and all the latter thus implies by way of maneuvers designed to eliminate it, maneuvers whose coercive nature we can no longer ignore—it is worth recalling that the first resistance analysis faces is that of discourse itself, insofar as it is first of all a discourse of opinion, and that all psychological objectification proves to be intimately tied to this discourse. This is, in effect, what motivated the remarkable simultaneity with which the psychoanalytic practice of the burgraves of analysis came to a standstill in the 1920s: for by then they knew both too much and not enough about it to get their patients, who scarcely knew less about it, to recognize the truth.

But the principle adopted at that time of granting primacy to the analysis of resistance hardly led to a favorable development. For the reason that giving top priority to an operation doesn't suffice to make it reach its objective when one is unclear as to what that objective is.

Now the analysis of resistance was designed precisely to reinforce the subject's objectifying position, to so great an extent, indeed, that this directive now permeates the principles that are supposed to be applied in the conduct of a standard treatment.

Far from having to maintain the subject in a state of self-observation, therefore, one must know that by inviting him to adopt such a position one enters a circle of misunderstanding that nothing in the treatment, or even in the analytic literature, will be able to shatter. Any intervention that moves in this direction can thus only be justified by a dialectical aim—namely, to demonstrate that it amounts to an impasse.

But I will go further and say that you cannot both carry out this objectification of the subject yourself and speak to him as you should. And for a reason, which is not simply that you can't, as the English proverb has it, have your cake and eat it too—that is, adopt two different approaches to the same objects whose consequences are mutually exclusive. But for the deeper reason that is expressed in the saying "you can't serve two masters," that is, conform your being to two actions that lead in opposite directions.

For objectification in psychological matters is subject, at its very core, to a law of misrecognition that governs the subject not only as observed, but also as observer. In other words, it is not about him that you must speak to him, for he can do this well enough himself, and in doing so, it is not even to you that he speaks. While it is to him that you must speak, it is literally about some-thing else—that is, about some-thing other than what is at stake when he speaks of himself—which is the thing that speaks to you. Regardless of what he says, this thing will remain forever inaccessible to him if, being speech addressed to you, it cannot elicit its response in you, and if, having heard its message in this inverted form, you cannot, in re-turning it to him, give him the twofold satisfaction of having recognized it and of making him recognize its truth.   420

Can't we then know the truth that we know in this way? *Adæquatio rei et intellectus*—thus has the concept of truth been defined since there were thinkers who lead us into the pathways of their thought. Intellects like ours will certainly measure up to the thing that speaks to us, nay, that speaks in us; and even when it hides behind a discourse that says nothing merely to make us speak, it would be shocking indeed if the thing did not find some-one to speak to.

I hope you will be so lucky; we must speak about it now, and those who put the thing into practice have the floor.

Interlude

But don't expect too much here, for ever since the psychoanalytic thing became an accepted thing and its servants started having their hands mani-cured, the housecleaning they have been performing makes do with sacri-fices to good taste, which, as far as ideas—which psychoanalysts have never had in abundance—are concerned, is certainly convenient: ideas on sale for everyone will make up the balance of what each person is lacking in. We are sufficiently abreast of things to know that *chosisme* is hardly in good taste—which is our way of sidestepping the question.

"Why go off in search of something other than the ego you distinguish, when you forbid us to see it?" it may be objected. "So we objectify it. What's wrong with that?" Here the delicate shoes move stealthily forward to deliver the following kick in the face: "Do you think, then, that the ego can be taken as a thing? We'd never entertain any such notion."

From thirty-five years of cohabitation with the ego under the roof of the second Freudian topography—including ten years of a rather stormy relationship, finally legitimized by the ministry of Miss Anna Freud in a marriage whose social credit has done nothing but grow ever since, so much so that people assure me it will soon request the Church's blessing—in short, from the most sustained work of psychoanalysts, you will draw nothing more than this drawer.

It is true that it is chock-full of old novelties and new antiques, the sheer mass of which is at least entertaining. The ego is a function, the ego is a synthesis, a synthesis of functions, a function of synthesis. It is autonomous! That's a good one! It's the latest fetish introduced into the holy of holies of a practice that is legitimated by the superiority of the superiors. It does the job as well as any other, everyone realizing that it is always the most outmoded, dirty, and repulsive object that best fulfills this function—this function being entirely real. That this object should gain for its inventor the veneration it does where it is in operation is just barely tolerable, but the most amazing thing is that in enlightened circles it has earned him the prestige of having returned psychoanalysis to the fold of the laws of general psychology. It is as if His Excellency the Aga Khan, not content with receiving his weight in gold—which in no way diminishes the esteem in which he is held in cosmopolitan society—were to be awarded the Nobel Prize for, in exchange, distributing to his followers the precise rules for pari-mutuel.

But the latest find is the best: the ego, like everything else we have been handling of late in the human sciences, is an op-er-a-tion-al notion.

At this point I appeal, before those in the audience, to this naive *chosisme* which keeps them sitting so properly in their seats, listening to me despite the barrage of calls to serve, so that they might, with me, agree to put a stop to this op [*stopper c't o-pé*].

In what respect does this op rationally distinguish what one makes of the notion of the ego in analysis from the common usage of any other thing, of this lectern, to take the first thing at hand? It distinguishes them so little that I am confident I can show that the discourses about them—and that is what is at stake—coincide point for point.

For this lectern, no less than the ego, is dependent on the signifier, namely on the word, which—generalizing its function compared to the pulpit of quarrelsome memory and to the Tronchin table of noble pedigree—is responsible for the fact that it is not merely a tree that has been felled, cut down to size, and glued back together by a cabinetmaker, for reasons of commerce tied to need-creating fashions that maintain its exchange value, assuming it is not led too quickly to satisfy the least superfluous of those needs by the final use to which wear and tear will eventually reduce it: namely, fuel for the fire.

422

Moreover, the significations to which the lectern refers are in no way less dignified than those of the ego, and the proof is that they occasionally envelop the ego itself, if it is by the functions Heinz Hartmann attributes to the ego that one of our semblables may become our lectern: namely, maintain a position suitable enough for him to consent to it. An operational function, no doubt, that will allow the said semblable to display within himself all the possible values of this lectern as a thing: from the hefty rent charged for its use that kept and still keeps the standing of the little hunchback of the rue Quincampoix above both the vicissitudes and the very memory of the first great speculative crash of modern times, through all the purposes of everyday convenience, of furnishing a room, of transfer for cash or assignment of interest, to its use—and why not? it has happened before—as firewood.

But that isn't all, for I am willing to lend my voice to the true lectern so that it might deliver a lecture on its existence, which, even though it is instrumental, is individual; on its history, which, however radically alienated it may seem to us, has left all the written traces a historian might require: documents, texts, and bills from suppliers; and on its very destiny, which, though inert, is dramatic, since a lectern is perishable, is engendered by labor, and has a fate subject to chance, obstacles, misadventures, prestige, and even fatalities whose index it becomes; and it is destined to an end of which it need know nothing for it to be the lectern's own, since we all know what it is.

But it would be nothing more than sheer banality if, after this prosopopeia, one of you dreams that he is this lectern, whether or not it is endowed with the gift of speech. And since the interpretation of dreams has become a well known, if not a widespread, practice, there would be no reason to be surprised if—by deciphering the use as a signifier that this lectern has taken on in the rebus in which the dreamer immures his desire, and by analyzing the more or less equivocal reference implied by this use to the significations the lectern's consciousness has awakened in him, with or without its lecture—we reached what might be called the lectern's "preconscious."

423

At this point I hear a protest, which I am not sure how to name, even though it is totally predictable: for, in effect, it concerns that which has no name in any language [*langue*], and which, generally manifesting itself in the ambiguous mollifying motion of "the total personality," comprises everything that leads us to be publicly ridiculed in psychiatry for our worthless phenomenology and in society for our stationary "progressivism." The protest is that of the beautiful soul, no doubt, but in forms suited to the wishy-washy being, wry manner, and tenebrous approach of the modern intellectual, whether on the right or left. Indeed, it is in this quarter that the fictional protest of those that disorder causes to proliferate finds its noble alliances. Let us listen rather to the tone of this protest.

The tone is measured but serious: neither the preconscious nor consciousness, we are told, belongs to the lectern, but to we who perceive the desk and give it its meaning—all the more easily, moreover, since we ourselves have made the thing. But even if a more natural being were at stake, we should never thoughtlessly debase in consciousness the high form which, however feeble we may be in the universe, assures us an imprescriptible dignity in it—look up "reed" in the dictionary of spiritualist thought.

I must admit that Freud incites me to be irreverent here by the way in which, in a passing remark somewhere, as if without touching on it, he speaks about the modes of spontaneous provocation that are usual when universal consciousness goes into action. And this relieves me of any constraint about pursuing my paradox.

Is the difference between the lectern and us, as far as consciousness is concerned, so very great then if, in being brought into play between you and me, the lectern can so easily acquire a semblance of consciousness that my sentences could allow us to mistake the one for the other? Being placed with one of us between two parallel mirrors, it will be seen to reflect indefinitely, which means that it will be far more like the person who is looking than we think, since in seeing his image repeated in the same way, he too truly sees himself through another's eyes when he looks at himself, since without the other, his image, he would not see himself seeing himself.

424

In other words, the ego's privileged status compared to things must be sought elsewhere than in this false recurrence to infinity of the reflection which constitutes the mirage of consciousness, and which, despite its utter uselessness, still titillates those who work with thought enough for them to see in it some supposed progress in interiority, whereas it is a topological phenomenon whose distribution in nature is as sporadic as the dispositions of pure exteriority that condition it, even if it is true that man has helped spread them with such immoderate frequency.

How, moreover, can we separate the term "preconscious" from the affectations of this lectern, or from those which are potentially or actually found in any other thing and which, by adjusting themselves so exactly to my affections, will become conscious along with them?

I am willing to accept that the ego, and not the lectern, is the seat of perceptions, but it thus reflects the essence of the objects it perceives and not its own essence, insofar as consciousness is supposedly its privilege, since these perceptions are, for the most part, unconscious.

It is no accident, moreover, that I have detected the origin of the protest that I must address here in the bastardized forms of phenomenology that cloud the technical analyses of human action, especially those required in medicine. If their cheap material, to borrow a term Jaspers uses in his assessment of psychoanalysis, really is what gives his work its style, and its weight to him as the epitome of the cast-iron spiritual advisor and tin-plate guru, they are not useless—indeed, their use is always the same, namely, to create a diversion.

They are used here, for example, in order to avoid discussing the important point that the lectern does not talk, which the upholders of the false protest want to know nothing about, because my lectern, hearing me grant them the point, would immediately begin to speak.

The other's Discourse   425

"In what way, then, is the ego you treat in analysis better than the lectern that I am?" it would ask them.

"For if its health is defined by its adaptation to a reality that is quite frankly regarded as being measured against the ego, and if you need the alliance of 'the healthy part of the ego' in order to eliminate discordances with reality (in the other part of the ego, no doubt)—which only appear to be discordances due to your principle of regarding the analytic situation as simple and innocuous, and concerning which you won't stop until you have made the subject see them as you see them—isn't it clear that there is no way to discern which is the healthy part of the subject's ego except by its agreement with your point of view? And, since the latter is assumed to be healthy, it becomes the measure of things. Isn't it similarly clear that there is no other criterion of cure than the complete adoption by the subject of your measure? This is confirmed by the common admission by certain serious authors that the end of analysis is achieved when the subject identifies with the analyst's ego.

"Certainly, the fact that such a view can spread and be accepted so calmly leads one to think that, contrary to the commonly held view that it is easy to impress the naive, it is much easier for the naive to impress others. And the hypocrisy revealed in the declaration—whose repentant tone appears with such curious regularity in this discourse—that we should speak to the subject in 'his own language,' gives one still further pause for thought regarding the depth of this naïveté. We still have to overcome the nausea we feel at the idea it suggests of employing baby talk, without which well informed parents would believe themselves incapable of inculcating their lofty reasons in the poor little guys that have to be made to keep quiet! These are simple attentions people consider necessary because, according to the notion projected by analytic imbecility, neurotics supposedly have weak egos.

"But we are not here to dream between nausea and vertigo. The fact remains that, although I may be a mere lectern in speaking to you, I am the ideal patient; for not so much trouble has to be taken with me—the results are obtained immediately, I am cured in advance. Since the point is simply to replace my discourse with yours, I am a perfect ego, since I have never had any other discourse, and I leave it to you to inform me of the things to which my adjustment controls do not allow you to adapt me directly— namely, of everything other than your eyesight, your height, and the dimensions of your papers."

Not a bad speech for a lectern, I'd say. I must be kidding, of course. In what it said under my command, it did not have its say. For the reason that it itself was a word; it was "me" [*moi*] as grammatical subject. Well, that's one rank achieved, one worth being picked up by the opportunistic soldier in the ditch of an entirely eristic claim, but which also provides us with an illustration of the Freudian motto, which, expressed as "La où était ça, le *je* doit être," would confirm, to our benefit, the feeble character of a translation that substantifies the *Ich*, by giving a "t" to *doit* translating *soll*, and fixes the price of the *Es* according to the rate of the ç. The fact remains that the lectern is not an ego, however eloquent it was, but a means that I have employed in my discourse.

But, after all, if we envision its virtue in analysis, the ego, too, is a means, and they can be compared.

As the lectern so pertinently mentioned, it has the advantage over the ego of not being a means of resistance, and that's precisely why I chose it to prop up my discourse and proportionately mitigate whatever resistance a greater interference of my ego in Freud's words might have given rise to in you—satisfied as I would already be if the resistance you must be left with, despite this effacement, led you to find what I am saying "interesting." It's no accident that this expression, in its euphemistic use, designates what interests us only moderately, and manages to come full circle in its antithesis, by which speculations of universal interest are called "disinterested."

But were what I am saying to come to interest you personally—as they say, filling out an antonomasia with a pleonasm—the lectern would soon be in pieces for us to use as a weapon.

Well, all of that applies to the ego, except that its uses seem to be reversed in their relation to its states. The ego is a means of the speech addressed to you from the subject's unconscious, a weapon for resisting its recognition; it is fragmented when it conveys speech and whole when it serves not to hear it.   427

Indeed, the subject finds the signifying material of his symptoms in the disintegration of the imaginary unity that the ego constitutes. And it is from the sort of interest the ego awakens in him that come the significations that turn his discourse away from it.

Imaginary Passion

This interest in the ego is a passion whose nature was already glimpsed by the traditional moralists, who called it *amour-propre*, but whose dynamics in relation to one's own body image only psychoanalytic investigation could analyze. This passion brings to every relation with this image, constantly represented by my semblable, a signification which interests me so greatly— that is, which makes me so dependent on this image—that it links all the objects of my desires to the other's desire, more closely than to the desire they arouse in me.

I am talking about objects as we expect them to appear in a space structured by vision—that is, objects characteristic of the human world. As to the knowledge on which desire for these objects depends, men are far from confirming the expression that says they see no further than the end of their nose; on the contrary, their misfortune is such that their world begins at the end of their nose, and they can apprehend their desire only by means of the same thing that allows them to see their nose itself: a mirror. But no sooner has this nose been discerned than they fall in love with it, and this is the first signification by which narcissism envelops the forms of desire. It is not the only signification, and the growing importance of aggressiveness in the firmament of analytic concerns would remain obscure if we confined our attention to this one alone.

This is a point I believe I myself have helped elucidate by conceptualizing the so-called dynamics of the "mirror stage" as the consequence of man's generic prematurity at birth, leading at the age indicated to the jubi-

428 lant identification of the individual who is still an infant with the total form in which this reflection of the nose is integrated—namely, with the image of his body. This operation—which is carried out in an approximate manner that might be off by a nose [*faite à vue de nez*], an apt expression here, in other words, falling more or less into the same category as the "aha!" that enlightens us about the chimpanzee's intelligence, amazed as we always are to detect the miracle of intelligence on our peers' faces—does not fail to bring deplorable consequences in its wake.

As a witty poet so rightly remarks, the mirror would do well to reflect a little more before sending us back our image. For at this point the subject has not yet seen anything. But let the same capture be reproduced under the nose of one of his semblables—the nose of a notary, for example—and Lord knows where the subject will be led by the nose, given the places such legal professionals are in the habit of sticking theirs. And whatever else we have—hands, feet, heart, mouth, even the eyes—that is so reluctant to follow is threatened by a breaking up of the team, whose announcement through anxiety could only lead to severe measures. Regroup!—an appeal to the power of this image which made the honeymoon with the mirror so jubilant, to the sacred union of right and left that is affirmed in it, as inverted as it may appear to be should the subject prove to be a bit more observant.

But what finer model of this union is there than the very image of the other, that is, of the notary in his function? It is thus that the functions of mastery, improperly called the ego's synthetic functions, institute on the basis of a libidinal alienation the subsequent development—namely, what I formerly termed the "paranoiac principle of human knowledge," according to which man's objects are subjected to a law of imaginary reduplication, evoking ratification by an indefinite series of notaries, which owes nothing to their professional federation.

But the signification that strikes me as decisive in the constitutive alienation of the ego's *Urbild* appears in the relation of exclusion that henceforth structures the dyadic ego-to-ego relationship in the subject. For should the imaginary coaptation of the one to the other bring about a complementary distribution of roles between, for example, the notary and the notarized party, an effect of the ego's precipitated identification with the other in the subject is that this distribution never constitutes even a kinetic harmony, but is instituted on the basis of a permanent "it's you or me" form of war in which the existence of one or the other of the two notaries in each of the

429 subjects is at stake. This situation is symbolized in the "So are you" of the transitivist quarrel, the original form of aggressive communication.

We can see to what the ego's language is reduced: intuitive illumination, recollective command, and the retorting aggressiveness of verbal echo. Let us add to this what the ego receives from the automatic scraps of everyday discourse: rote-learning and delusional refrain, modes of communication perfectly reproduced by objects scarcely more complicated than this lectern, a feed-back* construction for the former, a gramophone record, preferably scratched in the right place, for the latter.

It is, nevertheless, in this register that the systematic analysis of defense is proffered. It is corroborated by semblances of regression. The object-relation provides appearances of it, and this forcing has no other outcome than one of the three allowed by the technique currently in force. Either the impulsive leap into reality [réel] through the hoop of fantasy: acting out* in a direction that is ordinarily the opposite of suggestion. Or transitory hypomania due to ejection of the object itself, which is correctly described in the megalomaniacal intoxication which my friend Michael Balint, in an account so veracious as to make him a still better friend, recognizes as the index of the termination of an analysis according to current norms. Or in the sort of somatization constituted by mild hypochondria, discretely theorized under the heading of the doctor/patient relationship.

The dimension of a "two body psychology,"* suggested by Rickman, is the fantasy in which a "two ego analysis"* hides, which is as untenable as it is coherent in its results.

Analytic Action

This is why I teach that there are not only two subjects present in the analytic situation, but two subjects each of whom is provided with two objects, the ego and the other, the latter beginning with a lowercase o. Now, due to the singularities of a dialectical mathematics with which we must familiarize ourselves, their union in the pair of subjects S and A includes only four terms in all, because the relation of exclusion that obtains between a and a' reduces the two couples thus indicated to a single couple in the juxtaposition of the subjects.

In this game for four players, the analyst will act on the significant resistances that weigh down, impede, and divert speech, while himself introducing into the quartet the primordial sign of the exclusion that connotes the either/or of presence or absence which formally brings out death as included in the narcissistic *Bildung*. This sign is lacking, let it be noted in

430

passing, in the algorithmic apparatus of the modern logic that is called symbolic, demonstrating the dialectical inadequacy that renders it still unsuitable for formalizing the human sciences.

This means that the analyst concretely intervenes in the dialectic of analysis by playing dead—by "cadaverizing" his position, as the Chinese say—either by his silence where he is the Other with a capital O, or by canceling out his own resistance where he is the other with a lowercase o. In both cases, and via symbolic and imaginary effects, respectively, he makes death present.

Still, he must recognize and therefore distinguish his action in each of these two registers to know why he is intervening, at what moment the opportunity is presenting itself, and how to act on it.

The primordial condition for this is that the analyst should be thoroughly convinced of the radical difference between the Other to whom his speech should be addressed, and the second other who is the one he sees before him, about whom and by means of whom the first speaks to him in the discourse it pursues before him. For, in this way, the analyst will be able to be the one to whom this discourse is addressed.

The fable of my lectern and the usual practice of the discourse of conviction will show him clearly enough, if he thinks about it, that no word [*discours*]—whatever inertia it may be based on or whatever passion it may appeal to—is ever addressed to anyone except the wise to whom it is sufficient. Even what is known as an *ad hominem* argument is only regarded by the person who uses it as a seduction designed to get the other, in his authenticity, to accept what the person says [*parole*]; this speech constitutes a pact, whether it is made explicit or not, between the two subjects, but it is situated in either case beyond the reasons furnished in the argument.

In general, each person knows that others will remain, like himself, inaccessible to the constraints of reason, failing an a priori acceptance of a rule of debate that cannot function without an explicit or implicit agreement as to what is called its ground [*fonds*], which is almost always tantamount to a prior agreement regarding the stakes. What is called logic or law is never anything more than a body of rules that were laboriously worked out at a moment of history, duly dated and situated by a stamp of origin—whether agora or forum, church, or even political party. Thus I won't expect anything from these rules without the Other's good faith and, as a last resort, will only make use of them, if I see fit or am forced to, in order to beguile bad faith.

The Locus of Speech

The Other is, therefore, the locus in which is constituted the I who speaks along with he who hears, what is said by the one being already the reply, the other deciding, in hearing [*entendre*] it, whether the one has spoken or not.

But, in return, this locus extends as far into the subject as the laws of speech reign there, that is, well beyond the discourse that takes its watchwords from the ego, since Freud discovered its unconscious field and the laws that structure it.

It is not because of some mystery concerning the indestructibility of certain childhood desires that the laws of the unconscious determine analyzable symptoms. The subject's imaginary shaping by his desires—which are more or less fixated or regressed in relation to the object—is too inadequate and partial to provide the key.

The necessary and sufficient reason for the repetitive insistence of these desires in the transference and their permanent remembrance in a signifier that repression has appropriated—that is, in which the repressed returns—is found if one accepts the idea that in these determinations the desire for recognition dominates the desire that is to be recognized, preserving it as such until it is recognized.

Indeed, the laws of remembering and symbolic recognition are different in their essence and manifestation from the laws of imaginary reminiscence—that is, from the echo of feeling or instinctual imprinting (*Prägung*)—even if the elements organized by the former as signifiers are borrowed from the material to which the latter give signification.

To grasp the nature of symbolic memory, it suffices to have studied once, as I had people do in my seminar, the simplest symbolic sequence, that of a linear series of signs connoting the presence/absence alternative, each sign being chosen at random by whatever pure or impure means adopted. If this sequence is then elaborated in the simplest way, isolating three-term sequences to generate a new series, syntactical laws arise that impose on each term of this new series certain exclusions of possibility until the compensations demanded by its antecedents have been satisfied.

Freud's discovery went right to the heart of this determination by the symbolic law, for in the unconscious—which, he insisted, was quite different from everything that had previously been designated by that name—he recognized the instance of the laws on which marriage and kinship are based, establishing the Oedipus complex as its central motivation already in

432

the *Traumdeutung*. This is what now allows me to tell you why the motives of the unconscious are limited to sexual desire, a point on which Freud was quite clear from the outset and from which he never deviated. Indeed, it is essentially on sexual relations [*liaison*]—by regulating them according to the law of preferential marriage alliances and forbidden relations—that the first combinatory for exchanges of women between family lines relies, developing the fundamental commerce and concrete discourse on which human societies are based in an exchange of gratuitous goods and magic words.

The concrete field of individual preservation, on the other hand, through its links with the division not of labor, but of desire and labor—already manifest right from the first transformation that introduced human signification into food and up to the most highly developed forms of the production of consumable goods—sufficiently shows that it is structured in the master/slave dialectic, in which we can recognize the symbolic emergence of the imaginary struggle to the death that I defined above as the ego's essential structure; it is hardly surprising, then, that this field is exclusively reflected in this structure. In other words, this explains why the other great generic desire, hunger, is not represented, as Freud always maintained, in what the unconscious preserves in order to get it recognized.

433

Thus Freud's intention, which was quite legible to anyone who didn't confine himself to merely parroting Freud's texts, became increasingly clear when he promoted the topography of the ego; his intention was to restore, in all its rigor, the separation—right down to their unconscious interference—between the field of the ego and that of the unconscious he discovered first, by showing that the former is in a "blocking" position in relation to the latter, the former resisting recognition of the latter through the effect of its own significations in speech.

Here lies the contrast between the significations of guilt, whose discovery in the subject's action dominated the first phase in the history of psychoanalysis, and the significations of the subject's affective frustration, instinctual inadequacy, and imaginary dependence that dominate its current phase.

It isn't going very far to say that the latter significations, whose predominance is now consolidating through a forgetting of the former significations, promise us a preparatory course in general infantilization; for psychoanalysis is already allowing large-scale practices of social mystification to claim legitimacy by appealing to analytic principles.

Symbolic Debt

Will our action go so far, then, as to repress the very truth that it implies in its practice? Will it put this truth back to sleep—a truth that Freud, in the passion of the Rat Man, forever offers up so that we may recognize it, should we increasingly turn our vigilance away from it—namely, that the stone guest who came, in symptoms, to disturb the banquet of his desires was fashioned out of acts of treachery and vain oaths, broken promises and empty words, whose constellation presided over a man's birth?

For the green grape of speech by which the child received the authentication of the nothingness of existence from a father too early, and the grapes of wrath that responded to the words of false hope with which his mother lured him in feeding him with the milk of her true despair, set his teeth on edge more than if he had been weaned from an imaginary jouissance or even deprived of some real attentions.   434

Will we escape unscathed from the symbolic game in which the real misdeed pays the price for imaginary temptation? Will we turn our attention away from what becomes of the law when, by virtue of having been intolerable to the subject's loyalty, it is misrecognized by him already when it is still unknown to him, and from what becomes of the imperative when, having presented itself to him through imposture, it is challenged in his heart before being discerned? In other words, will we turn our attention away from the mainsprings that, in the broken link of the symbolic chain, raise from the imaginary the obscene, ferocious figure in which the true signification of the superego must be seen?

It should be understood here that my criticism of a kind of analysis that claims to be an analysis of resistance, and is reduced ever more to the mobilization of the defenses, bears solely on the fact that it is as disoriented in its practice as it is in its principles, and is designed to remind analysts of their legitimate ends.

The maneuvers involving dyadic complicity that this form of analysis forces itself to implement to achieve happiness and success can have value in our eyes only if they reduce the resistance, stemming from the effects of prestige in which the ego asserts itself, to the speech that is owned [*s'avoue*] at a certain moment of analysis, which is the analytic moment.

I believe that it is in the owning [*l'aveu*] of this speech, of which transference is the enigmatic actualization, that analysis must refind its center along with its gravity; and let no one imagine from what I said earlier that I conceptualize this speech as some mystical mode reminiscent of karma. For what is striking in the moving drama of neurosis is the absurd aspects of a disconcerted symbolization whose case of mistaken identity seems more derisory the more one delves into it.

Adæquatio rei et intellectus: the homonymic enigma that can be brought out in the genitive, *rei*—which without even changing accents can be the genitive of the word *reus*, meaning the party to the case in a lawsuit, specifically the accused, and metaphorically he who has incurred a debt—surprises us by providing, in the end, a formulation for this singular correspondence [*adéquation*] that I raised as a question for our intellect and that finds its answer in the symbolic debt for which the subject is responsible as a subject of speech.

435   *The Training of Analysts to Come*

In taking up anew my analysis of the ways in which speech is able to recover the debt it engenders, I will thus return to the structures of language that are so manifestly recognizable in the earliest discovered mechanisms of the unconscious.

We need but thumb through the pages of Freud's work for it to become abundantly clear that he regarded a history of languages [*langue*] and institutions, and the resonances—whether attested to or not in human memory—of literature and of the significations involved in works of art, as necessary to an understanding of the text of our experience; indeed, Freud himself found his inspiration, ways of thinking, and arsenal of techniques therein. But he also believed it wasn't superfluous to make them a condition for instituting the teaching of psychoanalysis.

The fact that this condition has been neglected, even in the selection of analysts, cannot be unconnected with the results we see around us; it indicates to us that it is only by articulating Freud's requirements in terms of technique that we will be able to satisfy them. It is with an initiation into the methods of the linguist, the historian, and, I would add, the mathematician that we should now be concerned if a new generation of practitioners and researchers is to recover the meaning and motor force of the Freudian experience. This generation will also find in these methods a way to avoid social-psychological objectification, in which the psychoanalyst seeks, in his uncertainty, the substance of what he does, whereas it can provide him with no more than an inadequate abstraction in which his practice gets bogged down and dissolves.

Such reform will require an institutional undertaking, for it can only be sustained by means of constant communication with disciplines that would define themselves as sciences of intersubjectivity, or by the term "conjectural sciences," a term by which I indicate the kind of research that is now changing the implication of the "human sciences."

But such a direction can only be maintained by a true teaching, that is, teaching that constantly subjects itself to what is known as renewal. For the pact instituting analytic experience must take into account the fact that this experience instates the very effects that capture it, diverting it from the subject.

436

Thus, in exposing magical thinking, people don't see that it is magical thinking and, in fact, an alibi for thoughts about wielding power that are ever ready to bring about their own rejection in an action that is sustained only by its connection with truth.

Freud is referring to this connection with truth when he declares that it is impossible to meet three challenges: to educate, govern, and psychoanalyze. Why are they impossible, if not for the fact that the subject can only be missed in these undertakings, slipping away in the margin Freud reserves for truth?

For in these undertakings truth proves to be complex in its essence, humble in its offices and foreign to reality, refractory to the choice of sex, akin to death and, on the whole, rather inhuman, Diana perhaps . . . Actaeon, too guilty to hunt the goddess, prey in which is caught, O huntsman, the shadow that you become, let the pack go without hastening your step, Diana will recognize the hounds for what they are worth . . .

Notes

1. This text was first published in *L'Évolution psychiatrique* 1 (1956): 225–52.

2. (Added in 1966:) This rewritten paragraph predates a line of thought I have since explored.

3. Namely, "Es ist Kulturarbeit etwa wie die Trockenlegung der Zuydersee." "It is a civilizing task like the drying out of the Zuider Zee."

4. One can but wonder what demon inspired the author of the extant French translation, whoever it was, to render it as "Le moi doit déloger le ça" ("The ego must dislodge the id"). It is true that one can savor in it the tone of an analytic quarter in which people know how to carry out the sort of operation it evokes.

The Instance of the Letter in the Unconscious

or Reason Since Freud

"Of Children Who Are Wrapped in Swaddling Bands"
O cities of the sea, I behold in you your citizens, women as well as men,
tightly bound with stout bonds around their arms and legs by folk who will
have no understanding of [y]our speech; and you will only be able to give
vent to your griefs and sense of loss of liberty by making tearful complaints,
and sighs, and lamentation one to another; for those who bind you will not
have understanding of your speech nor will you understand them.[1]
—Leonardo Da Vinci

While the theme of the third volume of *La Psychanalyse*[2] commissioned this
contribution by me, I owe this deference to what will be discovered here by
introducing it in situating it between writing and speech—it will be halfway
between the two.

Writing is in fact distinguished by a prevalence of the *text* in the sense
that we will see this factor of discourse take on here—which allows for the
kind of tightening up that must, to my taste, leave the reader no other way
out than the way in, which I prefer to be difficult. This, then, will not be a
writing in my sense of the term.

The fact that I contribute something wholly new at each class of my seminar has heretofore prevented me from providing such a text, except in one
class, which has nothing particularly outstanding about it in terms of the
series, and is only worth referring to for an idea of its overall level.

For the urgency that I am now taking as a pretext for leaving that aim
behind merely covers over the problem that, in maintaining it at the level at
which I must present my teachings here, it might stray too far from speech,
whose very different measures are essential to the training I seek to effect.

This is why I took the opportunity presented to me at that time by an
invitation to meet with the philosophy group of the Fédération des étudiants
ès lettres[3] to make an appropriate adjustment to my exposé—its necessary
generality matching the extraordinary character of their interest, but its sole

object encountering the connivance of their common background, a literary background, to which my title pays homage.

Indeed, how could we forget that Freud constantly, and right until the end, maintained that such a background was the prime requisite in the training of analysts, and that he designated the age-old *universitas litterarum* as the ideal place for its institution?[4]

Thus this reference to the real-life context of my lecture, by showing whom I tailored it for, also marked those to whom it is not addressed.

I mean: none of those who, for whatever reason in psychoanalysis, allow their discipline to take advantage of some false identity.

This is a vice of habit and its effect on the mind is such that its true identity may appear among them as just one more diversion, whose refined redoubling one hopes will not escape the notice of subtler minds.

It is thus that we observe with curiosity the beginnings of a new tack concerning symbolization and language in the *International Journal of Psycho-Analysis,* a great many wetted fingers leafing through works by Sapir and Jespersen. These exercises are still green around the edges, but it is above all the tone that is missing. A certain seriousness always raises a smile when it enters the domain of veracity.

And how could a contemporary psychoanalyst not sense, in coming upon speech, that he had reached this domain, when it is from speech that analytic experience receives its instrument, its frame, its material, and even the background noise of its uncertainties?

I. The Meaning of the Letter   495

My title conveys the fact that, beyond this speech, it is the whole structure of language that psychoanalytic experience discovers in the unconscious. This is to alert prejudiced minds from the outset that the idea that the unconscious is merely the seat of the instincts may have to be reconsidered.

But how are we to take the letter here? Quite simply, literally [*à la lettre*].

By "letter" I designate the material medium [*support*] that concrete discourse borrows from language.

This simple definition assumes that language is not to be confused with the various psychical and somatic functions that serve it in the speaking subject.

The primary reason for this is that language, with its structure, exists prior to each subject's entry into it at a certain moment in his mental development.

Let us note that, although the deficits of aphasia are caused by purely anatomical lesions in the cerebral systems that provide the mental center for these functions, they prove, on the whole, to be distributed between the two aspects of the signifying effect of what I am calling here "the letter" in the creation of signification.[5] This point will become clearer in what follows.

And the subject, while he may appear to be the slave of language, is still more the slave of a discourse in the universal movement of which his place is already inscribed at his birth, if only in the form of his proper name.

496   Reference to the experience of the community as the substance of this discourse resolves nothing. For this experience takes on its essential dimension in the tradition established by this discourse. This tradition, long before the drama of history is inscribed in it, grounds the elementary structures of culture. And these very structures display an ordering of exchanges which, even if unconscious, is inconceivable apart from the permutations authorized by language.

With the result that the ethnographic duality of nature and culture is giving way to a ternary conception of the human condition—nature, society, and culture—the last term of which may well be reduced to language, that is, to what essentially distinguishes human society from natural societies.

But I shall neither take sides here nor take this as a point of departure, leaving to their own obscurity the original relations between the signifier and labor. To settle accounts with the general function of *praxis* in the genesis of history by way of a quip, I will confine myself to mentioning that the very society that wished to restore the hierarchy responsible for the relations between production and ideological superstructures to its rightful political place, alongside the privilege of the producers, has nevertheless failed to give birth to an Esperanto whose relations to socialist reality [*réel*] would have ruled out from the start any possibility of literary formalism.[6]

For my part, I will put my faith in only those premises whose value has already been proven, in that they have allowed language to attain the status in experience of a scientific object.

This is what permits linguistics[7] to present itself in the pilot position in this domain, around which a reclassification of the sciences is signaling, as
497   is usually the case, a revolution in knowledge; only the necessities of communication have made me term this domain, in the theme of this volume of *La Psychanalyse*, "the sciences of man"—despite the confusion that may hide behind it.

To pinpoint the emergence of the discipline of linguistics, I will say that, as in the case of every science in the modern sense, it consists in the constitutive moment of an algorithm that grounds it. This algorithm is the following:

$$\frac{S}{s}$$

It is read as follows: signifier over signified, "over" corresponding to the bar separating the two levels.

The sign written in this way should be attributed to Ferdinand de Saussure, although it is not reduced to this exact form in any of the numerous schemas in which it appears in the printed version of the various lectures from the three courses he gave in 1906–7, 1908–9, and 1910–11, which a group of his devoted disciples collected under the title, *Cours de linguistique générale*—a publication of prime importance for the transmission of a teaching worthy of the name, that is, that one can stop only on its own movement.

This is why it is legitimate for us to credit him for the formalization $\frac{S}{s}$, which characterizes the modern stage of linguistics, despite the diversity between schools of linguistics.

The major theme of this science is thus based, in effect, on the primordial position of the signifier and the signified as distinct orders initially separated by a barrier resisting signification.

This is what makes possible an exact study of the connections characteristic of the signifier, and of the magnitude of their function in generating the signified.

For this primordial distinction goes well beyond the debate over the arbitrariness of the sign, such as it has been elaborated since the reflections of Antiquity, and even beyond the impasse, already sensed at that time, which opposed the one-to-one correspondence between word and thing, even in the act of naming—despite the appearances suggested by the role imputed to the index finger pointing to an object as an infant learns its mother tongue, or in the use of so-called concrete academic methods in the study of foreign languages [*langues*]. 498

We can take things no further along this path than to demonstrate that no signification can be sustained except by reference to another signification.[8] This ultimately leads us to the remark that there is no existing language [*langue*] whose ability to cover the field of the signified can be called into question, one of the effects of its existence as a language [*langue*] being that it fulfills all needs there. Were we to try to grasp the constitution of the object in language, we could but note that this constitution is found only at the level of the concept—which is very different from any nominative—and that the *thing* [*chose*], when quite obviously reduced to the noun, splits into the double, divergent ray of the cause in which the thing has taken shelter in French, and of the nothing [*rien*] to which the thing has abandoned its Latin dress (*rem*).

These considerations, as existent as they may be to philosophers, divert us from the locus whence language questions us about its very nature. And we will fail to sustain this question as long as we have not jettisoned the illusion that the signifier serves [*répond à*] the function of representing the signified, or better, that the signifier has to justify [*répondre de*] its existence in terms of any signification whatsoever.

For even if it is reduced to this latter formulation, the heresy is the same—the heresy that leads logical positivism in search of the "meaning of meaning,"* as its objective is called in the language [*langue*] in which its devotees snort. It can be seen here how this sort of analysis can reduce the text the most highly charged with meaning to insignificant trifles. Only mathematical algorithms resist this process; they are considered to be devoid of meaning, as they should be.[9]

499   The fact remains that if we were able to subtract solely the notion of the parallelism of its upper and lower terms from the algorithm $\frac{S}{s}$, each term only being taken globally, it would remain the enigmatic sign of a total mystery. Which, of course, is not the case.

In order to grasp its function, I will begin by reproducing the faulty illustration by which its usage is classically introduced:

TREE

We can see here how it lends itself to the kind of direction indicated above as erroneous.

In my lecture, I replaced this illustration with another, which can be considered more correct only because it exaggerates in the incongruous dimension psychoanalysts have not yet altogether given up, because of their justified sense that their conformism derives its value from it alone. Here is the other illustration:

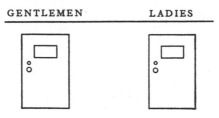

Here we see that, without greatly extending the scope of the signifier involved in the experiment—that is, by simply doubling the nominal type through the mere juxtaposition of two terms whose complementary mean-   500
ings would seem to have to reinforce each other—surprise is produced by the precipitation of an unexpected meaning: the image of two twin doors that symbolize, with the private stall offered Western man for the satisfaction of his natural needs when away from home, the imperative he seems to share with the vast majority of primitive communities that subjects his public life to the laws of urinary segregation.

The point is not merely to silence the nominalist debate with a low blow, but to show how the signifier in fact enters the signified—namely, in a form which, since it is not immaterial, raises the question of its place in reality. For in having to move closer to the little enamel plaques that bear it, the squinting gaze of a nearsighted person might be justified in wondering whether it is indeed here that we must see the signifier, whose signified would in this case be paid its last respects by the solemn procession in two lines from the upper nave.

But no contrived example can be as telling as what is encountered in the lived experience of truth. Thus I have no reason to be unhappy I invented the above, since it awoke in the person the most worthy of my trust a childhood memory which, having come serendipitously to my attention, is best placed here.

A train arrives at a station. A little boy and a little girl, brother and sister, are seated across from each other in a compartment next to the outside window that provides a view of the station platform buildings going by as the train comes to a stop. "Look," says the brother, "we're at Ladies!" "Imbecile!" replies his sister, "Don't you see we're at Gentlemen."

Aside from the fact that the rails in this story materialize the bar in the Saussurian algorithm in a form designed to suggest that its resistance may be other than dialectical, one would have to be half-blind to be confused as to the respective places of the signifier and the signified here, and not to follow from what radiant center the signifier reflects its light into the darkness of incomplete significations.

For the signifier will raise Dissension—that is merely animal in kind and destined to the natural fog of forgetfulness—to the immeasurable power of ideological warfare, which is merciless to families and a torment to the gods. To these children, Gentlemen and Ladies will henceforth be two homelands toward which each of their souls will take flight on divergent wings, and regarding which it will be all the more impossible for them to reach an agreement since, being in fact the same homeland, neither can give ground regarding the one's unsurpassed excellence without detracting from the other's glory.

Let us stop there. It sounds like the history of France. Which it is more humane to recall here, and rightly so, than that of England, destined to flip from the Large to the Small End of Dean Swift's egg.

It remains to be grasped up what steps and down what corridor the S of the signifier, visible here in the plurals [*hommes* and *dames*] by which it focuses its welcome beyond the train window, must pass to impress its curves upon the ducts by which—like hot air and cold air—indignation and scorn hiss on this side.

One thing is certain: this access must not, in any case, carry any signification with it if the algorithm, $\frac{S}{s}$, with its bar is appropriate to it. For insofar as the algorithm itself is but a pure function of the signifier, it can reveal only a signifying structure in this transfer.

Now the structure of the signifier is, as is commonly said of language, that it is articulated.

This means that its units—no matter where one begins in tracing out their reciprocal encroachments and expanding inclusions—are subject to the twofold condition of being reduced to ultimate differential elements and of combining the latter according to the laws of a closed order.

These elements, the decisive discovery of linguistics, are *phonemes*; we must not look for any *phonetic* constancy in the modulatory variability to which this term applies, but rather for the synchronic system of differential couplings that are necessary to discern vocables in a given language [*langue*]. This allows us to see that an essential element in speech itself was predestined to flow into moveable type which, in Didots or Garamonds squeezing into lowercases, renders validly present what I call the "letter"— namely, the essentially localized structure of the signifier.

The second property of the signifier, that of combining according to the laws of a closed order, affirms the necessity of the topological substratum, of which the term I ordinarily use, "signifying chain," gives an approximate idea: links by which a necklace firmly hooks onto a link of another necklace made of links.

Such are the structural conditions that define the order of the signifier's constitutive encroachments up to the unit immediately above the sentence as grammar, and the order of the signifier's constitutive inclusions up to the verbal locution as the lexicon.

In the limits within which these two approaches to understanding linguistic usage are confined, it is easy to see that only signifier-to-signifier correlations provide the standard for any and every search for signification; this is indicated by the notion of "usage" of a taxeme or semanteme, which refers to contexts just one degree above that of the units in question.

But it is not because grammatical and lexical approaches are exhausted at a certain point that we must think that signification rules unreservedly beyond it. That would be a mistake.

For the signifier, by its very nature, always anticipates meaning by deploying its dimension in some sense before it. As is seen at the level of the sentence when the latter is interrupted before the significant term: "I'll never . . .," "The fact remains . . .," "Still perhaps . . ." Such sentences nevertheless make sense, and that sense is all the more oppressive in that it is content to make us wait for it.[10]

But the phenomenon is no different, which—making her appear, with the sole postponement of a "but," as comely as the Shulamite, as honest as a virtuous maiden—adorns and readies the Negress for the wedding and the poor woman for the auction block.

Whence we can say that it is in the chain of the signifier that meaning *insists*, but that none of the chain's elements *consists* in the signification it can provide at that very moment.

The notion of an incessant sliding of the signified under the signifier thus comes to the fore—which Ferdinand de Saussure illustrates with an image resembling the wavy lines of the upper and lower Waters in miniatures from manuscripts of Genesis. It is a twofold flood in which the landmarks—fine streaks of rain traced by vertical dotted lines that supposedly delimit corresponding segments—seem insubstantial.

All our experience runs counter to this, which made me speak at one point in my seminar on the psychoses of the "button ties" [*points de capiton*] required by this schema to account for the dominance of the letter in the dramatic transformation that dialogue can effect in the subject.[11]

But while the linearity that Saussure considers to be constitutive of the

503

chain of discourse—in accordance with its emission by a single voice and with the horizontal axis along which it is situated in our writing—is in fact necessary, it is not sufficient. It applies to the chain of discourse only in the direction in which it is oriented in time, even being taken up therein as a signifying factor in all languages [*langues*] in which the time of "Peter hits Paul" is reversed when the terms are inverted.

But it suffices to listen to poetry, which Saussure was certainly in the habit of doing,[12] for a polyphony to be heard and for it to become clear that all discourse is aligned along the several staves of a musical score.

Indeed, there is no signifying chain that does not sustain—as if attached to the punctuation of each of its units—all attested contexts that are, so to speak, "vertically" linked to that point.

Thus, if we take up the word *arbre* (tree) again, this time not in its nominal isolation, but at the endpoint of one of these punctuations, we see that it is not simply because the word *barre* (bar) is its anagram that it crosses the bar of the Saussurian algorithm.

504   For broken down into the double specter of its vowels and consonants, it calls up—with the robur-oak [*robre*] and the plane tree [*platane*]—the significations of strength and majesty that it takes on in our flora. Tapping all the symbolic contexts in which it is used in the Hebrew of the Bible, it erects on a barren hill the shadow of the cross. Next it reduces to a capital Y, the sign of dichotomy—which, without the illustration that historiates armorials, would owe nothing to the tree, however genealogical it claims to be. Circulatory tree, arbor vitae of the cerebellum, lead tree or silver amalgam [*arbre de Diane*], crystals precipitated into a tree that conducts lightning, is it your countenance that traces our destiny for us in the fire-scorched tortoiseshell, or your flash that brings forth from an infinite night that slow change in being in the Ἐν Πάντα of language:

> No! says the Tree, it says No! in the scintillating
> Of its superb head

verses that I consider to be as legitimately heard in the harmonics of the tree as their reverse:

> Which the storm treats universally
> As it does a blade of grass.

For this modern verse is organized according to the same law of the parallelism of the signifier, whose concert governs both primitive Slavic epic poetry and the most refined Chinese poetry.

This can be seen in the common mode of beings [*l'étant*] from which the tree and the blade of grass are chosen, so that the signs of contradiction—saying "No!" and "treat as"—can come into being here, and so that, through the categorical contrast between the particularity of "superb" and the "universally" of its reduction, the indiscernible scintillating of the eternal instant may be accomplished in the condensation of *tête* (head) and *tempête* (storm).

But all this signifier can only operate, it may be objected, if it is present in the subject. I answer this objection by assuming that he has shifted to the level of the signified.

For what is important is not whether the subject know more or less about it. (If GENTLEMEN and LADIES were written in a language [*langue*] with which the little boy and girl were unfamiliar, their quarrel would simply be more exclusively a quarrel over words, but it would be no less ready to take on signification for all that.)

What this structure of the signifying chain discloses is the possibility I have—precisely insofar as I share its language [*langue*] with other subjects, that is, insofar as this language [*langue*] exists—to use it to signify *something altogether different* from what it says. This is a function of speech that is more worthy of being pointed out than that of disguising the subject's thought (which is usually indefinable)—namely, the function of indicating the place of this subject in the search for truth.   505

I need but plant my tree in a locution, *grimper à l'arbre*, or even project onto it the derisive light that a descriptive context gives the word, *arborer*, to not let myself be imprisoned in some sort of *communiqué* of the facts, however official it may be, and if I know the truth, convey it, despite all the censors, *between-the-lines* using nothing but the signifier that can be constituted by my acrobatics through the branches of the tree. These acrobatics may be provocative to the point of burlesque or perceptible only to the trained eye, depending on whether I wish to be understood by the many or the few.

The properly signifying function thus depicted in language has a name. We learned this name in our childhood grammar book on the last page, where the shade of Quintilian, relegated to some phantom chapter to convey final considerations on style, seemed suddenly to hasten its voice due to the threat of being cut off.

It is among the figures of style, or tropes—from which the verb "to find" [*trouver*] comes to us—that this name is, in fact, found. This name is *metonymy*.

I shall refer only to the example of it given there: "thirty sails." For the worry I felt, over the fact that the word "ship" [*bateau*] that was hiding therein seemed to split its presence there in two by having been able to borrow its figurative sense from the very rehashing of this example, veiled [*voilait*] not so much those illustrious sails [*voiles*] as the definition they were supposed to illustrate.

The part taken for the whole—I said to myself, if the thing is supposed to be based on reality [*réel*]—leaves us with hardly any idea what we are to conclude about the size of the fleet these thirty sails are nevertheless supposed to gauge: for a ship to have but one sail is very rare indeed.

506   This shows that the connection between ship and sail is nowhere other than in the signifier, and that metonymy is based on the *word-to-word* nature of this connection.[13]

I shall designate as metonymy the first aspect of the actual field the signifier constitutes, so that meaning may assume a place there.

The other aspect is *metaphor*. Let me illustrate it immediately; Quillet's dictionary seemed appropriate to me to provide a sample that would not be suspected of being deliberately selected, and I didn't pursue the farce any farther than Victor Hugo's well-known verse, "His sheaf was neither miserly nor hateful . . .," with which I presented metaphor, when the time came for it, in my seminar on the psychoses.

Let us say that modern poetry and the Surrealist school led us to take a major step forward here by showing that any conjunction of two signifiers could just as easily constitute a metaphor, if an additional condition—that of the greatest disparity of the images signified—weren't required for the

507   production of the poetic spark, in other words, for metaphoric creation to occur.

Of course, this radical position is based on the so-called "automatic writing" experiment, which would not have been attempted without the assurance its pioneers drew from Freud's discovery. But it remains marked by confusion because the doctrine behind it is false.

Metaphor's creative spark does not spring forth from the juxtaposition of two images, that is, of two equally actualized signifiers. It flashes between two signifiers, one of which has replaced the other by taking the other's place in the signifying chain, the occulted signifier remaining present by virtue of its (metonymic) connection to the rest of the chain.

One word for another: this is the formula for metaphor, and if you are a poet you will make it into a game and produce a continuous stream, nay, a dazzling weave of metaphors. You will, moreover, obtain the intoxicating effect of Jean Tardieu's dialogue that goes by this title, due solely to the demonstration it provides of the radical superfluousness of all signification to a perfectly convincing representation of bourgeois comedy.

In Hugo's verse, it is obvious that not the slightest light emanates from the assertion that a sheaf is neither miserly nor hateful, because it is clear that the sheaf has no more the merit than the demerit of these attributes, since miserliness and hatred, along with the sheaf, are properties of Booz, who exercises them when he uses the sheaf as he sees fit, without making his feelings known to it.

If "his sheaf" refers back to Booz, as is clearly the case nevertheless, it is because it replaces him in the signifying chain—at the very place that awaited him, because it had been raised up a step by the clearing away of miserliness and hatred. But the sheaf has thus cleared this place of Booz, ejected as he now is into the outer darkness where miserliness and hatred harbor him in the hollow of their negation.

But once *his* sheaf has thus usurped his place, Booz cannot go back to it, the slender thread of the little "his" that attaches him to it being an additional obstacle thereto, because it binds this return with a title of ownership that would detain him in the heart of miserliness and hatred. His asserted generosity is thus reduced to *less than nothing* by the munificence of the sheaf which, being drawn from nature, knows neither our reserve nor our rejections, and even in its accumulation remains prodigal by our standards.

But if, in this profusion, the giver disappears with the gift, it is only to reemerge in what surrounds the figure of speech in which he was annihilated. For it is the radiance of fecundity—which announces the surprise the poem celebrates, namely, the promise of acceding to paternity that the old man receives in a sacred context.

Thus it is between a man's proper name qua signifier and the signifier that metaphorically abolishes it that the poetic spark is produced, and it is all the more effective here in bringing about the signification of paternity in that it reproduces the mythical event through which Freud reconstructed the path along which the mystery of paternity advances in the unconscious of every man.

The structure of modern metaphor is no different. Hence the jaculation, "Love is a pebble laughing in the sun," recreates love in a dimension that I have said strikes me as tenable, as opposed to its ever imminent slippage into the mirage of some narcissistic altruism.

508

We see that metaphor is situated at the precise point at which meaning is produced in nonmeaning—that is, at the passage which, as Freud discovered, when crossed in the opposite direction, gives rise to the word that is "the word" ["*le mot*"] par excellence in French, the word that has no other patronage there than the signifier *esprit*[14]—and at which it becomes palpable that, in deriding the signifier, man defies his very destiny.

But to return to metonymy now, what does man find in it, if it must be more than the power to skirt the obstacles of social censure? Doesn't this form, which gives oppressed truth its field, manifest a certain servitude that is inherent in its presentation?

It's worth taking the time to read a book in which Leo Strauss, from the land that has traditionally offered asylum to those who have chosen freedom, reflects on the relations between the art of writing and persecution.[15] By honing in on the sort of connaturality that ties this art to this condition, he allows us to glimpse something that imposes its form here, in the effect of truth on desire.

But haven't we been feeling for a while now that, in following the paths of the letter to reach the Freudian truth, we are getting hot, its flames spreading all around us?

Of course, as it is said, the letter kills while the spirit gives life. I don't disagree, having had to pay homage somewhere here to a noble victim of the error of seeking in the letter, but I also ask how the spirit could live without the letter. The spirit's pretensions would nevertheless remain indisputable if the letter hadn't proven that it produces all its truth effects in man without the spirit having to intervene at all.

This revelation came to Freud, and he called his discovery the unconscious.

II. The Letter in the Unconscious

In Freud's complete works, one out of three pages presents us with philological references, one out of two pages with logical inferences, and everywhere we see a dialectical apprehension of experience, linguistic analysis becoming still more prevalent the more directly the unconscious is involved.

Thus what is at stake on every page in *The Interpretation of Dreams* is what I call the letter of discourse, in its texture, uses, and immanence in the matter in question. For this book inaugurates both Freud's work and his royal road to the unconscious. And we are informed of this by Freud, whose confession in letters to Fliess that have since been made public, when he launches this book toward us in the early days of this century,[16] merely confirms what he continued to proclaim to the end: that the whole of his discovery lies in this no-holds-barred expression of his message.

The first clause, articulated already in the introductory chapter because its   510
exposition cannot be postponed, is that the dream is a rebus. And Freud stipulates that it must be understood quite literally [*à la lettre*], as I said earlier. This is related to the instance in the dream of the same "literating" (in other words, phonemic) structure in which the signifier is articulated and analyzed in discourse. Like the unnatural figures of the boat on the roof, or the man with a comma for a head, which are expressly mentioned by Freud, dream images are to be taken up only on the basis of their value as signifiers, that is, only insofar as they allow us to spell out the "proverb" presented by the oneiric rebus. The linguistic structure that enables us to read dreams is at the crux of the "signifierness of dreams," at the crux of the *Traumdeutung*.

Freud shows us in every possible way that the image's value as a signifier has nothing to do with its signification, giving as an example Egyptian hieroglyphics in which it would be ridiculous to deduce from the frequency in a text of a vulture (which is an aleph) or a chick (which is a vau) indicating a form of the verb "to be" and plurals, that the text has anything whatsoever to do with these ornithological specimens. Freud takes his bearings from certain uses of the signifier in this writing that are effaced in ours, such as the use of determinatives, where a categorical figure is added as an exponent to the literal figuration of a verbal term; but this is only to bring us back to the fact that we are dealing with writing where even the supposed "ideogram" is a letter.

But psychoanalysts who have no training in linguistics don't need the current confusion regarding the term "ideogram" to believe in a symbolism deriving from natural analogy, or even from instinct's coaptational image. This is so true that, apart from the French school, which attends to this, it is with a statement like "reading coffee grounds is not the same as reading hieroglyphics" that I must recall to its own principles a technique whose pathways cannot be justified unless they aim at the unconscious.

It must be said that this is admitted only reluctantly, and that the mental vice denounced above enjoys such favor that the contemporary psychoanalyst can be expected to say that he decodes before resolving to take the journey with Freud (turn at the statue of Champollion, says the guide) that is necessary for him to understand that he deciphers—the latter differing in   511
that a cryptogram only takes on its full dimensions when it is in a lost language [*langue*].

Taking this journey simply amounts to going further in the *Traumdeutung*.

Entstellung, translated as "transposition"—which Freud shows to be the general precondition for the functioning of the dream—is what I designated earlier, with Saussure, as the sliding of the signified under the signifier, which is always happening (unconsciously, let us note) in discourse.

But the two aspects of the signifier's impact on the signified are also found here:

Verdichtung, "condensation," is the superimposed structure of signifiers in which metaphor finds its field; its name, condensing in itself the word *Dichtung*, shows the mechanism's connaturality with poetry, to the extent that it envelops poetry's own properly traditional function.

Verschiebung or "displacement"—this transfer of signification that metonymy displays is closer to the German term; it is presented, right from its first appearance in Freud's work, as the unconscious' best means by which to foil censorship.

What distinguishes these two mechanisms, which play a privileged role in the dream-work, *Traumarbeit*, from their homologous function in discourse? Nothing, except a condition imposed upon the signifying material, called *Rücksicht auf Darstellbarkeit*, which must be translated as "consideration of the means of staging" (the translation by "role of the possibility of representation" being overly approximate here). But this condition constitutes a limitation operating within the system of writing, rather than dissolving the system into a figurative semiology in which it would intersect the phenomena of natural expression. This would probably allow us to shed light on problems with certain types of pictography, which we are not justified in regarding as evolutionary stages simply because they were abandoned in writing as imperfect. Let us say, then, that dreams are like the parlor game in which each person, in turn, is supposed to get the spectators to guess some well-known saying or variant of it solely by silent gestures. The fact that dreams have speech at their disposal makes no difference since, for the unconscious, speech is but one staging element among others. It is precisely when games and dreams alike run up against the lack of taxemic material by which to represent logical relationships such as causality, contradiction, hypothesis, and so on that they prove they have to do with writing, not mime. The subtle procedures dreams end up using to represent these logical connections—in a much less artificial way than games usually employ—are taken up specifically in Freud's work, where it is once again confirmed that the dream-work proceeds in accordance with the laws of the signifier.

512

The rest of the dream revision is termed "secondary" by Freud, taking on its value from what is at stake: they are fantasies or daydreams, *Tagtraum*, to use the term Freud prefers to use to situate them in their wish-fulfilling function (*Wunscherfüllung*). Given that these fantasies may remain unconscious, their distinctive feature is clearly their signification. Now, Freud tells us that their role in dreams is either to serve as signifying elements for the statement of the unconscious thought (*Traumgedanke*), or to be used in the secondary revision that occurs—that is, in a function not to be distinguished, he says, from our waking thought (*von unserem wachen Denken nicht zu unterscheiden*). No better idea of this function's effects can be given than by comparing it to patches of colorwash which, when applied here and there on a stencil, can make stick figures—which are rather unprepossessing in themselves—in a rebus or hieroglyphics look more like a painting of people.

I apologize for seeming to spell out Freud's text myself; it is not merely to show how much is to be gained by not lopping off parts of it. It is to be able to situate what has happened in psychoanalysis in terms of its earliest reference points, which are fundamental and have never been revoked.

Right from the outset, people failed to recognize the constitutive role of the signifier in the status Freud immediately assigned to the unconscious in the most precise and explicit ways.

The reason for this was twofold, the least perceived being, naturally, that this formalization was not sufficient by itself to bring people to recognize the instance of the signifier, because when the *Traumdeutung* was published it was way ahead of the formalizations of linguistics for which one could no doubt show that it paved the way by the sheer weight of its truth. 513

The second reason is merely the flip side of the first, for if psychoanalysts were fascinated exclusively by the significations highlighted in the unconscious, it was because these significations derived their most secret attraction from the dialectic that seemed to be immanent in them.

I demonstrated to those who attend my seminar that the apparent changes of direction or rather changes in tack along the way—that Freud, in his primary concern to ensure the survival of his discovery along with the basic revisions it imposed upon our knowledge, felt it necessary to apply to his doctrine—were due to the need to counteract the ever-accelerating effects of this partiality.

For, I repeat, given the situation he found himself in, where he had nothing corresponding to the object of his discovery that was at the same level of scientific maturity, he at least never failed to maintain this object at the level of its ontological dignity.

The rest was the work of the gods and took such a course that analysis today finds its bearings in the imaginary forms I have just shown to be sketched out through inverse printing on the text they mutilate. It is to them that the analyst's aim now adapts, confusing them, in the interpretation of dreams, with the visionary liberation of the hieroglyphic aviary, and seeking more generally to verify the exhaustion of the analysis in a sort of "scanning"*[17] of these forms wherever they appear—with the idea that they bear witness both to the exhaustion of the regressions and to the remodeling of "the object-relation" that is supposed to typify the subject.[18]

514

The technique that is based on such positions can give rise to many varied effects, which are quite difficult to criticize behind their therapeutic aegis. But an internal critique can emerge from the flagrant discordance between the mode of operation by which the technique legitimizes itself—namely, the fundamental rule of psychoanalysis, all the instruments of which, starting with "free association," derive their justification from its inventor's conception of the unconscious—and the complete ignorance reigning there of this very conception of the unconscious. The most trenchant supporters of this technique let themselves off the hook here with a mere flourish: the fundamental rule must, they say, be observed all the more religiously since it is only the fruit of a lucky accident. In other words, Freud never really knew what he was doing.

A return to Freud's texts shows, on the contrary, the absolute coherence between his technique and his discovery, and this coherence allows us to situate his procedures at their proper level.

This is why any rectification of psychoanalysis requires a return to the truth of that discovery, which is impossible to obscure in its original moment.

For in the analysis of dreams, Freud intends to give us nothing other than the laws of the unconscious in their broadest extension. One of the reasons why dreams were the most propitious here is, Freud tells us, that they reveal these laws no less in normal subjects than in neurotics.

In neither, however, does the efficacy of the unconscious cease upon awakening. Psychoanalytic experience consists in nothing other than establishing that the unconscious leaves none of our actions outside its field. The presence of the unconscious in the psychological order—in other words, in the individual's relational functions—nevertheless deserves to be more precisely defined. It is not coextensive with that order, for we know that, while unconscious motivation manifests itself just as much in conscious psychical effects as in unconscious ones, conversely it is elementary to note that a

large number of psychical effects that are legitimately designated as unconscious, in the sense of excluding the characteristic of consciousness, nevertheless bear no relation whatsoever, by their nature, to the unconscious in
the Freudian sense. It is thus only due to an incorrect use of the term that
"psychical" and "unconscious" in this sense are confused, and that people
thus term psychical what is actually an effect of the unconscious on the
soma, for example.

The point is, therefore, to define the topography of this unconscious. I
say that it is the very topography defined by the algorithm: 515

$$\frac{S}{s}$$

What it has permitted me to elaborate concerning the impact of the signifier on the signified allows for its transformation into:

$$f(S)\frac{1}{s}$$

It is on the basis of the copresence in the signified not only of the elements
of the horizontal signifying chain but also of its vertical dependencies, that
I have demonstrated the effects, distributed in accordance with two fundamental structures, in metonymy and metaphor. We can symbolize them by:

$$f\,(S\ldots S')\,S \cong S\,(-)\,s$$

that is, metonymic structure, indicating that it is the signifier-to-signifier
connection that allows for the elision by which the signifier instates lack of
being [*le manque de l'être*] in the object-relation, using signification's referral
[*renvoi*] value to invest it with the desire aiming at the lack that it supports.
The — sign placed in ( ) manifests here the maintenance of the bar—which,
in the first algorithm, denotes the irreducible nature of the resistance of signification as constituted in the relations between signifier and signified.[19]

Now we turn to

$$f\left(\frac{S'}{S}\right)S \cong S\,(+)\,s$$

metaphoric structure, indicating that it is in the substitution of signifier for signifier that a signification effect is produced that is poetic or creative, in other words, that brings the signification in question into existence.[20] The + sign in ( ) manifests here the crossing of the bar, ——, and the constitutive value of this crossing for the emergence of signification.

516   This crossing expresses the condition for the passage of the signifier into the signified, whose moment I pointed out above by provisionally conflating it with the place of the subject.

It is the function of the subject, thus introduced, on which we must now dwell since it lies at the crux of our problem.

"I am thinking, therefore I am" (*cogito ergo sum*) is not simply the formulation in which the link between the transparency of the transcendental subject and his existential affirmation is constituted, at the historical apex of reflection on the conditions of science.

Perhaps I am only object and mechanism (and so nothing more than phenomenon), but assuredly, insofar as I think so, I am—absolutely. Philosophers certainly made important corrections here—namely, that in that which is thinking (*cogitans*), I am never doing anything but constituting myself as an object (*cogitatum*). The fact remains that through this extreme purification of the transcendental subject, my existential link to its project seems irrefutable, at least in the form of its actuality, and that "*cogito ergo sum*" *ubi cogito, ibi sum*, overcomes this objection.

Of course, this limits me to being there in my being only insofar as I think that I am in my thought; to what extent I really think this concerns me alone and, if I say it, interests no one.[21]

Yet to avoid it on the pretext of its philosophical semblances is simply to demonstrate one's inhibition. For the notion of the subject is indispensable even to the workings of a science such as strategy in the modern sense, whose calculations exclude all "subjectivism."

It is also to deny oneself access to what might be called the Freudian universe—in the sense in which we speak of the Copernican universe. Indeed, Freud himself compared his discovery to the so-called Copernican revolution, emphasizing that what was at stake was once again the place man assigns himself at the center of a universe.

517   Is the place that I occupy as subject of the signifier concentric or eccentric in relation to the place I occupy as subject of the signified? That is the question.

The point is not to know whether I speak of myself in a way that conforms to what I am, but rather to know whether, when I speak of myself, I am the same as the self of whom I speak. And there is no reason not to bring in the term "thought" here. For Freud uses the term to designate the elements at stake in the unconscious, that is, in the signifying mechanisms I just pointed to there.

It is nonetheless true that the philosophical *cogito* is at the center of the mirage that renders modern man so sure of being himself in his uncertainties about himself, and even in the distrust he has long since learned to exercise regarding the pitfalls of pride.

Now if, turning the weapon of metonymy against the nostalgia that it serves, I stop myself from seeking any meaning beyond tautology, and if, in the name of "war is war" and "a penny's a penny," I resolve to be only what I am, how can I escape here from the obvious fact that I am in this very act?

And how—in going to the other, metaphoric, pole of the signifying quest, and dedicating myself to becoming what I am, to coming into being—can I doubt that, even if I were to lose myself there, I am there?

Now it is on these very points, where the obvious is subverted by the empirical, that the trick of the Freudian conversion lies.

This signifying game of metonymy and metaphor—up to and including its active tip [*pointe*] that "cotter-pins" my desire to a refusal of the signifier or to a lack of being, and links my fate to the question of my destiny—this game is played, in its inexorable subtlety, until the match is over, where I am not because I cannot situate myself there.

That is, it wasn't going very far to say the words with which I momentarily dumbfounded my audience: I am thinking where I am not, therefore I am where I am not thinking. These words render palpable to an attentive ear with what elusive ambiguity the ring of meaning flees from our grasp along the verbal string.

What we must say is: I am not, where I am the plaything of my thought; I think about what I am where I do not think I am thinking.

This two-sided mystery can be seen to intersect the fact that truth is evoked only in that dimension of ruse whereby all "realism" in creation derives its virtue from metonymy, as well as this other fact that access to   518
meaning is granted only to the double elbow of metaphor, when we hold in our hand their one and only key: namely, the fact that the S and *s* of the Saussurian algorithm are not in the same plane, and man was deluding himself in believing he was situated in their common axis, which is nowhere.

At least until Freud made this discovery. For if what Freud discovered isn't precisely that, it is nothing.

The contents of the unconscious, in their deceptive ambiguity, supply us no reality in the subject more consistent than the immediate; it is from truth that they derive their virtue in the dimension of being: *Kern unseres Wesen* is Freud's own expression.

Metaphor's two-stage mechanism is the very mechanism by which symptoms, in the analytic sense, are determined. Between the enigmatic signifier of sexual trauma and the term it comes to replace in a current signifying chain, a spark flies that fixes in a symptom—a metaphor in which flesh or function is taken as a signifying element—the signification, that is inaccessible to the conscious subject, by which the symptom may be dissolved.

And the enigmas that desire—with its frenzy mimicking the gulf of the infinite and the secret collusion whereby it envelops the pleasure of knowing and of dominating in jouissance—poses for any sort of "natural philosophy" are based on no other derangement of instinct than the fact that it is caught in the rails of metonymy, eternally extending toward the *desire for something else*. Hence its "perverse" fixation at the very point of suspension of the signifying chain at which the screen-memory is immobilized and the fascinating image of the fetish becomes frozen.

There is no other way to conceive of the indestructibility of unconscious desire—given that there is no need which, when its satiation is prohibited, does not wither, in extreme cases through the very wasting away of the organism itself. It is in a kind of memory, comparable to what goes by that name in our modern thinking-machines (which are based on an electronic realization of signifying composition), that the chain is found which *insists* by reproducing itself in the transference, and which is the chain of a dead desire.

It is the truth of what this desire has been in his history that the subject cries out through his symptom, as Christ said that stones themselves would have cried out, had the children of Israel not lent them their voices.

519   And this is also why psychoanalysis alone allows us to differentiate in memory the function of remembering. The latter, rooted in the signifier, resolves the Platonic aporias of reminiscence through the ascendancy of history in man.

One need but read *Three Essays on the Theory of Sexuality*—which is covered over for the masses by so many pseudo-biological glosses—to note that Freud has all accession to the object derive from a dialectic of return.

Having thus begun with Holderlin's νόστος, Freud arrives less than twenty years later at Kierkegaard's repetition; that is, his thought, in submitting at the outset to the humble but inflexible consequences of the talking cure* alone, was never able to let go of the living servitudes that, starting from the royal principle of the Logos, led him to rethink the deadly Empedoclean antinomies.

And how, if not on the "other scene" Freud speaks of as the locus of the dream, are we to understand his recourse as a man of science to a *Deus ex machina* that is less derisory in that here it is revealed to the spectator that the machine directs the director himself? How can we fathom the fact that a scientist of the nineteenth century valued more highly than all his other works his *Totem and Taboo*—with its obscene, ferocious figure of the primordial father, who is inexhaustibly redeemed in the eternal blinding of Oedipus—before which contemporary ethnologists bow as before the development of an authentic myth, unless we realize that he had to bow to a force of evidence that went beyond his prejudices?

Similarly, the imperious proliferation of particular symbolic creations—such as what are called the sexual theories of children—which account for even the smallest details of the neurotic's compulsions, answer to the same necessities as do myths.

This is why, to bring you to the precise point of the commentary on Freud's work I am developing in my seminar, little Hans, left in the lurch at the age of five by the failings of his symbolic entourage, and faced with the suddenly actualized enigma to him of his sex and his existence, develops—under the direction of Freud and his father, who is Freud's disciple—all the possible permutations of a limited number of signifiers in the form of a myth, around the signifying crystal of his phobia.

We see here that, even at the individual level, man can find a solution to   520
the impossible by exhausting all possible forms of the impossibilities that are encountered when the solution is put into the form of a signifying equation. This is a striking demonstration that illuminates the labyrinth of a case study which thus far has been used only as a scrap heap. It also makes us grasp that the nature of neurosis is revealed in the fact that a symptom's development is coextensive with its elimination in the treatment: whether phobic, hysterical, or obsessive, neurosis is a question that being raises for the subject "from where he was before the subject came into the world" (this subordinate clause is the very expression Freud uses in explaining the Oedipus complex to little Hans).

At stake here is the being that appears in a split second in the emptiness of the verb "to be" and, as I said, this being raises its question for the subject. What does that mean? It does not raise it *before* the subject, since the subject cannot come to the place where being raises it, but being raises it *in* the subject's *place*—in other words, being raises the question in that place *with* the subject, just as one raises a problem *with* a pen and as antiquity's man thought *with* his soul.

Freud brought the ego into his doctrine in this way, defining it by the resistances that are specific to it.[22] I have tried to get people to understand that these resistances are imaginary in nature, like the coaptational lures that ethology shows us in display or combat in animal behavior, these lures being reduced in man to the narcissistic relation introduced by Freud and elaborated by me in "The Mirror Stage." While Freud—by situating in this ego the synthesis of the perceptual functions in which the sensorimotor selections are integrated—seems to agree with the tradition that delegates to the ego the task of answering for reality, this reality is simply all the more included in the suspension of the ego.

For this ego, distinguished first for the imaginary inertias it concentrates against the message of the unconscious, operates only by covering over the displacement the subject is with a resistance that is essential to discourse as such.

521   This is why an exhaustion of the defense mechanisms, as palpable as Fenichel renders it in his *Problems of Psychoanalytic Technique* because he is a practitioner (whereas his whole theoretical reduction of the neuroses and psychoses to genetic anomalies in libidinal development is pure platitude), turns out to be the other side of unconscious mechanisms, without Fenichel accounting for or even realizing it. Periphrasis, hyperbaton, ellipsis, suspension, anticipation, retraction, negation, digression, and irony, these are the figures of style (Quintilian's *figurae sententiarum*), just as catachresis, litotes, antonomasia, and hypotyposis are the tropes, whose names strike me as the most appropriate ones with which to label these mechanisms. Can one see here mere manners of speaking, when it is the figures themselves that are at work in the rhetoric of the discourse the analysand actually utters?

By obstinately characterizing resistance as having an emotional permanence, thereby making it foreign to discourse, contemporary psychoanalysts simply show that they have succumbed to one of the fundamental truths Freud rediscovered through psychoanalysis. Which is that we cannot confine ourselves to giving a new truth its rightful place, for the point is to take up our place in it. The truth requires us to go out of our way. We cannot do so by simply getting used to it. We get used to reality [*réel*]. The truth we repress.

Now it is especially necessary to the scholar, the sage, and even the quack, to be the only one who knows. The idea that deep within the simplest of souls—and, what's more, in the sickest—there is something ready to blossom is one thing. But that there may be someone who seems to know as much as them about what we ought to make of it . . . come to our rescue yon categories of primitive, pre-logical, and archaic thought—nay, of magical thought, so convenient to attribute to others! It is not fitting that these country bumpkins should keep us breathless by posing enigmas to us that prove overly clever.

To interpret the unconscious as Freud did, one would have to be, as he was, an encyclopedia of the arts and muses, as well as an assiduous reader of the *Fliegende Blätter*. And the task would become no easier were we to put ourselves at the mercy of a thread spun of allusions and quotations, puns   522 and equivocations. Must we make a career out of "antidoted fanfreluches"?

Indeed, we must resolve to do so. The unconscious is neither the primordial nor the instinctual, and what it knows of the elemental is no more than the elements of the signifier.

The three books that one might call canonical with regard to the unconscious—the *Traumdeutung*, *The Psychopathology of Everyday Life*, and *Jokes (Witz) and their Relation to the Unconscious*—are but a web of examples whose development is inscribed in formulas for connection and substitution (though multiplied tenfold by their particular complexity, diagrams of them sometimes being provided by Freud outside the main body of the text), which are the formulas I give for the signifier in its *transference* function. For in the *Traumdeutung* it is in terms of such a function that the term *Übertragung*, or transference, which later gave its name to the mainspring of the intersubjective link between analysand and analyst, is introduced.

Such diagrams are not solely constitutive in neurosis of each of the symptoms, but they alone allow us to encompass the thematic of its course and resolution—as the major case histories provided by Freud demonstrate admirably.

To fall back on a more limited fact, but one that is more manageable as it provides a final seal with which to close these remarks, I will cite the 1927 article on fetishism and the case Freud reports there of a patient for whom sexual satisfaction required a certain shine on the nose (*Glanz auf der Nase*).[23] The analysis showed that he owed it to the fact that his early English-speaking years had displaced the burning curiosity that attached him to his mother's phallus—that is, to that eminent want-to-be, whose privileged signifier Freud revealed—into a "glance at the nose,"* rather than a "shine on the nose"* in the forgotten language [*langue*] of his childhood.

It was the abyss, open to the thought that a thought might make itself heard in the abyss, that gave rise to resistance to psychoanalysis from the outset—not the emphasis on man's sexuality, as is commonly said. The lat-

523 ter is the object that has clearly predominated in literature throughout the
ages. And the evolution of psychoanalysis has succeeded by a comical stroke
of magic in turning it into a moral instance, the cradle and waiting area of
oblativity and attraction. The soul's Platonic steed, now blessed and enlightened, goes straight to heaven.

The intolerable scandal when Freudian sexuality was not yet holy was
that it was so "intellectual." It was in this respect that it showed itself to be
the worthy stooge of all those terrorists whose plots were going to ruin
society.

At a time when psychoanalysts are busy refashioning a right-thinking
psychoanalysis, whose crowning achievement is the sociological poem of
the "autonomous ego," I would like to say, to those who are listening to me,
how they can recognize bad psychoanalysts: by the word they use to depre-
cate all research on technique and theory that furthers the Freudian experience in its authentic direction. That word is "intellectualization"—execrable
to all those who, living in fear of putting themselves to the test by drinking
the wine of truth, spit on men's bread, even though their spittle can never
again have any effect but that of leavening.

III. The Letter, being, and the other

Is what thinks in my place, then, another ego? Does Freud's discovery represent the confirmation, at the level of psychological experience, of
Manichaeism?[24]

There can, in fact, be no confusion on this point: what Freud's research
introduced us to was not some more or less curious cases of dual personality. Even at the heroic era I have been describing—when, like animals in the
age of fairy tales, sexuality spoke—the diabolical atmosphere that such an
orientation might have given rise to never materialized.[25]

524 The goal Freud's discovery proposes to man was defined by Freud at the
height of his thought in these moving terms: *Wo Es war, soll Ich werden.*
Where it was, I must come into being.

This goal is one of reintegration and harmony, I might even say of
reconciliation (*Versöhnung*).

But if we ignore the self's radical eccentricity with respect to itself that
man is faced with—in other words, the very truth Freud discovered—we
will renege on both the order and pathways of psychoanalytic mediation; we
will make of it the compromise operation that it has, in effect, become—
precisely what both the spirit and letter of Freud's work most repudiate.

For, since he constantly points out that compromise is behind all the miseries his analysis assuages, we can say that resorting to compromise, whether explicit or implicit, disorients all psychoanalytic action and plunges it into darkness.

But neither does it suffice to rub shoulders with the moralistic tartufferies of our time or to be forever spouting forth about the "total personality" in order to have said anything articulate about the possibility of mediation.

The radical heteronomy that Freud's discovery shows gaping within man can no longer be covered over without whatever tries to hide it being fundamentally dishonest.

Which other is this, then, to whom I am more attached than to myself [*moi*], since, at the most assented to heart of my identity to myself, he pulls the strings?

His presence can only be understood in an alterity raised to the second power, which already situates him in a mediating position in relation to my own splitting from myself, as if from a semblable.

If I have said that the unconscious is the Other's discourse (with a capital O), it is in order to indicate the beyond in which the recognition of desire is tied to the desire for recognition.

In other words, this other is the Other that even my lie invokes as a guarantor of the truth in which my lie subsists.

Here we see that the dimension of truth emerges with the appearance of language.

Prior to this point, we have to admit the existence—in the psychological relation, which can be precisely isolated in the observation of animal behavior—of subjects, not because of some projective mirage, it being the psychologist's vacuous watchword to hack this phantom to pieces, but because of the manifested presence of intersubjectivity. In the animal hidden in his lookout, in the well-laid trap, in the straggler ruse by which a runaway separated from the flock throws a raptor off the scent, something more emerges than in the fascinating erection of display or combat. Yet there is nothing here that transcends the function of a lure in the service of a need, or that affirms a presence in that beyond-the-veil where the whole of Nature can be questioned about its design.

525

For the question to even arise (and we know that it arose for Freud in *Beyond the Pleasure Principle*), there must be language.

For I can lure my adversary with a movement that runs counter to my battle plan, and yet this movement has its deceptive effect only insofar as I actually make it for my adversary.

But in the proposals by which I initiate peace negotiations with him, what my negotiations propose is situated in a third locus which is neither my speech nor my interlocutor.

This locus is nothing but the locus of signifying convention, as is seen in the comedy of the distressed complaint of the Jew to his pal: "Why are you telling me you are going to Cracow so I'll believe you are going to Lemberg, when you really are going to Cracow?"

Of course the aforementioned flock-movement can be understood in the conventional register of a game's strategy, where it is on the basis of a rule that I deceive my adversary; but here my success is assessed as connoting betrayal—that is, it is assessed in the relationship to the Other who is the guarantor of Good Faith.

Here the problems are of an order whose heteronomy is simply ignored if it is reduced to some "awareness of others," or whatever people choose to call it. For the "existence of the other" having, not long ago, reached the ears of Midas, the psychoanalyst, through the partition that separates him from the phenomenologists' confabs, the news is now being whispered through the reeds: "Midas, King Midas, is the other of his patient. He himself said so."

What sort of breakthrough is that? The other—which other?

Which other was the young André Gide aiming at when he defied the landlady, in whose care his mother had placed him, to treat him as a responsible being by unlocking right in front of her—with a key that was fake only insofar as it opened all locks of the same kind—the lock that she herself considered to be the worthy signifier of her educational intentions? Was it she who would later intervene and to whom the child would laughingly say: "Do you really think a lousy padlock can ensure my obedience?" But by simply remaining out of sight and waiting until that evening before lecturing the kid, after giving him a suitably cold reception upon his return home, it was not simply a female other whose angry face she showed him, but another André Gide, one who was no longer really sure, either then or even later when he thought back on it, what he had wanted to do—who had been changed right down to his very truth by the doubt cast on his good faith.

Perhaps it would be worth dwelling on this realm of confusion—which is simply that in which the whole human *opera buffa* is played out—to understand the pathways by which analysis proceeds, not only to restore order here but also to instate the conditions for the possibility of its restoration.

Kern unseres Wesen, "the core of our being"—it is not so much that Freud commands us to target this, as so many others before him have done with the futile adage "Know thyself," as that he asks us to reconsider the pathways that lead to it.

Or, rather, the "this" which he proposes we attain is not a this which can be the object of knowledge, but a this—doesn't he say as much?—which constitutes my being and to which, as he teaches us, I bear witness as much and more in my whims, aberrations, phobias, and fetishes, than in my more or less civilized personage.

Madness, you are no longer the object of the ambiguous praise with which the sage furnished the impregnable burrow of his fear. And if he is, after all, not so badly ensconced there, it is because the supreme agent at work since time immemorial, digging its tunnels and maze, is reason itself, the same Logos he serves.

Then how do you explain the fact that a scholar like Erasmus, with so little talent for the "commitments" that solicited him in his age, as in any other, could hold such an eminent place in the revolution brought about by a Reformation in which man has as much of a stake in each man as in all men?   527

It is by touching, however lightly, on man's relation to the signifier—in this case, by changing the procedures of exegesis—that one changes the course of his history by modifying the moorings of his being.

It is precisely in this respect that anyone capable of glimpsing the changes we have lived through in our own lives can see that Freudianism, however misunderstood it has been and however nebulous its consequences have been, constitutes an intangible but radical revolution. There is no need to go seeking witnesses to the fact:[26] everything that concerns not just the human sciences, but the destiny of man, politics, metaphysics, literature, the arts, advertising, propaganda—and thus, no doubt, economics—has been affected by it.

But is this anything more than the dissonant effects of an immense truth where Freud has traced a pure path? It must be said here that a technique that takes advantage of the psychological categorization alone of its object is not following this path, as is the case of contemporary psychoanalysis apart from a return to the Freudian discovery.

Thus the vulgarity of the concepts by which its practice shows its mettle, the embroidery of Freudery [*fofreudisme*] which is now mere decoration, and what must be called the discredit in which it prospers, together bear witness to the fundamental repudiation of that discovery.

Through his discovery, Freud brought the border between object and being that seemed to mark the limits of science within its ambit.

This is the symptom of and prelude to a reexamination of man's situation in the midst of beings [*dans l'étant*], as all the postulates of knowledge have   528 heretofore assumed it to be—but please don't be content to classify the fact that I am saying so as a case of Heideggerianism, even prefixed by a "neo-" that adds nothing to the trashy style by which it is common to spare oneself any reflection with the quip, "Separate that out for me from its mental jet-sam."

When I speak of Heidegger, or rather when I translate him, I strive to preserve the sovereign signifierness of the speech he proffers.

If I speak of the letter and being, if I distinguish the other from the Other, it is because Freud suggests them to me as the terms to which resistance and transference effects refer—effects against which I have had to wage unequal battle in the twenty years that I have been engaged in the practice that we all, repeating after Freud, call impossible: that of psychoanalysis. It is also because I must help others avoid losing their way there.

It is to prevent the field they have inherited from falling fallow, and to that end to convey that if the symptom is a metaphor, it is not a metaphor to say so, any more than it is to say that man's desire is a metonymy. For the symptom *is* a metaphor, whether one likes to admit it or not, just as desire *is* a metonymy, even if man scoffs at the idea.

Thus, if I am to rouse you to indignation over the fact that, after so many centuries of religious hypocrisy and philosophical posturing, no one has yet validly articulated what links metaphor to the question of being and metonymy to its lack, something of the object of this indignation must still be there—something that, as both instigator and victim, corresponds to it: namely, the man of humanism and the irremediably contested debt he has incurred against his intentions.

T.t.y.e.m.u.p.t.

May 14–26, 1957

Related to this article is a presentation I made on April 23, 1960, to the Philosophical Society regarding the paper Mr. Perelman gave there on his theory of metaphor as a rhetorical function—found in his *Traité de l'argumentation*.

My presentation is included as an appendix (Appendix II) in this volume [*Écrits* 1966].

Notes

1. *Codice Atlantico*, 145. r. a., trans. Louise Servicen (Paris: Gallimard), vol. II, 400.

2. The theme was "Psychoanalysis and the sciences of man."

3. The talk took place on May 9, 1957, in the Descartes Amphitheater at the Sorbonne, and discussion continued afterward over drinks.

4. "Die Frage der Laienanalyse," *GW* XIV, 281–83.

5. This point—so useful in overturning the concept of "psychological function," which obscures everything related to the matter—becomes clear as day in the purely linguistic analysis of the two major forms of aphasia classified by one of the leaders of modern linguistics, Roman Jakobson. See the most accessible of his works (coauthored by Morris Halle), *Fundamentals of Language* ('s Gravenhage and New York: Mouton, 1956), part II, chapters 1 to 4; see too the collection of translations into French of his works that we owe to Nicolas Ruwet, *Essais de linguistique générale* (Paris: Minuit, 1963).

6. Recall that discussion about the need for a new language in communist society really did take place, and that Stalin, much to the relief of those who lent credence to his philosophy, put an end to it as follows: language is not a superstructure.

7. By "linguistics" I mean the study of existing languages [*langues*] as regards their structure and the laws they reveal; this does not include the theory of abstract codes (incorrectly placed under the heading of communication theory), so-called information theory (originating in physics), or any more or less hypothetically generalized semiology.

8. Cf. St. Augustine's *De Magistro;* I analyzed the chapter "De significatione locutionis" in my seminar on June 23, 1954.

9. Thus I. A. Richards, author of a book about procedures appropriate for reaching this objective, shows us their application in another book. He selects for his purposes a page from Meng Tzu (Mencius, to the Jesuits) and calls the piece *Mencius on the Mind*, given its object. The guarantees provided of the purity of the experiment are nothing compared to the luxury of the approaches employed. And the man of letters, an expert on the traditional Canon that contains the text, is met right on the spot in Peking where our demonstration-model wringer has been transported, regardless of the cost.

But we will be no less transported, though less expensively, upon witnessing the transformation of a bronze, which gives off bell-tones at the slightest contact with thought, into a rag with which to wipe clean the slate of the most depressing British psychologism. And not, alas, without quickly identifying it with the author's own brain—all that remains of his object or of him after he has exhausted the meaning [*sens*] of the one and the common sense of the other.

10. It is in this respect that verbal hallucination, when it takes this form, sometimes opens a door that communicates with the Freudian structure of psychosis—a door which was hitherto missed since it went unnoticed (see my Seminar from 1955–1956).

11. I did so on June 6, 1956, taking as an example the first scene of *Athaliah*, incited, I confess, by an allusion—made in passing by a highbrow* critic in *The New Statesman and Nation*—to the "supreme bitchery" of Racine's heroines, designed to dissuade us from making reference to Shakespeare's savage tragedies, which has become compulsory in analytic circles where such references serve to whitewash the vulgarity of Philistinism.

12. (Added in 1966:) The publication by Jean Starobinski, in *Le Mercure de France* (February 1964), of the notes left by Saussure on anagrams and their hypogrammatical use, from the Saturnine verses to the writings of Cicero, provide the corroboration I didn't have at the time.

13. I pay homage here to what this formulation owes to Roman Jakobson, that is, to his written work, in which a psychoanalyst can always find something to structure his own experience, and which renders superfluous the "personal communications" that I could tout as much as anyone else.

Indeed, one can recognize in such oblique forms of allegiance the style of that immortal couple, Rosencrantz and Guildenstern, who are a set that cannot be broken up, not even by the imperfection of their destiny, for it lasts by the same method as Jeannot's knife, and for the very reason for which Goethe praised Shakespeare for presenting the character in their doublet: all by themselves they are the whole *Gesellschaft*, Society in a nutshell (*Wilhelm Meisters Lehrjahre*, Vol. 5, ed. Trunz [Hamburg: Christian Wegner Verlag], 299)—I mean the International Psychoanalytical Association.

(We should extract the whole passage from Goethe: Dieses leise Auftreten, dieses Schmiegen und Biegen, dies Jasagen, Streicheln und Schmeicheln, dieses Behendigkeit, dies Schwänzein, diese Allheit und Leerheit, diese rechtliche Schurkerei, diese Unfähigleit, wie kann sie durch einen Menschen ausgedruckt werden? Es sollten ihrer wenigstens ein Dutzend sein, wenn man sie haben könnte; denn sie bloss in Gesellschaft etwas, sie sind die Gesellschaft.)

Let us be grateful, in this context, to the author of "Some Remarks on the Role of Speech in Psycho-Analytic Technique" (*IJP* XXXVII, 6 [1956]: 467) for taking the trouble to point out that his remarks are "based on" work by him that dates back to 1952. This no doubt explains why he has assimilated nothing of the work published since then, but which he is nevertheless aware of since he cites me as its publisher (*sic*. I know what "editor"* means).

14. *Esprit* is clearly the equivalent of the German *Witz* with which Freud marked the aim of his third fundamental book on the unconscious. The far greater difficulty of finding an equivalent in English is instructive: "wit," weighed down by a discussion running from Davenant and Hobbes to Pope and Addison, left its essential virtues to "humor," which is something else. The only other choice is "pun," but its meaning is too narrow.

15. Leo Strauss, *Persecution and the Art of Writing* (Glencoe, Illinois: The Free Press, 1957).

16. See the correspondence, in particular, letters 107 and 119 selected by its editors.

17. This is the procedure by which a study ensures results through a mechanical exploration of the entire extent of its object's field.

18. (Added in 1966:) By referring only to the development of the organism, the typology neglects the structure in which the subject is caught up in fantasy, the drive, and sublimation, respectively. I am currently developing the theory of this structure.

19. The sign $\cong$ designates congruence.

20. Since S′ designates, in this context, the term that produces the signifying effect (or signifierness), one can see that the term is latent in metonymy and patent in metaphor.

21. Things are altogether different if—in raising a question like "Why are there philosophers?"—I become more candid than usual, since I am raising not only a question that philosophers have been asking themselves since time immemorial, but also the one in which they are perhaps the most interested.

22. (Added in December 1968:) This and the next paragraph were rewritten solely to achieve greater clarity of expression.

23. "Fetischismus," *GW* XIV, 311.

24. One of my colleagues went as far as this thought in wondering if the id (*Es*) of Freud's last doctrine wasn't in fact the "bad ego." (Added in 1966:) You see the kind of people I had to work with.

25. Note, nevertheless, the tone with which people spoke in that period of the impish pranks of the unconscious: *Der Zufall und die Koboldstreiche des Unbewussten* ("Chance and the Impish Pranks of the Unconscious"), one of Silberer's titles, which would be absolutely anachronistic in the present context of soul-managers.

26. I'll highlight the most recent in what flowed quite smoothly from François Mauriac's pen, in the *Figaro littéraire* on May 25, by way of an apology for refusing "to tell us his life story." If one can no longer undertake to do this with the old enthusiasm, the reason, he tells us, is that, "for half a century, Freud, whatever we may think of him," has left his mark there. And after briefly yielding to the received idea that it would be to submit to the "history of our body," Mauriac quickly returns to what his writer's sensibility could not help but let slip out: our discourse, in endeavoring to be complete, would publish the deepest confessions of the souls of all our loved ones.

On a Question Prior to Any Possible Treatment of Psychosis

This article contains the most important material from the seminar I gave during the first two terms of the 1955–1956 academic year, the material from the third term thus having been excluded. It was published in volume 4 of La Psychanalyse.

Hoc quod triginta tres per annos in ipso loco studui, et Sanctae Annae Genio loci, et dilectae juventuti, quae eo me sectata est, diligenter dedico.

I. Toward Freud

1. Half a century of Freudianism applied to psychosis has left the latter still to be reconceptualized, in other words, *in statu quo ante*.

We might say that, prior to Freud, discussion of psychosis was unable to move beyond a theoretical framework that presented itself as psychology and was merely a "laicized" residue of what I will call the long metaphysical coction of science in the School (with the capital S our reverence owes it).

Now if our science, concerning the *phusis*, in its ever purer mathematization, retains from this cuisine no more than a stench so subtle that one may legitimately wonder whether a substitution of person has not occurred, the same cannot be said concerning the *antiphusis* (that is, the living apparatus that one hopes is capable of taking the measure of the said *phusis*), whose smell of burnt fat indubitably betrays the age-old practice of preparing brains in that cuisine.

Thus the theory of abstraction, necessary to account for knowledge, has become fixed in an abstract theory of the subject's faculties, which the most radical sensationalist question begging has been unable to render more functional with regard to subjective effects.

The ever-renewed attempts to correct its results by the various counter-

532   weights of affect must, in fact, remain futile as long as one neglects to ask whether or not it is indeed the same subject that is affected.

2. This is the question one learns to avoid once and for all on one's school (with a lowercase s) bench: for even if alternations in the identity of the *percipiens* are accepted, the latter's function in constituting the unity of the *perceptum* is not challenged. Thus diversity of structure in the *perceptum* affects only a diversity of register in the *percipiens*—in the final analysis, that of the *sensoriums*. This diversity is always surmountable, in principle, provided the *percipiens* remains at a level commensurate with reality.

This is why those whose task it is to answer the question raised by the existence of the madman have been unable to stop themselves from interposing between it and them those same school benches, which they find, in this case, to be a convenient wall behind which to take shelter.

Indeed, I would dare to lump together, so to speak, all positions on the matter, whether mechanistic or dynamic, whether they see the genesis of madness as based on the organism or the psyche, and its structure as based on disintegration or conflict. Yes, all of them, however ingenious they may be, insofar as, in the name of the obvious fact that a hallucination is a *perceptum* without an object, they confine themselves to asking the *percipiens* to account for this *perceptum*, without realizing that, in doing so, they skip a step—that of inquiring whether the *perceptum* itself bequeaths a univocal meaning to the *percipiens* who is asked here to explain it.

This step should nevertheless seem legitimate in any unbiased examination of verbal hallucination, in that the latter is not reducible, as we shall see, to any particular *sensorium*, and especially not to any *percipiens* insofar as the *percipiens* would give it its unity.

Indeed, it is a mistake to take verbal hallucination to be auditory in nature, when it is theoretically conceivable that it not be auditory at all (in the case of a deaf-mute, for example, or of some nonauditory register of hallucinatory spelling out of words), but above all if we consider that the act of hearing is not the same when it aims at the coherence of the verbal chain—namely, its overdetermination at each instant by the deferred action [*après-coup*] of its sequence, and the suspension at each instant of its value upon the advent of a meaning that is always susceptible to postponement

533   [*renvoi*]—and when it adjusts to sound modulation in speech, for the purpose of acoustic analysis, whether tonal or phonetic, or even of musical power.

These highly abbreviated remarks would seem to suffice to bring out the different subjectivities we must consider when investigating the *perceptum* (and the extent to which they are misunderstood in patient interviews and the nosology of "voices").

But it might be claimed that we can reduce these differences in subjectivity to levels of objectification in the *percipiens*.

This is not so, however. For it is at the level at which subjective "synthesis" confers upon speech its full meaning that the subject manifests all the paradoxes to which he falls victim in this singular perception. The fact that these paradoxes already appear when it is the other who proffers speech is sufficiently manifested in the subject by the possibility of obeying the other insofar as the latter's speech orders him to listen and to be on guard; for by simply listening in, the subject falls under the sway of a suggestion from which he can only escape by reducing the other to being no more than the mouthpiece of a discourse that is not his own or of an intention that he sets aside in his discourse.

But more striking still is the subject's relation to his own speech, in which what is important is somewhat masked by the purely acoustic fact that he cannot speak without hearing himself. Nor is there anything special in the behavior of consciousness about the fact that he cannot listen to himself without becoming divided. Clinicians did better when they figured out that verbal motor hallucinations are often accompanied by the subject's own partial phonatory movements. Yet they did not articulate the crucial point, which is that, since the *sensorium* is indifferent in the production of a signifying chain:

(a) the signifying chain imposes itself, by itself, on the subject in its dimension as voice;
(b) it takes on, as such, a reality proportionate to the time, which is perfectly observable in experience, involved in its subjective attribution;
(c) and its own structure, qua signifier, is determinant in this attribution, which is distributive as a rule—that is, it has several voices and thus renders equivocal the supposedly unifying *percipiens*.

3. I will illustrate what I have just said with a phenomenon taken from one of my clinical presentations from 1955–1956, the very year of the seminar whose work I am presenting here. Let us say that such a find can only be the reward for complete, albeit enlightened, submission to the patient's properly subjective positions, positions which are all too often forced by being reduced in the doctor/patient dialogue to the morbid process, thus increas-

534

ing the difficulty of fathoming them due to a not unjustified reticence on the subject's part.

It was a case of one of those shared delusions [*délires à deux*]—the typical case of which is the mother/daughter couple, as I showed long ago—in which a feeling of being intruded upon, that had developed into a delusion of being watched, was but the development of the defense characteristic of an affective binary relation, open as such to every alienation.

It was the daughter who, during my examination, presented me—as proof of the insults to which she and her mother were subjected by their neighbors—a fact concerning the boyfriend of their female neighbor who was supposedly harassing them with her onslaughts, after they had had to break off an intimate friendship with her that was at first kindly received. This man—who was thus an indirect party to the situation and, moreover, a rather secondary figure in the patient's allegations—had, according to her, flung at her the offensive term "Sow!" as he passed her in the hallway of their apartment building.

On hearing this, and being hardly inclined to see in it a retort to "Pig!" that would be too easy to extrapolate in the name of a projection which in such cases is never anything more than the psychiatrist's own projection, I asked her straight out what in herself had been proffered the moment before. Not in vain, for she conceded with a smile that, upon seeing the man, she had murmured the following words which, if she is to be believed here, gave no cause for offense: "I've just been to the pork butcher's . . ."

At whom were these words aimed? She was hard pressed to say, giving me the right to help her. For their literal meaning, we cannot neglect the fact, among others, that the patient had suddenly taken leave of her husband and her in-laws—and thus given a marriage her mother disapproved of a conclusion that had not changed in the interim—due to the conviction she had formed that these country bumpkins were planning nothing less, in order to finish off this good-for-nothing city girl, than to carve her up piece by piece.

But what difference does it make whether or not one has to resort to the fantasy of the fragmented body in order to understand how the patient, a prisoner of the dyadic relationship, was responding once again here to a situation that was beyond her?

For our present purposes, it is enough that the patient admitted that the sentence was allusive, even though she was unable for all that to demonstrate anything other than perplexity over which of the two people present or the one person absent was targeted by the allusion. For it thus appears that the "I," as subject of the sentence in direct speech, left in abeyance—in accordance with its function as a "shifter," as it is called in linguistics¹—the designation of the speaking subject for as long as the allusion, in its conjuratory intention no doubt, itself remained oscillating. After a pause, this uncertainty came to an end with the apposition of the word "sow," itself too loaded with invective to follow the oscillation isochronously. This is how the discourse managed to realize its rejecting intention in the hallucination. In the locus where the unspeakable object was rejected into the real, a word made itself heard because, in coming to the place of what has no name, it was unable to follow the subject's intention without detaching itself from it by the dash that introduces the reply—opposing its disparaging antistrophe to the grumbling of the strophe that was thus restored to the patient with the index of the I, resembling in its opacity the exclamations of love, when, running short of signifiers to call the object of its epithalamion, it employs the crudest imaginary means:

"I'll eat you up . . ."

"My sweetie! [*Chou!*]"

"You'll love it . . ."

"You dog, you! [*Rat!*]"

4. I mention this example here only to show in a real life case that the function of unrealization is not entirely located in the symbol. For in order for its irruption in the real to be incontrovertible, the symbol need but present itself, as it commonly does, in the form of a broken chain.²

We also see here the effect every signifier has, once it is perceived, of   536
arousing in the *percipiens* an assent composed of the awakening of the *percipiens'* hidden duplicity by the signifier's manifest ambiguity.

Of course, all of this can be considered to be a mirage from the classic perspective of the unifying subject.

But it is striking that this perspective, reduced to itself, offers only such impoverished views regarding hallucination, for example, that the work of a madman, as remarkable as Judge Schreber proves to be in his *Memoirs of My Nervous Illness*,³ after being well received, even before Freud, by psychiatrists, can be regarded, even after Freud, as a text worth reading as an introduction to the phenomenology of psychosis, and not simply for beginners.⁴

This work provided me with the basis for a structural analysis in my 1955–1956 seminar on Freudian structures in the psychoses when, following Freud's advice, I reexamined it.

The relation between the signifier and the subject that this analysis uncovers can be found—as is apparent in this preamble—in the very appearance of the phenomena, provided that, coming back to it from Freud's experience, one knows where it leads.

But, if properly carried out, an approach that starts from the phenomenon leads back to this point, as was the case for me when my initial study of paranoia thirty years ago brought me to the threshold of psychoanalysis.[5]

537   Nowhere, in fact, is the fallacious conception of a psychical process in Jaspers' sense—in which a symptom is merely an index—more irrelevant than in dealing with psychosis, because nowhere is the symptom more clearly articulated in the structure itself, assuming one knows how to read it.

This makes it incumbent upon us to define this process by the most radical determinants of man's relation to the signifier.

5. But we need not have reached this stage to be interested in the variety of forms verbal hallucinations assume in Schreber's *Memoirs*, or to recognize in them differences quite other than those by which they are "classically" classified, according to the way they involve the *percipiens* (the degree of his "belief") or the latter's reality ("auditivation"): namely, differences that stem instead from their speech structure, insofar as this structure is already in the *perceptum*.

If we consider the text of the hallucinations alone, a distinction immediately arises for the linguist between code phenomena and message phenomena.

Belonging to the code phenomena, in this approach, are the voices that use the *Grundsprache*, which I translate as "basic language" [*langue-de-fond*], and which Schreber describes (S. 13)[6] as "a vigorous though somewhat antiquated German, which is especially characterized by its great wealth of euphemisms." Elsewhere (S. 167) he ruefully refers to "its form, which is authentic on account of its characteristics of noble distinction and simplicity."

These code phenomena are specified in locutions that are neological in both their form (new compound words, though the compounding here takes place in accordance with the rules of the patient's mother tongue) and usage. Hallucinations inform the subject of the forms and usages that constitute the neo-code: the subject owes to them, for example, first and foremost, the term *Grundsprache* that designates this neo-code.

We are dealing here with something fairly akin to the messages that linguists call "autonymous," insofar as it is the signifier itself (and not what it signifies) that is the object of the communication. However, this peculiar

538   but normal relation of the message to itself is redoubled here, in that these messages are taken to be borne by beings whose relations are enunciated by

the messages themselves, in modes that prove to be quite analogous to the connections between signifiers. The term *Nervenanhang*, which I translate as "nerve-annexation," and which also comes from these messages, illustrates this remark insofar as passion and action between these beings are reduced to those annexed or disannexed nerves, but also insofar as these nerves, just like the divine rays (*Gottesstrahlen*) with which they are homogeneous, are nothing but the entification of the spoken words they bear (S. 130, which the voices formulate as: "Do not forget that the nature of the rays is that they must speak").

This is the system's relation to its own constitution as signifier, which should be filed under the question of metalanguage and which, in my opinion, demonstrates the impropriety of this notion if it is intended to define elements differentiated within language.

Let us note, on the other hand, that we are presented here with phenomena that have mistakenly been called intuitive due to the fact that the effect of signification anticipates the development of signification therein. What is actually involved is an effect of the signifier, insofar as its degree of certainty (second degree: signification of signification) takes on a weight proportional to the enigmatic void that first presents itself in the place of signification itself.

What is amusing in this case is that it is precisely to the extent that the signifier's high tension drops for the subject—that is, that the hallucinations turn into refrains, mere repetitions whose emptiness is imputed to beings devoid of intelligence and personality, or who are even altogether effaced from the register of being—it is to this very extent, as I was saying, that the voices highlight the *Seelenauffassung*, the "soul-conception" (in the basic language); this conception is manifested in a catalog of thoughts that is not unworthy of a book of classical psychology. This catalog is tied to a pedantic intention on the part of the voices, which does not stop the subject from making highly relevant comments on it. Note that the source of terms is always carefully referenced in these comments; for example, when the subject uses the word *Instanz* (S. 30 note; see also notes on pages 11 to 21), he emphasizes in a note: "this expression . . . is mine."

This is why the primordial importance of memory-thoughts (*Erinnerungsgedanken*) in the psychical economy does not escape him, and he immediately offers proof of this in the poetic and musical use of modulating reprise.

Our patient, who provides the priceless description of this "soul-conception" as "a somewhat idealized representation which souls had

539

formed of human life and thought" (S. 164), thinks that he has "gained insight into the nature of human thought processes and human feelings for which many a psychologist might envy me" (S. 167).

I would agree all the more readily in that, unlike them, he does not imagine that he has wrested this knowledge, whose scope he assesses so humorously, from the nature of things, and in that, while he thinks that he must make use of it, it is, as I have just indicated, on the basis of a semantic analysis![7]

But to return to the thread of my argument, let us turn to the phenomena that I will contrast with the preceding ones as message phenomena.

The latter are interrupted messages, by means of which a relationship is sustained between the subject and his divine interlocutor, a relationship to which the messages give the form of a challenge* or an endurance test.

Indeed, his partner's voice limits the messages in question to the beginning of a sentence whose complement of meaning poses, moreover, no problem to the subject, except for its harassing, offensive character, which is usually so idiotic as to discourage him. The valiance he displays by not faltering in his reply, and even in eluding the traps he is led into, is not the least important aspect for our analysis of the phenomenon.

But I will dwell here again on the very text of what might be called the hallucinatory provocation (or better, protasis). The subject gives us the following examples of such a structure (S. 217),

1. *Nun will ich mich* . . . ("Now I shall . . ."),
2. *Sie sollen nämlich* . . . ("You were to . . ."),
3. *Das will ich mir* . . . ("I shall . . ."),

540   to take only these three—to which he must reply with their significant supplement, which to him is not open to doubt, namely:

1. "resign myself to being stupid,"
2. "be exposed (a word of the basic language) as denying God, as given to voluptuous excesses," not to mention other things,
3. "think about that first."

One might note that each sentence is interrupted at the point at which the group of words that one might call "index-terms" ends, the latter being those designated by their function in the signifier, according to the terminology employed above, as shifters*—that is, the terms in the code that indicate the subject's position on the basis of the message itself.

After which, the properly lexical part of the sentence—in other words, the part that includes the words the code defines by their use, whether it is the shared code or the delusional code—remains elided.

Aren't we struck by the predominance of the signifier's function in these two orders of phenomena, and even incited to seek what lies at the root of the association they constitute: that of a code constituted by messages about the code and of a message reduced to what, in the code, indicates the message?

All this would have to be carefully transcribed onto a graph,[8] the graph with which I have tried this year to represent the signifier's internal connections, insofar as they structure the subject.

For there is a topology here that is altogether different from the topology we might be led to imagine by the requirement of an immediate parallelism between the form of the phenomena and their pathways in the central nervous system.

But this topology—which follows the lines laid down by Freud when, after opening up the field of the unconscious with dreams, he set out to describe the dynamics of the unconscious, without feeling bound by any concern for cortical localization—is precisely what may best prepare the questions we should ask when investigating the surface of the cerebral cortex.

For it is only after linguistic analysis of the phenomenon of language that one can legitimately establish the relation it constitutes in the subject and at the same time delimit the order of "machines" (in the purely associative sense this term takes on in network theory in mathematics) that can bring about this phenomenon.   541

It is no less remarkable that it was the Freudian experience that led the author of these lines in the direction presented here. Let us examine, then, what this experience contributes to our question.

II. After Freud

1. What did Freud contribute here? I began by stating that, regarding the problem of psychosis, his contribution led to backsliding.

This is immediately apparent in the simplistic character of the mainsprings invoked in conceptions that all boil down to the following fundamental schema: how can the inside be shifted outside? Indeed, even though the subject here encompasses an opaque id, it is nevertheless as an ego—that is, and this is clearly expressed in the current psychoanalytic orientation, as the same inexhaustible *percipiens*—that he is invoked in explaining psychosis. This *percipiens* has total power over its no less unchanged correlate, reality, and the model for this power is derived from a fact accessible to everyday experience, that of affective projection.

For what is noteworthy about current theories is the absolutely uncritical way in which the mechanism of projection is put to use in them. Everything objects to it, yet nothing stops them, least of all the obvious clinical fact that there is no relation between affective projection and its supposed delusional effects—between, for example, the jealousy of the unfaithful spouse and the jealousy of the alcoholic.

Freud, in the essay in which he interprets the Schreber case, which is read badly when it is reduced to the rehashings that followed it, uses the form of a grammatical deduction in order to present the switching involved in the relation to the other in psychosis. He employs the different ways of negating the proposition, "I love him," from which it follows that the negative judgment is structured in two stages: the first is a reversal of the value of the verb ("I hate him") or inversion of the gender of the agent or object ("It is not me—or It is not him—but her," or vice versa); the second is a reversal of subjects ("He hates me," "It is her that he loves," "It is she who loves me"). But no one pays any attention to the logical problems formally involved in this deduction.

Furthermore, while Freud in this text expressly dismisses the mechanism of projection as insufficient to account for the problem—entering at this point into a very long, detailed, and subtle discussion of repression, which offers us, all the same, some toothing stones for our problem—suffice it to say that these toothing stones continue to stand out inviolate above the clouds of dust raised on the psychoanalytic construction site.

2. After that, Freud contributed "On Narcissism." It was put to the same use, namely, to a sort of pumping—a sucking in and spewing out, depending on the stages of the theorem—of libido by the *percipiens*, which is thereby capable of inflating and deflating a windbag reality.

Freud provided the first theory of the way in which the ego is constituted on the model of the other in the new subjective economy determined by the unconscious; the response was to acclaim the rediscovery in this ego of the good old reliable *percipiens* and of the synthesizing function.

Is it surprising that the only use made of it regarding psychosis was to definitively foreground the notion of "loss of reality"?

That's not all. In 1924 Freud wrote an incisive article, "The Loss of Reality in Neurosis and Psychosis," in which he directs our attention back to the fact that the problem is not that of the loss of reality, but of the mainspring of what takes its place. His words fell on deaf ears, since the problem had already been resolved: the prop room is inside and the props are taken out as the need arises.

Such is, in fact, the schema with which even Katan remains satisfied—in

his studies in which he examines so attentively the stages of Schreber's psychosis, guided by his concern to penetrate the prepsychotic phase—when he
highlights the defense against instinctual temptation, against masturbation
and homosexuality in this case, in order to justify the upsurge of hallucinatory phantasmagoria, which he considers to be a curtain interposed by the
operation of the *percipiens* between the tendency and its real stimulus.

What a relief this simplicity would have been to me at one time, if I had
thought it sufficed to explain the problem of literary creation in psychosis!

543

3. Yet can any problem still constitute an obstacle to the discourse of
psychoanalysis, when the fact that a tendency gets expressed in reality is
considered indicative of regression in the couple they form? What could
possibly tire minds that let people talk to them of regression, without distinguishing between regression in structure, regression in history, and
regression in development (which Freud always differentiates as topographical, temporal, or genetic)?

I shall refrain from spending time here taking inventory of the confusion.
It is old hat to those whom I train and would be of no interest to others. I
will confine myself to pointing out, for their common meditation, the
sense of unfamiliarity that is produced—in those whose speculation has
condemned itself to go around in circles between development and
entourage—by the simple mention of characteristics that are nevertheless
the very framework of the Freudian edifice: namely, the equivalence
Freud maintains of the imaginary function of the phallus in the two sexes
(long the despair of fans of false "biological," that is naturalist, windows); the castration complex considered to be a normative phase of the
subject's assumption [*assomption*] of his own sex; the myth of the killing
of the father rendered necessary by the constitutive presence of the
Oedipus complex in every personal history; and, "last but not . . .,"*
the splitting brought about in love life by the instance, indeed the repetitive instance, of the object that is always to be refound as unique. Must we
again recall the fundamentally dissident nature of Freud's notion of
the drive, the theoretical disjunction between the tendency, its direction,
and its object, and not only its original "perversion" but its involvement
in a conceptual systematic, a systematic whose place Freud indicated,
from the very beginning of his work, under the heading of the sexual theories of children?

Is it not clear that we have been far from all that for a long time now, in
an educational naturism that no longer has any other principle than the

notion of gratification and its counterpart, frustration, which is nowhere mentioned in Freud's work?

544   The structures revealed by Freud no doubt continue to sustain—not only in their plausibility, but also in the way they are handled—the vague dynamisms with which contemporary psychoanalysis claims to orient its flow. A forsaken technique would merely be more capable still of performing "miracles"—were it not for the extra dose of conformism that reduces its effects to those of an ambiguous combination of social suggestion and psychological superstition.

4. It is even striking that a demand for rigor is found only in those people whom the course of things keeps out of the mainstream in some respect, such as Ida Macalpine, who gives us cause to marvel, encountering, as we do in reading her work, a sound thinker.

Her critique of the cliché that confines itself to the factor of the suppression of a homosexual drive—which is, moreover, altogether undefined—to explain psychosis is brilliant, and she demonstrates it amply in the Schreber case itself. Homosexuality, which is supposedly the determining factor in paranoiac psychosis, is actually a symptom articulated in the psychotic process.

This process had begun long before the first sign of it appeared in Schreber in the form of one of those hypnopompic ideas—which, in their fragility, present us with tomographies (as it were) of the ego—an idea whose imaginary function is sufficiently indicated to us by its form: that it would "be *beautiful* to be a woman submitting to the act of copulation" [S. 36].

Macalpine, to introduce a valid criticism here, nevertheless seems to neglect the fact that, although Freud places considerable stress on the homosexual question, it is in order to show, first of all, that it conditions the idea of grandeur in delusion; but, more essentially, he indicates in it the mode of alterity by which the subject's metamorphosis occurs—in other words, the place where his successive delusional "transferences" occur. She would have done better to put her trust in the reason why Freud here again stubbornly insists on a reference to the Oedipus complex, which she does not accept.

This difficulty would have led her to discoveries that would certainly have been illuminating to us, for everything still remains to be said about the function of what is known as the inverted Oedipus complex. Macalpine prefers to reject all recourse to Oedipus here, making up for it with a pro-
545   creation fantasy found in children of both sexes in the form of pregnancy

fantasies—which, moreover, she considers to be related to the structure of hypochondria.[9]

This fantasy is, indeed, essential, and I will even add that in the first case in which I obtained this fantasy in a man, it was by a means that marked an important milestone in my career, and he was neither a hypochondriac nor a hysteric.

Macalpine feels—rather subtly, indeed surprisingly so given the way things are today—a need to tie this fantasy to a symbolic structure. But in order to find a structure independent of the Oedipus complex, she goes off in search of ethnographic references, her assimilation of which is hard to gauge in her text. This involves the "heliolithic" theme, which has been championed by one of the most eminent supporters of the English diffusionist school. I am aware of the merit of these conceptions, but they do not seem to me to even remotely corroborate Macalpine's idea that asexual procreation is a "primitive" conception.[10]

Macalpine's error is seen elsewhere, in the fact that she arrives at a result that is diametrically opposed to the result she is seeking.

By isolating a fantasy in a dynamic that she terms intrapsychic, in accordance with the conception of transference she introduces, she ends up designating the psychotic's uncertainty about his own sex as the sensitive spot where the analyst must intervene, contrasting the felicitous effects of intervening there with the catastrophic effect—which is, in fact, constantly found in work with psychotics—of any suggestion that goes in the direction of getting the subject to recognize his latent homosexuality.

Now, uncertainty about one's own sex is a common feature in hysteria, whose diagnostic encroachments Macalpine points out.

The fact is that no imaginary formation is specific[11] or determinant in either the structure or dynamics of a process. And this is why one condemns oneself to missing both of them when, in the hope of grasping them better, one flouts the symbolic articulation that Freud discovered at the same time as the unconscious that is, in effect, consubstantial with the unconscious. The necessity of this articulation is what he indicates to us in his methodical reference to the Oedipus complex.

5. How can we hold Macalpine responsible for such neglect when, rather than being remedied, it has continued to grow in psychoanalysis?

That is why, in order to define the minimal split, which is certainly called for, between neurosis and psychosis, psychoanalysts are reduced to deferring to the ego's responsibility regarding reality: this is what I call leaving the problem of psychosis *in statu quo ante.*

One point was, however, very precisely designated as the bridge across the border between the two domains.

Analysts have even emphasized it in the most inordinate way concerning the question of transference in psychosis. It would be uncharitable to repeat here what has been said on the subject. I shall simply take the opportunity of paying homage to Macalpine's intelligence, when she sums up a position in line with the genius deployed in psychoanalysis today in these terms: in short, psychoanalysts claim to be able to cure psychosis in all cases in which psychosis is not involved.[12]

It is on this point that Midas, laying down the law one day regarding the cases in which psychoanalysis is indicated, expressed himself thus: "It is clear that psychoanalysis is possible only with a subject for whom there is an other!" And Midas crossed the bridge back and forth thinking it to be a wasteland. How could he have done otherwise, since he was unaware that the river lay there?

The term "other," never before heard by the psychoanalytic people, had no other meaning for them than the whispering of the reeds.

III. With Freud

1. It is rather striking that a dimension that is felt to be that of something-Other [*Autre-chose*] in so many of the experiences men have—not at all without thinking about them, rather in thinking about them, but without thinking that they are thinking, and like Telemachus thinking of the expense—has never been thought out to the point of being suitably stated by those whom the idea of thought assures that they are thinking.

Desire, boredom, confinement, revolt, prayer, wakefulness (I would like us to pause here, since Freud explicitly refers to the latter by mentioning, in the middle of his text on Schreber, a passage from Nietzsche's *Zarathustra*),[13] and panic are evidence of the dimension of this Elsewhere and draw our attention to it, not as mere moods that deadpan thinkers can put in their place, but much more so as permanent principles of collective organizations, without which it does not seem human life can maintain itself for long.

It is probably not out of the question that the most thinkable one who thinks-about-thinking, thinking that he himself is this Other-thing [*Autre-chose*], may have always been unable to tolerate this possible competition.

But this aversion becomes perfectly clear once the conceptual connection, which nobody had yet thought of, was made between this Elsewhere and the locus, present for all of us and closed to each of us, in which Freud discovered that, without us thinking about it, and thus without anyone being able to think he thinks about it better than anyone else, it [*ça*] thinks. It thinks rather badly, but it thinks steadily. It is in these very terms that Freud announces the unconscious to us: thoughts that, while their laws are not exactly the same as those of our everyday thoughts, whether noble or vulgar, are certainly articulated.

There is no longer any way, therefore, to reduce this Elsewhere to the imaginary form of a nostalgia for some lost or future Paradise; what one finds there is the paradise of the child's loves, where—baudelaire de Dieu!—scandalous things happen.

Moreover, if any doubt still remained in our minds, Freud called the locus of the unconscious *ein anderer Schauplatz*, another scene, borrowing a term that had struck him in a text by Fechner (who, in his experimentalism, is not at all the realist our textbooks suggest he is); Freud repeats it some twenty times in his early works.

This spray of cold water having hopefully sharpened our wits, let us move on to the scientific formulation of the subject's relation to this Other.

2. "In order to set down our ideas" and orient the souls who are lost here, I shall apply the said relation to the previously introduced **L** schema, which I will simplify as follows:

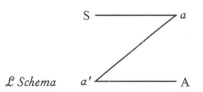

£ Schema

This schema signifies that the condition of the subject, S (neurosis or psychosis), depends on what unfolds in the Other, A. What unfolds there is articulated like a discourse (the unconscious is the Other's discourse [*discours de l'Autre*]), whose syntax Freud first sought to define for those fragments of it that reach us in certain privileged moments, such as dreams, slips, and witticisms.   549

Why would the subject be interested in this discourse if he were not a party to it? He is, indeed, insofar as he is drawn to the four corners of the schema: namely, S, his ineffable and stupid existence; *a*, his objects; *a´*, his ego, that is, his form as reflected in his objects; and A, the locus from which the question of his existence may arise for him.

For it is an experiential truth for psychoanalysis that the question of the subject's existence arises for him, not in the kind of anxiety it provokes at the level of the ego, which is only one element of his cortege, but as an articulated question—"What am I there?"—about his sex and his contingency in being: namely, that on the one hand he is a man or a woman, and on the other that he might not be, the two conjugating their mystery and knotting it in symbols of procreation and death. The fact that the question of his existence envelops the subject, props him up, invades him, and even tears him apart from every angle, is revealed to the analyst by the tensions, suspense, and fantasies that he encounters. It should be added that this question is articulated in the Other in the form of elements of a particular discourse. It is because these phenomena are organized in accordance with the figures of this discourse that they have the fixity of symptoms and that they are legible and dissolve when deciphered.

3. I must therefore emphasize the fact that this question is not presented in the unconscious as ineffable and that this question is a calling into question there—that is, that prior to any analysis this question is articulated there in discrete elements. This is of capital importance, for these elements are the ones that linguistic analysis obliges us to isolate as signifiers, and they are grasped here functioning in their purest form at what is simultaneously the most unlikely and likely point:

550

- the most unlikely, since their chain is found to subsist in an alterity with respect to the subject, which is as radical as that of the still indecipherable hieroglyphics in the desert's solitude;
- the most likely, because only here can their function—that of inducing signification into the signified by imposing their structure on it—appear quite unambiguously.

For the furrows opened up by the signifier in the real world will certainly seek out the gaps—in order to widen them—that the real world as an entity [*étant*] offers the signifier, so much so that an ambiguity may well persist as to whether the signifier does not, in fact, follow the law of the signified here.

But this is not the case at the level of the calling into question, not of the subject's place in the world, but of his existence as a subject, a calling into question which, starting with him, will extend to his within-the-world relation to objects, and to the existence of the world, insofar as its existence, too, can be called into question beyond its order.

4. It is of the utmost importance to observe—in the experience of the unconscious Other where Freud is our guide—that the question does not find its outlines in protomorphic proliferations of the image, in vegetative intumescences, or in animastic halos radiating from the palpitations of life.

This is the whole difference between Freud's orientation and that of Jung's school, which latches onto such forms: *Wandlungen der libido*. These forms may be brought to the fore in a mantic, for they can be produced using the proper techniques (promoting imaginary creations such as reveries, drawings, etc.) in a situable site. This site can be seen on my schema stretched between *a* and *a'*—that is, in the veil of the narcissistic mirage, which is eminently suited to sustaining whatever is reflected in it through its effects of seduction and capture.

If Freud rejected this mantic, it was at the point at which it neglects the guiding function of a signifying articulation, which operates on the basis of its internal law and of material subjected to the poverty that is essential to it.

Similarly, it is precisely to the extent that this style of articulation has been maintained, by virtue of the Freudian Word [*verbe*], even if it has been dismembered, in the community that claims to be orthodox, that such a profound difference persists between the two schools—although, given where things now stand, neither school is in a position to say why. As a result, the level of their practice will soon seem to be reduced to the distance between the forms of reverie found in the Alps and the Atlantic.

To borrow a formulation that delighted Freud when he heard it from Charcot, "That doesn't stop it from existing," it here being the Other, in its place, A.

For if the Other is removed from its place, man can no longer even sustain himself in the position of Narcissus. The *anima*, like a rubber band, snaps back to the *animus* and the *animus* to the animal, who between S and *a* maintains considerably closer "foreign relations" with its *Umwelt* than our own, without our being able to say, moreover, that its relation with the Other is nil, but simply that we only ever see it in sporadic sketches of neurosis.

5. The **L** of the calling-into-question of the subject in his existence has a combinatory structure that must not be confused with its spatial aspect. In this respect, it is the signifier itself that must be articulated in the Other, especially in its quaternary topology.

To support this structure, we find here the three signifiers where the Other may be identified in the Oedipus complex. They suffice to symbolize the significations of sexual reproduction, under the relational signifiers of love and procreation.

The fourth term is given by the subject in his reality, foreclosed as such in the system and entering into the play of signifiers only in the form of the dummy [*mort*], but becoming the true subject as this play of signifiers makes him signify.

Indeed, this play of signifiers is not inert, since it is animated in each particular case [*partie*] by the whole ancestral history of real others that the denomination of signifying Others involves in the Subject's contemporaneity. Furthermore, insofar as this play is properly instituted above and beyond each case, it already structures the three instances in the subject—(ideal) ego, reality, and superego—which were determined by Freud's second topography.

552   Moreover, the subject enters the game as the dummy [*mort*], but it is as a living being that he plays it; it is in his life that he must play the suit he calls trump at some point. He will do so by using a set* of imaginary figures, selected from among the innumerable forms of animastic relations, the choice of which involves a certain arbitrariness, since, in order to cover the symbolic ternary homologically, it must be numerically reduced.

To do so, the polar relation—by which the specular image (of the narcissistic relationship) is linked, as unifying, to the set of imaginary elements of the so-called fragmented body—provides a couple that is not merely readied by a natural fit between development and structure to serve as a homologue for the symbolic Mother/Child relation. While the imaginary couple of the mirror stage, through the counter-natural features it manifests, must be related to a specific prematurity of birth in man, it proves appropriate for providing the imaginary triangle with the base that the symbolic relation may, in some sense, overlap (see the R schema).

Indeed, it is by means of the gap in the imaginary opened up by this prematurity, and in which the effects of the mirror stage proliferate, that the human animal is *capable* of imagining himself mortal—which does not mean that he could do so without his symbiosis with the symbolic, but rather that, without the gap that alienates him from his own image, this symbiosis with the symbolic, in which he constitutes himself as subject to death, could not have occurred.

6. The third term of the imaginary ternary—the one where the subject is identified, on the contrary, with his living being—is nothing but the phallic

image, whose unveiling in this function is not the least scandalous facet of the Freudian discovery.

I will now inscribe here, as a conceptual visualization of this double ternary, what I shall henceforth call the R schema, which represents the lines that condition the *perceptum*—in other words, the object—insofar as these lines circumscribe the field of reality rather than merely depending on it.

Thus, in considering the vertices of the symbolic triangle—I as the ego-ideal, M as the signifier of the primordial object, and P [for *père*] as the position in A of the Name-of-the-Father—we can see how the homologous pinning of the signification of the subject S under the signifier of the phallus may have repercussions on the support of the field of reality delimited by the quadrangle M*i*m*I. The other two vertices of this quadrangle, *i* and *m*, represent the two imaginary terms of the narcissistic relation: the ego [*m* for *moi*] and the specular image.

R Schema

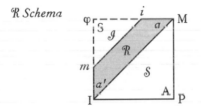

We can thus situate between *i* and M—that is, in *a*—the extremities of the segments S*i*, S*a*¹, S*a*², S*a*ⁿ, and SM, where we place figures of the imaginary other in the relationships of erotic aggression where they are realized. Similarly, we can situate between *m* and I, that is in *a*´, the extremities of segments S*m*, S*a*´¹, S*a*´², S*a*´ⁿ, and SI, where the ego is identified, from its specular *Urbild* to the paternal identification involved in the ego-ideal.[14]

Those who attended my 1956–1957 seminar know the use I made of the imaginary ternary laid out here—whose vertex, I, is really constituted by the child, qua desired—in order to restore to the notion of the Object Relation,[15] somewhat discredited by the mass of nonsense that the term has been used to validate in recent years, the capital of experience that legitimately belongs to it.

In effect, this schema allows us to show the relations that refer not to preoedipal stages—which are not, of course, nonexistent, but are analytically unthinkable (as is sufficiently obvious in Melanie Klein's faltering but not altogether misguided work)—but to the pregenital stages insofar as they are organized by the retroactive effect of the Oedipus complex.

The whole problem of the perversions consists in conceiving how the child, in its relationship with its mother—a relationship that is constituted in analysis not by the child's biological dependence, but by its dependence on her love, that is, by its desire for her desire—identifies with the imaginary object of her desire insofar as the mother herself symbolizes it in the phallus.

555 The phallocentrism produced by this dialectic is all that need concern us here. It is, of course, entirely conditioned by the intrusion of the signifier in man's psyche and strictly impossible to deduce from any preestablished harmony between this psyche and the nature it expresses.

This imaginary effect, which can be felt as a discordance only on the basis of a belief in a normativity proper to instinct, nevertheless gave rise to the long quarrel—which is now dead, but not without leaving wreckage in its wake—concerning the primary or secondary nature of the phallic phase. Even apart from the extreme importance of the question, this quarrel would warrant our interest due to the dialectical exploits it imposed on Ernest Jones in order to maintain, with the claim that he was in complete agreement with Freud, a position that was diametrically opposed to Freud's—namely, a position that made him, with certain minor qualifications no doubt, the champion of the British feminists, enamored of their "to each his own" principle: boys have the dick, girls have the c . . .

7. Freud thus unveiled the imaginary function of the phallus as the pivotal point in the symbolic process that completes, *in both sexes*, the calling into question of one's sex by the castration complex.

The current obscuring of this function of the phallus (reduced to the role of a part-object) in the analytic chorus is simply the continuation of the profound mystification in which culture maintains its symbol—in the sense in which paganism itself presented it only at the culmination of its most secret mysteries.

In the subjective economy, commanded as it is by the unconscious, it is, in effect, a signification that is evoked only by what I call a metaphor—to be precise, the paternal metaphor.

And this brings us back, since it is with Macalpine that I have chosen to dialogue, to her need to refer to a "heliolithism," by which she claims to see procreation codified in a preoedipal culture, where the father's procreative function is eluded.

Anything that can be put forward along these lines, in whatever form, will only better highlight the signifying function that conditions paternity.

For in another debate dating back to the time when psychoanalysts still puzzled over doctrine, Ernest Jones, with a remark that was more relevant than his aforementioned one, contributed a no less inappropriate argument.

Indeed, concerning the state of beliefs in some Australian tribe, he refused to admit that any collectivity of men could overlook the fact of experience that—except in the case of an enigmatic exception—no woman gives birth without having engaged in coitus, or even be ignorant of the requisite lapse of time between the two events. Now the credit that seems to me to be quite legitimately granted to human capacities to observe reality [*réel*] is precisely what has not the slightest importance in the matter.

For, if the symbolic context requires it, paternity will nevertheless be attributed to the woman's encounter with a spirit at such and such a fountain or at a certain rock in which he is supposed to dwell.

This is clearly what demonstrates that the attribution of procreation to the father can only be the effect of a pure signifier, of a recognition, not of the real father, but of what religion has taught us to invoke as the Name-of-the-Father.

Of course, there is no need of a signifier to be a father, any more than there is to be dead, but without a signifier, no one will ever know anything about either of these states of being.

Let me remind those who cannot be persuaded to seek in Freud's texts something to complement the wisdom that their coaches dispense to them, how insistently Freud stresses the affinity of the two signifying relations I just mentioned, whenever the neurotic subject (especially the obsessive) manifests this affinity through the conjunction of their themes.

How, indeed, could Freud fail to recognize such an affinity, when the necessity of his reflection led him to tie the appearance of the signifier of the Father, as author of the Law, to death—indeed, to the killing of the Father—thus showing that, if this murder is the fertile moment of the debt by which the subject binds himself for life to the Law, the symbolic Father, insofar as he signifies this Law, is truly the dead Father.

IV. Schreber's Way

1. We can now enter into the subjectivity of Schreber's delusion.

The signification of the phallus, as I said, must be evoked in the subject's imaginary by the paternal metaphor.

This has a precise meaning in the economy of the signifier, whose formalization I can only recall to mind here, but which is familiar to those who attend the seminar I am giving this year on unconscious formations.

Namely, *the formula for metaphor*, or *for signifying substitution*:

$$\frac{S}{\cancel{S'}} \cdot \frac{\cancel{S'}}{x} \longrightarrow S\left(\frac{1}{s}\right)$$

Here the capital Ss are signifiers, x is the unknown signification, and s is the signified induced by the metaphor, which consists in the substitution in the signifying chain of S for S´. The elision of S´, represented in the formula by the fact that it is crossed out, is the condition of the metaphor's success.

This applies thus to the metaphor of the Name-of-the-Father, that is, the metaphor that puts this Name in the place that was first symbolized by the operation of the mother's absence.

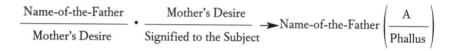

$$\frac{\text{Name-of-the-Father}}{\text{Mother's Desire}} \cdot \frac{\text{Mother's Desire}}{\text{Signified to the Subject}} \longrightarrow \text{Name-of-the-Father}\left(\frac{A}{\text{Phallus}}\right)$$

Let us now try to conceive of a circumstance of the subjective position in which what responds to the appeal to the Name-of-the-Father is not the absence of the real father, for this absence is more than compatible with the presence of the signifier, but the lack of the signifier itself.

This is not a conception for which nothing has prepared us. The signifier's presence in the Other is, in effect, a presence that is usually closed off to the subject, because it usually persists there in a repressed (*verdrängt*) state, and insists from that place so as to be represented in the signified by means of its repetition automatism (*Wiederholungszwang*).

Let us extract from several of Freud's texts a term that is sufficiently articulated in them to render them unjustifiable if it does not designate in them a function of the unconscious that is distinct from the repressed. Let us take as demonstrated what constituted the crux of my seminar on the psychoses—namely, that this term, *Verwerfung*, refers to the most necessary implication of Freud's thought when it grapples with the phenomenon of psychosis.

It is articulated in this register as the absence of *Bejahung*—the judgment of attribution—which Freud posits as a necessary precedent for any possible application of *Verneinung* [negation], the latter, in contrast with *Bejahung*, being the judgment of existence; meanwhile, the whole article in which he separates out this *Verneinung* as an element of analytic experience demonstrates in *Verneinung* the owning [*aveu*] of the very signifier that *Verneinung* annuls.

The primordial *Bejahung* thus also bears on the signifier, and other texts allow us to recognize this, in particular, Letter 52 of Freud's correspondence with Fliess, in which it is expressly isolated as the term for an original perception by the name "sign," *Zeichen.*

I will thus take *Verwerfung* to be "foreclosure" of the signifier. At the point at which the Name-of-the-Father is summoned—and we shall see how—a pure and simple hole may thus answer in the Other; due to the lack of the metaphoric effect, this hole will give rise to a corresponding hole in the place of phallic signification.

This is the only form in which it is possible for us to conceptualize something whose outcome Schreber presents to us as that of an injury which he is in a position to reveal only in part, and in which, he says, the term "soul murder" (*Seelenmord*, S. 22), along with the names Flechsig and Schreber, plays an essential role.[16]

It is clear that what we are presented with here is a disturbance that occurred at the inmost juncture of the subject's sense of life. The censorship, which mutilated the text of his *Memoirs* before the addition announced by Schreber to the rather roundabout explanations that he tried to give of the disturbance's process, inclines me to think that he associated facts that could not be published due to the conventions of the time with the names of   559 people who were still alive. The following chapter [chapter 3] is thus missing in its entirety and, to exercise his perspicacity, Freud had to confine himself to the allusion to *Faust, Der Freischütz*, and Byron's *Manfred*, the latter work (from which he assumes Ahriman, the name of one of the manifestations of God in Schreber's delusion, was borrowed) seeming to him to derive its full value in this reference from its theme: the hero dies from the curse borne in him by the death of the object of fraternal incest.

For my part—since like Freud I have chosen to trust in a text which, except for these mutilations, regrettable as they are, remains a document whose guarantees of credibility place it among the finest—it is in the most highly developed form of the delusion, with which the book coincides, that I will try to demonstrate a structure that will prove to be similar to the psychotic process itself.

2. Following this line of approach, I will observe—with the hint of surprise that Freud sees as the subjective connotation of the unconscious when recognized—that the delusion deploys its whole tapestry around the power of

creation attributed to the words of which the divine rays (*Gottesstrahlen*) are the hypostasis.

This begins as a leitmotiv in the first chapter, where the author first dwells on what is shocking to thought about the act of bringing something into existence out of nothing, flying, as it does, in the face of the evidence that experience provides to thought of the transformations of matter in which reality finds its substance.

He emphasizes this paradox by contrasting it with ideas that are more familiar to the man he assures us he is, as if there were any need for it: a *gebildet* German of the Wilhelmine era, raised on Haeckelian metascientism, to support which he provides a list of readings, an occasion for us to fill out, by reading them, what Gavarni somewhere calls a courageous idea of Man.[17]

560   It is in this very paradox, reflected by the intrusion of a thought, for him hitherto unthinkable, that Schreber sees the proof that something must have happened that did not proceed from his own mind: a proof which, it seems, only the question begging highlighted above in the psychiatrist's position gives us the right to resist.

3. Having said this, let us for our part confine our attention to a sequence of phenomena that Schreber establishes in chapter 15 (S. 204–15).

At this point in the book we know that the support for his side in the forced game of thought (*Denkzwang*), which God's words constrain him to play (see section I.5 above), has a dramatic stake. God, whose powers of ignorance become apparent later, considering the subject to have been annihilated, leaves him in the lurch (*liegen lassen*)—a threat to which we will return further on.

The fact that the effort to reply—which the subject is thus stuck on, so to speak, in this way in his being as a subject—eventually fails at a moment of "thinking nothing" (*Nichtsdenken* [S. 205]), which certainly seems to be the most humanly merited of rests (Schreber says [S. 47]), leads, according to him, to:

(a) What he calls the bellowing-miracle (*Brüllenwunder*), a cry torn from his breast that surprises him beyond all warning, whether he is alone or with others who are horrified by the image he offers them of his mouth suddenly agape before the unspeakable void, abandoned by the cigar that was stuck there a moment before;

(b) The cries of "help" (*"Hülfe" rufen*), made by "those of God's nerves separated from the total mass," whose woeful tone is explained by the greater distance to which God withdraws [S. 206];

(two phenomena in which the subjective rending is indistinguishable enough from its signifying mode for me not to belabor the point);

(c) The imminent appearance—in the occult zone of the perceptual field, in the hallway, or in the next room—of manifestations which, though not extraordinary, strike the subject as produced for him;

(d) The appearance, at the next stage, from afar—in other words, out of the range of the senses, in the park, *in the real*—of miraculous creations, that is, newly created beings, which, as Macalpine perspicaciously notes, always belong to flying species: birds or insects.

Don't these latter meteors of the delusion appear as the trace of a furrow,   561
or as a halo effect, showing the two moments at which, from out of its darkness, the signifier   which has fallen silent in the subject   first makes a glimmer of signification spring forth at the surface of the real, and then causes the real to become illuminated with a flash projected from below its underpinning of nothingness?

Thus, at the height of these hallucinatory effects, these creatures—which are the only ones that deserve to be called "hallucinations" if we rigorously apply the criterion that the phenomenon appear *in reality*—advise us to reconsider in their symbolic solidarity the trio of Creator, Creature, and Created that separates out here.

4. Indeed, it is from the position of the Creator that we will arrive at that of the Created, which subjectively creates the former.

Unique in his Multiplicity, Multiple in his Unity (these are the attributes by which Schreber, like Heraclitus, defines him), this God—broken down, in effect, into a hierarchy of realms, which warrants a separate study of its own—degrades into beings that pilfer disannexed identities.

Immanent in these beings, whose capture by their inclusion in Schreber's being threatens his integrity, God is not without the intuitive prop of a hyperspace, in which Schreber sees even signifying transmissions being conducted along filaments (*Fäden*) that materialize the parabolic trajectory by which they enter his cranium through the occiput (S. 315).

Yet, as time goes by, God, in his manifestations, allows the field of beings devoid of intelligence to expand ever further, beings who do not know what they are saying, inane beings, such as those "miracled birds," those "talking birds," those "forecourts of heaven" (*Vorhöfe des Himmels* [S. 19]), in which Freud's misogyny detected at first glance the silly geese that young girls were considered to be in the ideals of his time, finding his view confirmed by the proper names[18] the subject later gives them. Suffice it to say that, in my view, they are far more representative by virtue of their surprise at the similarity of vocables and the purely homophonic equivalences on which they rely in using them (Santiago = Carthago, Chinesenthum = Jesum Christum, etc., S. 210).

Similarly, God's being in its essence withdraws ever further into the space that conditions it, a withdrawal that can be intuited in the increasing slowness of his speech, which even goes as far as a halting, stammered articulation of every letter of a word (S. 223). Indeed, were we to follow solely what this process indicates, we would regard this unique Other—with which the subject's existence is linked—as suited above all for emptying the places (S. 196 note) in which the murmuring of words unfolds, were Schreber not careful to inform us, in addition, that this God is foreclosed from every other aspect of the exchange. He apologizes for doing so, but however sorry he may be about it, he nevertheless has to observe it: God is not simply impermeable to experience; he is incapable of understanding a living man; he grasps him only from the outside (which certainly seems to be his essential mode); all interiority is closed off to him. A "writing-down-system" (*Aufschreibesystem* [S. 126])—in which acts and thoughts are preserved—recalls, of course, in a displaced way, the notebook kept by the guardian angel from our catechized childhood, but beyond that we should note the absence of any trace of the sounding of loins or hearts (S. 20).

Again, in the same way, after the purification of souls (*Laüterung*) has abolished every remnant of their personal identity in them, everything will be reduced to the eternal subsistence of this verbiage, which is the sole means God has for knowing the very works that men's ingenuity has constructed (S. 300).

How could I fail to note here that the grandnephew of the author of *Novae species insectorum* (Johann Christian Daniel von Schreber) points out that none of the miracled creatures is of a new species, or to add—in opposition to Macalpine, who sees in them the Dove that conveys the fruitful tidings of the Logos from the Father's lap to the Virgin—that they remind me, rather, of the species a magician produces from out of the opening of his waistcoat or sleeve in great numbers?

This leads me at last to the surprising conclusion that the subject who has

fallen prey to these mysteries does not hesitate, Created being though he be, to   563
use words to deal with the dismayingly silly traps set by his Lord, or to stand
his ground in the face of the destruction he believes his Lord capable of initiating against him or anyone else, by virtue of a right that legitimates his doing
so in the name of the Order of Things (*Weltordnung*). The fact that this right
is on his side is the reason for this unique victory of a creature whom a chain
of disturbances has made succumb to his creator's "perfidy" (this word, which
he lets slip out not without reservations, is in French in the original: S. 226).

Isn't this recalcitrant created being, who holds out against his fall owing
to the sole support of his Word and to his faith in speech, a strange counterpart to Malebranche's continuous creation?

This would warrant another look at the authors covered on the
Baccalaureate exam in philosophy, for we have perhaps been overly dismis-
sive of those who did not help pave the way for *homo psychologicus*, in which
our era finds the measure of a humanism that is—don't you think?—perhaps somewhat pedestrian.

Between Malebranche and Locke the cleverer is the crazier . . .

Yes, but which one is it? There's the rub, my dear colleague. Come on,
drop that stiff manner. When will you feel at ease, then, here where you are
on your home turf?

5. Let us now try to locate the subject's position, as it is constituted here in
the symbolic order, on the ternary that maps it in my R schema.

It seems to me, then, that if the Created, I, takes the place here of the Law
in P, which is left vacant, the place of the Creator is designated here by this
liegen lassen, this fundamental leaving in the lurch, in which the absence that
allowed the primordial symbolization, M, of the mother to be constructed
appears to be unveiled, by virtue of the foreclosure of the Father.

Between the two, a line—which would culminate in the Creatures of
speech occupying the place of the child who doesn't come, dashing the subject's hopes (see my postscript further on)—would thus be conceived as
skirting the hole excavated in the field of the signifier by the foreclosure of
the Name-of-the-Father (see the I schema, page 571 [page 202] below).

It is around this hole, where the subject lacks the support of the signify-   564
ing chain, and which need not, as can be observed, be ineffable to induce
panic, that the whole struggle in which the subject reconstructed himself
took place. He conducted this struggle honorably, and the "vaginas of

heaven" (another meaning of the word *Vorhöfe* mentioned above)—the cohort of miracled young girls who laid siege to the edges of the hole— commented on it in the clucks of admiration wrung from their harpies' throats: "*Verfluchter Kerl!* One hell of a fellow!" In other words: What a great guy! Alas! It was by way of antiphrasis.

6. For in the field of the imaginary, a gap had already recently opened up for him in response to the absence of the symbolic metaphor, a gap that could only find a way to be eliminated in the carrying out of *Entmannung* (emasculation).

This was at first horrifying to the subject, then it was accepted as a reasonable compromise (*vernünftig*, S. 177), and thereafter as an irremissible resolve (S. 179 note) and a future motive for a redemption concerning the entire world.

Although we still are not off the hook regarding the term *Entmannung*, it will surely be less of a hindrance to us than it is to Macalpine, given her standpoint, as I have described it. No doubt she thought she was clarifying things by substituting the word "unmanning"* for "emasculation,"* which the translator of volume III of the *Collected Papers* had innocently believed to suffice to render it; she even went so far as to try to ensure that the translation was altered in the authorized version then being prepared. Perhaps she was struck by some imperceptible etymological suggestion that differentiated the two terms, despite their identical usage.[19]

But to what avail? When she rejects as *impropère*[20] the calling into question of an organ which, in referring to the *Memoirs*, she considers to be destined only to a peaceful reabsorption into the subject's entrails, does she mean by this to depict the timorous slyness in which it takes refuge close to the body when he shivers with cold, or the conscientious objection the description of which the author of *The Satyricon* maliciously lingers over?

Or could it perhaps be that she erroneously believes that the castration complex has always had something to do with real castration?

She is no doubt justified in noticing the ambiguity there is in regarding as equivalent the subject's transformation into a woman (*Verweiblichung*) and castration [*éviration*] (for this is certainly the meaning of *Entmannung*). But she does not see that this ambiguity is that of the very subjective structure which produces it here: the latter implies that what borders, at the imaginary level, on the subject's transformation into a woman is precisely what makes him forfeit any inheritance from which he may legitimately expect the allotment of a penis to his person. This because, whereas being and having are mutually exclusive in theory, they overlap, at least as far as the result is concerned, when a lack is at stake. Which does not prevent the distinction between them from being decisive in what follows.

As we can perceive if we note that the patient is destined to become a woman not because he is foreclosed from the penis, but because he has to be the phallus.

The symbolic parity *Mädchen* = *Phallus*—or, in English, the equation Girl = Phallus, in the words of Fenichel,[21] this equation providing him the theme of a worthy, albeit somewhat confused, essay—finds its root in the imaginary paths by which the child's desire manages to identify with the mother's want-to-be, into which she herself was, of course, inducted by the symbolic law in which this want is constituted.

It is as a result of the same mainspring that, whether they like it or not, women in reality [*réel*] serve as objects for exchanges ordained by the elementary structures of kinship, which are sometimes perpetuated in the imaginary, while what is simultaneously transmitted in the symbolic order is the phallus.

7. Here the identification, whatever it may be, by which the subject assumed [*assumé*] his mother's desire, triggers, as a result of being shaken up, the dissolution of the imaginary tripod (note that it was in his mother's apartment, where he had taken refuge, that the subject had his first attack of anxious confusion with suicidal raptus: S. 39–40).   566

Divination by the unconscious no doubt warned the subject very early on that, unable to be the phallus the mother is missing, there remained the solution of being the woman that men are missing.

This is the meaning of his fantasy, his account of which has often been commented on and which I quoted above from the incubation period of his second illness—namely, the idea "that it would be beautiful to be a woman submitting to the act of copulation" [S. 36]. This is precisely the *pons asinorum* of the Schreberian literature.

Yet this solution was premature at the time because, regarding the *Menschenspielerei* (a term that appeared in the basic language, meaning, in our contemporary idiom, brawling among men) that normally would have ensued, any attempt by Schreber to call upon real men was bound to fall flat, as it were, since they became as improbable as Schreber himself—that is, as devoid as he was of any phallus. This is because a stroke was omitted in the subject's imaginary—no less for them than for him—the stroke, parallel to the outline of their figure, that can be seen in a drawing by little Hans, which is familiar to connoisseurs of children's drawings. It was because others were, from then on, no more than "images of men cobbled together 1, 2, 3" [*"images d'hommes torchées à la six-quatre-deux"*]—to combine, in this translation of *flüchtig hingemachte Männer*, Niederland's remarks on the uses of *hinmachen* and Édouard Pichon's inspired translation of the expression into French.[22]

The upshot being that matters might have stagnated in a rather dishonorable fashion, had the subject not succeeded in brilliantly saving the day.

He himself articulated the way out (in November 1895, that is, two years after the beginning of his illness) with the term *Versöhnung*. The word has the meaning of expiation or propitiation and, given the characteristics of the basic language, must be drawn even more toward the primitive meaning of *Sühne*, that is, sacrifice; instead, people have emphasized its meaning as compromise (reasonable compromise, with which the subject explains the accepting of his destiny; see page 564 [page 196] above).

Here Freud, going well beyond the subject's own rationalization, admits paradoxically that the "reconciliation" (since this flat meaning of the term *Versöhnung* is the one that was chosen in the French translation) highlighted by the subject finds its mainspring in the underhanded dealings of the partner involved in this reconciliation—namely, in the consideration that God's wife contracts, in any case, an alliance that would satisfy the most pernickety pride.

I think we can say that Freud failed to live up to his own standards here, and in the most contradictory way, in that he accepts as a turning point of the delusion what he refused in his general conception—namely, to make the homosexual theme depend on the idea of grandeur (I will assume that my readers are familiar with his text).

The reason for this failure is found in necessity, that is, in the fact that Freud had not yet formulated "On Narcissism: an Introduction" [1914].

8. Three years after 1911 he probably would not have missed the true reason for the reversal in Schreber's sense of indignation—initially aroused in him by the idea of *Entmannung*—which was precisely the fact that in the interval *the subject had died*.

This, at least, was the event that the voices—always informed by the right sources and ever constant in their information service—made known to him after the fact, complete with the date and name of the newspaper in which the event was announced in the obituaries (S. 81).

We, on the other hand, can make do with the evidence provided by the medical certificates, which depict the patient to us as sunk in a catatonic stupor at the relevant time.

As is commonly the case, his memories of this time are plentiful. Thus we know that, modifying the custom according to which one departs this life feet first, our patient, so as to do it only in transit, took pleasure in keeping his feet out of it—that is, stuck out the window, under the tendentious pretext of exposing them to the cold (S. 172)—thus reviving perhaps (I will leave this to be gauged by those who will only be interested here in the imaginary avatar) the direction of his birth.

568

But this is not a career that one takes up at a full fifty years of age without becoming disoriented to some degree. Hence the faithful portrait that the voices, annalists I would say, gave him of himself as a "leper corpse leading another leper corpse" (S. 92), a truly brilliant description, it must be admitted, of an identity reduced to a confrontation with its psychical double, but which, moreover, renders patent the subject's regression—a topographical, not a genetic, regression—to the mirror stage, insofar as the relationship to the specular other is reduced here to its mortal impact.

This was also the time at which his body was merely an aggregate of colonies of foreign "nerves," a sort of dump for detached fragments of his persecutors' identities (S. chapter XIV).

It seems to me that the relation of all this to homosexuality, which is certainly manifest in the delusion, requires a more advanced set of rules regarding the theoretical use that can be made of this reference.

It holds great interest, since it is certain that the use of this term in interpretation may cause serious damage if it is not informed by the symbolic relations that I consider determinant here.

9. I believe that this symbolic determination is demonstrated in the form in which the imaginary structure comes to be restored. At this stage, the imaginary structure presents two facets that Freud himself distinguished.

The first is that of a transsexualist practice, not at all unworthy of being related to "perversion," the features of which have been presented in many case histories since that time.[23]

Furthermore, I must point out how the structure I am isolating here may shed light on the highly unusual insistence displayed by the subjects of these case histories on obtaining their father's authorization for, one might even say his hands-on assistance with, their demands for the most radical rectifications.

Be that as it may, we see our subject give himself over to an erotic activity which, he emphasizes, is strictly reserved for solitude, but whose satis-

569

factions he nevertheless admits to—satisfactions his image in the mirror gives him, when, dressed in the cheap adornments of feminine finery, nothing in the upper part of his body, he says, seems to him incapable of convincing any possible aficionado of the female bust (S. 280).

To which we must link, I believe, the development, alleged to be an endosomatic perception, of the so-called nerves of female pleasure in his own integument, particularly in those zones where they are supposed to be erogenous in women [S. 274].

One remark he makes—the remark that if he were to incessantly contemplate woman's image, and never detach his thoughts from the prop of something feminine, God's sensuality would be all the better served—turns our attention to the other facet of his libidinal fantasies.

This facet links the subject's feminization to the coordinate of divine copulation.

Freud very clearly saw in this the sense of mortification, when he stressed everything that links "soul-voluptuousness" (*Seelenwollust*), which is included in it, to "bliss" [*béatitude*] (*Seligkeit*), insofar as the latter is the state of deceased souls (*abschiedenen Wesen*).

The fact that the now blessed voluptuousness should become the soul's bliss is, indeed, an essential turning point, and Freud, it should be noted, stresses its linguistic motivation when he suggests that the history of his language [*langue*] might shed some light on it.[24]

This is simply to make a mistake regarding the dimension in which the letter manifests itself in the unconscious, and which, in accordance with its own literal instance, is far less etymological (or diachronic, to be precise) than homophonic (synchronic). Indeed, there is nothing in the history of the German language [*langue*] that would allow us to relate *selig* to *Seele*, or to relate the happiness that transports lovers to "heaven"—insofar as it is this happiness to which Freud refers in the aria he quotes from *Don Giovanni*—to the happiness promised to the so-called "blessed" souls by their stay in heaven. The dead are *selig* in German only by virtue of a borrowing from Latin, and because of the Latin phrase "of blessed memory" (*beatae memoriae, seliger Gedächtnis*). Their *Seelen* have more to do with the lakes (*Seen*) in which they sojourned at one time than with anything like their bliss. The fact is that the unconscious is concerned more with the signifier than with the signified, and that the phrase, "*feu mon père*" ("my late father"), may mean there that my father was the fire of God [*le feu de Dieu*], or even give the order for him to be shot: Fire!

But this digression aside, the fact remains that we are, here, in a beyond of the world, which easily accommodates an indefinite postponement of the realization of its goal.

Once Schreber has completed his transformation into a woman, the act of divine fecundation will assuredly take place, although it is clear that God could not compromise himself by taking an obscure journey through the organs (S. 3). (Let us not forget God's aversion to the living being.) It is thus through a spiritual operation that Schreber will feel awakening in him the embryonic germ, whose stirrings he already experienced in the early stages of his illness.

The new spiritual humanity of the Schreberian creatures will be entirely engendered through his womb, of course, so that the rotten and condemned humanity of the present age may be reborn. This is clearly a sort of redemption—since this is how the delusion has been cataloged—but it aims only at the creature of the future, for the creature of the present is struck by a decadence that is correlative to the captation of the divine rays by the voluptuousness that rivets them to Schreber (S. 51–2).

In this, the mirage dimension becomes visible. It is further highlighted by the indefinite amount of time for which the promise is postponed, and is profoundly conditioned by the absence of mediation to which the fantasy bears witness. For we can see that this fantasy parodies the situation of the last surviving couple who, following some human catastrophe, would find themselves confronted with what is total in the act of animal reproduction, holding as they would the power to repopulate the earth.

Here again one can place under the sign of the creature the turning point from which the line flees along its two branches, that of narcissistic jouissance and that of ideal identification—but in the sense in which its image is the decoy of the imaginary capture in which the two branches are rooted. And here, too, the line revolves around a hole, the very hole in which "soul-murder" has installed death.

Was this other gulf formed by the simple effect in the imaginary of the   571
futile appeal made in the symbolic to the paternal metaphor? Or must we conceive of it as produced at one remove by the elision of the phallus, which the subject would like to reduce, in order to resolve it, to the lethal gap of the mirror stage? The link, which this time is a genetic one, between this stage and the symbolization of the Mother insofar as she is primordial would certainly have to be evoked to explain this solution.

Can we locate the geometrical points of the R schema on a schema of the subject's structure at the end of the psychotic process? I shall try to do so in the I schema below.

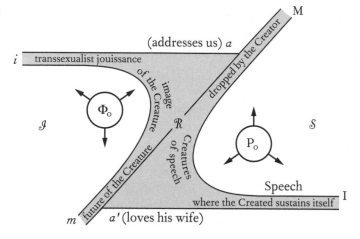

I Schema

This schema no doubt suffers from the excess endemic to any formalization that is presented in the intuitive realm.

In other words, the distortion that it manifests between the functions identified here by the letters transferred to it from the R schema can only be gauged on the basis of its use in restarting the dialectic.

Let me simply point out here—in the double curve that resembles a hyperbola except for the slippage of the two curves along one of the guiding lines of their asymptote—the link made palpable, in the double asymptote that unites the delusional ego to the divine other, of their imaginary divergence in space and time to the ideal convergence of their conjunction. And let us not overlook the fact that Freud himself had an intuition of such a form, since he himself introduced the term *asymptotisch* in this context.[25]

The entire width of the real creature, on the other hand, is interposed for the subject between the narcissistic jouissance of his image and the alienation of speech in which the ego-ideal has taken the place of the Other.

The schema shows that the final state of the psychosis does not represent the frozen chaos encountered in the aftermath of an earthquake, but rather the bringing to light of lines of efficiency that makes people talk when it is a problem with an elegant solution.

It materializes in a signifying way what lies at the crux of the true fruitfulness of Freud's research. For it is a fact that without any other support or prop than a written document—which is not only a testimony to, but also a product of, this final state of the psychosis—Freud shed the first light on the very evolution of the psychotic process, allowing us to elucidate its proper determination, by which I mean the only organicity that is essentially involved in this process: the organicity that motivates the structure of signification.

Condensed in the form of this schema, the relations emerge by which the signifier's induction effects, impacting the imaginary, bring about the upheaval in the subject that clinicians refer to as the "twilight of the world," necessitating new signifying effects in response.

In my seminar I showed that the symbolic succession of the anterior realms, and then the posterior realms of God, the lower and the upper, Ahriman and Ormuzd, and their shifts in "policy" (a word of the basic language) with respect to the subject, provide these very responses at the various stages of the imaginary dissolution—which, moreover, the patient's memories and the medical certificates connote sufficiently—in order to restore order in the subject there.

Regarding the question that I am foregrounding here concerning the signifier's alienating impact, I will refer to the low point that came on a night in July of 1894 when Ahriman, the lower God, revealing himself to Schreber in the most impressive trappings of his power, addressed him with a simple and, according to the subject, common word of the basic language: *Luder!*[26]

To translate the word we must do more than simply look it up in the Sachs-Villatte dictionary, to which the French translator confined his efforts. Niederland's reference to "lewd" in English, meaning whore, does not seem acceptable to me as an attempt to convey the sense of spineless or slut, which is what it means when used as an obscene insult.

But if we take into account the archaism indicated as characteristic of the basic language, I believe we can justifiably link this term to the root of the French *leurre*, and of the English "lure,"* which is certainly the best *ad hominem* address to be expected coming from the symbolic: the Other with a capital O can be awfully impertinent.

There remains the disposition of the field **R** in the schema, inasmuch as this disposition represents the conditions in which reality was restored for the subject: for him a sort of island, the consistency of which is imposed on him after proving its constancy,[27] which, to my mind, is linked to what makes it inhabitable for him, but which also distorts it—namely, eccentric reshapings of the imaginary, **I**, and of the symbolic, **S**, which reduce reality to the field of the skew between them.

The subordinate conception that we must have of the function of reality in the process, in both its cause and effects, is what is important here.

I cannot elaborate here on the question, which is nevertheless crucial, of what we are for the subject, we whom he addresses as readers, nor on the question of what remains of his relationship with his wife, for whom his book was initially intended, whose visits during his illness were always

573

greeted by him with the most intense emotion, and for whom, he asserts, alongside the most decisive admission of his delusional vocation, "I retain my former love in full" (S. 179 note).

The maintenance of the trajectory, *Saa'A*, in the I schema symbolizes there the opinion I have formed, on the basis of my examination of this case, that the relation to the other qua relation to one's semblable, and even a relation as elevated as that of friendship in the sense in which Aristotle makes it the essence of the conjugal link, are perfectly compatible with the skewing of the relation to the Other with a capital O and all the radical anomalies it brings with it—qualified, improperly but not without some relevance as a first approximation, in the old clinical jargon as a "partial delusion."

Nonetheless, it would be better to consign this schema to the garbage heap, if, like so many others, it prompted anyone to forget, because of an intuitive image, the analysis on which this image is based.

Indeed, one need but think about it to realize how satisfied Macalpine—my interlocutor here whose authentic reflection I will praise now one last time—would be with it, by simply misrecognizing what made me construct it.

What I am asserting here is that, in recognizing the drama of madness, reason is doing what it likes best, *sua res agitur*, because it is in man's relation to the signifier that this drama is situated.

The danger people mention of becoming as mad as the patient no more intimidates me than it did Freud.

Like Freud, I hold that we must listen to the speaker, when what is at stake is a message that does not come from a subject beyond language, but from speech beyond the subject. For it is then that we will hear this speech, which Schreber picked up in the Other, when from Ahriman to Ormuzd, from the evil God to the absent God, it carries the summons in which the very law of the signifier is articulated: "*Aller Unsinn hebt sich auf!*" "All nonsense cancels itself out!" (S. 182–83 and 312).

Here we encounter anew (leaving to those who will concern themselves with me later the task of figuring out why I have left it in abeyance for ten years) what I said in my dialogue with Henri Ey: "Not only can man's being not be understood without madness, but it would not be man's being if it did not bear madness within itself as the limit of his freedom."[28]

V. Postscript

Following in Freud's footsteps, I teach that the Other is the locus of the kind of memory he discovered by the name "unconscious," memory that he

regards as the object of a question that has remained unanswered, insofar as
it conditions the indestructibility of certain desires. I will answer this question with the conception of the signifying chain, inasmuch as—once this
chain has been inaugurated by primordial symbolization (made manifest in
the *Fort! Da!* game, which Freud elucidated as lying at the origin of repetition automatism)—it develops in accordance with logical connections whose
hold on that which is to be signified, namely, the being of entities, is exerted
through the signifying effects I describe as metaphor and metonymy.

It is an accident in this register and in what occurs in it—namely, the
foreclosure of the Name-of-the-Father in the place of the Other—and the
failure of the paternal metaphor that I designate as the defect that gives psychosis its essential condition, along with the structure that separates it from
neurosis.

This thesis, which I am contributing here as a question prior to any possible treatment of psychosis, has a dialectic that can be pursued beyond this
point: but I shall stop it here and say why.

First, because it is worth indicating what can be discovered by my halting
here.

A perspective that does not distinguish Schreber's relationship with God
on the basis of its subjective impact marks this relationship with negative features which make it appear as a mixture rather than as a union of being with
being, and which—in the voracity that accommodates disgust there and in the
complicity that tolerates its exaction—show nothing, to call things by their
rightful names, of the Presence and Joy that illuminate mystical experience.
This opposition is not only demonstrated but founded by the astonishing
absence in this relationship of the *Du*, in French of the *Tu*—certain languages   576
[*langues*] reserving a vocable (e.g., Thou*) for God's appeal and for the
appeal to God—which is the signifier of the Other in speech.

We are familiar with the false modesties that are considered proper in science in this regard; they accompany pedantry's false thoughts when it
invokes the ineffability of lived experience, or even "morbid consciousness," in order to disarm the effort it spares itself—namely, the effort that is
required at the point at which it is not ineffable precisely because it [*ça*]
speaks; at which lived experience, far from separating us, is communicated;
and at which subjectivity surrenders its true structure, that structure in
which what can be analyzed is identical to what can be articulated.

Thus from the same vantage point to which delusional subjectivity has
brought us, I will turn to scientific subjectivity: I mean the subjectivity that
the scientist at work in science shares with the man of the civilization that

supports it. I will not deny that I have seen enough on this score in our time to wonder about the criteria by which this man—with a discourse on freedom that must certainly be called delusional (I devoted one of my seminars to it), with a concept of the real in which determinism is no more than an alibi that quickly becomes anxiety provoking when one tries to extend its field to chance (I had my audience experience this in a preliminary experiment), and with a belief that unites men, half the universe at least, under the symbol of Father Christmas (which no one can overlook)—would stop me from situating him, by legitimate analogy, in the category of social psychosis which, if I am not mistaken, Pascal established before me.

There is no doubt but that such a psychosis may turn out to be compatible with what is called an orderly state of affairs, but that does not authorize the psychiatrist, even if he is a psychoanalyst, to trust in his own compatibility with this orderly state to believe that he is in possession of an adequate idea of the *reality* to which his patient supposedly proves to be unequal.

Under these conditions, he would perhaps do better to jettison this idea from his assessment of the foundations of psychosis: which brings us back to the objective of its treatment.

To gauge the length of the path that separates us from it, suffice it to mention the mass of delays with which its pilgrims have marked it. Everyone knows that no discussion of the mechanism of transference, however learned it may be, has succeeded in stopping it from being conceived in practice as a relationship whose terms are purely dyadic and whose substratum is utterly confused.

If we simply consider transference on the basis of its fundamental nature as a repetition phenomenon, let me raise the question of what it is repeating in the persecuting persons Freud designates as its effect here.

I can just imagine the lame reply: "Following your approach, a paternal failing no doubt." In this vein, there has been no shortage of accounts of every kind: and the psychotic's "entourage" has been minutely scrutinized for all the so-called biographical and characterological tidbits the anamnesis enabled people to extract from the *dramatis personae*, even from their "interpersonal relations."[29]

Let us nevertheless proceed according to the structural terms I have outlined.

For psychosis to be triggered, the Name-of-the-Father—*verworfen*, foreclosed, that is, never having come to the place of the Other—must be summoned to that place in symbolic opposition to the subject.

It is the lack of the Name-of-the-Father in that place which, by the hole that it opens up in the signified, sets off a cascade of reworkings of the signifier from which the growing disaster of the imaginary proceeds, until the level is reached at which signifier and signified stabilize in a delusional metaphor.

But how can the Name-of-the-Father be summoned by the subject to the only place from which it could have come into being for him and in which it has never been? By nothing other than a real father, not at all necessarily by the subject's own father, but by One-father [*Un-père*].

Yet this One-father must still come to that place to which the subject could not summon him before. For this, the One-father need but situate himself in a tertiary position in any relationship that has as its base the imaginary couple *a-a´*—that is, ego-object or ideal-reality—involving the subject in the field of eroticized aggression that it induces.

We should try to detect this dramatic conjuncture at the beginning of each case of psychosis. Whether the conjuncture presents itself to a woman who has just given birth, in her husband's face, to a penitent confessing her sins in the person of her confessor, or to a girl in love in her encounter with "the young man's father," it will always be found, and it will be found more easily if one allows oneself to be guided by "situations" in the novelistic sense of the term. It should be noted in passing that these situations are the novelist's true resource—namely, the resource that brings out the "depth psychology" to which no psychological perspective can give him access.[30]

To move on now to the principle of foreclosure (*Verwerfung*) of the Name-of-the-Father, it must be admitted that the Name-of-the-Father redoubles in the Other's place the very signifier of the symbolic ternary, insofar as it constitutes the law of the signifier.

Provisionally admitting this can cost nothing, it seems, to those who—in their quest for the "environmental" coordinates of psychosis—wander like lost souls from the frustrating mother to the overfeeding mother, feeling nevertheless that in directing their attention to the father's situation, they are burning, as one says in the game of hide-the-thimble.

Even so, in this groping search for a paternal failing—the range of which is unsettling, including as it does the thundering father, the easy-going father, the all-powerful father, the humiliated father, the rigid father, the pathetic father, the stay-at-home father, and the father on the loose—it would probably be excessive to expect the following remark to provide a jolt of any kind: The effects of prestige that are at stake in all of this—and in which (thank heaven!) the ternary relation of the Oedipus complex is not

578

entirely omitted, since the mother's reverence is regarded as decisive in it—
boil down to the rivalry between the two parents in the subject's imaginary.
In other words, they boil down to what is articulated in the question that
regularly, not to say obligatorily, seems to be raised in any self-respecting
childhood: "Whom do you love more, daddy or mommy?"

My aim in drawing this parallel is not to reduce anything; quite the contrary, for this question—in which the child never fails to concretize the
disgust he feels at his parents' childishness—is precisely the question with
which the real children, who are the parents (in this sense, there are no other
children in the family but the parents), try to mask the mystery of their
union, or disunion as the case may be: namely, the mystery of what their kid
clearly knows to be the real problem and poses to himself as such.

People will say that they are emphasizing the bond of love and respect by
which the mother does or does not situate the father in his ideal place. It is
curious, I would reply first, that they do not make much of the same bonds
in the opposite direction, proving that the theory is complicit in the veil
thrown over the parents' coitus by childhood amnesia.

But what I want to stress is that we should concern ourselves not only
with the way the mother accommodates the father as a person, but also with
the importance she attributes to his speech—in a word, to his authority—in
other words, with the place she reserves for the Name-of-the-Father in the
promotion of the law.

Further still, the father's relation to this law must be considered in its own
right, for one will find in it the reason for the paradox whereby devastating
effects of the paternal figure are found with particular frequency in cases
where the father really functions as a legislator or boasts that he does—
whether he is, in fact, one of the people who makes the laws or presents himself as a pillar of faith, as a paragon of integrity or devotion, as virtuous or
a virtuoso, as serving a charitable cause whatever the object or lack thereof
that is at stake, as serving the nation or birth rate, safety or salubrity, legacy
or law, the pure, the lowest of the low, or the empire. These are all ideals that
provide him with all too many opportunities to seem to be at fault, to fall
short, and even to be fraudulent—in short, to exclude the Name-of-the-
Father from its position in the signifier.

This result can be obtained with still less, and no one who practices child
analysis will deny that children see right through hypocritical behavior, so
much so that it can be devastating to them. But who articulates that the lie
thus perceived implies a reference to the constitutive function of speech?

It thus turns out that a little severity is not excessive if we are to give the

579

most accessible experience its true meaning. The consequences that may be   580
expected of it in clinical examination and analytic technique can be gauged
elsewhere.

I am giving here only what is needed to perceive the clumsiness with
which the best inspired authors handle what they find most valuable in
following Freud on the ground of the preeminence that he grants to the
transference of the relation to the father in the genesis of psychosis.

Niederland provides a remarkable example of this when he draws attention to the delusional genealogy Schreber attributes to Flechsig. This
genealogy is constructed with the names of Schreber's own ancestors,
Gottfried, Gottlieb, Fürchtegott, and, above all, Daniel, which is handed
down from father to son and whose meaning in Hebrew he gives in order
to show—in their convergence on the name of God (*Gott*)—a symbolic
chain that is important in that it manifests the function of the father in the
delusion.[31]

But failing to distinguish in it the instance of the Name-of-the-Father—
and to recognize it, it obviously does not suffice that it be visible here to the
naked eye—Niederland misses the opportunity to grasp the chain in which
the erotic aggressions experienced by the subject are woven together, and
thereby to contribute to putting what must properly be termed "delusional
homosexuality" in its place.

How, then, could he have dwelt on what is concealed in the statement
quoted above from the first lines of Schreber's second chapter[32]—one of
those statements so obviously made in order not to be heard that they must
catch our ear. What, to take it literally, is the meaning of the fact that the
author equally links the names Flechsig and Schreber to soul murder in his
bid to take us to the crux of the abuse of which he is the victim? We must
leave something for future commentators to elucidate.

Just as uncertain is the attempt, made by Niederland in the same article,
to specify—starting with the subject this time, no longer with the signifier
(these terms are, of course, foreign to him)—the role of the paternal function in triggering the delusion.

Indeed, if Niederland claims that what occasioned the psychosis was   581
the mere assumption [*assomption*] of paternity by the subject, which is the
theme of his essay, then it is contradictory on his part to regard as equivalent the disappointment Schreber mentions of his hopes of becoming a
father and his appointment to the High Court, his title as *Senätspräsident*
emphasizing the quality of (conscripted) Father that it assigns him—this
being the sole reason Niederland gives for his second illness, the first being

explained analogously by our author by the failure of his candidacy for the Reichstag.

Whereas reference to the tertiary position, to which the signifier of paternity is summoned in all such cases, would be correct and would eliminate this contradiction.

But from the standpoint of my thesis, it is the primordial foreclosure (*Verwerfung*) that dominates everything with its problem, and the preceding considerations do not leave me unprepared.

For if we refer to the work of Daniel Gottlob Moritz Schreber—the founder of an Institute of Orthopedics at the University of Leipzig, an educator, or, better still, an "educationalist"* as they say in English, a social reformer "with an apostle-like mission to bring health, happiness and bliss to the masses" (sic, *Memoirs*, 1)[33] through physical culture, the initiator of those allotment gardens, intended to preserve in the employee a vegetable garden idealism, which in Germany are still known as *Schrebergärten*, not to mention the forty editions of *Medical Indoor Gymnastics*, of which the little "men cobbled together 1, 2, 3" that illustrate it are more or less explicitly mentioned by Schreber (S. 166)—we will be able to consider as having been exceeded the limits at which the native and the natal give way to nature, the natural, naturism, and even naturalization; at which virtue turns into vertigo, legacy into league, and salvation into saltation; at which the pure verges on the evil realm; and at which we will not be surprised if the child, like the apprentice sailor of Prévert's famous catch, sends packing (*verwerfe*) the whale of imposture, after having, according to the wit of this immortal piece, seen right through the pop [*percé la trame de père en part*].

582 There can be no doubt that the figure of Professor Flechsig, with his researcher's gravity (Macalpine's book contains a photograph that shows him profiled against a colossal enlargement of a cerebral hemisphere), did not succeed in supplementing the suddenly perceived void constituted by the inaugural *Verwerfung* (*"Kleiner Flechsig!"* "Little Flechsig!" proclaim the voices).

At least, this is Freud's conception, insofar as it designates the transference the subject developed to Flechsig as the factor that precipitated the subject into psychosis.

Thanks to which, a few months later, the divine jaculations make their concert heard in the subject in order to tell the Name-of-the-Father to go fuck itself, with the Name of God[34] right behind it, and to found the Son in his certainty that at the end of his trials, he could do no better than to "go"[35] on the whole world (S. 226).

The last word with which our century's "inner experience" has yielded

us its computation was thus articulated fifty years ahead of its time by the   583
theodicy to which Schreber was exposed: "God is a whore."[36]

This is the term in which the process by which the signifier was "unleashed" in the real culminates, after the Name-of-the-Father began to collapse—the latter being the signifier which, in the Other, qua locus of the signifier, is the signifier of the Other qua locus of the law.

I will leave this question prior to any possible treatment of the psychoses at that for the time being. It is a question that introduces, as we see, the conception to be formed of the handling of the transference in such treatment.

To say what we can do in this area would be premature, because it would now be to go "beyond Freud," and it is out of the question to go beyond Freud when psychoanalysis after Freud has, as I have said, returned to a pre-Freudian stage.

At least this is what keeps me from any other objective than that of restoring access to the experience Freud discovered.

For to use the technique he instituted outside the experience to which it applies is as stupid as to toil at the oars when one's ship is stuck in the sand.

December 1957–January 1958

Notes

1. Roman Jakobson borrows this term from Jespersen to designate those words in the code that take on meaning only from the coordinates (attribution, date, and place of emission) of the message. According to Pierce's classification, they are "index-symbols." Personal pronouns are the best example: the difficulties involved in their acquisition and their functional deficiencies illustrate the problematic generated by these signifiers in the subject. (Roman Jakobson, "Shifters, Verbal Categories, and the Russian Verb," Russian Language Project, Department of Slavic Languages and Literatures, Harvard University, 1957.)

2. See the seminar held February 8, 1956, in which I discussed the example of the "normal" vocalization of "la paix du soir."

3. *Denkwürdigkeiten eines Nervenkranken, von Dr. jur. Daniel Paul Schreber, Senätspräsident beim kgl. Oberlandesgericht Dresden a-D.* (Leipzig: Oswald Mutze, 1903), a French

translation of which I prepared for the use of my group.

4. This is, notably, the opinion expressed by the authors of the English translation of these *Memoirs*, which was published the year of my seminar (see *Memoirs of My Nervous Illness*, trans. Ida Macalpine and Richard Hunter, London: W. M. Dawson & Sons), in their introduction, p. 25. They also give an account of the book's success on pages 6–10.

5. This was my doctoral thesis in medicine, entitled *De la psychose paranoïaque dans ses rapports avec la personnalité*, which Professor Heuyer, in a letter to me, judged very pertinently in these terms: "One swallow does not make a summer," adding, in connection with my bibliography, "If you've read all that, I pity you." In fact, I had read it all.

6. The parentheses including the letter S followed by numbers will be used here to refer to the corresponding page of the origi-

nal edition of the *Denkwürdigkeiten*, the original pagination being fortunately provided in the margins of the English translation.

7. Note that my homage here is merely an extension of that of Freud, who did not shy away from recognizing in Schreber's delusion itself a foreshadowing of the theory of the libido (*GW* VIII, 315).

8. See *Écrits* 1966, 808.

9. He who wishes to prove too much goes astray. Thus Macalpine—who, by the way, advisedly dwells on the nature, said by the patient himself to be far too persuasive (S. 39), of the suggestive enthusiasm in which Professor Flechsig indulges (everything indicates that he was usually calmer) with Schreber regarding the benefits of a sleep-cure that he proposes to him—Macalpine, as I was saying, interprets at length the themes of procreation, which she considers to have been suggested by this discourse (see *Memoirs*, "Translators' Analysis of the Case," page 396, lines 12 and 21). She bases her case on the use of the verb "to deliver,"* to designate the effect on his problems to be expected from the treatment, and on that of the adjective "prolific,"* with which she translates, extremely loosely I might add, the German term, *ausgiebig*, applied to the sleep in question.

Now the term "to deliver"* is indisputable considering what it translates, for the simple reason that there is nothing here to translate. I scoured the German text searching for it. The verb was simply forgotten by either the author or the typesetter, and Macalpine, in her work of translation, restored it for us unbeknown to herself. The happiness she must later have felt upon finding that it fit the bill so well was surely well deserved!

10. *Memoirs*, 361, 379–80.

11. I would ask Macalpine (see *Memoirs*, 391–92) whether the number nine, insofar as it is involved in such diverse durations as nine hours, nine days, nine months, and nine years, which she underscores at every point in the patient's anamnesis—finding it again in the time on the clock up until which his anxiety postponed the beginning of the afore-mentioned sleep-cure, and even in the hesitation between four and five days that recurs several times in one and the same period of his personal recollection—must be conceived as forming part as such (that is, as a symbol) of the imaginary relation she isolates as a procreation fantasy.

The question is of concern to everyone, for it differs from the use Freud, in the Wolf Man case, makes of the form of the Roman numeral V, presumably recalled as having been seen at the end of the clock hand during a scene the Wolf Man witnessed at age one and a half, finding it anew in the opening and shutting of a butterfly's wings, in a girl's spread legs, etc.

12. See *Memoirs*, 13–19.

13. "Before Sunrise," "Vor Sonnenaufgang," in *Also sprach Zarathustra*, Part III. It is the fourth song in this third part.

14. It is interesting to situate object *a* in the R schema so as to shed light on what it contributes regarding the field of reality (a field that bars it).

However much emphasis I have placed on developing it since I wrote this article—by stating that this field functions only when obturated by the screen of fantasy—it still requires a great deal of attention.

There may be some point in indicating that—while it was enigmatic at the time, even though it is perfectly legible to anyone who knows what came later, as is the case if one claims to be basing oneself on it—what the R schema lays flat is a cross-cap.

In particular, the points—and I did not choose the letters that correspond to them at random (or for fun)—*m* M and *i* I, which are those by which the only valid cut in this schema (the cut $\overrightarrow{mi}$, $\overrightarrow{MI}$) is framed, suffice to indicate that this cut isolates a Möbius strip in the field.

This says it all, since this field will henceforth be the mere placeholder of the fantasy whose entire structure is provided by this cut.

I mean that only the cut reveals the structure of the entire surface, because it is able to detach from it the following two heterogeneous elements (noted in my algorithm ($\$\Diamond a$)

of fantasy):$— the barred S of the strip to be expected here where it in fact turns up, that is, covering the field **R** of reality—and *a*, which corresponds to the fields **I** and **S**.

It is thus as representation's representative in fantasy—that is, as the originally repressed subject—that $, the barred S of desire, props up the field of reality here; and this field is sustained only by the extraction of object *a*, which nevertheless gives it its frame.

Measuring in increments [*échelons*] that are all vectorialized by an intrusion into the field **R** of the field **I** alone, which is articulated clearly in my text only as the effect of narcissism, shows that it is obviously out of the question that I wanted to bring back in, through some back door, the notion that these effects ("system of identifications," as we read) can theoretically ground reality in any way whatsoever.

Those who have attended my topological presentations (which are justified by nothing but the structure, that remains to be articulated, of fantasy) must surely know that there is nothing measurable that need be preserved in the structure of the Möbius strip, and that this structure boils down—like the real with which we are concerned here—to the cut itself.

This note indicates the current stage of my topological work (July 1966).

15. The title of that seminar.

16. Here is the text: *Einleitend habe ich dazu zu bemerken, dass bei der Genesis der betreffenden Entwicklung deren erste Anfänge weit, vielleicht bis zum 18. Jahrhundert zurückreichen, einertheils* die Namen Flechsig und Schreber (my emphasis) *(wahrscheinlich nicht in der Beschränkung auf je ein Individuum der betreffenden Familien) und anderntheils der Begriff des* Seelenmords (in "*Sperrdruck*" [emphasized] in the original) *eine Hauptrolle spielen.*

17. See, in particular, Ernst Haeckel's *Natürliche Schöpfungsgeschichte* (Berlin, 1872) and Otto Casari's *Urgeschichte der Menschheit* (Leipzig: Brockhaus, 1877).

18. The relationship between the proper name and the voice must be situated in language's two-axis structure of message and

code, to which I have already referred. See section I.5 above. It is this structure that makes puns on proper names into witticisms.

19. *Memoirs*, 398.

20. This is the spelling of the English word currently in use in Hugues Salel's admirable verse translation of the first ten songs of the *Iliad*; it should suffice to ensure that this spelling survives in French.

21. "Die symbolische Gleichung Mädchen = Phallus," *Int. Zeitschrift für Psychoanalyse* XXII (1936), since translated into English as "The Symbolic Equation: Girl = Phallus" and published in *PQ* XX, 3 (1949): 303–24. French allows us to translate the term more appropriately as *pucelle* ["maid," "maiden," or "virgin"].

22. See W. G. Niederland, "Three Notes on the Schreber Case," *PQ* XX, 4 (1951): 579–91. Édouard Pichon is the author of the translation into French of these terms as "Shadows of men thrown together 1, 2, 3."

23. See Jean-Marc Alby's highly remarkable thesis, "Contribution à l'étude du transsexualisme," Paris, 1956.

24. See Freud, *Psychoanalytische Bemerkungen über einem autobiographisch beschriebenen Fall von Paranoia*, *GW* VIII, 264, fn1.

25. Freud, *GW* VIII, 284 and note.

26. S. 136.

27. At the acme of imaginary dissolution, the subject showed, in his delusional apperception, odd recourse to the following criterion of reality, which is to always return to the same place, and why the stars eminently represent it: this is the theme designated by his voices as "tying-to-the-planets" (*Anbinden an Erden*, S. 125).

28. "Remarks on Psychical Causality" (Paper given on September 28, 1946, at the Journées de Bonneval); see *Écrits* 1966, 151–93.

29. See André Green's thesis, *Le milieu familial des schizophrènes* (Paris, 1957), a work whose clear merit would not have suffered if surer landmarks had guided him toward greater success—in particular, in approaching what he bizarrely terms "psychotic fracture."

30. I wish the best of luck to the student of mine who followed up this remark, wherein literary criticism can rest assured it holds a thread that will not lead it astray.

31. Niederland, "Three Notes."

32. This sentence is quoted in the footnote on page 558 [page 213, note 16] above.

33. In a note on the same page, Macalpine quotes the title of one of this author's books, *Glückseligkeitslehre für das physische Leben des Menschen*, namely, "Course in Blessed Felicity for the Physical Life of Men."

34. S. 194. *Die Redensart "Ei verflucht" ... war noch ein Uberbleibsel der Grundsprache, in welcher die Worte "Ei verflucht, das sagt sich schwer" jedesmal gebraucht werden, wenn irgend ein mit der Weltordnung unerträgliche Erscheinung in das Bewusstsein der Seelen trat, ʒ. B. "Ei verflucht, das sagt sich schwer, dass der liebe Gott sich f ... lässt."*

35. I think I can borrow this euphemism from the *Grundsprache*'s own register, which the voices and Schreber himself nevertheless uncharacteristically dispense with here.

I think I can better fulfill the duties of scientific rigor by pointing out the hypocrisy which, in this detour as in others, reduces what Freudian experience demonstrates to something benign, nay, inane. I mean the indefinable use ordinarily made of references like the following: "At this moment in his analysis, the patient regressed to the anal phase." I'd like to see the analyst's face if the patient started "straining," or even just slobbering, on his couch.

All this is but a concealed return to the sublimation that finds shelter in the *inter urinas et faeces nascimur*, implying here that this sordid origin concerns only our bodies.

What analysis uncovers is something altogether different. It is not man's rags, but his very being that takes up its position among the scraps in which his first frolics found their cortege—inasmuch as the law of symbolization, in which his desire must become engaged, catches him in its net by the position as part-object in which he offers himself up on coming into the world, into a world where the Other's desire lays down the law.

This relationship is, of course, clearly articulated by Schreber in what he relates—to put it in such a way as to leave no room for ambiguity—to the act of shitting: namely, the fact of feeling the elements of his being, whose dispersal into the infinitude of his delusion constitutes his suffering, coming together in it.

36. In the form: *Die Sonne ist eine Hure* (S. 384). For Schreber, the sun is God's central aspect. The inner experience I am speaking of here is a reference to Georges Bataille's work. In *Madame Edwarda*, he describes the odd extremity of this experience.

The Direction of the Treatment and the Principles of Its Power

Paper given at the Royaumont Colloquium held July 10–13, 1958[1]

I. Who Analyzes Today?

1. People say that an analysis bears the marks of the analysand as a person as if it were self-evident. But they think they are being audacious if they take an interest in the effects that the analyst as a person may have on an analysis. This, at least, explains the shudder that runs through us when trendy remarks are made about countertransference, which contribute, no doubt, to masking its conceptual impropriety: just think of the highminded-ness we display when we show that we ourselves are made of the same clay as those we shape!

That was a nasty thing to say. Yet it barely suffices for those it targets, given that people now go about proclaiming, under the aegis of psycho-analysis, that they are working toward "the patient's emotional reeduca-tion" [22].[2]

Situating the analyst's action at this level implies a position based on a principle, with respect to which anything that might be said about counter-transference, even if it were not futile, would merely serve as a diversion. For the imposture that I wish to dislodge here now lies beyond this.[3]

I am not, for all that, denouncing the anti-Freudian aspects of contempo-rary psychoanalysis. Indeed, we should be grateful to the partisans of the latter for throwing down their mask in this regard, priding themselves, as

they do, on going beyond what they, in fact, know nothing about, having
586 retained just enough of Freud's doctrine to sense how significantly what
they are led to enunciate about their experience diverges from it.

I intend to show how the inability to authentically sustain a praxis results,
as is common in the history of mankind, in the exercise of power.

2. Assuredly, a psychoanalyst directs the treatment. The first principle of
this treatment, the one that is spelled out to him before all else, and which he
finds throughout his training, so much so that he becomes utterly imbued
with it, is that he must not direct the patient. The direction of conscience, in
the sense of the moral guidance a faithful Catholic might find in it, is radically excluded here. If psychoanalysis raises problems for moral theology,
they are not those of the direction of conscience—which, let me remind
you, also raises problems.

The direction of the treatment is something else altogether. It consists,
first of all, in getting the subject to apply the fundamental rule of psychoanalysis, that is, the directives whose presence at the heart of what is called
"the analytic situation" cannot be neglected, under the pretext that the subject would best apply them without thinking about it.

These directives are initially laid out to the patient in the form of instruc-
tions which, however little the analyst comments on them, convey, even in
the very inflections of his statement of them, the doctrine the analyst himself has arrived at. Which does not mean that the analyst remains unscathed
by the mass of prejudices that await him in the patient, based on the idea the
latter has been allowed to form of the procedures and aim of the psychoanalytic enterprise by the spreading of notions about analysis in his culture.

This is already enough to show us that, from the initial directives on, the
problem of direction cannot be formulated along the lines of univocal communication—a fact that forces us to go no further in our discussion of this
stage and to shed light on it by what follows it.

Let us simply state that, if we reduce it to its truth, this stage consists in
getting the patient to forget that it is merely a matter of words, but that this
does not excuse the analyst for forgetting it himself [16].

3. In any case, I announced that I intended to approach the topic from the
analyst's vantage point.
587 Let us say that in the capital outlay involved in the common enterprise,
the patient is not alone in finding it difficult to pay his share. The analyst too
must pay:

- pay with words no doubt, if the transmutation they undergo due to the analytic operation raises them to the level of their effect as interpretation;
- but also pay with his person, in that, whether he likes it or not, he lends it as a prop for the singular phenomena analysis discovered in transference;
- can anyone forget that he must pay for becoming enmeshed in an action that goes right to the core of being (*Kern unseres Wesens*, as Freud put it [6]) with what is essential in his most intimate judgment: could he alone remain on the sidelines?

Let those who support my cause not be concerned at the thought that I am exposing myself here once again to adversaries who are always only too happy to dismiss me for my metaphysics.

For it is at the heart of their claim to be satisfied with effectiveness that a statement like "the analyst cures not so much by what he says and does as by what he is" [22] can be made. Nobody, apparently, demands an explanation from the author for such a remark, any more than one appeals to his sense of modesty when, with a tired smile directed at the ridicule he incurs, he puts his trust in goodness, his own goodness (we must be good, there being no transcendence in this context), to put an end to a dead-end debate about transference neurosis.[4] But who would be so cruel as to question someone buckling under the weight of his luggage, when his posture clearly indicates that it is full of bricks?

Yet being is being, regardless of who invokes it, and we have the right to ask what it is doing here.

4. So I shall cross-examine the analyst again, insofar as I myself am one, in order to note that the more his being is involved, the less sure he is of his action.

As an interpreter of what is presented to me in words or deeds, I choose my own oracle and articulate it as I please, sole master of my ship after God;   588
and while, of course, I am far from able to weigh the whole effect of my words, I am well aware of the fact and strive to attend to it. In other words, I am always free in the timing and frequency, as well as in the choice of my interventions, so much so that it seems that the rule has been entirely designed so as not to interfere in any way with my activity as an executor— to which corresponds the aspect of "material," which is how my action here takes up what it produces.

5. In handling transference, on the other hand, my freedom is alienated by the splitting my person undergoes in it, and everyone knows that it is here that

the secret of analysis must be sought. This does not prevent people from believing they are making progress with the following learned remark: that psychoanalysis must be studied as a situation involving two persons. To be sure, conditions are placed on it that restrict its movements, but the situation thus conceived nevertheless serves to articulate (and with no more artifice than the aforementioned "emotional reeducation") the principles for training the so-called "weak" ego, by an ego that one likes to believe capable of carrying out such a project because it is strong. That such a view is not expressed without a certain embarrassment is shown by the strikingly clumsy repentances that are offered, like that of the author who specifies that he does not compromise on the need for a "cure from the inside" [22].[5] But it is all the more significant to observe that the subject's assent, referred to in this passage, comes only secondarily, from an effect that was at first imposed.

It is not for my own pleasure that I point out these deviations, but rather to use their pitfalls as markers for our route.

In fact, every analyst (even those who wander off course in this way) always experiences the transference in wonder at this least expected effect of a relationship between two people that would seem to be like any other. He tells himself that he has to deal with a phenomenon for which he is not responsible, and we know with what insistence Freud stressed the spontaneity of its appearance in the patient.

589   For some time now, analysts—in the heartrending revisions they treat us to—have willingly insinuated that this insistence, with which they for so long built a wall around themselves, expressed a flight on Freud's part from the commitment that the notion of situation presupposes. "We are, you see, up to date," they seem to say.

But it is rather the facile excitement of their gesture in dumping feelings, which they class under the heading of their countertransference, onto one side of the scales—the situation balancing out due to the weight of those feelings—that to me is evidence of a troubled conscience corresponding to a failure to conceptualize the true nature of transference.

One cannot reason from the fantasies the analysand gets propped up to the analyst's person in the same way as an ideal player guesses his opponent's intentions. There is probably always an element of strategy, but one should not be deceived by the metaphor of the mirror, appropriate as it may be to the smooth surface the analyst presents to the patient. An impassive face and sealed lips do not have the same purpose here as in bridge. Instead, the analyst enlists the aid of what in bridge is called the dummy [*le mort*], but he does so in order to bring out the fourth player who is to be the analysand's partner here, and whose hand the analyst, by his maneuvers, strives to get the analysand to guess: such is the restraint—of abnegation, as it were—that is imposed on the analyst by the stakes of the game in analysis.

One might pursue the metaphor by deducing his game therefrom according to whether he places himself "to the right" or "to the left" of the patient—in other words, in a position to play his cards after or before the fourth player, that is, before or after the latter by using the dummy.

But what is certain is that the analyst's feelings have only one possible place in the game, that of the dummy; and that if the dummy is revived the game will proceed without anyone knowing who is leading it.

This is why the analyst is less free in his <u>strategy</u> than in his <u>tactics</u>.

6. Let us go further. The analyst is even less free in what dominates both his strategy and tactics—namely, his politics, where he would do better to take his bearings from his want-to-be than from his being.

To put it another way: his action concerning the patient will escape him along with the idea he forms of his action, as long as he does not reconsider its point of departure in terms of what makes his action possible and does not preserve the paradox of its quadripartition, in order to revise at the core the structure by which all action intervenes in reality.

For contemporary psychoanalysts, this relationship to reality is self-evident. They gauge the patient's defections from it using the authoritarian principle that has been employed by educators since time immemorial. They simply rely on training analysis to ensure its maintenance at a sufficient rate among analysts, about whom one can't help feeling that, in facing the problems of humanity that are addressed to them, their views are sometimes a bit parochial. This is merely to push the problem back to an individual level.

And it is hardly reassuring—when they describe the procedure of analysis as the reduction in the subject of deviations, attributed to his transference and his resistances, but mapped in relation to reality—to hear them gush about the "perfectly simple situation" that is provided by analysis as a means of assessing those deviations. Come now! The educator is hardly ready to be educated if he can judge so superficially an experience that he, too, must nevertheless have undergone.

From such an assessment, one assumes that these analysts would have provided this experience with other means if they had had to depend on their own sense of reality to invent it themselves: a priority shocking to imagine. They half-suspect as much, and that is why they are so punctilious about preserving its forms.

590

One understands why, in order to prop up so obviously precarious a conception, certain individuals on the other side of the Atlantic felt the need to introduce a stable value here, a standard by which to measure reality [*réel*]: the autonomous ego*. It is the supposedly organized set of the most disparate functions that lend their support to the subject's feeling of innateness. It is regarded as autonomous because it is supposed to be sheltered from the person's internal conflicts ("nonconflictual sphere"*) [14].

One recognizes here a worn-out mirage that the most academic introspective psychology had already rejected as untenable. Yet this regression is celebrated as a return to the fold of "general psychology."

Be that as it may, it solves the problem of the analyst's being.[6] A team of egos*, no doubt less equal than autonomous (but by what stamp of origin do they recognize each other in the sufficiency of their autonomy?), offers itself to Americans to guide them toward happiness*, without upsetting the autonomies, whether egoistic or not, that pave with their nonconflictual spheres the American way* of getting there.

7. Let me summarize. If an analyst dealt only with resistances, he would look twice before hazarding an interpretation, which he in fact does, but this prudence would suffice.

However, this interpretation, if he gives it, will be received as coming from the person the transference imputes him to be. Will he agree to take advantage of this error concerning who he is? Psychoanalytic morals do not forbid it, on the condition that he interpret this effect, failing which the analysis would remain at the level of crude suggestion.

This is an indisputable position, except that the analyst's speech is still heard as coming from the transferential Other, and the subject's exit from the transference is thus postponed *ad infinitum*.

It is therefore because of what the subject imputes the analyst to be (his being being elsewhere) that an interpretation may come back to the place from which it can bear upon the distribution of responses.

But who will say what the analyst is there, and what remains of him when he is up against the wall of the task of interpreting? Let him dare say it himself if the fact that he is a man is all he has by way of an answer. Whether he has any or not would then be all there is to it: yet it is here that he beats a retreat, not only on account of the impudence of the mystery, but because in this having, it is being that is at stake, and how! We shall see later that this "how" is no easy matter.

Thus he prefers to fall back on his ego, and on the reality about which he knows a thing or two. But here he is, then, at the level of "I" and "me" with his patient. How can he manage it if they're at each other's throats? It is here that we astutely count on the secret contacts we must have on the inside—named, in this case, the healthy part *of the ego*, the part that thinks like us.

We might conclude that this brings us back to our initial problem—namely, how to reinvent analysis.

Or to recast it: by treating transference as a particular form of resistance.   592

Many profess to do so. It is to them that I would ask the question that forms the title of this chapter: Who is the analyst? He who interprets by taking advantage of the transference? He who analyzes transference as resistance? Or he who imposes his idea of reality?

It is a question that may pinch a bit harder those to whom it is addressed, and be less easy to sidestep than the question, "Who is speaking?" which one of my students blared into their ears regarding the patient. For their impatient answer—"An animal of our species"—to a changed question would be more annoyingly tautological, to have to say: "Me [*moi*]."

And that's all there is to it.

II. What Is the Place of Interpretation?

1. The preceding does not answer all the questions that occur to a novice. But in gathering together the problems currently raised concerning the direction of an analysis, insofar as this currency reflects contemporary practice, I think I have kept everything in proportion.

Which is to say, the smaller place occupied by interpretation in present-day psychoanalysis—not that people no longer know the meaning of interpretation, but they seem to be embarrassed when they approach it. No author tackles interpretation without first distinguishing it from every other form of verbal intervention that does not constitute interpretation: explanations, gratifications, responses to demands, and so on. This process becomes revealing when it gets close to the center of interest. It stipulates that even something said to lead the subject to an insight* into one of his behaviors, especially its signification as resistance, may be given any other name, "confrontation," for example, if only confrontation of the subject with his own words, without deserving the name "interpretation," simply because it is a clarifying statement.

It is touching to see an author attempt to storm Gestalt theory to find in it a metaphor that would allow him to express what interpretation brings by way of resolution to an ambiguity of intention, and by way of closure to an   593
incompleteness that is nevertheless achieved only after the fact [2].

2. One senses that what is slippery here is the nature of the transmutation that occurs in the subject; this is all the more painful for thought in that it eludes thought at the very moment thought shifts into action. Indeed, no index suffices to show where interpretation operates, unless one accepts in all its radical implications a concept of the function of the signifier, which grasps where it is that the subject subordinates himself to the signifier to so great an extent that he is suborned by it.

In order to decipher the diachrony of unconscious repetitions, interpretation must introduce into the synchrony of signifiers that come together there something that suddenly makes translation possible—this is precisely what is allowed by the function of the Other in the possession of the code, it being in relation to that Other that the missing element appears.

This importance of the signifier in the localization of analytic truth appears implicitly when an author holds firmly to the internal coherence of analytic experience in defining aporias. One should read Edward Glover to gauge the price he pays for not having the term "signifier" at his disposal. In articulating the most relevant views, he finds interpretation everywhere, even in the banality of a medical prescription, being unable to set any limits to it. He even goes so far as to say, quite simply—without our being sure he knows what he is saying—that symptom formation is an inexact interpretation on the subject's part [13].

Conceived of in this way, interpretation becomes a sort of phlogiston: it is manifest in everything that is understood rightly or wrongly, as long as it feeds the flame of the imaginary, of that pure display which, going by the name of aggressiveness, flourishes in the technique of that period (1931—new enough to still be current today [13]).

It is only insofar as interpretation culminates in the here and now of this game that it can be distinguished from the reading of the *signatura rerum*, regarding which Jung tries to outdo Böhme. To follow it there would hardly suit the being of our analysts.

But to keep time with Freud requires a very different tablature, one for which it is useful to know how to take the clock apart.

594   3. My doctrine of the signifier is first of all a discipline, in which those I train have to familiarize themselves with the ways the signifier effects the advent of the signified, which is the only way of conceiving how it is that interpretation, by inscribing itself therein, can produce anything new.

For interpretation is not grounded in some assumption of divine archetypes, but in the fact that the unconscious has the radical structure of language and that a material operates in the unconscious according to certain laws, which are the same laws as those discovered in the study of natural languages [*langues*]—that is, languages [*langues*] that are or were actually spoken.

The phlogiston metaphor, which was suggested to me a moment ago by Glover, derives its appropriateness from the error it evokes: signification no more emanates from life than phlogiston escapes from bodies in combustion. We should speak of signification rather as of the combination of life with the O atom of the sign[7]—the sign insofar as it first of all connotes presence *or* absence, by essentially introducing the *and* that links them, since in connoting presence or absence, it institutes presence against a background of absence, just as it constitutes absence in presence.

One will recall that with characteristic sureness of step in his field, Freud, seeking a model of repetition automatism, stopped at the crossroads formed by a game of occultation and an alternating scansion of two phonemes, whose conjugation by a child made a striking impression on him.

At the same time, we also see in the game that the value of the object is insignificant (the object the child causes to appear and disappear), and that phonetic perfection is less important than phonemic distinction—no one would dispute that Freud was right to translate it immediately by the *Fort!* *Da!* of the German he as an adult spoke [9].

This is the point of insemination for a symbolic order that preexists the infantile subject and in accordance with which he has to structure himself.

4. I will spare myself the task of providing the rules of interpretation. It is not that they cannot be formulated, but their formulations presuppose developments that I cannot presume to be known, since I cannot give a condensed account of them here.

I will confine myself to remarking that, in reading the classical commentaries on interpretation, I always regret how little is made of the very facts people supply.

To give an example, everyone acknowledges in his own way that to confirm that an interpretation is well founded, it is not the conviction with which it is received by the subject that counts, its well-foundedness instead being gauged by the material that emerges afterward.

But psychologizing superstition has such a powerful grip on our minds that people always seek out the phenomenon of well-foundedness in the subject's assent, entirely overlooking the consequences of what Freud says about *Verneinung* [negation] as a form of avowal—to say the least,

595

negation by the subject cannot be treated as equivalent to drawing a blank.

This is how theory translates the way in which resistance is engendered in practice. It is also what I am trying to convey when I say that there is no other resistance to analysis than that of the analyst himself.

5. The problem is that contemporary authors seem to have gotten the sequence of analytic effects backward. According to them, interpretation is but hesitant stammering compared to the opening up of a broader relationship in which, at last, we understand each other ("from the inside," no doubt).

Interpretation becomes necessary here because the subject's weakness requires our assistance. It is also something that is very difficult to get his weakness to swallow without rejecting it. It is both at once—in other words, a very awkward means.

But what we have here is only the effect of the analyst's passions: his fear, which is not of making a mistake but of displaying his ignorance; his taste, which is not to satisfy but not to disappoint; his need, which is not to govern but to keep the upper hand. It has nothing to do with countertransference on the part of this or that analyst; it has to do with the consequences of the dyadic relation, if the therapist does not overcome it, and how could he overcome it when he views it as the ideal of his action?

Primum vivere, no doubt: a break must be avoided. That the practice of common decency should be classified as a technique to be taught so that breaks are avoided is one thing. But to confuse this physical necessity, the patient's presence at his appointment, with an analytic relationship is a mistaken notion that will mislead the novice for a long time.

6. From this point of view, transference becomes the analyst's security, and the subject's relation to reality [*réel*] becomes the terrain on which the outcome of the battle is determined. Interpretation, which was postponed until the transference was consolidated, now becomes subordinate to its liquidation.

As a result, interpretation is absorbed into a kind of "working through"*—that one can quite simply translate by "work of transference" [*travail du transfert*]—which serves as an alibi for a sort of revenge the analyst takes for his initial timidity, that is, for an insistence that opens the door to all kinds of forcing, placed under the banner of "strengthening the ego" [21–22].

7. But has anyone observed, in criticizing Freud's approach, as presented for example in the case of the Rat Man, that what surprises us as a preliminary indoctrination is due simply to the fact that Freud proceeds in exactly the opposite order? For he begins by introducing the patient to an initial situating of his position in reality [*réel*], even if this situating leads to a precipitation—I would even go so far as to say a systematization—of symptoms [8].

Another well-known example: Freud brings Dora to realize that she has done more than merely participate in the great disorder of her father's world, whose damaging consequences she complains of—she has made herself its linchpin, and it could not have continued without her connivance [7].

I have long stressed the Hegelian procedure at work in this reversal of positions of the beautiful soul in relation to the reality he accuses. The point is not to adapt him to it, but to show him that he is only too well adapted to it, since he assists in its very fabrication.

But the path to be followed with the other ends here. For the transference has already done its job, demonstrating that what is at stake is something altogether different than relations between the ego and the world.

Freud does not always seem to find his way about very well in the transference in the cases he describes. And that is why they are so precious.

597

For he immediately recognized that the crux [*principe*] of his power lay in the transference—in which respect it did not differ from suggestion—but also that this power only gave him a way out of the problem on the condition that he not use it, for it was then that it took on its whole transferential development.

From then on he no longer addressed the person who was in his proximity, which is why he refused to work face to face with him.

Interpretation in Freud's work is so bold that, in popularizing it, we no longer recognize its import as mantic. When Freud exposes a tendency—what he calls *Trieb*, which is altogether different from an instinct—the freshness of the discovery prevents us from seeing the advent of a signifier that the *Trieb* in itself implies. But when Freud brings to light what can only be called the subject's lines of fate, what we ponder is Tiresias' face confronting the ambiguity where his verdict operates.

For the lines that are divined here have so little to do with the subject's ego, or with anything he may make present here and now in the dyadic relation, that in the case of the Rat Man, it is by a direct hit on the pact that presided over his parents' marriage (that is, on something that occurred well before the Rat Man was born) that Freud finds several conditions intermingled in it—honor just barely saved, emotional betrayal, social compromise, and prescribed debt, of which the great compulsive scenario that led the patient to him seems to be the cryptographic copy—and finally manages to explain the impasses in which the Rat Man's moral life and desire go astray.

But the most striking thing about it is that access to this material was rendered possible only by an interpretation in which Freud relies too heavily on the idea that the Rat Man's father had prohibited his son from marrying the girl to whom he was sublimely devoted, in order to explain the impossibility that seems to have blocked this relationship for him in every way. An interpretation which, to say the least, is inexact, since it is contradicted by the reality it presumes, but which is nevertheless true in the sense that, in it, Freud evinces an intuition that anticipates my own contribution regarding the function of the Other in obsessive neurosis. I have demonstrated that this function may be served, in obsessive neurosis, by a dead man [*un mort*], and that in this case it could not be better served than by the father, insofar as the Rat Man's father had, by his death, acceded to the position Freud recognized as that of the absolute Father.

8. I will ask those who have read my work and who have attended my seminar to forgive me for citing examples with which they are already familiar.

I am doing so not only because I cannot make use of my own analyses to demonstrate the level interpretation reaches—when the interpretation, proving to be coextensive with the subject's history, cannot be communicated in the communicating milieu in which many of my analyses take place without the risk of betraying the subject's identity. For I have succeeded at times in saying enough about a case without saying too much, that is, in conveying my example without anyone, except the person in question, recognizing it.

Nor is it because I regard the Rat Man as a case that Freud cured—for if I were to add that I do not think that the analysis is entirely unconnected with the tragic conclusion of his story by death on the battlefield, what an opportunity for contempt I would be offering to those who wish to find fault!

What I am saying is that it is in a direction of the treatment, ordered, as I have just shown, in accordance with a process that begins with rectification of the subject's relations with reality [*réel*], and proceeds to development of the transference and then to interpretation, that is situated the horizon at which the fundamental discoveries, which we are still living off, surrendered themselves to Freud concerning the dynamics and structure of obsessive neurosis. Nothing more, but nothing less either.

598

The question now is whether we have lost this horizon by reversing this order.

9. What we can say is that the new pathways by which the approach laid out by the discoverer has supposedly been authenticated are proof of terminological confusion that can only be exposed in particular cases. I will thus take an example that has already contributed to my teaching; it has, of course, been chosen from a first-rate author who, by virtue of his background, is particularly attuned to the dimension of interpretation. I am referring to Ernst Kris and to a case which—he does not hide the fact—he took over from Melitta Schmidcberg [15].

It concerns a subject inhibited in his intellectual life and particularly incapable of publishing his research on account of an impulse to plagiarize, which, it seems, he was unable to control. Such was the subjective drama.

599

Melitta Schmideberg had understood it as the recurrence of an adolescent delinquency [25]; the subject stole sweets and books, and it was from this angle that she had undertaken the analysis of the unconscious conflict.

Ernst Kris gently approaches the case anew in accordance with a more methodical interpretation, one that proceeds from the surface to the depths, he says. The fact that he credits this interpretation to "ego* psychology" à la Hartmann, whose supporter he felt he had to become, is incidental to an assessment of what takes place. Ernst Kris changes perspective on the case and claims to give the subject insight* for a new departure on the basis of a fact that is merely a repetition of his compulsion, but regarding which Kris quite commendably does not content himself with what the patient says. And when the patient claims to have taken, in spite of himself, the ideas for a piece that he has just completed from a book which, on being remembered, enabled him to check it after the fact, Kris looks at the evidence and discovers that nothing has apparently gone beyond what is implied by a shared field of research. In short, having assured himself that his patient is not a plagiarist when he thinks he is, he sets out to show him that he wants to be one in order to prevent himself from really being one—which is what we call analyzing the defense before the drive, the latter being manifested here in an attraction to others' ideas.

This intervention may be presumed to be erroneous, owing simply to the fact that it presupposes that defense and drive are concentric, the one being molded, as it were, around the other.

What proves that it is, in fact, erroneous is the very thing Kris thinks confirms his intervention—namely, that just when he feels he can ask the patient what he thinks of the tables being turned in this way, the patient, daydreaming for a moment, replies that for some time, on leaving his sessions, he has wandered along a street full of attractive little restaurants, scrutinizing their menus in search of his favorite dish: fresh brains.

An admission which, rather than sanctioning the felicity of the intervention by way of the material it contributes, seems to me to have the corrective value of an acting out* in the very report he gives of it.

The post-session condiment the patient sniffs out seems to me rather to tell the dinner host that the condiment had been sorely lacking during the meal. However compulsive he may be about smelling it, it is a hint*; being a transitory symptom, no doubt, it warns the analyst that he is barking up the wrong tree.

Indeed, you are barking up the wrong tree, I would continue, addressing the late Ernst Kris, as I remember him at the Marienbad Congress where, the day after my address on the mirror stage, I took my leave, anxious as I was to get a feeling for the spirit of the time—a time full of promises—at the Olympics in Berlin. He kindly objected, "ça ne se fait pas!" ("That isn't done!"), having already acquired that penchant for the respectable that perhaps influenced his approach here.

Was this what misled you, Ernst Kris, or was it simply that while your intentions may have been upright, and your judgment indubitably so as well, things themselves were askew?

It's not the fact that your patient doesn't steal that is important here. It's that he doesn't . . . Not "doesn't": it's that he steals *nothing*. And that's what you should have conveyed to him.

Contrary to what you believe, it's not his defense against the idea of stealing that makes him believe he is stealing. It's that he may have an idea of his own which never occurs to him or barely crosses his mind.

It is thus useless to engage him in a process of separating out what more or less original ideas his friend filches from him when they chew the fat together, which God himself could not determine.

Couldn't this craving for fresh brains refresh your own concepts, and remind you of the function of metonymy in Roman Jakobson's work? I shall return to this later.

You speak of Melitta Schmideberg as if she had confused delinquency with the id. I am not so sure, and the wording of the title of the article in which she discusses this case suggests a metaphor to me.

You treat the patient as if he were obsessed, but he throws you a line with his food fantasy, giving you the opportunity to be a quarter-of-an-hour

ahead of the nosology of your time by providing a diagnosis of anorexia   601
nervosa [*anorexie mentale*]. You would simultaneously refresh, by giving
them back their true meaning, this couple of terms which current usage has
reduced to the dubious status of an etiological indication.

Anorexia, in this case, concerns the mental realm, concerns the desire on
which the idea lives, and this leads us to the scurvy that rages on the raft on
which I embark him with the skinny virgins.

Their symbolically motivated refusal seems to me to have a good deal to
do with the patient's aversion to what he thinks. His daddy, you tell us, was
not very resourceful when it came to ideas. Could it be that the grandfather,
who was celebrated for his ideas, disgusted him of them? How can we
know? You are surely right to make the signifier "grand," included in the
kinship term ["grandfather"], nothing less than the origin of the rivalry
played out with the father over who could catch the biggest [*le plus grand*]
fish. But this purely formal challenge* seems to me rather to mean: nothing
doing.

Your progress, supposedly from the surface, thus has nothing in common
with subjective rectification, highlighted above in Freud's method, where,
moreover, it isn't motivated by any kind of topographical priority.

The fact is that this rectification is also dialectical in Freud's work. It
takes off from the subject's own words in order to come back to them, which
means that an interpretation can be exact only by being . . . an interpretation.

To side here with the objective situation is going too far, if only because
plagiarism is relative to the customs in force.[8]

But the idea that the surface is the level of the superficial is itself dan-
gerous.

Another topology is necessary if we are not to be mistaken as to the place
of desire.

To wipe desire off the map [*carte*] when it is already covered over in the   602
patient's landscape is not the best way of following Freud's teaching.

Nor is it a way of getting rid of depth, for it is on the surface that depth
is seen, as when one's face breaks out in pimples on holidays.

III. Where Do We Stand Regarding Transference?

1. We must look to the work of my colleague, Daniel Lagache, for an accurate history of the writings devoted—around Freud while he was pursuing
his work and since he bequeathed it to us—to transference, which Freud discovered [18]. Lagache's work aims to go much further, by introducing

structural distinctions into the phenomenon's function that are essential for its critique. Suffice it to recall the highly relevant alternative he presents—regarding the ultimate nature of transference—between the need for repetition and the repetition of need.

Such work, whose consequences I believe I have been able to draw out in my teaching, shows very clearly, by means of the ordering it introduces, to what extent the aspects on which discussion focuses are often partial, and particularly to what extent the ordinary use of the term "transference," even in psychoanalysis, cannot free itself from its most questionable approach, which is also its crudest: to make transference into the succession or sum total of positive or negative feelings the patient has for his analyst.

To assess where we stand regarding transference in our scientific community, it could be said that there has been no agreement nor light shed on the following points where they would, nevertheless, seem necessary: Is it the same effect of the relation with the analyst that is manifested in the initial infatuation observed at the beginning of treatment and in the web of satisfactions that make this relation so difficult to break off when transference neurosis seems to go beyond strictly analytic means? And is it the relation with the analyst and its fundamental frustration which, in the second phase of analysis, sustains the scansion—frustration, aggression, and regression—in which the most fruitful effects of analysis are supposed to occur? How is the subordination of phenomena to be conceptualized when their movement is traversed by fantasies that openly involve the figure of the analyst?

603

The reason for these persistent obscurities has been formulated in an exceptionally perspicacious study: at each of the stages at which an attempt has been made to reappraise the problems of transference, the divergences in technique that made this task so urgent have not given way to a true critique of the notion itself [20].

2. The notion I want to get at here is so central to analytic action that it may serve as a gauge of the partiality of the theories that have taken the time to conceptualize it. That is, we will not be misled if we judge their partiality on the basis of the handling of transference these theories imply. This pragmatism is justified. For the handling of transference and one's notion of it are one and the same, and however little this notion is elaborated in practice, it cannot but align itself with the partialities of the theory.

On the other hand, the simultaneous existence of these partialities does not necessarily mean that they complete each other. This confirms the fact that they suffer from a central defect.

In order to introduce a little order here already, I will reduce these partialities of the theory to three, even if it means giving in to taking sides to some degree, less serious as it is only for the purposes of exposition.

3. I will link geneticism—in the sense that it tends to ground analytic phenomena in the developmental moments involved in those phenomena and to feed on the so-called direct observation of the child—to a specific technique, one that centers this procedure on the analysis of the defenses.

This link is obvious from a historical perspective. One might even say that it has no other foundation, since it is constituted only on the basis of the failure of the solidarity it presupposes.

One can locate its beginnings in the legitimate credence lent to the notion of an unconscious ego with which Freud reoriented his doctrine. To move from that notion to the hypothesis that the defense mechanisms that were grouped under ego functioning ought themselves to be able to reveal a comparable law of appearance—one that even corresponds to the succession of phases by which Freud had attempted to connect the emergence of the drives with physiology—was the step Anna Freud, in her book *The Ego and the Mechanisms of Defense* [4], proposed to take in order to put it to the test of experience.   604

It could have occasioned a fruitful critique of the relations between development and the obviously more complex structures Freud introduced into psychology. But the sights were lowered; it was so much more tempting to try to insert the defense mechanisms into the observable stages of sensorimotor development and progressive abilities of intelligent behavior—those mechanisms supposedly separating out in the course of their progress.

One might say that the hopes Anna Freud placed in such an exploration were dashed: nothing emerged from this line of approach that could inform technique, even though the details gleaned from a type of child observation informed by analysis were sometimes very suggestive.

The notion of pattern*, which serves here as an alibi for the failed typology, sponsors a technique which, in seeking to detect a pattern* that isn't current, willingly judges it on the basis of its deviation from a pattern* that finds in its conformism the guarantees of its conformity. One cannot recall without a sense of shame the criteria of success in which this trumped-up work culminates: the achievement of a higher income and the safety valve of an affair with one's secretary, regulating the release of forces that are strictly under wraps in marriage, career, and political community. These do not seem to me to be of sufficient dignity to require an appeal—articulated in the analyst's planning* and even in his interpretation—to the Discord of the life and death instincts, even if only to decorate one's words with the pretentious term "economic," and to pursue it, in an utter and complete misunderstanding of Freud's thought, as the play of a couple of forces that are homologous in their opposition.

4. The second trend where we see what slips away from transference seems less degraded in its analytic relief—namely, that based on object relations.

This theory, however much it has degenerated in France in recent years, has, like geneticism, a noble origin. It was Karl Abraham who opened up this field and the notion of the part-object is his original contribution. This is not the place to demonstrate its value. I am more interested in indicating its connection with the partiality of that aspect of transference which Abraham isolates, promoting it in its opacity as the ability to love—as if that were a constitutional facet of the patient in which one could read the degree of his curability, and, in particular, the only aspect concerning which the treatment of psychosis would fail.

In fact, we have two equations here: the so-called sexual transference (*Sexualübertragung*) is at the heart of the love that in French has been called *amour objectal*, object love (*Objektliebe*); and the capacity for transference is a measure of the patient's access to reality [*réel*]. I cannot stress too strongly that this merely begs the question.

In contradistinction to the presuppositions of geneticism, which is supposed to be based on an order of formal emergences in the subject, Abraham's perspective can be explained by a finality that is authorized because it is instinctual, in that it is embellished by the maturation of an ineffable object, the Object with a capital O, that governs the phase of "objectality" (significantly distinguished from objectivity by its affective substance).

This ectoplasmic conception of the object quickly revealed its dangers when it degenerated into the crude dichotomy expressed in the opposition between pregenital character and genital character.

This elementary theme was summarily developed by attributing to pregenital character a slew of features—projective unrealism, greater or lesser degrees of autism, restriction of satisfactions by the defenses, and the wrapping of the object in doubly protective insulation when it comes to the destructive effects that connote it—in other words, an amalgamation of all the defects in the object-relation with a view to showing the reasons for the extreme dependence of the subject that results therefrom. A picture that would be useful, despite its tendency to be confused, if it did not seem designed to serve as a negative for the puerility of the following: "the passage from the pregenital form to the genital form," in which the drives "are no longer characterized by an uncontrollable, unlimited, unconditional need for possession, involving a destructive element. They are truly tender and loving, and if the subject still does not prove to be 'oblative'—that is, disinterested—and if these objects" (here the author recalls my remarks) "are just as profoundly narcissistic objects as they were before, he is now capable of comprehension and adaptation to the other. Moreover, the intimate structure of these object relations shows that the object's own pleasure is indispensable to the subject's happiness. The object's preferences, desires, and needs (what a hodgepodge!)[y] are taken into consideration to the highest degree."

However, this does not prevent the ego from having "a stability that runs no risk of being compromised by the loss of a significant Object. It remains independent of its objects."

"Its organization is such that the mode of thought it employs is essentially logical. It does not spontaneously present regression to an archaic mode of apprehending reality, affective thinking and magical belief playing only an absolutely secondary role here; symbolization does not go beyond the extent and importance it has in normal life (!!).[10] The style of relations between subject and object is one of the most highly evolved (*sic*)."[11]

This is the promise held out to those who "at the end of a successful analysis . . . realize the enormous difference between what they used to believe sexual joy to be and what they now experience" [21, page 55].

One is led to understand that for those who have this joy from the outset, "genital relations are, in short, untroubled" [21].

Untroubled except for conjugating themselves irresistibly in the verb "to bang your behind on the chandelier," which marks a place here for the future scholiast to find his eternal opportunity.

5. Although we must agree with Abraham when he suggests that the typical object-relation is manifested in the activity of the collector, perhaps the rule of that relation is not given in this edifying antinomy, but is to be sought, rather, in some impasse that is constitutive of desire as such.

What makes it such that the object presents itself as broken and decomposed is perhaps something other than a pathological factor. And what does this absurd hymn to the harmony of genital relations have to do with reality [*réel*]?

Must we erase the Oedipal drama from our experience when it had to be forged by Freud precisely to explain the barriers and debasements (*Erniedrigungen*) so common in the sphere of love, even the most fulfilled?

607

Is it our job to disguise Eros, the black God, as the Good Shepherd's curly-haired sheep?

Sublimation may be at work in the "oblation" that radiates from love, but we should try to go a little further into the structure of the sublime and not confuse it with the perfect orgasm—an equation Freud, in any case, opposed.

The worst thing is that the souls who overflow with the most natural tenderness are led to wonder whether they satisfy the delusional normalism of the genital relation—an unheralded burden which we have loaded onto the shoulders of the innocent, like those cursed by the Evangelist.

Yet in reading our work, should any of it survive into a time when people will no longer know what these effervescent words corresponded to in practice, people might imagine that our art was designed to revive sexual hunger in those afflicted with retardation of the sexual gland—to the physiology of which we have, nevertheless, made no contribution, and of which we need know very little indeed.

6. At least three sides are needed to make a pyramid, even a heretical one. The side that closes the dihedron I have described here in the gap left in the conception of transference, strives, one might say, to join the edges together.

If transference derives its power from being brought back to the reality of which the analyst is the representative, and if the goal is to ripen the Object in the hothouse of a confined situation, the analysand is left with only one object to sink his teeth into, if you will allow me the expression, and that is the analyst.

Hence the third mistake on my list—the notion of intersubjective introjection—because it is unfortunately installed in a dyadic relation.

For we are certainly dealing with a unitive pathway, concerning which the various theoretical sauces that accompany it, depending on the topography they refer to, can but retain the metaphor, varying it according to the level of the operation regarded as serious: introjection for Ferenczi, identification with the analyst's superego for Strachey, and terminal narcissistic trance for Balint.

608

I am trying to draw attention to the substance of this mystical consummation and if, once again, I must criticize what is happening right in front of my nose, it is because analytic experience is known to draw its strength from the particular.

The importance given in treatment to the fantasy of phallic devouring, the brunt of which is borne by the image of the analyst, seems worthy of note to me because it tallies so well with a conception of the direction of the treatment that is entirely based on setting the distance between the patient and the analyst, the latter as the object of the dyadic relation.

For, however deficient the theory with which an author systematizes his technique, the fact remains that he really does analyze people, and that the coherence revealed in the error is the guarantor here of the wrong turn practice has taken.

It is the privileged function of the signifier "phallus" in the subject's way of being present in desire that is illustrated here, but in an experience that might be called blind—failing any orientation regarding the true relations in the analytic situation, which, like any other situation involving speech, can only be crushed if one tries to inscribe it in a dyadic relation.

Since the nature of symbolic incorporation is not recognized, for good reason, and since it is ruled out that anything real should be consummated in analysis, it is clear—from the elementary landmarks of my teaching— that anything that occurs that is not imaginary can no longer be recognized. For it is not necessary to know the floor plan of a house to bang one's head against its walls: indeed, one can do so very well without it.

I myself suggested to this author, at a time when we used to discuss things, that if one confines oneself to an imaginary relation between objects there remains nothing but the dimension of distance to order it. I wasn't expecting him to agree with me.

To make distance the sole dimension in which the neurotic's relations with the object are played out generates insurmountable contradictions that can be seen clearly enough both in the system and in the opposite directions different authors derive from the same metaphor to organize their impressions. Too much and too little distance from the object sometimes appear to be confounded so thoroughly as to become confused. And it was not distance from the object, but rather its excessive intimacy with the subject that seemed to Ferenczi to characterize the neurotic.

609

What determines what each author means is his technique, and the technique of "bringing-together" [rapprocher], however priceless an effect the untranslated French term may have in a paper written in English, reveals in practice a tendency that verges on obsession.

It is hard to believe that the ideal prescribed by this author of reducing this distance to zero ("nil" in English) stops him from seeing that his theoretical paradox converges here.

Be that as it may, there is no doubt that this distance is taken as a universal parameter, regulating variations in the technique (however incomprehensible the debate on their magnitude may seem) for dismantling neurosis.

What such a conception owes to the specific conditions of obsessive neurosis is not to be ascribed entirely to the object.

It does not even seem to have to its credit any notable privilege regarding the results it obtains in the treatment of obsessive neurosis. For if I can, as Kris did, mention an analysis which I took over from another analyst, I can attest that such a technique, in the hands of an analyst of indisputable talent, succeeded in producing—in a clinical case of pure obsession in a man—the irruption of an infatuation which, while Platonic, was no less unbridled, and which proved no less irreducible even though it was directed at the first object of the same sex that happened to be at hand in his circle.

To speak of transitory perversion here may satisfy a militant optimist, but only at the cost of failing to recognize, in this atypical restoration of the overly neglected third party to the relation, that one should not pull too hard on the strings of proximity in the object-relation.

7. There is no limit to the eroding of analytic technique through its deconceptualization. I have already referred to what was found in a "wild" analysis, about which, to my pained astonishment, no supervisor had become alarmed. To be able to smell one's analyst seemed in one work to be an achievement to be taken literally, as an indication of the felicitous outcome of the transference.

One can perceive here a sort of involuntary humor, which is what makes the example so valuable. It would have delighted Jarry. It is, in fact, merely the consequence one can expect from comprehending the development of the analytic situation in terms of reality [*réel*]: and it is true that, taste apart, the olfactory is the only dimension that allows one to reduce distance to zero (nil*), this time in reality [*réel*]. Whether it provides a guide for the direction of the treatment and the principles of its power is more dubious.

But that a stale smell should waft into a technique that is conducted largely by "following one's nose," as they say, is not simply ridiculous. The students who attend my seminar will recall the smell of urine that marked the turning point in a case of transitory perversion, which I dwelt on in order to criticize this technique. It cannot be said that the turning point was unconnected with the incident that motivated the case study, since it was in looking through a crack in the wall of a water* closet to spy on a woman pissing that the patient suddenly transposed his libido, without anything, it seems, predestining it for this—infantile emotions bound up with the fantasy of the phallic mother having until then taken the form of a phobia [23].

It is not a direct connection, however, no more than it would be correct to see in this voyeurism an inversion of the exhibition involved in the atypia of the phobia—which was the correct diagnosis—underlying the patient's anxiety at being teased for being too tall.

As I said, the analyst to whom we owe this remarkable publication proves her rare perspicacity by returning again and again, to the point of tormenting the patient, to the interpretation she made of a certain suit of armor—which appeared in a dream chasing him and armed, moreover, with a syringe containing insecticide—as a symbol of the phallic mother.

"Should I have talked about his father instead?" she wondered. She justified not doing so by the fact that the real father had been deficient [carence] in the patient's history.

My students can deplore here the fact that the teaching of my seminar was unable to help her at the time, since they know by what principles I have taught them to distinguish between the phobic object as an all-purpose signifier to make up for [suppléer] the Other's lack and the fundamental fetish in every perversion as an object perceived in the signifier's cut.

Failing that, shouldn't this gifted novice have recalled the dialogue between the suits of armor in André Breton's "Discours sur le peu de réalité"? That would have put her on the right track.   611

But how could we hope for such a thing when this analysis was, in supervision, given a direction that inclined her to constantly harass the patient to bring him back to the real situation? How can we be surprised that, unlike the Queen of Spain, the analyst has legs, when she herself emphasizes it in the harshness of her calls to order, that is, to the present?

Naturally, this procedure played a part in the benign outcome of the acting out* under examination here: since the analyst—who was, moreover, aware of the fact—was thus constantly intervening in a castrating manner.

But why, then, attribute this role to the mother, when everything in the anamnesis of this case indicates that she always acted, rather, as a go-between?

The faltering Oedipus complex was compensated for, but always in the form, which is disarming here in its naïveté, of an entirely forced, if not arbitrary, reference to the analyst's husband—a situation encouraged here by the fact that it was he, himself a psychiatrist, who provided the analyst with this particular patient.

This is not a common situation. In any case, it is to be impugned as lying outside the analytic situation.

My reservations about its outcome are not entirely due to the graceless detours of the treatment, and the patient's joke—probably not devoid of malice—about the fee for the last session being misappropriated to pay for debauchery is not a bad omen for the future.

The question that can be raised is that of the boundary between analysis and reeducation when the very process of analysis is guided by a predominant solicitation of its real effects. This can be seen by comparing the biographical facts in this case with the transference formations: the contribution made by the deciphering of the unconscious is truly minimal. So minimal that one wonders whether the lion's share of the unconscious does not remain intact in the encystment of the enigma which—labeled transitory perversion here—is the subject of this instructive paper.

8. Lest the lay reader be misled, let me say that I wish in no way to disparage a work to which Virgil's epithet *improbus* can rightly be applied.

My only purpose is to warn analysts of the decline their technique suffers when they misrecognize the true place in which its effects are produced.

While they are tireless in their attempts to define it, one cannot say that in falling back on positions of modesty, or even taking fictions as their guide, the analytic experience they develop is always unfruitful.

Geneticism-based research and direct observation are far from having cut themselves off from a properly analytic spirit. When I discussed object-relation themes one year in my seminar, I showed the value of a conception in which child observation is nourished by the most accurate reconsideration of the function of mothering in the genesis of the object: I mean the notion of the transitional object, introduced by D. W. Winnicott, which is key in explaining the genesis of fetishism [27].

The fact remains that flagrant uncertainties in the reading of the major Freudian concepts correspond to weaknesses that plague analytic practice.

What I want to convey is that the more impasses researchers and groups encounter in conceptualizing their action in its authenticity, the more they end up forcing their action into the direction of the exercise of power.

They substitute this power for the relation to being where their action takes place, making its means—especially those of speech—fall from their veridical eminence. This is why it is a sort of return of the repressed, however strange it may be, which—owing to pretensions hardly disposed to encumber themselves with the dignity of these means—occasions the linguistic error of referring to being as though it were a fact of reality, when the discourse that reigns there rejects any questioning that a fine platitude would not have already recognized.

IV. How to Act with One's Being

1. The question of the analyst's being arose very early in the history of analysis. And it should come as no surprise that it was introduced by the analyst most tormented by the problem of analytic action. Indeed, it can be said that Ferenczi's article, "Introjection and Transference," dating back to 1909 [3], was inaugural here and that it anticipated by many years all the themes later developed on the basis of the second topography.

Although Ferenczi conceives of transference as the introjection of the doctor's person into the patient's subjective economy, it is not introjection of this person as a prop for a repetitive compulsion or ill-adapted behavior, or as a fantasy figure. What he means is the absorption into the subject's economy of everything the psychoanalyst makes present in the duo as the here and now of an incarnated problematic. Doesn't Ferenczi reach the extreme conclusion that the treatment can only be complete if the doctor avows to the patient the sense of abandonment the doctor himself is liable to suffer?[17]

2. Must one pay this comical price for the subject's want-to-be to simply be recognized as the heart of analytic experience, as the very field in which the neurotic's passion is deployed?

Apart from the Hungarian school, whose embers are now dispersed and soon to be mere ashes, only the English, with their cold objectivity, have been able to articulate this gap—to which the neurotic, in wanting to justify his existence, attests—and hence to implicitly distinguish the relation to the Other, in which being finds its status, from the interpersonal relation, with its warmth and lures.

It should suffice to cite Ella Sharpe and her pertinent remarks in following the neurotic's true concerns [24]. The strength of her remarks lies in a sort of naïveté reflected in the justly famous brusqueness of her style as both therapist and writer. She is quite out of the ordinary in going as far as vainglory when she requires the analyst to be omniscient if he is to read the intentions of the analysand's discourse correctly.

We must credit her for having given a literary background pride of place in training institutes, even if she does not seem to realize that, in the mini-

613

614 mal reading list she proposes, there is a predominance of imaginative works in which the phallus as a signifier plays a central role beneath a transparent veil. This simply proves that her choice is no less guided by analytic experience than her recommendation is felicitous.

3. It is again by the British, whether by birth or by adoption, that the end of analysis has been most categorically defined as the subject's identification with the analyst. Certainly, opinion varies as to whether it is his ego or superego that is involved. It is not that easy to master the structure Freud isolated in the subject, unless you distinguish therein the symbolic from the imaginary and the real.

Let us simply say that statements made with such a view to affront are not forged without some pressure on those who proffer them. The dialectic of fantasy objects promoted in practice by Melanie Klein tends to be translated in the theory in terms of identification.

For these objects, whether part-objects or not, but certainly signifying objects—the breast, excrement, and the phallus—are no doubt won or lost by the subject; he is destroyed by them or preserves them, but above all he *is* these objects, according to the place where they function in his fundamental fantasy. This form of identification merely demonstrates the pathology of the path down which the subject is pushed in a world where his needs are reduced to exchange values—this path itself finding its radical possibility only in the mortification the signifier imposes on his life by numbering it.

4. It would seem that the psychoanalyst, if he is simply to help the subject, must be spared this pathology, which, as we see, depends on nothing less than an iron-clad law.

This is why people imagine that a psychoanalyst should be a happy man. Indeed, is it not happiness that people ask him for, and how could he give it, commonsense asks, if he does not have a bit of it himself?

It is a fact that we do not proclaim our incompetence to promise happiness in an era in which the question of how to gauge it has become so complicated—in the first place, because happiness, as Saint-Just said, has become a political factor.

615 To be fair, humanist progress from Aristotle to St. Francis (de Sales) did not fill the aporias of happiness.

It is a waste of time, as we know, to look for a happy man's shirt, and what is called a happy shade is to be avoided for the ills it propagates.

It is certainly in the relation to being that the analyst has to find his operating level, and the opportunities training analysis offers him for this purpose are not only to be calculated as a function of the problem which is supposedly already resolved for the analyst who is guiding him.

There are misfortunes of being that the prudence of colleges and the false shame that ensures domination dare not excise from one.

An ethics must be formulated that integrates Freud's conquests concerning desire: one that would place at the forefront the question of the analyst's desire.

5. If one is attuned to the resonance of earlier work, one cannot fail to be struck by the decline in analytic speculation, especially in this area.

Because they understand a lot of things, analysts on the whole imagine that to understand is an end in itself, and that it can only be a happy end.* The example of physical science may show them, however, that the most impressive successes do not require that one know where one is going.

To think, it is often better not to understand; and one can gallop along, understanding for miles and miles, without the slightest thought being produced.

This, indeed, was how the behaviorists began: "give up understanding." But since they had no other thoughts concerning our particular subject matter, which is *antiphusis*, they adopted the course of using, without understanding it, what we understand—a source of renewed pride for us.

A sample of the kind of morality we are capable of producing is provided by the notion of oblativity. It is an obsessive's fantasy misunderstood by oneself: "everything for the other, my semblable," one propounds with this notion, without recognizing here the anxiety that the Other (with a capital O) inspires by not being a semblable.

6. I don't claim to teach psychoanalysts what thinking is. They know. But it   616
is not as if they came to understand it by themselves. They learned their lesson from psychologists. Thought is a first try at action, they dutifully repeat. (Freud himself falls into this trap, which does not stop him from being a doughty thinker, whose action culminates in thought.)

In truth, to analysts thought is an action that undoes itself. This leaves some hope that, if one makes them think about it by taking it up again, they will come to rethink it.

7. The analyst is the man to whom one speaks and to whom one speaks freely. That is what he is there for. What does this mean?

Everything that can be said about the association of ideas is mere dressing up in psychologistic clothing. Induced plays on words are far removed from it; because of their protocol, moreover, nothing could be less free.

The subject invited to speak in analysis does not really display a great deal of freedom in what he says. Not that he is bound by the rigor of his associations: they no doubt oppress him, but it is rather that they lead to a free speech, a full speech that would be painful to him.

Nothing is to be feared more than saying something that might be true. For it would become entirely true if it were said, and Lord knows what happens when something can no longer be cast into doubt because it is true.

Is that the procedure used in analysis—a progress of truth? I can already hear the philistines whispering about my intellectualistic analyses: whereas I, to the best of my knowledge, am at the very forefront in preserving what is unsayable there.

I know better than anyone that we listen for what lies beyond discourse, if only I take the path of hearing, not that of auscultating. Yes, certainly not the path of auscultating resistance, blood pressure, opisthotonos, pallor, and adrenal discharge (*sic*) by which a stronger (*resic*) ego should be reformed: what I listen to is based on hearing [*ce que j'écoute est d'entendement*].

Hearing does not force me to understand. The fact remains that what I hear is a discourse, even if it is as seemingly nondiscursive as an interjection. For an interjection is linguistic in nature and not an expressive cry. It is a part of speech that is just as important as any other in its syntactic effects in a given language [*langue*].

617 In what I indubitably hear, I have nothing to find fault with if I understand none of it, or if I do understand something I am sure to be mistaken. This need not stop me from responding to it. That's what happens outside analysis in such cases. Instead I keep quiet. Everybody agrees that I frustrate the speaker—him first, but me too. Why?

If I frustrate him it is because he is asking [*demande*] me for something. To answer him, in fact. But he knows very well that it would be but words. And he can get those from whomever he likes. It's not even certain that he'd be grateful to me if they were fine words, let alone if they were lousy. It's not these words he's asking for [*demande*]. He is simply demanding of me . . ., by the very fact that he is speaking: his demand is intransitive—it brings no object with it.

Of course, his demand is deployed against the backdrop of an implicit demand, the one for which he is here: the demand for me to cure him, to reveal him to himself, to introduce him to psychoanalysis, to help him qualify as an analyst. But, as he knows, this demand can wait. His present demand has nothing to do with that—it is not even his own, for after all I am the one who offered to let him speak. (Only the subject is transitive here.)

In short, I have succeeded in doing what in the field of ordinary commerce people would like to be able to do with such ease: out of supply [*offre*] I have created demand.

8. But it is, one might say, a radical demand.

Ida Macalpine is no doubt right in wanting to seek the motor force of transference in the fundamental rule of psychoanalysis alone. But she errs in attributing the unobstructed path toward infantile regression to the absence of all objects [20]. This would rather seem to be an obstacle thereto, for, as everyone knows—child analysts more than anyone—it takes a lot of little objects to keep up a relationship with a child.

By means of demand, the whole past begins to open up, right down to earliest infancy. The subject has never done anything but demand, he could not have survived otherwise, and we take it from there.

This is the way that analytic regression can occur and does in fact present itself. People talk about it as if the subject began acting like a child. That no doubt happens, and such playacting does not bode very well. It differs, in any case, from what is usually observed in what passes for regression. For regression displays nothing other than a return to the present of signifiers used in demands that have exceeded their statute of limitations.

618

9. To return to our point of departure, this situation explains primary transference and the love by which it is sometimes declared.

For if love is giving what you don't have, it is certainly true that the subject can wait to be given it, since the psychoanalyst has nothing else to give him. But he does not even give him this nothing, and it is better that way— which is why he is paid for this nothing, preferably well paid, in order to show that otherwise it would not be worth much.

Although primary transference most often remains little more than a shadow, that doesn't stop this shadow from dreaming and reproducing its demand when there is nothing left to demand. This demand will simply be all the purer since it is empty.

It may be objected that the analyst nevertheless gives his presence, but I believe that his presence is initially implied simply by his listening, and that this listening is simply the condition of speech. Why would analytic technique require that he make his presence so discreet if this were not, in fact, the case? It is later that his presence will be noticed.

In any case, the most acute sense of his presence is tied to a moment at which the subject can only remain silent—that is, when he backs away from even the shadow of demand.

Thus the analyst is he who sustains demand, not, as people say, to frustrate the subject, but in order to allow the signifiers with which the latter's frustration is bound up to reappear.

10. It is worth recalling that it is in the oldest demand that primary identification is produced, the one that occurs on the basis of the mother's omnipotence—namely, the one that not only makes the satisfaction of needs dependent upon the signifying apparatus, but also that fragments, filters, and models those needs in the defiles of the signifier's structure.

Needs become subordinate to the same conventional conditions as does the signifier in its double register: the synchronic register of opposition between irreducible elements, and the diachronic register of substitution and combination, through which language, while it does not fulfill all functions, structures everything in interpersonal relations.

Hence the oscillation found in Freud's statements concerning relations between the superego and reality. The superego is not, of course, the source of reality, as he says somewhere, but it lays down its pathways, before refinding in the unconscious the first ideal marks in which the tendencies are constituted as repressed in the substitution of the signifier for needs.

11. There is thus no need to look any further for the mainspring of identification with the analyst. That identification may assume very different forms, but it will always be an identification with signifiers.

As an analysis proceeds, the analyst deals in turn with all the articulations of the subject's demand. But, as I will explain later, he must respond to them only from his position in the transference.

Who, in fact, doesn't emphasize the importance of what might be called analysis' permissive hypothesis? But we need no particular political regime for that which is not forbidden to become obligatory.

Analysts who might be said to be fascinated by the consequences of frustration merely maintain a position of suggestion that reduces the subject to going back through his demand. That must be what they mean by emotional reeducation.

Goodness is no doubt more necessary there than it is elsewhere, but it

619

cannot cure the evil it engenders. The analyst who wants what is good for the subject repeats what he was trained in and sometimes even twisted by. The most aberrant education has never had any other motive than the subject's own good.

A theory of analysis is conceived, which—unlike the delicate articulation of Freudian analysis—reduces the mainspring of symptoms to fear. It engenders a practice on which what I have elsewhere called the obscene, ferocious figure of the superego is stamped, and in which there is no other way out of transference neurosis than to sit the patient down by the window and point out the bright side of things to him, adding: "Go for it. You're a good kid now" [22].

V. Desire Must Be Taken Literally   620

1. A dream, after all, is but a dream, we hear people say these days [22]. Does it mean nothing that Freud recognized desire in dreams?

Desire, not tendencies. For we must read the *Traumdeutung* [*The Interpretation of Dreams*] to know what is meant by what Freud calls "desire" there.

We must pause at the vocable *Wunsch*, and its English translation, "wish,"* to distinguish them from the French *désir* [desire], given that the sound of damp firecrackers with which the German and English words fizzle out suggests anything but concupiscence. Their French equivalent is *voeu*.

These *voeux* may be pious, nostalgic, annoying, or mischievous. A lady may have a dream that is motivated by no other desire than to provide Freud, who has explained to her his theory that dreams are desires, with proof that they are nothing of the kind. What we must keep in mind here is that this desire is articulated in a very cunning discourse. But in order to understand what desire means in Freud's thought, it is just as important to perceive the consequences of the fact that he was satisfied to recognize the dream's desire and the confirmation of his law in that cunning discourse.

For he takes its eccentricity still further, since a dream of being punished may, if it likes, signify a desire for what the punishment suppresses.

But let us not stop at the labels on the drawers, although many people confuse them with the fruits of science. Let us read the texts; let us follow Freud's thinking in the twists and turns it imposes on us, and not forget that, in deploring them himself compared with an ideal of scientific discourse, he claims that he was forced into them by his object of study.[13]

We see then that this object is identical to those twists and turns, since at the first turning point of his book, when dealing with an hysteric's dream, he stumbles upon the fact that, by displacement, in this case specifically by allusion to another woman's desire, a desire from the day before is satisfied in the dream—a desire that is sustained in its eminent position by a desire that is of quite a different order, since Freud characterizes it as the desire to have an unsatisfied desire [7].[14]

621

One should try and count the number of referrals [*renvois*] made here to bring desire to a geometrically higher power. A single index would not suffice to characterize the exponent. For it would be necessary to distinguish two dimensions in these referrals: a desire for desire, in other words, a desire signified by a desire (the hysteric's desire to have an unsatisfied desire is signified by her desire for caviar: the desire for caviar is its signifier), is inscribed in the different register of a desire substituted for a desire (in the dream, the desire for smoked salmon, characteristic of the patient's female friend, is substituted for the patient's own desire for caviar, which constitutes the substitution of a signifier for a signifier).[15]

2. What we thus find is in no way microscopic, no more than there is any need of special instruments to recognize that a leaf has the structural features of the plant from which it has been detached. Even if one had never seen a plant with its leaves, one would realize at once that a leaf is more likely to be part of a plant than a piece of skin.

The desire in the hysteric's dream, but also any other bit of nothing in its place in this text by Freud, summarizes what the whole book explains about mechanisms said to be unconscious—condensation, sliding, etc.—by attesting to their common structure: namely, desire's relation to the mark of language that specifies the Freudian unconscious and decenters our conception of the subject.

I think that my students will appreciate the kind of access I provide here to the fundamental opposition between the signifier and the signified, language's powers stemming from that opposition, as I show them. While conceptualizing the exercise of those powers, I nevertheless leave them with their work cut out for them.

622

Let me recall to mind here the automatic functioning of the laws by which the following are articulated in the signifying chain:

(a) the substitution of one term for another to produce a metaphorical effect;

(b) the combination of one term with another to produce a metonymical effect [17].

If we apply them here, we see that, insofar as in our patient's dream smoked salmon—the object of her friend's desire—is all the patient has to offer, Freud, in positing that smoked salmon has been substituted here for caviar, which he takes to be the signifier of the patient's desire, proposes that the dream be viewed as a metaphor of desire.

But what is metaphor if not a positive meaning effect, that is, a certain access gained by the subject to the meaning of her desire?

The subject's desire being presented here as what is implied by her (conscious) discourse, thus, as preconscious—which is obvious since her husband is willing to satisfy her desire, though it is important to the patient, who has persuaded him that she has such a desire, that he not do so, but you still have to be Freud to articulate this as the desire to have an unsatisfied desire—one still must go further to figure out what such a desire means in the unconscious.

For a dream is not the unconscious but, as Freud tells us, the royal road to it. This confirms that the unconscious proceeds on the basis of metaphorical effects. Dreams lay bare such effects. To whom? I shall return to that shortly.

Let us note for the moment that the desire in question, while signified as unsatisfied, is signified thusly by the signifier "caviar," insofar as the signifier symbolizes this desire as inaccessible; note too, however, that as soon as this desire slips, qua desire, into the caviar, the desire for caviar becomes this desire's metonymy—rendered necessary by the want-to-be in which this desire sustains itself.

Metonymy is, as I have been teaching you, an effect which is rendered possible by the fact that there is no signification that does not refer to another signification; the most common denominator of those significations is produced in it—namely, the scant meaning (commonly confused with what is meaningless), I repeat, the scant meaning that turns out to be at the root of this desire, conferring upon it the hint of perversion one is tempted to point to in the present case of hysteria.

The truth of this appearance is that desire is the metonymy of the want-to-be.   623

3. Let us now return to the book known in French as *The Science of Dreams* (*Traumdeutung*), though "Mantic" or, better still, "Signifierness" would be more suitable translations than "Science."

Freud in no way claims here to solve all the psychological problems dreams pose. Read it and you will note that Freud does not touch on such rarely explored questions (studies on space and time in dreams, on the sensory stuff of dreams, and on color or atonal dreams are rare or at least contribute little; are smell, taste, and the graininess of touch present like dizziness, turgidity, and heaviness are?). To say that Freud's doctrine is a psychology is a crude equivocation.

Freud can hardly be said to leave himself open to such an equivocation. He tells us, on the contrary, that he is only interested in the dream's "elaboration." What does that mean? Exactly what I translate as the dream's "linguistic structure." How could Freud have become aware of that structure when it was only later articulated by Ferdinand de Saussure? It is all the more striking that Freud anticipated it as that structure overlaps Freud's own terms. But where did he discover it? In a signifying flow whose mystery lies in the fact that the subject doesn't even know where to pretend to be its organizer.

To get him to refind himself therein as desiring is the opposite of getting him to recognize himself therein as a subject, for the brook of desire runs as if along a branch line of the signifying chain, and the subject must take advantage of a crossover in order to catch hold of his own feedback*.

Desire merely subjugates what analysis subjectivizes.

4. This brings me back to the question left unanswered above: "To whom does the dream reveal its meaning before the analyst comes on the scene?" This meaning exists prior both to its being read and to the science of its deciphering.

Both show that the dream is designed for the recognition—but my voice falters before finishing—of desire. For desire, assuming that Freud is right about the unconscious and that analysis is necessary, can only be grasped in interpretation.

But to return to what I was saying before, the elaboration of the dream is nourished by the desire . . . why does my voice fail to complete the thought?—for recognition—as if the second word ["recognition"] were extinguished which, when it was the first earlier, resorbed the other ["desire"] in its light. For it is not by sleeping that one gets oneself recognized. And the dream, Freud tells us, without seeming to see the slightest contradiction therein, serves above all the desire to go on sleeping. It involves the narcissistic withdrawal of libido into oneself and the decathexis of reality.

It is, in any case, a fact of experience that when my dream begins to coincide with my demand (not with reality, as is improperly said, which can safe-

624

guard my sleep)—or with what proves to be equivalent to it here, the other's demand—I wake up.

5. A dream, after all, is but a dream. Those who now disdain it as a tool in analysis have found, as we have seen, surer and more direct roads by which to bring the patient back to sound principles and normal desires, those that satisfy true needs. Which needs? Why, everyone's needs, my friend. If that is what frightens you, have faith in your psychoanalyst and climb the Eiffel Tower to see how beautiful Paris is. Too bad some people jump over the railing on the first deck, precisely those whose needs have all been restored to their proper proportions. A negative therapeutic reaction, I would call it.

Thank God not everyone takes refusal that far! Nevertheless, the symptom grows back like a weed: repetition compulsion.

But that, of course, is no more than a misconception: one does not get better because one remembers. One remembers because one gets better. Since this formulation was found, there has no longer been any question regarding the reproduction of symptoms, but only regarding the reproduction of analysts; the reproduction of patients has been resolved.

6. Thus a dream is but a dream. A certain psychoanalyst who has the nerve to teach has even gone so far as to write that dreams are produced by the ego. This proves that we run no great risk in wanting to wake men from their dreams: the latter are pursued in broad daylight and by those who rarely indulge in dreaming.

But even these men, if they are psychoanalysts, must read Freud on dreams, because otherwise it is not possible either to understand what he   625
means by the neurotic's desire, repression, the unconscious, interpretation, or analysis itself, or to close in on anything whatsoever related to his technique or doctrine. We shall see how much is contained in the short dream I borrowed above for the purposes of this discussion.

For the desire of our witty hysteric (Freud is the one who characterizes her as such)—I mean her waking desire, that is, her desire for caviar—is the desire of a woman who is fulfilled and yet does not want to be. For her butcher of a husband never neglects to dot the i's and cross the t's when it comes to providing her the kinds of satisfaction everyone needs; nor does he mince words with a painter who flatters him, God knows with what obscure intent, regarding his interesting mug, saying, "Nothing doing! A nice piece of ass is what you need, and if you expect me to get it for you, you can stick it you know where."

Here's a man a woman should have nothing to complain about, a genital character, who must appropriately ensure that when he fucks his wife, she has no need to jerk off afterward. Moreover, Freud does not hide from us the fact that she is very taken with him and teases him all the time.

But there it is: she does not want to be satisfied regarding her true needs alone. She wants other needs that are gratuitous and, in order to be quite sure that they are gratuitous, not to satisfy them. This is why the question "What does the witty butcher's wife desire?" can be answered as follows: "Caviar." But this answer is hopeless because she also does not want any.

7. This is not the whole of her mystery. Far from being imprisoned by this impasse, she finds the key to her freedom in it, the key to the field of the desires of all the witty hysterics in the world, whether butchers' wives or not.

This is what Freud perceives in one of those sidelong glances by which he discovers the truth, shattering in passing the abstractions with which positivist thinkers willingly explain everything: in this case, imitation, a concept so dear to Tarde. We must bring to bear in this particular case the linchpin Freud provides here of hysterical identification. If our patient identifies with her friend, it is insofar as she is inimitable in her unsatisfied desire for that salmon—may God damn it if it is not He himself who smokes it!

Thus the patient's dream is a response to her friend's request [*demande*], which is to come dine at the patient's house. And what could possibly make her friend want to do so, apart from the fine dinners served there, if not the fact—not overlooked by the butcher's wife—that her husband always praises her friend? Now, as her friend is thin, her figure is not likely to attract him, relishing only curves as he does.

Couldn't it be that he too has a desire that remains awry when all in him is satisfied? It is the same mechanism that, in the dream, thwarts her own request [*demande*] due to her friend's desire.

For despite the precision with which the request [*demande*] is symbolized by the newborn accessory, the telephone, it is all for naught. The patient's call does not go through; a fine thing it would be, indeed, for the other [her friend] to fatten up so that her husband could feast on her!

But how can another woman be loved (doesn't the mere fact that her husband holds her friend in high regard suffice to give the patient pause for thought?) by a man who cannot be satisfied with her (he being an "ass man" [*l'homme à la tranche de postérieur*])? This is the precise formulation of the question that is, generally speaking, the question involved in hysterical identification.

8. The subject becomes this question here. In this respect, the woman identifies with the man and the slice [*tranche*] of smoked salmon comes to occupy
the place of the Other's desire.

This desire not sufficing for anything (how can all the people be served
with this single slice of smoked salmon?), "I must, in the end (and at the end
of the dream), give up my desire to throw a dinner party (that is, give up my
search for the Other's desire, which is the secret of my own). Everything
goes wrong, and you say that a dream is the fulfillment of a desire! How do
you explain that one, professor?"

Challenged in this way, psychoanalysts stopped responding a long time
ago, having themselves given up pondering their patients' desires; analysts
reduce their patients' desires to demands, which simplifies the task of con-
verting them into the analysts' own demands. "Isn't that the reasonable road
to take?"—so they adopted it.

But sometimes desire cannot be conjured away quite so easily, being all
too visible, smack in the middle of the scene on the banquet table as we see
it here, in the form of a salmon, which happens to be a pretty fish; it suffices
to present it, as they do in restaurants, under a thin cloth for the unveiling to
equal that carried out at the culmination of the mysteries of Antiquity.

To be the phallus, even a somewhat skinny one—isn't that the final identification with the signifier of desire?

That doesn't seem self-evident in the case of a woman, and there are
those among us who prefer to have nothing further to do with this
obscure discourse. Are we going to have to spell out the role of the signifier only to find ourselves saddled with the castration complex and—God
spare us!—penis envy, when Freud, having come to this crossing, no
longer knew which way to turn, perceiving only the desert of analysis
beyond it?

Yes, but he led them to that crossing, and the place was less infested than
transference neurosis, which reduces you to chasing the patient away, begging him to go slowly so as to take his flies with him.

9. Let us nevertheless articulate what structures desire.

Desire is what manifests itself in the interval demand excavates just shy
of itself, insofar as the subject, articulating the signifying chain, brings to
light his lack of being [*manque à être*] with his call to receive the complement
of this lack from the Other—assuming that the Other, the locus of speech,
is also the locus of this lack.

What it is thus the Other's job to provide—and, indeed, it is what he does

627

not have, since he too lacks being—is what is called love, but it is also hate and ignorance.

Those passions for being are, moreover, evoked by any demand beyond the need articulated in that demand, and the more the need articulated in that demand is satisfied, the more the subject remains deprived of those passions.

Furthermore, the satisfaction of need appears here only as a lure in which the demand for love is crushed, throwing the subject back into a kind of sleep in which he haunts the limbo realm of being, letting it speak in him. For the being of language is the nonbeing of objects, and the fact that desire was discovered by Freud in its place in dreams—which have always been the bane of all attempts by thought to situate itself in reality—suffices to instruct us.

To be or not to be, to sleep, perchance to dream—even the supposedly simplest dreams of the child (as "simple" as the analytic situation, no doubt) simply display miraculous or forbidden objects.

628

10. But the child does not always fall asleep in this way in the bosom of being, especially if the Other, which has its own ideas about his needs, interferes and, instead of what it does not have, stuffs him with the smothering baby food it does have, that is, confuses the care it provides with the gift of its love.

It is the child who is the most lovingly fed who refuses food and employs his refusal as if it were a desire (anorexia nervosa).

This is an extreme case where one grasps as nowhere else that hate is the payback for love, but where it is ignorance that is not pardoned.

Ultimately, by refusing to satisfy the mother's demand, isn't the child requiring the mother to have a desire outside of him, because that is the pathway toward desire that he lacks?

11. Indeed, one of the principles that follows from these premises is that:

- if desire is an effect in the subject of the condition—which is imposed on him by the existence of discourse—that his need pass through the defiles of the signifier;
- and if, as I intimated above, by opening up the dialectic of transference, we must establish the notion of the Other with a capital O as being the locus of speech's deployment (the other scene, *ein anderer Schauplatz*, of which Freud speaks in the *Traumdeutung*);

then it must be posited that, as a characteristic of an animal at the mercy of language, man's desire is the Other's desire.

This concerns a totally different function than that of primary identification mentioned above, for it does not involve the assumption by the subject of the other's insignia, but rather the condition that the subject find the constitutive structure of his desire in the same gap opened up by the effect of signifiers in those who come to represent the Other for him, insofar as his demand is subjected to them.

Perhaps we can catch a glimpse in passing of the reason for this effect of occultation that caught our attention regarding the recognition of desire in the dream. The desire in the dream is not owned [*assumé*] by the subject who says "I" in his speech. Articulated, nevertheless, in the locus of the Other, it is discourse—a discourse whose grammar Freud began to enunciate as such. This is why the wishes it constitutes have no optative inflection to alter the indicative in which they are formulated.

A linguistic point of view would allow us to see that what is called the aspect of the verb is here that of the perfective [*accompli*] (the true meaning of *Wunscherfüllung* [wish-fulfillment]).

It is this ex-sistence (*Entstellung*)[16] of desire in the dream that explains how the dream's signifierness masks its desire, whereas its motive vanishes as being simply problematic.

629

---

12. Desire is produced in the beyond of demand, because in linking the subject's life to its conditions, demand prunes it of need. But desire is also excavated in the [area] shy of demand in that, as an unconditional demand for presence and absence, demand evokes the want-to-be in the three figures of the nothing that constitutes the ground for the demand for love, for the hatred that goes so far as to negate the other's being, and for the unspeakableness of what is not known [*s'ignore*] in its request. In this aporia incarnate—of which one might metaphorically say that demand borrows its heavy soul from the hardy offshoots of the wounded tendency, and its subtle body from death as it is actualized in the signifying sequence—desire asserts itself as an absolute condition.

Less still than the nothing that circulates in the round of significations that stir men up, desire is the wake left behind by its trajectory and like the signifier's brand on the speaking subject's shoulder. It is not so much a pure passion of the signified as a pure action of the signifier, which stops at the moment when the living being, having become a sign, renders this action meaningless [*insignifiante*].

630 This moment of cutting is haunted by the form of a bloody scrap: the pound of flesh that life pays in order to turn it into the signifier of signifiers, which it is impossible to restore, as such, to the imaginary body; it is the lost phallus of embalmed Osiris.

13. The function of this signifier as such in desire's quest is, as Freud detected, the key to what we need to know in order to terminate our analyses—and no artifice can make up for it if we are to achieve this end.

To give some idea of this function, I will describe an incident that occurred at the end of the analysis of an obsessive, that is, after a great deal of work in which I did not confine myself to "analyzing the subject's aggressiveness" (in other words, to pounding away at his imaginary aggressions), but in which he was made to recognize the part he had played in the destructive game foisted by one of his parents on the other parent's desire. He surmised his powerlessness to desire without destroying the Other, thus destroying his own desire insofar as it was the Other's desire.

To arrive at this stage, he was shown how at every moment he manipulated the situation so as to protect the Other, by our exhausting in the transference work [travail de transfert] (Durcharbeitung) all the artifices of a verbalization that distinguished the other from the Other (with a lowercase o and a capital O), and that, from the spectator's box reserved for the Other's (with a capital O) boredom, made him arrange the circus games between the two others (little a and the ego, its shadow).

Of course, it was not enough to go around in circles in some well-explored area of obsessive neurosis to bring him to this traffic circle, or to know this traffic circle in order to lead him to it by a route that is never the most direct. One does not simply need the blueprints to a reconstructed labyrinth, nor even a pile of blueprints that have already been worked up. What is needed above all is the general combinatory that no doubt governs their variety, but that also, even more usefully, accounts for the illusions or, better, shifts in the labyrinth that take place right before one's very eyes. For there is no shortage of either in obsessive neurosis, which is an architecture of contrasts that have not yet been sufficiently noticed and that cannot simply be attributed to differing facades. Amid so many seductive, insurgent, and impassive attitudes, we must grasp the anxieties that are bound up with performance, the grudges that do not prevent generosity (imagine claiming
631 that obsessives are lacking in oblativity!), and the mental infidelities that sustain infrangible loyalties. All this moves as a unit in an analysis, though not without local wilting; the great mass of it nevertheless remains.

Here my subject was at the end of his rope, having reached the point of playing a game of three-card monte with me that was of a rather peculiar kind, in that it revealed a structure of desire.

Let's say that being of mature years, as the comical expression goes, and of a disillusioned turn of mind, he would have willingly misled me into thinking his menopause was the cause of the impotence that struck him, and accused me of the same.

In fact, redistributions of libido are not brought about without certain objects losing their position, even if the position itself is permanent.

In short, he was impotent with his mistress and, having gotten it into his head to use his discoveries about the function of the potential third party in the couple, he suggested that she sleep with another man to see.

Now, if she remained in the place assigned to her by his neurosis, and if his analysis affected her in that position, it was because of the peace she had no doubt made long ago with the patient's desires, but even more so with the unconscious postulates maintained by those desires.

It will thus come as no surprise that, without wasting any time—indeed, that very night—she had a dream, which she recounted to our crestfallen patient hot off the presses.

In the dream she had a phallus—she sensed its shape under her clothing—which did not prevent her from having a vagina as well, nor, especially, from wanting this phallus to enter it.

On hearing this, my patient's powers were immediately restored and he demonstrated this brilliantly to his shrewd paramour.

What interpretation is indicated here?

You will have guessed from the request [demande] my patient had made of his mistress that he had been trying for a long time to get me to ratify his repressed homosexuality.

This was an effect of Freud's discovery of the unconscious, one that he was very quick to anticipate: among the regressive demands, the demand for fables will be sated with the truths spread by analysis itself. Analysis, upon its return from America, exceeded his expectations.

But I remained, as you may well have expected, rather off-putting on that point.

Note that the dreamer was no more indulgent in this regard, since her scenario excluded any coadjutor. This would guide even a novice to trust only in the text, if he is trained according to my principles.   632

Yet I am not analyzing her dream, but rather its effect on my patient.

It would run counter to my practice to get him to see in the dream a truth that is less widely known in analytic history as it is one of my own contributions: that the refusal of castration, if there is any such thing, is first and foremost a refusal of the Other's castration (of the mother's, first of all).

True opinion is not science, and conscience without science is but complicity with ignorance. Our science is transmitted only by articulating what is particular in the situation.

Here the situation is unique in showing the figure that I state in these terms: unconscious desire is the Other's desire—since the dream was designed to satisfy the patient's desire beyond his request [*demande*], as is suggested by the fact that it succeeds in doing so. Although it is not one of the patient's dreams, it may be no less valuable to us since, while it was not addressed to me as it was to the analysand, it addressed the analysand just as well as the analyst could have.

It was an opportunity to get the patient to grasp the function the phallus as a signifier serves in his desire. For it is as a signifier that the phallus operates in the dream in order to enable him to recover the use of the organ it represents, as I will show by the place the dream aims at in the structure in which his desire is caught up.

Apart from what the woman dreamt, there is the fact that she talked to him about it. Was the fact that she presented herself, in this discourse, as having a phallus the only way in which her erotic value was restored to her? Having a phallus was not, in effect, enough to restore to her an object position that allowed her to fit a fantasy on the basis of which my patient, as an obsessive, could maintain his desire in an impossibility that preserved its metonymic conditions. The latter governed a game of escape in his choices that analysis had disturbed, but which the woman restored here by a ruse, the crudeness of which concealed a subtlety that perfectly illustrates the science included in the unconscious.

For, to my patient, it was of no use to have this phallus, since his desire was to be it. And the woman's desire yields to his desire here, by showing him what she does not have.

633   Undiscriminating case studies always make much of any sign of a castrating mother, however small the role the anamnesis gives her. She looms large here, as expected.

People think that their job is then done. But it's of no value in interpretation, where to invoke it would not have taken us very far, except to bring the patient back to the very point where he wound his way between a desire and contempt for that desire: certainly, his ill-tempered mother's contempt for the overly ardent desire whose image his father bequeathed him.

But this would have taught him less about it than what his mistress *said* to him: that having this phallus in her dream didn't stop her from desiring it. Which is why his own want-to-be was touched.

That lack results from an exodus: his being is always elsewhere. He has "tucked it away," one might say. Am I saying this to explain the difficulty of his desire? No, rather to say that his desire is for difficulty.

Let us not, therefore, be misled by the guarantee the subject received from the fact that the dreamer had a phallus and would not have to take it from him—even if to point out, learnedly, that such a guarantee is too strong not to be fragile.

For that would be precisely to fail to recognize that this guarantee would not require so much weight if it did not have to be (im)printed in a sign, and that it is by displaying this sign as such, by making it appear where it cannot be, that this guarantee has its effect.

The condition of desire that especially grabs the obsessive is the very mark by which he finds desire spoiled, the mark of origin of its object—contraband.

A singular mode of grace which is figured only on the basis of a disavowal of nature. A favor is hidden here that is always kept waiting in our subject. And it is by dismissing this favor that one day he will let it enter.

14. The importance of preserving the place of desire in the direction of the treatment requires one to position this place in relation to the effects of demand, the only effects that are currently considered to be at the crux of the power of the treatment.

Indeed, the fact that the genital act must find its place in desire's unconscious articulation is the discovery of analysis, and it is precisely why no one has ever thought of giving in to the patient's illusion that to facilitate his demand for the satisfaction of need would be of any help to him. (Still less to authorize it with the classic *coïtus normalis dosim repetatur.*)

634

Why do people think differently in believing it to be more essential for the progress of the treatment to work in any way whatsoever on other demands, under the pretext that they are regressive?

Let us begin once again with the notion that the subject's own speech is a message to him, first of all, because it is produced in the Other's locus. It originates in that locus and is worded as such not only because his demand is submitted to the Other's code, but because his demand is dated by this Other's locus (and even time).

This can be clearly read in the subject's most freely given speech. He

invokes his wife or his master, so that they have his word with a *tu es . . .,*
"you are . . ." (the one or the other), without declaring what he himself is
otherwise than by murmuring an order of murder against himself that the
equivocation of the French brings to one's ear.

Although it always shows through in demand, as we see here, desire is
nevertheless beyond demand. It is also shy of another demand in which the
subject, echoing in the other's locus, would like not so much to efface his
dependence by a payback agreement as to fix the very being he proposes
there.

This means that it is only from a kind of speech [*une parole*] that would
remove the mark the subject receives from what he says that he might obtain
the absolution that would return him to his desire.

But desire is nothing but the impossibility of such speech, which, in
replying to the first speech can merely redouble its mark by consummating
the split (*Spaltung*) the subject undergoes by virtue of being a subject only
insofar as he speaks.

(This is symbolized by the slanted bar of noble bastardy, which I assign
to the S of the subject in order to indicate that it is this specific subject: $.)[17]

635   The regression people foreground in analysis (temporal regression, no
doubt, providing one specifies that it has to do with the time of remembering) concerns only the (oral, anal, etc.) signifiers of demand, and involves
the corresponding drive only through them.

Reducing this demand to its place may produce the appearance of a
reduction of desire owing to the mitigation of need.

But this is really only the effect of the analyst's heavy-handedness. For
if demand's signifiers have sustained the frustrations on which desire is fixated (Freud's *Fixierung*), it is only in their place that desire is exacting
[*assujetissant*].

Whether it intends to frustrate or to gratify, any response to demand in
analysis reduces transference to suggestion.

There is a relation between transference and suggestion, as Freud discovered: transference is also a suggestion, but a suggestion that operates
only on the basis of the demand for love, which is not a demand based on
any need. The fact that this demand is constituted as such only insofar as the
subject is the subject of the signifier is what allows it to be misused by reducing it to the needs from which these signifiers have been borrowed—which
is what psychoanalysts, as we see, do not fail to do.

But identification with demand's omnipotent signifier, of which I have
already spoken, must not be confused with identification with the object of

the demand for love. The demand for love is also a regression, as Freud insists, when he makes it into the second form of identification, which he distinguished in his second topography when he wrote *Group Psychology and the Analysis of the Ego*. But it is another kind of regression.

Here is the exit* that allows us to leave suggestion behind. Identification with the object as a regression, because it begins with the demand for love, opens up the sequence of transference (opens it up, not closes it)—that is, the pathway by which the identifications that punctuate this regression by stopping it can be exposed.

But this regression is no more dependent on the need in demand than sadistic desire is explained by anal demand, for to believe that a turd is in itself a noxious object is but an ordinary lure of understanding. ("Understanding" in the harmful sense the word takes on in Jaspers' work. "You understand . . ." is an introductory phrase by which someone who has nothing to convey thinks he can impress someone who understands nothing.) But the demand to be a shit—now there's something that it is preferable to view from a different angle when the subject reveals himself there. It's the "misfortune of being" I referred to above.

636

Whoever cannot carry his training analyses to this turning point—at which it is revealed, with trembling, that all the demands that have been articulated in the analysis (and more than any other the one that was at its core, the demand to become an analyst, which now comes to maturity) were merely transferences designed to keep in place a desire that was unstable or dubious in its problematic—such a person knows nothing of what must be obtained from the subject if he is to be able to ensure the direction of an analysis, or merely offer a well-advised interpretation in it.

These considerations confirm that it is natural to analyze transference. For transference is already, in itself, an analysis of suggestion, insofar as transference places the subject, with regard to his demand, in a position he occupies only because of his desire.

It is only in order to maintain this transference framework that frustration must prevail over gratification.

The subject's resistance, when it opposes suggestion, is but a desire to maintain his desire. As such, his resistance should be considered positive transference, since it is desire that maintains the direction of the analysis, quite apart from the effects of demand.

As you can see, these propositions are rather different from the received opinions on the matter. If they lead people to think that something has gone awry somewhere, I will have succeeded in my aim.

15. This is the place for a few remarks on symptom formation.

Freud—starting with his demonstrative study of such subjective phenomena as dreams, slips, and jokes, which, he says quite categorically, are structurally identical to symptoms (but, of course, to our scientists, all this is clearly inadequate for the experience they have acquired—and by what pathways!—for them to even dream of returning to it)—Freud, as I was saying, stressed again and again that symptoms are overdetermined. To the foolish acolyte engaged in the daily drumbeating that promises the imminent reduction of analysis to its biological bases, this is obvious enough; it is so easy to say that he does not even hear it. "Is that all you've got?" he asks.

637

Let us leave aside my remarks on the fact that overdetermination is only conceivable, strictly speaking, within the structure of language. What does this mean, as far as neurotic symptoms are concerned?

It means that interference will occur in the effects that correspond in a subject to a particular demand from the effects of a position that he maintains as a subject in relation to the other (here, his semblable).

"That he maintains as a subject" means that language allows him to regard himself as the stagehand, or even the director, of the entire imaginary capture of which he would otherwise be nothing more than the living marionette.

Fantasy is the very illustration of this original possibility. This is why any temptation to reduce fantasy to imagination, that doesn't admit to its failure, is a permanent misconception, a misconception from which the Kleinian school, which has certainly carried things very far here, is not free, having failed to even glimpse the category of the signifier.

However, the notion of unconscious fantasy no longer presents any difficulty once it is defined as an image set to work in the signifying structure.

Let us say that, in its fundamental use, fantasy is the means by which the subject maintains himself at the level of his vanishing desire, vanishing inasmuch as the very satisfaction of demand deprives him of his object.

"Oh, these neurotics are so fussy! What is to be done with them? These people are incomprehensible, upon my word," as one family man put it.

But this is precisely what has been said for a long time—indeed, what has always been said—and analysts haven't gotten any further. The simpleminded call it the irrational, since they haven't even realized that Freud's discovery is ratified by the fact that it first takes it as certain that the real is rational—which, in itself, is enough to cut the ground out from under our exegetes—and then by noting that the rational is real. As a result, Freud can articulate that what presents itself as not very reasonable in desire is an effect of the passage of the rational qua real—that is, of language—into the real, insofar as the rational has already traced its circumvallation there.

For the paradox of desire is not the neurotic's privilege; it is rather that he takes the existence of this paradox into account in his way of dealing with desire. This does not give him such a bad ranking in the order of human dignity, and it does no honor to mediocre analysts (this is not an assessment, but an ideal formulated in a definite wish made by the interested parties) who, on this point, fail to achieve the same dignity: a surprising distance that analysts have always noted in veiled terms by talking about "other analysts," without our knowing how the latter can be distinguished, since they would never have thought of doing so themselves, if they hadn't first had to oppose the deviation of the former.

638

16. It is, then, the neurotic's position with respect to desire—let us say, to abbreviate, fantasy—that marks with its presence the subject's response to demand, in other words, the signification of his need.

But this fantasy has nothing to do with the signification in which it interferes. Indeed, this signification comes from the Other, insofar as it depends on the Other whether or not demand is met. But fantasy comes in here only to find itself on the return path of a broader circuit, a circuit that, in carrying demand to the limits of being, makes the subject wonder about the lack in which he appears to himself as desire.

It is incredible that certain features of man's action as such, which have always been obvious enough, have not been highlighted here by analysis. I am talking about what makes man's action the deed that finds support in his epic poem. The analyst reduces this dimension of exploit, performance, and solution strangled by the symbol, what thus makes it symbolic (but not in the alienating sense this term commonly denotes)—the very reason why people speak of *passage à l'acte* [acting out], that Rubicon whose characteristic desire is always camouflaged in history in favor of its success, everything to which the experience of what the analyst calls "acting out"* gives him a quasi-experimental access, since he holds its entire artifice in his hands—the analyst reduces it at best to a relapse on the subject's part, at worst to a mistake on the therapist's part.

One is stupefied by the analyst's false shame in the face of action—a shame that no doubt conceals true shame, the shame he has regarding an action, his own action, one of the highest of actions, when it stoops to abjection.

639   For what else, in fact, is it, when by intervening the analyst degrades the transference message he is there to interpret into a fallacious signification of reality [*réel*] that is nothing but mystification?

For the point at which the contemporary analyst claims to grasp transference is the distance he defines between fantasy and the so-called "well-adapted response." Well-adapted to what if not to the Other's demand? And why would this demand have any more or less consistency than the response obtained, if the analyst didn't believe he was authorized to deny [*dénier*] all value to fantasy in using the yardstick he takes from his own reality?

Here the very pathway by which he proceeds betrays him, when it is necessary for him to insert himself into fantasy by this pathway and offer himself up as an imaginary Host [*hostie*] to fictions in which an idiotic desire proliferates—an unexpected Ulysses who offers himself up as fodder so that Circe's pigsty may prosper.

Let it not be said that I am defaming anyone here, for it is the precise point at which those who cannot articulate their practice in any other way are themselves sufficiently concerned to question what they are doing: "Aren't fantasies the area in which we provide the subject with the gratification in which the analysis becomes bogged down?" This is the question they keep repeating to themselves with the inescapable insistence of an unconscious torment.

17. Thus, at best, the contemporary analyst leaves his patient at the point of purely imaginary identification—of which the hysteric remains captive, because her fantasy implies ensnarement in it.

This is the very point from which Freud, throughout the first part of his career, wished to extricate the hysteric too quickly by forcing the call for love onto the object of identification (for Elisabeth von R., her brother-in-law [5]; for Dora, Herr K.; for the young homosexual woman in the case of female homosexuality, he sees the problem more clearly, but errs when he regards himself as the object aimed at in reality [*réel*] by the negative transference).

It was not until the chapter on identification in *Group Psychology and the Analysis of the Ego* that Freud clearly distinguished the third form of identification, which is conditioned by its function of sustaining desire and is therefore specified by the indifference of its object.

But our psychoanalysts insist: this indifferent object is the substance of the object—eat of my body, drink of my blood (this profane evocation flows from their pens). The mystery of the analysand's redemption lies in this imaginary effusion, of which the analyst is the sacrificial object [*l'oblat*].   640

How can the ego, whose aid they claim to enlist here, not suffer, in effect, from the blows of the further alienation they induce in the subject? Long before Freud came on the scene, psychologists knew, even if they did not express it in these terms, that while desire is the metonymy of the want-to-be, the ego is the metonymy of desire.

This is how the terminal identification occurs, in which analysts take such pride.

Whether the identification involves their patient's ego or superego, they aren't sure, or rather, they couldn't care less, but what the patient identifies with is their strong ego.

Freud foresaw this result very clearly in the text I just mentioned, when he showed that the most insignificant object may play the role of an ideal in the genesis of a leader.

It is not in vain that analytic psychology is increasingly turning toward group psychology and even group psychotherapy.

Let us observe its effects in the analytic group itself. It is not true that analysands undergoing training analysis model themselves on the image of their analyst, regardless of the level at which one wishes to detect that image. It is rather that analysands of the same analyst are linked to each other by a feature that may be quite secondary in the psychical economy of each of them, but upon which the analyst's inadequacy in his work is clearly stamped.

Thus the analyst according to whom the problem of desire can be reduced to lifting the veil off of fear, leaves all those he has guided wrapped in this shroud.

18. Thus we have now reached the tricky crux of this power that is ever open to a blind direction. It is the power to do good—no power has any other end—and that is why power has no end. But something else is at stake here: truth, the only truth, the truth about the effects of truth. Once Oedipus set off down this path, he had already given up power.

Where, then, is the direction of the treatment headed? Perhaps we need but question its means to define it in its soundness.

Let us note: 641

(1) that speech possesses all the powers here, the specific powers of the treatment;

(2) that, with the fundamental rule of psychoanalysis, the analyst is far from directing the subject toward full speech, or toward a coherent discourse—rather, the analyst leaves the subject free to have a go at it;

(3) that this freedom is what the subject tolerates least easily;

(4) that demand is exactly what is bracketed in analysis, it being ruled out that the analyst satisfy any of the subject's demands;

(5) that since no obstacle is put in the way of the subject's owning [*aveu*] of his desire, it is toward this owning that he is directed and even channeled;

(6) that resistance to this owning can, in the final analysis, be related here to nothing but desire's incompatibility with speech.

There may still be a few people, even in my usual audience, who are surprised to find such propositions in my discourse.

One senses here the terrible temptation the analyst must face to respond to demand, however minimally.

How, moreover, is the analyst to prevent the subject from attributing this response to him, in the form of a demand to get better, and in accordance with the horizon of a discourse that the subject has all the more reason to impute to him given that our authority has wrongly adopted this discourse?

Who will now relieve us of this tunic of Nessus we have spun for ourselves in maintaining that analysis responds to all the desiderata of demand, and by widely circulated norms? Who will sweep this enormous pile of dung out of the Augean Stables of analytic literature?

What silence must the analyst now impose upon himself if he is to make out, rising above this bog, the raised finger of Leonardo's "St. John the Baptist," if interpretation is to find anew the forsaken horizon of being in which its allusive virtue must be deployed?

19. Since the point is to take desire, and since it can only be taken literally [*à la lettre*], since it is the letter's snare that determines, nay overdetermines, its place as a heavenly bird, how can we fail to require the bird catcher to first be a man of letters?

Who among us has attempted to articulate the importance of the "literary" element in Freud's work, apart from a professor of literature in Zurich who has begun to spell it out?

This is merely an indication. Let us go further. Let us question how things should stand with the analyst (with the analyst's "being"), as far as his own desire is concerned.

Who would still be so naive as to see Freud as the conventional Viennese bourgeois who so astonished André Breton by not manifesting any obsession with the Bacchanalian? Now that we have nothing but his works, will we not recognize in them a river of fire, which owes nothing to François Mauriac's artificial river?

Who was more able than him, when avowing his dreams, to spin the thread on which the ring that unites us with being slides, and make its brief shine glow in closed hands, passing it from the one to the other in the swiftly shifting game of human passion?

Who has inveighed as much as this scholar against the monopolization of jouissance by those who load the burdens of need onto others' shoulders?

Who, as fearlessly as this clinician, so firmly rooted in the everydayness of human suffering, has questioned life as to its meaning   not to say that it has none, which is a convenient way of washing one's hands of the matter, but to say that it has only one, that in which desire is borne by death?

A man of desire, a desire he followed against his will down pathways where it is reflected in feeling, dominating, and knowing, but whose unparalleled signifier he and he alone—like an initiate at the defunct mysteries—succeeded in unveiling: the phallus, the receiving and giving of which are equally impossible for the neurotic, whether he knows that the Other does not have it, or that the Other does have it, because in both cases the neurotic's desire is elsewhere—to be it. And whether male or female, man must accept to have and not have it, on the basis of the discovery that he isn't it.

It is here that is inscribed the final *Spaltung* by which the subject is linked to Logos, and about which Freud was beginning to write [12], giving us, at the final point of an oeuvre that has the dimensions of being, the solution to "infinite" analysis, when his death applied to it the word "Nothing."

Note and References   643

This paper represents a selection from my ongoing seminar. My talk at the colloquium and the responses it received resituated the paper in the context of my teaching.

During the talk I presented a graph that precisely articulates the directions proposed here for the field of analysis and its handling.

Below, the reader will find, in alphabetical order by author, the references indicated in my text by numbers in brackets.

I have used the following abbreviations:

GW: *Gesammelte Werke*, by Freud, published by Imago Publishing, London. The Roman numerals that follow refer to the volume.

SE: The Standard Edition of the Complete Psychological Works of Sigmund Freud, the English translation of Freud's works, published by Hogarth Press, London. Again, the Roman numerals refer to the volume.

IJP: International Journal of Psycho-Analysis.

PQ: The Psycho-Analytic Quarterly.

RFP: Revue Française de Psychanalyse.

PDA: A work entitled La Psychanalyse d'aujourd'hui ["Contemporary Psychoanalysis"] (Paris: PUF, 1956), which I refer to only because of the naive simplicity with which the tendency to degrade the direction of the treatment and the principles of its power in psychoanalysis is presented in it. Designed, no doubt, to circulate outside the psychoanalytic community, it serves as an obstacle inside it. Thus I don't mention its authors, who make no properly scientific contribution in it.

[1] Abraham, Karl, "Die psychosexuellen Differenzen der Hysterie und der Dementia praecox" (1st International Congress of Psychoanalysis, Salzburg, April 26, 1908), Centralblatt für Nervenheilkunde und Psychiatrie, number 2, July 1908, Neue folge, Bd. 19: 521–33, and in Klinische Beiträge zur Psychoanalyse (Leipzig, Vienna, Zurich: Int. Psych. Verlag, 1921); "The Psycho-Sexual Differences between Hysteria and Dementia Praecox," Selected Papers (London: Hogarth Press, 1927): 64–79.

[2] Devereux, Georges, "Some Criteria for the Timing of Confrontations and Interpretations," *IJP* XXXII, 1 (1951): 19–24.

[3] Ferenczi, Sandor, "Introjektion und Übertragung," 1909, Jahrbuch für psychoanalytische Forschungen I: 422–57; "Introjection and Transference," Sex in Psycho-Analysis (New York: Basic Books, 1952): 35–93.

[4] Freud, Anna, Das Ich und die Abwehrmechanismen, Chapter IV, "Die Abwehrmechanismen." See Versuch einer Chronologie, 60–63 (Vienna: Intern. psychoanal. Verlag, 1936); The Ego and the Mechanisms of Defence (London: Hogarth Press, 1937); (New York: International Universities Press, 1946).

[5] Freud, Sigmund, Studien über Hysterie (1895), *GW* I; for the case of Elisabeth von R., see pages 196–251 and especially 125–27; Studies on Hysteria, *SE* II, 158–60.

[6] Freud, Sigmund, *Die Traumdeutung* (1900), *GW* II–III. See, in Chap. IV, "Die Traumentstellung," pages 152–56, 157, and 163–68; "Kern unseres Wesens," 609; *The Interpretation of Dreams*, *SE* IV, Chap. IV, "Distortion in Dreams," 146–50, 151, 157–62, and Chap. VII, 603.

[7] Freud, Sigmund, "Bruchstück einer Hysterie-Analyse (Dora)," finished   644
on January 24, 1901 (see letter 140 in *Aus den Anfängen*, the correspondence with Fliess originally published in London): *GW* V, 194–95 [*The Origins of Psychoanalysis* (New York: Basic Books, 1954), 325–26]; "Fragment of an Analysis of a Case of Hysteria," *SE* VII, 35–36.

[8] Freud, Sigmund, "Bemerkungen über einen Fall von Zwangsneurose" (1909), *GW* VII. See, in section 1.d, "Die Einführung ins Verständnis der Kur," pages 402–4, and the footnote on pages 404–5; in section 1.f, "Die Krankheitsveranlassung," namely, Freud's decisive interpretation concerning what I would translate as the subject of the illness; and 1.g, "Der Vaterkomplex und die Lösung der Rattenidee," 417–38, "Notes upon a Case of Obsessional Neurosis," *SE* X. See, section 1.d, "Initiation into the Nature of the Treatment," 178–81 and the footnote on 181; and sections 1.f, "The Precipitating Cause of the Illness," and 1.g, "The Father Complex and the Solution of the Rat Idea," 195–220.

[9] Freud, Sigmund, *Jenseits des Lustprinzips* (1920), *GW* XIII; see, if it is still necessary, pages 11–14 of Chapter II; *Beyond the Pleasure Principle*, *SE* XVIII, 14–16.

[10] Freud, Sigmund, *Massenpsychologie und Ich-Analyse* (1921), *GW* XIII, Chapter VII, "Die Identifizierung," especially pages 116–18; *Group Psychology and the Analysis of the Ego*, *SE* XVIII, 106–8.

[11] Freud, Sigmund, "Die endliche und die unendliche Analyse" (1937), *GW* XVI, 59–99, translated into French as "Terminated (!) analysis and interminable (!!) analysis" (my exclamation marks concern the standards employed in the translation into French of Freud's works. I am mentioning this translation because, according to the sixteenth volume of the *GW* that came out in 1950, it doesn't exist; see page 280), in *RFP* XI, 1 (1939): 3–38.

[12] Freud, Sigmund, "Die Ichspaltung im Abwehrvorgang," *GW* XVII, "Schriften aus dem Nachlass," 58–62. Manuscript dated January 2, 1938

(unfinished); "Splitting of the Ego in the Defensive Process," *Collected Papers* V, 372–75. [*SE* XXIII, 275–78.]

[13] Glover, Edward, "The Therapeutic Effect of Inexact Interpretation: A Contribution to the Theory of Suggestion," *IJP* XII, 4 (1931): 397–411.

[14] Hartmann, Kris, and Loewenstein, various team* contributions in *The Psychoanalytic Study of the Child* since 1946.

[15] Kris, Ernst, "Ego Psychology and Interpretation in Psychoanalytic Therapy," *PQ* XX, 1 (1951): 21–25. [Reprinted, with modifications, in *Selected Papers of Ernst Kris* (New Haven: Yale University Press, 1975), 237–51.]

[16] Lacan, Jacques, my paper for the Rome Congress (September 26–27, 1953), "Fonction et champ de la parole et du langage en psychanalyse" ["The Function and Field of Speech and Language in Psychoanalysis"], *La Psychanalyse* 1 (1956); *Écrits* 1966, 237–322.

[17] Lacan, Jacques, "L'instance de la lettre dans l'inconscient ou la raison depuis Freud" ["The Instance of the Letter in the Unconscious or Reason Since Freud"] (May 9, 1957), *La Psychanalyse* 3 (1957), 47–81; *Écrits* 1966, 493–528.

[18] Lagache, Daniel, "Le problème du transfert" ["The Problem of Transference"] (Paper given at the 14th Conference of French-speaking Psychoanalysts on November 1, 1951), *RFP* XVI, 1–2 (1952): 5–115.

[19] Leclaire, Serge, "À la recherche des principes d'une psychothérapie des psychoses" ["Search for Principles Guiding Psychotherapy with Psychotics"] (Bonneval Congress, April 15, 1957), *L'Évolution psychiatrique* 2 (1958): 377–419.

[20] Macalpine, Ida, "The Development of the Transference," *PQ* XIX, 4 (1950): 500–539, especially 502–8 and 522–28.

[21] *PDA*: see pages 51–52 (on "pregenital" and "genital"), passim (on the strengthening of the ego and the method for doing so), and 102 (on distance from the object as the principle of a method of treatment) [Maurice Bouvet, "La clinique psychanalytique. La relation d'objet"].

645

[22] *PDA*: see pages 133 (on emotional reeducation and the *PDA*'s opposition to Freud regarding the primordial importance of the two-person relation), 132 (on the cure "from the inside"), 135 (what is important . . . is not so much what the analyst says or does as what he is), 136, etc., passim, and 162 (on dismissing [the patient] at the end of the treatment), and 149 (on dreams) [Sacha Nacht, "La thérapeutique psychanalytique"].

[23] R.L. [Ruth Lebovici], "Perversion sexuelle transitoire au cours d'un traitement psychanalytique" ["Transitory Sexual Perversion in the Course of a Psychoanalytic Treatment"], *Bulletin d'activités de l'Association des Psychanalystes de Belgique* 25 (1956): 1–15 (118, rue Froissart, Brussels).

[24] Sharpe, Ella, "The Technique of Psychoanalysis," *Collected Papers on Psychoanalysis* (London: Hogarth Press, 1950). See pages 81 (on the need to justify one's existence) and 12–14 (on the background and techniques required of the analyst).

[25] Schmideberg, Melitta, "Intellektuelle Hemmung und Ess-störung," *Zeitschrift für psa. Pädagogik* VIII (1934). ["Intellectual Inhibition and Disturbances in Eating," *IJP* XIX (1938): 17–22.]

[26] Williams, J. D., *The Compleat Strategyst*, The Rand Series (New York, Toronto, London: McGraw Hill, 1966). [More recently: (New York: Dover, 1986).]

[27] Winnicott, D. W., "Transitional Objects and Transitional Phenomena," in *IJP* XXXIV, 2 (1953): 29–97.

Notes

1. This is the first of two papers I gave at the International Colloquium at the invitation of the Société Française de Psychanalyse; it was published in *La Psychanalyse* 6 (1961): 149–206.

2. Numbers in square brackets correspond to the references provided at the end of this paper.

3. To turn the term "dislodge" against the spirit of a society, a term that allows us to assess this spirit, for it translates the sentence in which Freud proved himself the equal of the pre-Socratics—*Wo Es war, soll Ich werden*—into French quite simply as *Le Moi doit déloger le ça*, "the ego must dislodge the id."

4. "Comment terminer le traitement analytique," *Revue Française de Psychanalyse* XVIII, 4 (1954): 519 and passim. To gauge the influence of such training, read: Charles-Henri Nodet, "Le psychanalyste," *L'Évolution psychiatrique* 4 (1957): 689–91.

5. I promise not to tire my readers any fur-

ther with such stupid formulations, which really only serve here to show what has become of analytic discourse. I apologized to the foreigners in the audience who no doubt had just as many stupid formulations available in their own language [*langue*], if not of quite the same platitudinous level.

6. In France the doctrinaire of being, quoted above, went straight to the following solution: the psychoanalyst's being is innate [22 (page 136)].

7. Rather than being vocalized as the letter symbolizing oxygen, evoked by the metaphor being played out, the "O" may be read as zero, insofar as this number symbolizes the essential function of place in the signifier's structure.

8. For example: in the United States, where Kris has achieved success, publication means title of ownership, and a seminar like mine would have to stake its claim to priority every week against the pillage it couldn't fail to occasion. In France, my ideas penetrate by way of infiltration into a group, in which people obey orders that prohibit my teachings. In being cursed there, ideas can only serve as decorations for a few dandies. Never mind: the void the ideas cause to resound, whether I am cited or not, makes another voice heard.

9. My parentheses.

10. My parentheses.

11. My parentheses.

12. (Added in 1966:) The penultimate sentence of this paragraph and the first line of the next paragraph have been rectified.

13. See letter 118 (September 11, 1899) to Fliess in *Sigmund Freud, Aus den Anfängen der Psychoanalyse* (London: Imago Publishing Company, 1950).

14. Here is the dream as it is presented in the patient's account on page 152 of *GW* II–III: "I want to throw a dinner party. But I only have a little smoked salmon left. I think of going out shopping, when I remember that it is Sunday afternoon and all the shops are closed. I tell myself that I'll call a few caterers on the phone. But the phone is out of order. Thus I have to give up my desire to throw a dinner party."

15. This is the reason Freud gives for the hysterical identification, specifying that smoked salmon plays for the friend the same role caviar plays for the patient.

16. It must not be forgotten that the term is used for the first time in the *Traumdeutung* on the subject of dreams, and that this use provides its meaning and, simultaneously, that of the term "distortion," which translates it when British analysts apply it to the ego. This remark allows us to evaluate the use made in France of the term "ego distortion" [*distortion du Moi*], which supporters of ego strengthening—insufficiently alerted to the "false cognates" English words constitute (words have so little importance, don't they?)—understand simply as . . . a twisted ego.

17. See ($\lozenge$D) and ($\lozenge a$) on my graph, reproduced in "Subversion of the Subject," page 817 [page 302] below. The sign $\lozenge$ registers the relations envelopment-development-conjunction-disjunction. The links it signifies in these two parentheses allow us to read the barred S as "S fading* in demand's cut," and "S fading* before the object of desire"—that is, drive and fantasy.

The Signification of the Phallus
Die Bedeutung des Phallus

The following is the unaltered text of a lecture I gave in German on May 9, 1958, at the Max Planck Society in Munich, having been invited to speak there by Professor Paul Matussek.

If one has any notion of the mentality then prevalent in not otherwise uninformed circles, one can imagine how my use of terms that I was the first to extract from Freud's work, such as "the other scene" (to cite one mentioned here), must have resounded.

If deferred action (*Nachtrag*), to take back another of these terms from the domain of the highbrow literati where they now circulate, makes this effort impracticable, it should be realized that they were unheard of at that time.

We know that the unconscious castration complex functions as a knot:

(1) in the dynamic structuring of symptoms, in the analytic sense of the term, in other words, in the dynamic structuring of what is analyzable in the neuroses, perversions, and psychoses;

(2) in regulating the development that gives its *ratio* to this first role: namely, the instating in the subject of an unconscious position without which he could not identify with the ideal type of his sex or even answer the needs of his partner in sexual relations without grave risk, much less appropriately meet the needs of the child who may be produced thereby.

There is an antinomy here that is internal to the assumption [*assomption*] by man (*Mensch*) of his sex: why must he assume the attributes of that sex only through a threat or even in the guise of a deprivation? In *Civilization and Its Discontents*, Freud, as we know, went so far as to suggest not a contingent but an essential disturbance of human sexuality, and one of his last articles concerns the irreducibility—in any finite (*endliche*) analysis—of the aftermath of the castration complex in the masculine unconscious and of *Penisneid* [penis envy] in woman's unconscious.

This is not the only aporia, but it is the first that Freudian experience and the metapsychology that resulted from it introduced into our experience of man. It cannot be solved by reducing things to biological data; the very necessity of the myth underlying the structuring brought on by the Oedipus complex demonstrates this sufficiently.

It would be mere artifice to invoke in this case some inherited forgotten experience, not only because such an experience is in itself debatable, but because it leaves the problem unsolved: what is the link between killing the father and the pact of the primordial law, if we include here the fact that castration is the punishment for incest?

It is only on the basis of clinical facts that the discussion can be fruitful. These facts reveal a relation between the subject and the phallus that forms without regard to the anatomical distinction between the sexes and that is thus especially difficult to interpret in the case of women and with respect to women, particularly as concerns the following four points:

(1) why a little girl considers herself, even for a moment, to be castrated, in the sense of deprived of a phallus, by someone whom she at first identifies as her mother—an important point—and then as her father, but in such a way that one must recognize therein a transference in the analytic sense of the term;

(2) why, more primordially, both sexes consider the mother to be endowed with a phallus, that is, to be a phallic mother;

(3) why, correlatively, the signification of castration in fact takes on its (clinically manifest) full weight in the formation of symptoms only on the basis of its discovery as the mother's castration;

(4) these three problems lead, finally, to the why and wherefore of the "phallic phase" in development. Freud, as we know, uses this term to refer to the first genital maturation insofar as, on the one hand, it would seem to be characterized by the imaginary dominance of the phallic attribute and by masturbatory jouissance and, on the other, he localizes this jouissance in the case of women in the clitoris, which is thus raised to the function of the phallus. He thus seems to exclude in both sexes any instinctual mapping of the vagina as the site of genital penetration until the end of this phase, that is, until the dissolution of the Oedipus complex.

687

This ignorance smacks of misrecognition in the technical sense of the term—all the more so in that it is sometimes fabricated. Could it correspond to anything other than the fable in which Longus depicts Daphnis and Chloe's initiation as dependent upon the explanations of an old woman?

This is what has led certain authors to regard the phallic phase as the effect of a repression, and the function assumed in it by the phallic object as a symptom. The problem begins when one asks, *which* symptom? Phobia, says one, perversion, says another, and sometimes the same person says both. In the latter case, the quandary is evident: not that interesting transmutations of the object of a phobia into a fetish do not occur, but if they are interesting it is precisely owing to their different places in the structure. It would be pointless to ask these authors to formulate this difference from the perspectives currently in favor that go by the name of "object relations." For on this subject they have no other reference than the approximate notion of part-object, which has never been subjected to criticism since Karl Abraham introduced it. This is unfortunate given the comfort it offers analysts today.

The fact remains that the now abandoned discussion of the phallic phase, if one rereads the surviving texts from 1928–32, is refreshing for the example it sets of doctrinal passion—making one nostalgic, given psychoanalysis' decline following its American transplantation.

Were one to merely summarize the debate, one could but distort the authentic diversity of positions taken up by Helene Deutsch, Karen Horney, and Ernest Jones, to mention only the most eminent.

The series of three articles Jones devoted to the subject is especially suggestive—if only for the first sighting on which he built, which is signaled by the term he introduced: "aphanisis." For in raising, quite rightly, the problem of the relation between castration and desire, he demonstrates his inability to recognize what he nevertheless closes in on so nearly that the term, which will soon provide us with the key, seems to emerge in his work due to its very absence.

Particularly amusing is the way he manages to extract from the very letter of Freud's text a position that is strictly contrary to it: a true model in a difficult genre.   688

Yet the question refuses to let itself be dodged, seeming to scoff at Jones' plea to reestablish the equality of natural rights (doesn't it push him to the point where he closes with the Biblical "Male and female created He them"?). What does he, in fact, gain by normalizing the function of the phallus as a part-object if he has to invoke its presence in the mother's body as an "internal object," a term based on fantasies revealed by Melanie Klein, and if he becomes still more unable to separate himself from her views, relating these fantasies to the recurrence, as far back as earliest infancy, of the Oedipal formation?

We will not be led astray if we reexamine the question by asking what could have led Freud to his obviously paradoxical position. For one has to admit that he was better guided than anyone in his recognition of the order of unconscious phenomena, of which he was the inventor, and that, in the absence of an adequate articulation of the nature of these phenomena, his followers were destined to lose their way to a greater or lesser degree.

It is on the basis of this wager—which I place at the crux of the commentary on Freud's work I have been pursuing for seven years—that I have been led to certain results: first and foremost, to promote the notion of the signifier as necessary to any articulation of the analytic phenomenon, insofar as it is opposed to that of the signified in modern linguistic analysis. Freud could not have taken into account modern linguistics, which postdates him, but I would maintain that Freud's discovery stands out precisely because, in setting out from a domain in which one could not have expected to encounter linguistics' reign, it had to anticipate its formulations. Conversely, it is Freud's discovery that gives the signifier/signified opposition its full scope: for the signifier plays an active role in determining the effects by which the signifiable appears to succumb to its mark, becoming, through that passion, the signified.

This passion of the signifier thus becomes a new dimension of the human condition in that it is not only man who speaks, but in man and through man that it [*ça*] speaks; in that his nature becomes woven by effects in which the structure of the language of which he becomes the material can be refound; and in that the relation of speech thus resonates in him, beyond anything that could have been conceived of by the psychology of ideas.

689

In this sense one can say that the consequences of the discovery of the unconscious have not yet been so much as glimpsed in analytic theory, although its impact has been felt in analytic praxis more than we realize, even if only in the form of people beating a retreat from it.

Let me make it clear that my emphasis on man's relation to the signifier as such has nothing to do with a "culturalist" position, in the ordinary sense of the term—the position Karen Horney, for example, anticipated in the debate over the phallus, a position Freud described as feminist. It is not man's relationship to language as a social phenomenon that is at issue, nor even anything resembling the ideological psychogenesis we are familiar with which is not superseded by peremptory recourse to the thoroughly metaphysical notion—with its question-begging appeal to the concrete—that derisively goes by the name of affect.

What is at issue is to refind—in the laws that govern this other scene (*ein anderer Schauplatz*), which Freud, on the subject of dreams, designates as the scene of the unconscious—the effects that are discovered at the level of the chain of materially unstable elements that constitutes language: effects that are determined by the double play of combination and substitution in the signifier, according to the two axes for generating the signified, metonymy and metaphor; effects that are determinant in instituting the subject. In the process, a topology, in the mathematical sense of the term, appears, without which one soon realizes that it is impossible to even note the structure of a symptom in the analytic sense of the term.

It speaks in the Other, I say, designating by "Other" the very locus evoked by recourse to speech in any relation in which such recourse plays a part. If it speaks in the Other, whether or not the subject hears it with his ear, it is because it is there that the subject finds his signifying place in a way that is logically prior to any awakening of the signified. The discovery of what it articulates in that place, that is, in the unconscious, enables us to grasp at the price of what splitting (*Spaltung*) he has thus been constituted.

The phallus can be better understood on the basis of its function here. In   690
Freudian doctrine, the phallus is not a fantasy, if we are to view fantasy as an imaginary effect. Nor is it as such an object (part , internal, good, bad, etc.) inasmuch as "object" tends to gauge the reality involved in a relationship. Still less is it the organ—penis or clitoris—that it symbolizes. And it is no accident that Freud adopted as a reference the simulacrum it represented to the Ancients.

For the phallus is a signifier, a signifier whose function, in the intrasub jective economy of analysis, may lift the veil from the function it served in the mysteries. For it is the signifier that is destined to designate meaning effects as a whole, insofar as the signifier conditions them by its presence as signifier.

Let us thus examine the effects of this presence. They include, first, a deviation of man's needs due to the fact that he speaks: to the extent that his needs are subjected to demand, they come back to him in an alienated form. This is not the effect of his real dependence (one should not expect to find here the parasitic conception represented by the notion of dependency in the theory of neurosis), but rather of their being put into signifying form as such and of the fact that it is from the Other's locus that his message is emitted.

What is thus alienated in needs constitutes an *Urverdrängung* [primal repression], as it cannot, hypothetically, be articulated in demand; it nevertheless appears in an offshoot that presents itself in man as desire (*das*

Begehren). The phenomenology that emerges from analytic experience is certainly of a kind to demonstrate the paradoxical, deviant, erratic, eccentric, and even scandalous nature of desire that distinguishes it from need. This fact is all too clear not to have been obvious to moralists worthy of the name since time immemorial, and the Freudianism of earlier days seemed obliged to give it its full status. Paradoxically, however, psychoanalysis now finds itself at the head of an age-old obscurantism that is even more boring as it denies this fact due to its ideal of theoretically and practically reducing desire to need.

That is why I must articulate this status here, beginning with demand, the specific characteristics of which are eluded in the notion of frustration (a notion Freud never used).

691   Demand in itself bears on something other than the satisfactions it calls for. It is demand for a presence or an absence. This is what the primordial relationship with the mother manifests, replete as it is with that Other who must be situated *shy of* the needs that Other can fulfill. Demand already constitutes the Other as having the "privilege" of satisfying needs, that is, the power to deprive them of what alone can satisfy them. The Other's privilege here thus outlines the radical form of the gift of what the Other does not have—namely, what is known as its love.

In this way, demand annuls (*aufhebt*) the particularity of everything that can be granted, by transmuting it into a proof of love, and the very satisfactions demand obtains for need are debased (*sich erniedrigt*) to the point of being no more than the crushing brought on by the demand for love (all of which is perfectly apparent in the psychology of early child-care, which our analyst/nannies have latched onto).

It is necessary, then, that the particularity thus abolished reappear *beyond* demand. And in fact it does reappear there, but it preserves the structure concealed in the unconditionality of the demand for love. By a reversal that is not simply a negation of the negation, the power of pure loss emerges from the residue of an obliteration. For the unconditionality of demand, desire substitutes the "absolute" condition: this condition in fact dissolves the element in the proof of love that rebels against the satisfaction of need. This is why desire is neither the appetite for satisfaction nor the demand for love, but the difference that results from the subtraction of the first from the second, the very phenomenon of their splitting (*Spaltung*).

One can see how a sexual relationship occupies this closed field of desire and plays out its fate there. This is because it is the field designed for the production of the enigma that this relationship gives rise to in the subject by doubly "signifying" it to him: the return of the demand it gives rise to, in the form of a demand concerning the subject of need; and the ambiguity presented concerning the Other in question in the proof of love that is demanded. The gap constituted by this enigma avers what determines it, namely, to put it as simply and clearly as possible, that for each of the partners in the relationship, both the subject and the Other, it is not enough to be subjects of need or objects of love—they must hold the place of the cause of desire.

This truth lies at the heart of all the defects found in the psychoanalytic field regarding sexual life. It also constitutes the condition of the subject's happiness there; and to disguise its gap by assuming that the virtue of the "genital" will   692 resolve it through the maturation of tenderness (that is to say, solely by recourse to the Other as reality), however pious the intent may be, is nonetheless fraudulent. It should be pointed out here that French analysts, with their hypocritical notion of genital oblativity, set a moralizing tone which, to the strains of Salvation Army bands, is pervading the entire landscape.

In any case, man cannot aim at being whole (at the "total personality," another premise with which modern psychotherapy veers off course), once the play of displacement and condensation to which he is destined in the exercise of his functions marks his relation, as a subject, to the signifier.

The phallus is the privileged signifier of this mark in which the role [part] of Logos is wedded to the advent of desire.

One could say that this signifier is chosen as the most salient of what can be grasped in sexual intercourse [copulation] as real, as well as the most symbolic, in the literal (typographical) sense of the term, since it is equivalent in intercourse to the (logical) copula. One could also say that, by virtue of its turgidity, it is the image of the vital flow as it is transmitted in generation.

All of these remarks still merely veil the fact that it can play its role only when veiled, that is, as itself a sign of the latency with which any signifiable is struck, once it is raised (aufgehoben) to the function of signifier.

The phallus is the signifier of this very Aufhebung, which it inaugurates (initiates) by its disappearance. That is why the demon of Αἰδώς (Scham)[1] springs forth at the very moment the phallus is unveiled in the ancient mysteries (see the famous painting in the Villa of the Mysteries in Pompeii).

It then becomes the bar with which the demon's hand strikes the signified, marking it as the bastard offspring of its signifying concatenation.

A condition of complementarity is thus produced in the instating of the subject by the signifier, which explains his Spaltung and the interventionist movement in which it is completed.

693   Namely:

(1) that the subject designates his being only by barring everything it signifies, as is seen in the fact that he wants to be loved for himself, a
mirage that is not dispelled by simply pointing out that it is grammatical (since it abolishes discourse);

(2) that the part of this being that is alive in the *urverdrängt* [primally
repressed] finds its signifier by receiving the mark of the phallus'
Verdrängung [repression] (owing to which the unconscious is language).

The phallus as a signifier provides the ratio [*raison*] of desire (in the
sense in which the term is used in "mean and extreme ratio" of harmonic
division).

I shall thus be using the phallus as an algorithm and I cannot, without
endlessly inflating my talk, do otherwise than rely on the echoes of the
experience that unites us to get you to grasp this usage.

The fact that the phallus is a signifier requires that it be in the place of the
Other that the subject have access to it. But since this signifier is there only
as veiled and as ratio [*raison*] of the Other's desire, it is the Other's desire as
such that the subject is required to recognize—in other words, the other
insofar as he himself is a subject divided by the signifying *Spaltung*.

The developments that appear in psychological genesis confirm the phallus' signifying function.

This allows us, first of all, to more correctly formulate Klein's finding
that the child apprehends from the outset that the mother "contains" the
phallus.

But development is ordained by the dialectic of the demand for love and
the test constituted by desire.

The demand for love can only suffer from a desire whose signifier is foreign to it. If the mother's desire *is* for the phallus, the child wants to be the
phallus in order to satisfy her desire. Thus the division immanent in desire
already makes itself felt by virtue of being experienced in the Other's desire,
in that this division already stands in the way of the subject being satisfied
with presenting to the Other the real [organ] he may *have* that corresponds
to the phallus; for what he has is no better than what he does not have, from
the point of view of his demand for love, which would like him to be the
phallus.

Clinical work shows us that the test constituted by the Other's desire is
decisive, not in the sense that the subject learns by it whether or not he has

a real phallus, but in the sense that he learns that his mother does not have one. This is the moment in experience without which no symptomatic consequence (phobia) or structural consequence (*Penisneid*) related to the castration complex can take effect. This seals the conjunction of desire, insofar as the phallic signifier is its mark, with the threat of or nostalgia based on not-having [*manque à avoir*].

Of course, its future depends on the law introduced by the father in this sequence.

But one can indicate the structures that govern the relations between the sexes by referring simply to the phallus' function.

These relations revolve around a being and a having which, since they refer to a signifier, the phallus, have contradictory effects: they give the subject reality in this signifier, on the one hand, but render unreal the relations to be signified, on the other.

This is brought about by the intervention of a seeming [*paraître*] that replaces the having in order to protect it, in one case, and to mask the lack thereof, in the other, and whose effect is to completely project the ideal or typical manifestations of each of the sexes' behavior, including the act of copulation itself, into the realm of comedy.

These ideals are strengthened by the demand they are capable of satisfying, which is always a demand for love, with the reduction of desire to demand as its complement.

Paradoxical as this formulation may seem, I am saying that it is in order to be the phallus—that is, the signifier of the Other's desire—that a woman rejects an essential part of femininity, namely, all its attributes, in the masquerade. It is for what she is not that she expects to be desired as well as loved. But she finds the signifier of her own desire in the body of the person to whom her demand for love is addressed. It should not be forgotten, of course, that the organ that is endowed with this signifying function takes on the value of a fetish thereby. But the result for a woman remains that two things converge on the same object: an experience of love that, as such (see above), ideally deprives her of what the object gives, and a desire that finds its signifier in this object. This is why one may find that a lack of satisfaction of sexual needs, in other words, frigidity, is relatively well tolerated by women, whereas the *Verdrängung* inherent in desire is less in them than in men.

In the case of men, on the other hand, the dialectic of demand and desire engenders effects regarding which one must once again admire Freud's sureness in situating them, in the precise articulations on which they depend,

694

695

under the heading of a specific debasement (*Erniedrigung*) in the sphere of love.

If, indeed, man is able to satisfy his demand for love in his relationship with a woman, inasmuch as the phallic signifier clearly constitutes her as giving in love what she does not have, conversely, his own desire for the phallus will make its signifier emerge in its residual divergence toward "another woman" who may signify this phallus in various ways, either as a virgin or as a prostitute. There results from this a centrifugal tendency of the genital drive in the sphere of love, which makes impotence much harder for him to bear, while the *Verdrängung* inherent in his desire is greater.

Still it should not be thought that the sort of infidelity that might appear to be constitutive of the masculine function is characteristic of him alone. For if one looks closely, the same split can be found in women, with the proviso that the Loving Other [*l'Autre de l'Amour*] as such—that is, the Other insofar as he is deprived of what he gives—is difficult to see in the backcourt where he replaces the being of the very man whose attributes she cherishes.

One might add here that male homosexuality, in accordance with the phallic mark that constitutes desire, is constituted along the axis of desire, while female homosexuality, on the contrary, as observation shows, is oriented by a disappointment that strengthens the axis of the demand for love. These remarks should be refined through a reexamination of the function of the mask, insofar as it dominates the identifications in which refusals of demand are resolved.

The fact that femininity finds refuge in this mask, by virtue of the *Verdrängung* inherent in desire's phallic mark, has the curious consequence of making virile display in human beings seem feminine.

Correlatively, one can glimpse the reason for a characteristic that has never been elucidated and that shows once again the depth of Freud's intuition: namely, why Freud claims there is only one libido, his text showing that he conceives of it as masculine in nature. The function of the phallic signifier touches here on its most profound relation: that by which the Ancients embodied therein the Nous and the Logos.

Note

1. The demon of Shame.

The Subversion of the Subject and the Dialectic of Desire in the Freudian Unconscious

This text represents my contribution to a conference on "La Dialectique," held at Royaumont from September 19 to 23, 1960. The conference was organized by the "Colloques philosophiques internationaux," and I was invited to participate by Jean Wahl.

It is the date of this text—which predates the Bonneval Colloquium from which the text that follows stemmed ["Position of the Unconscious" follows this one in *Écrits* 1966]—that leads me to publish it, in order to give the reader an idea how far my teaching has always been ahead of what I could make more widely available.

(The graph presented here was constructed for my seminar on unconscious formations. It was worked out particularly in relation to the structure of jokes, which I took as a point of departure, before a surprised audience. That was in the first term of the seminar, which was the last term of 1957. An account of the seminar, along with the graph provided here, was published at the time in the *Bulletin de psychologie*.)

A structure is constitutive of the praxis known as psychoanalysis. This structure cannot be immaterial to an audience like the one here today, which is supposed to be philosophically sophisticated.

The thesis that being a philosopher means being interested in what everyone is interested in without knowing it has the interesting peculiarity that its relevance does not imply that it can be settled either way. For it can only be settled if everyone becomes a philosopher.

I am talking about its philosophical relevance, for that is, in the end, the schema Hegel gave us of History in *The Phenomenology of Mind*.

Summarizing it in this way has the advantage of providing us with a mediation that is convenient for situating the subject: on the basis of a relationship to knowledge.

It is also convenient for demonstrating the ambiguity of such a relationship.

This same ambiguity is manifested by the effects of science in the contemporary universe.

The scientist himself is a subject, one who is particularly qualified in his constitution, as is shown by the fact that science did not come into the world all by itself (its birth was not without vicissitudes, and was preceded by a number of failures—abortion or prematurity).

Now this subject who must know what he is doing, or so we presume, does not know what is already, in fact, of interest to everyone regarding the effects of science. Or so it would appear in the contemporary universe, where everyone finds himself at the same level as the scientist as far as this point of ignorance is concerned.

In and of itself, this warrants our speaking of a subject of science—a notion to which an epistemology that can be said to display more pretension than success would like to measure up.

Hence—let it be noted here—the entirely didactic reference I have made to Hegel in order to convey, for my analytic training purposes, where things stand regarding the question of the subject such as psychoanalysis properly subverts it.

What qualifies me to proceed along this path is obviously my experience of this praxis. What made me decide to do so—those who follow my work will attest to this—is a failure of theory coupled with abuses in its transmission, which, while presenting no danger to the praxis itself, result, in both cases, in a total absence of scientific status. To raise the question of the minimal conditions required for such a status was not perhaps an impertinent point of departure. It has turned out to lead a long way.

I am not referring here to anything as broad in scope as a challenging of different societies' practices—in particular, to the stockpile of conclusions I have been forced to draw in order to counter the notorious deviations in analytic praxis that claim to be genuinely psychoanalytic in England and America.

What I will specifically try to define is subversion, and I apologize to this assembly, whose qualifications I mentioned earlier, for being unable to do more in its presence than elsewhere—namely, to take this assembly as such as the pivot of my demonstration, the onus being on me to justify taking such liberties with regard to it.

795   Nevertheless, I shall take advantage of your kindness in assuming we agree that a science cannot be conditioned upon empiricism.

Secondly, we encounter what has already been constituted, with a scientific label, by the name of psychology.

Which I challenge—precisely because, as I will show, the function of the subject, as inaugurated by Freudian experience, disqualifies from the outset what, going by the name "psychology," merely perpetuates an academic framework, no matter how one dresses up its premises.

Its criterion is the unity of the subject, which is one of the presuppositions of this sort of psychology; it should even be taken as symptomatic that this theme is ever more emphatically isolated, as if the return of a certain subject of consciousness [*connaissance*] were at stake, or as if the psychical had to obtain recognition as doubling the organism.

Here we must take as exemplary the idea in which a whole body of traditional thought comes together in accrediting a term, "state of consciousness," that is not without basis. Whether we're dealing with the states of enthusiasm described by Plato, the degrees of samadhi in Buddhism, or the experience (*Erlebnis*) one has under the influence of hallucinogens, it is important to know how much of this is authenticated by any theory.

Authenticated in the register of what consciousness includes by way of connaturality.

It is clear that Hegelian knowledge, in the logicizing *Aufhebung* [sublation] on which it is based, puts as little stock in these states as such as does modern science, which may recognize in them an object of experience, in the sense of an opportunity to define certain coordinates, but in no way an ascesis that could, so to speak, be "epistemogenic" or "noophoric."

It is in this respect that reference to them is relevant to us.

For I assume you are sufficiently informed about Freudian practice to realize that such states play no part in it; but what is not fully appreciated is the fact that this supposed "depth psychology" does not dream of using these states to obtain illumination, for example, or even assign any value to them along the path it sketches out.

For that is why—though it is not stressed—Freud steers clear of hypnoid states, even when it comes to explaining the phenomena of hysteria. That is the amazing thing: Freud prefers the hysteric's discourse to hypnoid states. What I have called "fertile moments" in my mapping of paranoiac knowledge [*connaissance*] is not a Freudian reference.

I have some difficulty in getting across—in a circle infatuated with the most incredible illogicality—what it means to interrogate the unconscious as I do, that is, to the point at which it gives a reply that is not some sort of ravishment or takedown, but is rather a "saying why."

If we conduct the subject anywhere, it is to a deciphering which assumes that a sort of logic is already operative in the unconscious, a logic in which, for example, an interrogative voice or even the development of an argument can be recognized.

The whole psychoanalytic tradition supports the view that the analyst's voice can intervene only if it enters at the right place, and that if it comes too early it merely produces a closing up.

In other words, a strain of psychoanalysis that is sustained by its allegiance to Freud cannot under any circumstances pass itself off as a rite of passage to some archetypal, or in any sense ineffable, experience. The day someone who is not simply a moron obtains a hearing for a view of this kind will be the day all limits will have been abolished. We are still a long way from that.[1]

Thus far we have merely broached our subject. For we must home in more precisely on what Freud himself articulates in his doctrine as constituting a "Copernican" step.

For such a step to be constituted, is it enough that a privilege should be revoked—in this case, the one that put the earth in the central place? Man's subsequent destitution from an analogous place due to the triumph of the idea of evolution gives one the sense that such revocation implies an advantage that is confirmed by its constancy.

797   But can we be so sure this is an advantage or real progress? Does anything make it seem that the other truth, if we may so term revealed truth, has seriously suffered as a result? Don't we realize that, by exalting the center, heliocentrism is no less of a lure than seeing the earth as the center, and that the existence of the ecliptic probably provided a more stimulating model of our relations with truth, before it lost much of its interest when it was reduced to being no more than the earth bowing assent?

In any case, it is not because of Darwin that men believe themselves to be any the less the best among the creatures, for it is precisely of this that he convinces them.

The use of Copernicus' name as a reference has more hidden resources that touch specifically on what has already just slipped from my pen regarding our relation to the true—namely, the emergence of the ellipse as being not unworthy of the locus from which the so-called higher truths take their name. The revolution is no less important even though it concerns only "celestial revolutions."

From that point on, to dwell on it no longer means simply revoking some idiotic notion stemming from the religious tradition, which, as can be seen well enough, is none the worse for it, but rather of tying more closely together the regime of knowledge and the regime of truth.

For if Copernicus' work, as others have remarked before me, is not as Copernican as we think it is, it is because the doctrine of double truth continues to offer shelter to a knowledge that, up until then, it must be said, appeared to be quite content with that shelter.

So here we are at the palpable border between truth and knowledge; and it might be said, after all, that at first sight our science certainly seems to have readopted the solution of closing the border.

Yet if the history of Science's birth is still a sufficiently burning question for us to be aware that at that border something shifted at that time, it is perhaps here that psychoanalysis distinguishes itself by representing a new seism that occurred there.

For let us reexamine from this angle the service we expect from Hegel's phenomenology: that of marking out an ideal solution—one that involves a permanent revisionism, so to speak, in which what is disturbing about truth is constantly being reabsorbed, truth being in itself but what is lacking in the realization of knowledge. The antinomy the Scholastic tradition posited as principial is here taken to be resolved by virtue of being imaginary. Truth is nothing but what knowledge can learn that it knows merely by putting its ignorance to work. This is a real crisis, in which the imaginary is eliminated in engendering a new symbolic form, to use my own categories. This dialectic is convergent and proceeds to the conjuncture defined as absolute knowledge. As it is deduced, this conjuncture can only be the conjunction of the symbolic with a real from which nothing more can be expected. What is this, if not a subject finalized in his self-identity? From which one can conclude that this subject is already perfect(ed) here and is the fundamental hypothesis of the entire process. He is named, in effect, as the substratum of this process; he is called *Selbstbewusstsein*, the being of the conscious, wholly conscious self.

798

Would that it were so! But the history of science itself—I mean of our science, since its inception, assuming we situate its first birth in Greek mathematics—presents itself, rather, in the form of detours that comply very little with this immanentism. And scientific theories—let us not be misled on this score by any resorption of the special theory of relativity into the general theory—do not, in any way, fit together according to the thesis/antithesis/synthesis dialectic.

Indeed, a number of creaks—confusedly given voice to by the great minds responsible for some of the cardinal changes in physics—remind us that, after all, it is elsewhere that the moment of truth must sound for this field of knowledge as for others.

Why wouldn't we think that the astonishing indulgence science is showing toward psychoanalytic hype may be due to the theoretical hope psychoanalysis offers—a hope that is not merely the result of the prevailing confusion?

I am not, of course, referring to the extraordinary lateral transference by which psychology reimmerses its categories in psychoanalysis to reinvigorate its lowly purposes of social exploitation. For the reason already stated, I regard the fate of psychology as irremediably sealed.

In any case, my two-pronged reference to Hegel's absolute subject and to science's abolished subject sheds the light necessary to accurately formulate Freud's dramatism: the return of truth to the field of science at the same time as it comes to the fore in the field of its praxis—repressed, it reappears there.

Who cannot see the distance that separates the unhappiness of consciousness—which, however deeply ingrained it may be in Hegel's work, can still be said to be but the suspension of knowing—from civilization's discontents in Freud's work, even if it is only in the inspiration of a sentence which is, as it were, disavowed, that Freud marks for us what, on reading it, cannot be articulated otherwise than the skewed relation that separates the subject from sex?

There is nothing, then, in my approach to situating Freud that owes anything to the judicial astrology in which the psychologist is immersed. Nothing that proceeds on the basis of quality, much less of intensity, or of any phenomenology from which idealism may draw reassurance. In the Freudian field, the words notwithstanding, consciousness is a characteristic that is as obsolete to us in grounding the unconscious—for we cannot ground it on the negation of consciousness (that unconscious dates back to Saint Thomas Aquinas)—as affect is unsuited to play the role of the protopathic subject, since it is a function without a functionary.

Starting with Freud, the unconscious becomes a chain of signifiers that repeats and insists somewhere (on another stage or in a different scene, as he wrote), interfering in the cuts offered it by actual discourse and the cogitation it informs.

In this formulation, which is mine only in the sense that it conforms as closely to Freud's texts as to the experience they opened up, the crucial term is the signifier, revived from ancient rhetoric by modern linguistics, in a doctrine whose various stages I cannot trace here, but of which the names Ferdinand de Saussure and Roman Jakobson stand for its dawn and its present-day culmination, not forgetting that the pilot science of structuralism in the West has its roots in Russia, where formalism first flourished. Geneva 1910 and Petrograd 1920 suffice to explain why Freud did not have this particular instrument at his disposal. But this historically motivated lacuna makes all the more instructive the fact that the mechanisms described by Freud as those of the primary process, by which the unconscious is governed, correspond exactly to the functions this school of linguistics believes determine the most radical axes of the effects of language, namely metaphor and metonymy—in other words, the effects of the substitution and combination of signifiers in the synchronic and diachronic dimensions, respectively, in which they appear in discourse.

Once the structure of language is recognized in the unconscious, what sort of subject can we conceive of for it?

In a concern for method, we can try to begin here with the strictly linguistic definition of *I* as signifier, where it is nothing but the shifter* or indicative that, qua grammatical subject of the statement, designates the subject insofar as he is currently speaking.

That is to say, it designates the enunciating subject, but does not signify him. This is obvious from the fact that there may be no signifier of the enunciating subject in the statement—not to mention that there are signifiers that differ from *I*, and not only those that are inadequately called cases of the first person singular, even if we add that it can be lodged in the plural invocation or even in the Self [*Soi*] of auto-suggestion.

I believe, for example, that I have detected the enunciating subject in the French signifier *ne*, said by grammarians to be "expletive," a term that already prefigures the incredible opinion of those among the best who regard its form as subject to sheer whimsy. Would that the weight I give it make them think twice, before it not but become obvious they have missed the point [*avant qu'il ne soit averé qu'ils n'y comprennent rien*]—take out that "not but" [*ne*] and my enunciation loses its force as an attack, *I* eliding me in the impersonal. Yet I fear that in this way they could not but come to vilify me [*Mais je crains ainsi qu'ils n'en viennent à me honnir*]—skip that "not but" [*n'*] and its absence, toning down my alleged fear to declare my repugnance to a timid assertion, reduces the emphasis of my enunciation by situating me in the statement.

But if I say "*tue*" (kill), because they are killing me, where am I situating myself if not in the *tu* on the basis of which I glare at them [*toise*]?

Don't sulk—I am merely referring obliquely to what I am reluctant to cover over with the inevitable map of clinical work.

Namely, the right way to answer the question "Who is speaking?" when the subject of the unconscious is at stake. For the answer cannot come from him if he doesn't know what he is saying, or even that he is speaking, as all of analytic experience teaches us.

Hence the place of the "inter-said" [*inter-dit*], constituted by the "intra-said" [*intra-dit*] of a between-two-subjects, is the very place at which the transparency of the classical subject divides, undergoing, as it does, the effects of fading* that specify the Freudian subject due to its occultation by an ever purer signifier; may these effects lead us to the frontiers where slips of the tongue and jokes become indistinguishable in their collusion, or even where elision is so much more allusive in driving presence back to its lair, that we are astonished the hunt for Dasein hasn't made any more of it.

Lest our hunt be in vain, we analysts must bring everything back to the cut qua function in discourse, the most significant being the cut that constitutes a bar between the signifier and the signified. Here we come upon the subject who interests us since, being bound up in signification, he seems to be lodging in the preconscious. This would lead us to the paradox of conceiving that discourse in an analytic session is worthwhile only insofar as it stumbles or even interrupts itself—were not the session itself instituted as a break in a false discourse, that is, in what discourse realizes when it becomes empty as speech, when it is no more than the worn coinage Mallarmé speaks of that is passed from hand to hand "in silence."

The cut made by the signifying chain is the only cut that verifies the structure of the subject as a discontinuity in the real. If linguistics enables us to see the signifier as the determinant of the signified, analysis reveals the truth of this relationship by making holes in meaning the determinants of its discourse.

This is the path by which an imperative can be fulfilled, the imperative Freud raised to the sublime stature of a pre-Socratic gnome in his formulation, "Wo Es war, soll Ich werden," which I have commented upon more than once, and which I am now going to inflect differently.

I will limit myself to examining one step in its grammar: "where it was . . ." [là où ce fut . . .]—what does that mean? If it were but this [ça] that might have been (to use the aoristic form), how to come to the same place in order to make myself be there, by stating it now?

But the French translation says: "Là où c'était . . ." Let us take advantage of the distinct imperfect it provides. Where it was just now, where it was for a short while, between an extinction that is still glowing and an opening up that stumbles, I can [peut] come into being by disappearing from my statement [dit].

An enunciation that denounces itself, a statement that renounces itself, an ignorance that sweeps itself away, an opportunity that self-destructs—what remains here if not the trace of what really must be in order to fall away from being?

A dream related by Freud in his article, "Formulations on the Two Principles of Mental Functioning," gives us a sentence, related to the pathos with which the figure of a dead father returning as a ghost would be invested: "He did not know he was dead."[2]

I have already used this sentence to illustrate the subject's relation to the signifier—through an enunciation that makes a human being tremble due to the vacillation that comes back to him from his own statement.

If this figure of the dead father subsists only by virtue of the fact that one does not tell him the truth of which he is unaware, what then is the status of the *I* on which this subsistence depends?

He did not know . . . He was to know a bit later. Oh! may that never happen! May *I* die rather than have him know. Yes, that's how I get there, where it was (to be): who knew, thus, that *I* was dead?

Being of non-being, that is how *I* comes on the scene as a subject who is conjugated with the double aporia of a veritable subsistence that is abolished by his knowledge, and by a discourse in which it is death that sustains existence.

Will we weigh this being against the being Hegel as subject forged— Hegel being the subject who, regarding history, adopts the discourse of absolute knowledge? We recall that Hegel admitted to having experienced the temptation of madness. Isn't our path the one that overcomes that, by going right to the truth of the vanity of this discourse?

I will not expound my doctrine on madness here. For I have included this eschatological excursion only to designate the gap that separates the two relations—Freudian and Hegelian—between the subject and knowledge.

And to show that there is no surer root of these relations than the different ways in which the dialectic of desire is distinguished in them.

For in Hegel's work it is desire (*Begierde*) that is given responsibility for the minimal link the subject must retain to Antiquity's knowledge [*connaissance*] if truth is to be immanent in the realization of knowledge. The "cunning of reason" means that, from the outset and right to the end, the subject knows what he wants.

It is here that Freud reopens the junction between truth and knowledge to the mobility out of which revolutions arise.

In this respect: that desire becomes bound up at that junction with the Other's desire, but that the desire to know lies in this loop.

Freud's biologism has nothing to do with the preachy abjection that wafts up to us from psychoanalytic headquarters.

And you had to be made to experience the death instinct, which is held in such abomination there, to get on the true wavelength of Freud's biology. For to evade the death instinct in his doctrine is not to know his doctrine at all.

On the basis of the approach I have prepared for you, you should recognize in the metaphor of the return to the inanimate—which Freud ascribes

to every living body—the margin beyond life that language assures the
human being of due to the fact that he speaks, and which is precisely the
margin where this being places in signifying position, not only those parts of
his body that lend themselves to this because they are exchangeable, but the
body itself. Thus it becomes apparent that the object's relation to the body
can in no way be defined as based on a partial identification that would have
to be totalized there, since, on the contrary, this object is the prototype of
the body's signifierness as the human being's ante.

Here I will take up the challenge made to me when people translate as
"instinct" what Freud calls *Trieb*—which "drive" would seem to translate
quite well into English, but which is avoided in the *Standard Edition*. In
French, my last resort would be *dérive* [drift], if I were unable to give the
bastardized term *pulsion* [drive or urge] its point of impact.

And so I insist on promoting the idea that, whether grounded or not in
biological observation, instinct—among the modes of knowledge [*connaissance*] required by nature of living beings so that they satisfy its needs—is
defined as a kind of [experiential] knowledge [*connaissance*] we admire
because it cannot become [articulated] knowledge [*un savoir*]. But in Freud's
work something quite different is at stake, which is a *savoir* certainly, but one
that doesn't involve the slightest *connaissance*, in that it is inscribed in a discourse of which the subject—who, like the messenger-slave of Antiquity,
carries under his hair the codicil that condemns him to death—knows neither the meaning nor the text, nor in what language [*langue*] it is written, nor
even that it was tattooed on his shaven scalp while he was sleeping.

This apologue barely exaggerates just how little the unconscious has to
do with physiology.

This can be gauged by crosschecking the contribution made by psychoanalysis to physiology since its inception: its contribution has been nil, even
as far as the sexual organs are concerned. No amount of fabulation will prevail against this balance sheet.

804   For, of course, psychoanalysis concerns the reality [*réel*] of the body and of
its imaginary mental schema. But to recognize their import in the perspective
authorized by "development," we must first realize that the more or less fragmented integrations that seem to account for the order of development, function first and foremost like elements of a heraldry, a heraldry of the body. This
is confirmed by the use that is made of them in reading children's drawings.

This is the crux—to which I shall return later—of the paradoxical privilege the phallus continues to have in the unconscious dialectic, the theory of
the part-object not sufficing to explain it.

Need I now say—if one understands the kind of support I have sought in Hegel's work by which to criticize a degradation of psychoanalysis that is so inept that it has no other claim to fame than that of being contemporary—that it is inadmissible that I should be accused of having been lured by a purely dialectical exhaustion of being, and that I can but hold a particular philosopher[3] responsible for authorizing this misunderstanding?

For far from giving myself over to some logicizing reduction where desire is at stake, I detect in desire's irreducibility to demand the very mainspring of what also prevents it from being reduced to need. To put it elliptically: it is precisely because desire is articulated that it is not articulable—by which I mean in the discourse that suits it, an ethical, not a psychological discourse.

I must now lay out for you in much greater detail the topology that I have developed in my teaching over the past few years, that is, introduce a certain graph, which, I should indicate, also serves purposes other than the one I have in mind here, having been constructed and perfected quite explicitly in order to map out on its different levels the most broadly practical structure of the data of analytic experience. It will serve here to show where desire is   805 situated in relation to a subject defined on the basis of his articulation by the signifier.

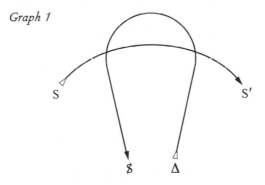

Graph 1

This is what might be called its elementary cell (see Graph 1). In it is articulated what I have called the "button tie" [*point de capiton*], by which the signifier stops the otherwise indefinite sliding of signification. The signifying chain is assumed to be borne by the vector $\overrightarrow{S.S'}$. Without even going into the subtleties of the negatively oriented direction in which its double intersection with the vector $\overrightarrow{\Delta.\$}$ occurs—only in this latter vector does one see the fish it hooks, a fish less suitable for representing what it withdraws from our grasp in its vigorous swimming than the intention that tries to drown it in the floodtide of pre-text, namely, the reality that is imagined in the ethological schema of the return of need.

The diachronic function of this button tie can be found in a sentence, insofar as a sentence closes its signification only with its last term, each term being anticipated in the construction constituted by the other terms and, inversely, sealing their meaning by its retroactive effect.

But the synchronic structure is more hidden, and it is this structure that brings us to the beginning. It is metaphor insofar as the first attribution is constituted in it—the attribution that promulgates "the dog goes meow, the cat goes woof-woof," by which, in one fell swoop, the child, by disconnecting the thing from its cry, raises the sign to the function of the signifier and reality to the sophistics of signification, and in his contempt for verisimilitude, makes necessary the verification of multiple objectifications of the same thing.

806   Does this possibility require the topology of a four-corners game? This sort of question seems innocent enough, but it may give us some trouble if the subsequent construction must depend on it.

I will spare you the stages by revealing directly the function of the two points of intersection in this elementary graph [see Graph 2]. The first, labeled A, is the locus of the treasure trove of signifiers, which does not mean of the code, for the one-to-one correspondence between a sign and a thing is not preserved here, the signifier being constituted on the basis of a synchronic and countable collection in which none of the elements is sustained except through its opposition to each of the others. The second, labeled s(A), is what may be called the punctuation, in which signification ends as a finished product.

Let us observe the dissymmetry between the one, which is a locus (a place, rather than a space), and the other, which is a moment (a scansion, rather than a duration).

Both are related to the offer to the signifier that is constituted by the hole is the real, the one as a hollow for concealment, the other as drilling toward a way out.

The subject's submission to the signifier, which occurs in the circuit that goes from s(A) to A and back from A to s(A), is truly a circle, inasmuch as the assertion that is established in it—being unable to close on anything but its own scansion, in other words, failing an act in which it would find its certainty—refers back only to its own anticipation in the composition of the signifier, which is in itself meaningless [insignifiante].

To be possible, the squaring of this circle only requires the completeness of the signifying battery installed in A, henceforth symbolizing the Other's locus. This allows us to see that this Other is but the pure subject of modern game strategy, and is as such perfectly accessible to the calculation of conjecture—in the sense that the real subject, in making his own calculations, need not take into account any so-called subjective (in the usual, that is, psychological, sense of the term) aberration, but only the inscription of a combinatory whose combinations may be exhaustively enumerated.

This squaring of the circle is nevertheless impossible, but solely because the subject constitutes himself only by subtracting himself from it and by decompleting it essentially, such that he must, at one and the same time,   807
count himself here and function only as a lack here.

The Other, as preliminary site of the pure subject of the signifier, occupies the key [*maîtresse*] position here, even before coming into existence here as absolute Master—to use Hegel's term with and against him. For what is omitted in the platitude of modern information theory is the fact that one cannot even speak of a code without it already being the Other's code; something quite different is at stake in the message, since the subject constitutes himself on the basis of the message, such that he receives from the Other even the message he himself sends. Thus the notations A and *s*(A) are justified.

Code messages and message codes separate out into pure forms in the psychotic subject, the subject who makes do with this preliminary Other alone.

Observe, as an aside, that this Other, distinguished as the locus of Speech, nevertheless emerges as Truth's witness. Without the dimension it constitutes, the deceptiveness of Speech would be indistinguishable from the feint, which, in fighting or sexual display, is nevertheless quite different. Deployed in imaginary capture, the feint is integrated into the play of approach and retreat that constituted the first dance, in which these two vital situations find their scansion, and the partners who fall into step with it find what I will dare to write as their "dancity." Moreover, animals show that they are capable of such behavior when they are being hunted down; they manage to throw their pursuers off the scent by briefly going in one direction as a lure and then changing direction. This can go so far as to suggest on the part of game animals the nobility of honoring the parrying found in the hunt. But an animal does not feign feigning. It does not make tracks whose deceptiveness lies in getting them to be taken as false, when in fact they are true—that is, tracks that indicate the right trail. No more than it effaces its tracks, which would already be tantamount to making itself the subject of the signifier.

All this has been articulated only in a confused way by philosophers who are nevertheless professional. But it is clear that Speech begins only with the passage from the feint to the order of the signifier, and that the signifier requires another locus—the locus of the Other, the Other as witness, the witness who is Other than any of the partners—for the Speech borne by the signifier to be able to lie, that is, to posit itself as Truth.

808   Thus Truth draws its guarantee from somewhere other than the Reality it concerns: it draws it from Speech. Just as it is from Speech that Truth receives the mark that instates it in a fictional structure.

The first words spoken decree, legislate, aphorize, and are an oracle; they give the real other its obscure authority.

Take just one signifier as an insignia of this omnipotence, that is, of this wholly potential power, of this birth of possibility, and you have the unary trait which—filling in the invisible mark the subject receives from the signifier—alienates this subject in the first identification that forms the ego-ideal.

This is inscribed by the notation I(A), which I must substitute, at this stage, for $, the barred S of the negatively oriented vector, moving $ from the vector's endpoint to its starting point (see Graph 2).

Graph 2

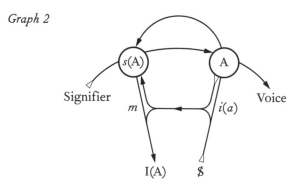

This is a retroversion effect by which the subject, at each stage, becomes what he was (to be) [*était*] before that, and "he will have been" is only announced in the future perfect tense.

Here arises the ambiguity of a misrecognizing that is essential to knowing myself [*un méconnaître essentiel au me connaître*]. For, in this "rear view," all the subject can be sure of is the anticipated image—which he had caught of himself in his mirror—coming to meet him. I won't go back over the function of my "mirror stage" here, the first strategic point I developed as an objection to the supposedly "autonomous ego" in favor in psychoanalytic theory, whose academic restoration justified the mistaken proposal to strengthen the ego in a type of treatment diverted thereafter toward successful adaptation—a phenomenon of mental abdication tied to the aging of the psychoanalytic group in the Diaspora owing to the war, and the reduction of an eminent practice to a *Good Housekeeping* seal of approval attesting to its suitability to the "American way of life."*[4]

Be that as it may, what the subject finds in this altered image of his body is the paradigm of all the forms of resemblance that will cast a shade of hostility onto the world of objects, by projecting onto them the avatar of his narcissistic image, which, from the jubilation derived from encountering it in the mirror, becomes—in confronting his semblables—the outlet for his most intimate aggressiveness.

It is this image that becomes fixed—this is the ideal ego—from the point at which the subject fixates as ego-ideal. The ego is thus a function of mastery, a game of bearing, and constituted rivalry. In the capture it undergoes due to its imaginary nature, the ego masks its duplicity; that is, consciousness, in which the ego assures itself an indisputable existence (a naïveté that is displayed in Fénelon's work), is in no way immanent in the ego, but rather transcendent, since consciousness is based on the ego-ideal as unary trait (the Cartesian cogito does not fail to recognize this).[5] As a result, the transcendental ego itself is relativized, implicated as it is in the misrecognition in which the ego's identifications originate.

This imaginary process, which goes from the specular image to the constitution of the ego along the path of subjectification by the signifier, is signified in my graph by the $\overrightarrow{i(a).m}$ vector, which is one-way but doubly articulated, first as a short circuit of the $\overrightarrow{\$.I(A)}$ vector, and second as a return route of the $\overrightarrow{A.s(A)}$ vector. This shows that the ego is only completed by being articulated not as the *I* of discourse, but as a metonymy of its signification (what Damourette and Pichon take as the "filled out" person, as opposed to the "ethereal" person, the latter being no other than the function I designated earlier as that of the shifter*).

The promotion of consciousness as essential to the subject in the historical aftermath of the Cartesian cogito is indicative, to my mind, of a misleading emphasis on the transparency of the *I* in action at the expense of the opacity of the signifier that determines it; and the slippage by which *Bewusstsein* serves to cover over the confusion of the *Selbst* actually reveals, in *The*

810   *Phenomenology of Mind*, that the reason for Hegel's error lies in his rigor.

The very movement that shifts the axis of the phenomenon of mind toward the imaginary relation to the other (that is, to the semblable connoted by a lowercase *a*), brings its effect to light: namely, the aggressiveness that becomes the balance arm of the scales around which the equilibrium of semblable to semblable decomposes in the relationship between Master and Slave, a relationship that is replete with all the cunning tricks by which reason advances its impersonal reign.

Regarding this slavery that inaugurates the roads to freedom—a myth rather than an actual genesis, no doubt—I can point here to what it hides precisely because I have revealed what it hides as no one had before.

The struggle that gives rise to this slavery is rightly called a struggle of pure prestige, and what is at stake—life itself—is well suited to echo the danger of the generic prematurity of birth, which Hegel was unaware of, and which I have situated as the dynamic mainspring of specular capture.

But death—precisely because it is dragged into the stakes (making this a more honest wager than Pascal's, though Hegel's too is a poker game, since limits are placed on how high the bid can be raised)—simultaneously shows what is elided by a preliminary rule as well as by the final settlement. For, in the final analysis, the loser must not perish if he is to become a slave. In other words, a pact always precedes violence before perpetuating it, and what I call the symbolic dominates the imaginary, allowing us to wonder whether or not murder really is the absolute Master.

For it is not enough to decide the question on the basis of its effect: Death. We need to know which death,[6] the one that life brings or the one that brings life.

Without criticizing the Hegelian dialectic for what it leaves out—the lack of a bond that would keep the society of masters together was pointed out long ago—I simply wish to stress what, on the basis of my own experience, strikes me as blatantly symptomatic in it, that is, as indicative of repression.

811   This is clearly the theme of the cunning of reason, whose seductiveness is in no wise lessened by the error I pointed out above. The work, Hegel tells us, to which the slave submits in giving up jouissance out of fear of death, is precisely the path by which he achieves freedom. There can be no more obvious lure than this, politically or psychologically. Jouissance comes easily to the slave, and it leaves work in serfdom.

The cunning of reason is a seductive notion because it echoes a well-known individual myth characteristic of obsessives, obsessive structure being known to be common among the intelligentsia. But even if someone in this category avoids the professor's bad faith, he cannot easily deceive himself that his work will grant him access to jouissance. Paying truly unconscious homage to the story as written by Hegel, he often finds his alibi in the death of the Master. But what of this death? He quite simply waits for it.

In fact, it is from the Other's locus where he situates himself that he follows the game, thus eliminating all risk to himself—especially the risk of a joust—in a "self-consciousness" for which death is but a joke.

I say this so that philosophers will not believe they can minimize the importance of the irruption constituted by what Freud said about desire.

And this on the pretext that demand, along with the effects of frustration, has buried everything that trickles down to them from a practice which has degenerated into an educative banality that is no longer even redeemed by its laziness.

Yes, the enigmatic traumas of the Freudian discovery are now considered to be merely suppressed cravings. Psychoanalysis is nourished by the observation of children and by the childishness of the observations. Let us skip the reports thus generated, edifying as they all are.

And devoid, as they all are now, of the slightest hint of humor.

Their authors are now far too concerned with obtaining a respectable position to leave any room for the irremediable ludicrousness the unconscious owes to its roots in language.

Yet it is impossible, for those who claim that discordance is introduced into the needs assumed to exist at the subject's origins by the way demand is received, to neglect the fact that there is no demand that does not in some respect pass through the defiles of the signifier.

And while the somatic *ananke* of man's inability to move, much less be self-sufficient, for some time after birth provides grounds for a psychology   812
of dependence, how can that psychology elide the fact that this dependence is maintained by a universe of language? Indeed, needs have been diversified and geared down by and through language to such an extent that their import appears to be of a quite different order, whether we are dealing with the subject or politics. In other words, to such an extent that these needs have passed over into the register of desire, with everything it forces us to face in this new experience of ours: the age-old paradoxes desire has created for moralists and the mark of the infinite that theologians find in it, not to mention the precariousness of its status, as expressed in its most recent form by Sartre—desire, a useless passion.

What psychoanalysis shows us about desire in what might be called its most natural function, since the survival of the species depends on it, is not only that it is subjected, in its agency, its appropriation, and even its very normality, to the accidents of the subject's history (the notion of trauma as contingency), but also that all this requires the assistance of structural elements—which, in order to intervene, can do very well without these accidents. The inharmonious, unexpected, and recalcitrant impact of these elements certainly seems to leave to the experience [of desire in its most natural function] a residue that drove Freud to admit that sexuality had to bear the mark of some hardly natural flaw.

We would be mistaken if we thought that the Freudian Oedipus myth puts an end to theology on the matter. For the myth does not confine itself to working the puppet of sexual rivalry. It would be better to read in it what Freud requires us to contemplate using his coordinates; for they boil down to the question with which he himself began: What is a Father?

"It is the dead Father," Freud replies, but no one hears him; and it is regrettable that, due to the mere fact that Lacan takes it up again under the heading of the "Name-of-the-Father," a situation that is hardly scientific should still deprive him of his normal audience.[7]

Yet analytic reflection has vaguely revolved around the problematic misrecognition of the function of the sire among certain primitive peoples, and psychoanalysts—rallying round the contraband flag of "culturalism"—have even argued about the forms of an authority about which it cannot even be said that any branch of anthropology has provided a definition of any importance.

Will we wait until we are confronted with a practice, which may in the course of time become standard practice, of artificially inseminating women who are at odds with phallicism with the sperm of some great man, before we deign to pronounce a verdict on the paternal function?

Yet the Oedipal show cannot run indefinitely in forms of society that are losing the sense of tragedy to an ever greater extent.

Let us begin with the conception of the Other as the locus of the signifier. No authoritative statement has any other guarantee here than its very enunciation, since it would be pointless for the statement to seek it in another signifier, which could in no way appear outside that locus. I formulate this by saying that there is no metalanguage that can be spoken, or, more aphoristically, that there is no Other of the Other. And when the Legislator (he who claims to lay down the Law) comes forward to make up for this, he does so as an impostor.

But the Law itself is not an impostor, nor is he who authorizes his actions on its basis.

The fact that the Father may be regarded as the original representative of the Law's authority requires us to specify by what privileged mode of presence he sustains himself beyond the subject who is led to really occupy the place of the Other, namely, the Mother. The question is thus pushed back a step.

It will seem strange that—in opening up here the incommensurate space all demand implies, since it is a request for love—I didn't allow for more "making" and debating on this point.

And that instead I focused it on what closes shy of it, due to the same effect of demand, to truly create the place of desire.

Indeed, it is quite simply, and I am going to say in what sense, as the Other's desire that man's desire takes shape, though at first only retaining a subjective opacity in order to represent need in it.

I will now explain in what way this opacity in some sense constitutes the substance of desire.

Desire begins to take shape in the margin in which demand rips away   814
from need, this margin being the one that demand—whose appeal can be unconditional only with respect to the Other—opens up in the guise of the possible gap need may give rise to here, because it has no universal satisfaction (this is called "anxiety"). A margin which, as linear as it may be, allows its vertiginous character to appear, provided it is not trampled by the elephantine feet of the Other's whimsy. Nevertheless, it is this whimsy that introduces the phantom of Omnipotence—not of the subject, but of the Other in which the subject's demand is instated (it's about time this idiotic cliché was, once and for all, and for all parties, put in its place)—and with this phantom, the necessity that the Other be bridled by the Law.

But I will stop here again in order to return to the status of desire, which presents itself as independent of the Law's mediation, because Law originates in desire—owing to the fact that, by an odd symmetry, desire reverses the unconditionality of the demand for love, in which the subject remains subjected to the Other, in order to raise it to the power of an absolute condition (in which "absolute" also implies "detachment").

Given the advantage won over the anxiety related to need, this detachment is successful right from its humblest mode—that in which it was glimpsed by a certain psychoanalyst in his work with children, which he called the "transitional object," in other words, the shred of blanket or beloved shard the child's lips or hands never stop touching.

This is, frankly, no more than an emblem; representation's representative in the absolute condition is in its proper place in the unconscious, where it causes desire in accordance with the structure of fantasy I will extract from it.

For it is clear here that man's continued nescience of his desire is not so much nescience of what he demands, which may after all be isolated, as nescience of whence he desires.

This is where my formulation that the unconscious is (the) discourse about the Other [*discours de l'Autre*] fits in, in which the *de* should be understood in the sense of the Latin *de* (objective determination): *de Alio in oratione* (you complete it: *tua res agitur*).

But we must also add that man's desire is the Other's desire [*le désir de l'homme est le désir de l'Autre*] in which the *de* provides what grammarians call a "subjective determination"—namely, that it is qua Other that man desires (this is what provides the true scope of human passion).

815   This is why the Other's question [*la question de l'Autre*]—that comes back to the subject from the place from which he expects an oracular reply—which takes some such form as *"Chè vuoi?,"* "What do you want?," is the question that best leads the subject to the path of his own desire, assuming that, thanks to the know-how of a partner known as a psychoanalyst, he takes up that question, even without knowing it, in the following form: "What does he want from me?"

Graph 3

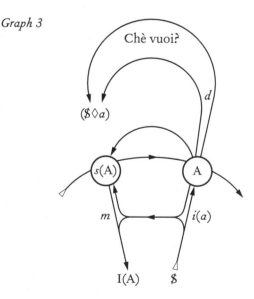

It is this superimposed level of structure that will nudge my graph (see Graph 3) toward its completed form, inserting itself there first like the out-

line of a question mark planted in the circle of the capital A, for Other, symbolizing the question it signifies with a disconcerting collineation.

Of what bottle is this the opener? Of what answer is it the signifier, the
master key?

It should be noted that a clue may be found in the clear alienation that
leaves it up to the subject to butt up against the question of his essence, in
that he may not misrecognize that what he desires presents itself to him as
what he does not want—a form assumed by negation in which misrecognition is inserted in a very odd way, the misrecognition, of which he himself
is unaware, by which he transfers the permanence of his desire to an ego that
is nevertheless obviously intermittent, and, inversely, protects himself from
his desire by attributing to it these very intermittences.

Of course, one may be surprised by the extent of what is accessible to
self-consciousness, on the condition that one has learnt it through another
channel. Which is certainly the case here.

For if we are to rediscover the pertinence of all this, a sufficiently sophisticated study, that can only be situated in the context of analytic experience,
must enable us to complete the structure of fantasy by essentially linking
here, regardless of its occasional elisions, the moment of a fading* or eclipse   816
of the subject—which is closely tied to the *Spaltung* or splitting he undergoes due to his subordination to the signifier—to the condition of an object
(whose privilege I have done no more than touch on above in reference to
diachrony).

This is what is symbolized by the abbreviation ($\lozenge a$), which I have introduced as an algorithm; and it is no accident that it breaks the phonemic element constituted by the signifying unit right down to its literal atom. For it
is designed to allow for a hundred and one different readings, a multiplicity
that is acceptable as long as what is said about it remains grounded in its
algebra.

This algorithm and the analogs of it used in the graph in no way contradict what I said earlier about the impossibility of a metalanguage. They are
not transcendent signifiers; they are indices of an absolute signification, a
notion which will, I hope, seem appropriate to the condition of fantasy
without further commentary.

The graph shows that desire adjusts to fantasy as posited in this way—
like the ego does in relation to the body image—but the graph also shows
the inversion of the misrecognitions on which the one and the other are
based, respectively. Thus closes the imaginary path, by which I must come
into being in analysis, where the unconscious was (to be) *itself.*

Let us say—borrowing the metaphor used by Damourette and Pichon about the grammatical ego and applying it to a subject to which it is better suited—that fantasy is really the "stuff" of the *I* that is primally repressed, because it can be indicated only in the fading* of enunciation.

Indeed, our attention is now drawn to the subjective status of the signifying chain in the unconscious or, better, in primal repression (*Urverdrängung*).

In my deduction, it is easier to understand why it was necessary to investigate the function on which the subject of the unconscious is based, because we realize that it is difficult to designate that subject anywhere as subject of a statement—and therefore as articulating it—when he does not even know he is speaking. Hence the concept of the drive, in which the subject is designated on the basis of a pinpointing that is organic, oral, anal, and so on, which satisfies the requirement that the more he speaks, the further he is from speaking.

817

Complete Graph

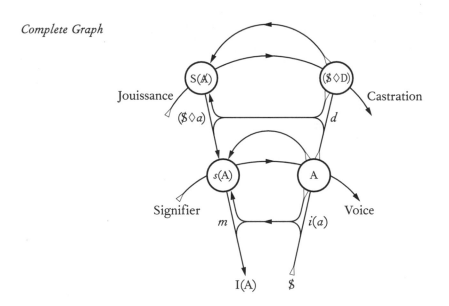

But while my complete graph allows us to situate the drive as the treasure trove of signifiers, its notation, ($◊D), maintains its structure by linking it to diachrony. The drive is what becomes of demand when the subject vanishes from it. It goes without saying that demand also disappears, except that the cut remains, for the latter remains present in what distinguishes the drive from the organic function it inhabits: namely, its grammatical artifice, so manifest in the reversals of its articulation with respect to both source and object. (Freud is a veritable wellspring on this point.)

The very delimitation of the "erogenous zone" that the drive isolates from the function's metabolism (the act of devouring involves organs other than the mouth—just ask Pavlov's dog) is the result of a cut that takes advantage of the anatomical characteristic of a margin or border: the lips, "the enclosure of the teeth," the rim of the anus, the penile groove, the vagina, and the slit formed by the eyelids, not to mention the hollow of the ear (I am avoiding going into embryological detail here). Respiratory erogeneity has been little studied, but it is obviously through spasms that it comes into play.

Let us note that this characteristic of the cut is no less obviously prevalent in the object described by analytic theory: the mamilla, the feces, the phallus (as an imaginary object), and the urinary flow. (An unthinkable list, unless we add, as I do, the phoneme, the gaze, the voice . . . and the nothing.) For isn't it plain to see that the characteristic of being partial, rightly emphasized in objects, is applicable not because these objects are part of a total object, which the body is assumed to be, but because they only partially represent the function that produces them?

A common characteristic of these objects as I formulate them is that they have no specular image, in other words, no alterity.[8] This is what allows them to be the "stuff" or, better put, the lining—without, nevertheless, being the flip side—of the very subject people take to be the subject of consciousness. For this subject, who thinks he can accede to himself by designating himself in the statement, is nothing but such an object. Ask someone with writer's block about the anxiety he experiences and he will tell you who the turd *is* in his fantasy.

It is to this object that cannot be grasped in the mirror that the specular image lends its clothes. A substance caught in the net of shadow, and which, robbed of its shadow-swelling volume, holds out once again the tired lure of the shadow as if it were substance.

What the graph now offers us is situated at the point at which every signifying chain takes pride in closing its signification. If we are to expect such an effect from unconscious enunciation, it is here in S(Ⱥ) and read as: signifier of a lack in the Other, a lack inherent in the Other's very function as the treasure trove of signifiers. And this is so insofar as the Other is called upon (*chè vuoi*) to answer for the value of this treasure, that is, to answer for its place in the lower chain certainly, but with the signifiers constitutive of the upper chain—in other words, in terms of the drive.

The lack at stake is one I have already formulated: that there is no Other of the Other. But is this characteristic of truth's Faithlessness really the last

818

word worth giving in answer to the question, "What does the Other want from me?" when we analysts are its mouthpiece? Surely not, and precisely because there is nothing doctrinal about our role. We need not answer for any ultimate truth, and certainly not for or against any particular religion.

It is already significant that I had to situate here [in S(Ⱥ)] the dead Father in the Freudian myth. But a myth is nothing if it props up no rites, and psychoanalysis is not the Oedipal rite—a point to be expanded on later.

No doubt a corpse is a signifier, but Moses' tomb is as empty for Freud as Christ's was for Hegel. Abraham revealed his mystery to neither of them.

819   For my part, I will begin with what the abbreviation S(Ⱥ) articulates, being first of all a signifier. My definition of the signifier (there is no other) is as follows: a signifier is what represents the subject to another signifier. This latter signifier is therefore the signifier to which all the other signifiers represent the subject—which means that if this signifier is missing, all the other signifiers represent nothing. For something is only represented to.

Now insofar as the battery of signifiers is, it is complete, and this signifier can only be a line that is drawn from its circle without being able to be counted in it. This can be symbolized by the inherence of a (-1) in the set of signifiers.

It is, as such, unpronounceable, but its operation is not, for the latter is what occurs whenever a proper name is pronounced. Its statement is equal to its signification.

Hence, by calculating this signification according to the algebra I use, namely:

$$\frac{S \text{ (signifier)}}{s \text{ (signified)}} = s \text{ (the statement)},$$

$$\text{with } S = (-1), \text{ we find: } s = \sqrt{-1}$$

This is what the subject is missing in thinking he is exhaustively accounted for by his cogito—he is missing what is unthinkable about him. But where does this being, who appears in some way missing from the sea of proper names, come from?

We cannot ask this question of the subject qua *I*. He is missing everything he needs in order to know the answer, since if this subject, *I*, was dead [*moi J'étais mort*], he would not know it, as I said earlier. Thus he does not know I'm alive. How, therefore, will *I* prove it to myself?

For I can, at most, prove to the Other that he exists, not, of course, with the proofs of the existence of God with which the centuries have killed him, but by loving him, a solution introduced by the Christian kerygma.

It is, in any case, too precarious a solution for us to even think of using it to circumvent our problem, namely: What am *I*?

I am in the place from which "the universe is a flaw in the purity of Non-Being" is vociferated.

And not without reason for, by protecting itself, this place makes Being itself languish. This place is called Jouissance, and it is Jouissance whose absence would render the universe vain.

Am I responsible for it, then? Yes, of course. Is this Jouissance, the lack of which makes the Other inconsistent, mine, then? Experience proves that   820 it is usually forbidden me, not only, as certain fools would have it, due to bad societal arrangements, but, I would say, because the Other is to blame—if he was to exist [*existait*], that is. But since he doesn't exist, all that's left for me is to place the blame on *I*, that is, to believe in what experience leads us all to, Freud at the head of the list: original sin. For even if we did not have Freud's express and sorrowful avowal, the fact remains that the myth we owe to him—the most recent in history—is of no more use than the myth of the forbidden fruit, except for the fact (and this is not one of its assets as a myth) that, being more succinct, it is considerably less stultifying.

But what is not a myth, although Freud formulated it just as early on as he formulated the Oedipus myth, is the castration complex.

In the castration complex we find the mainspring of the very subversion I am trying to articulate here by means of its dialectic. For this complex, which was unknown as such until Freud introduced it into the formation of desire, can no longer be ignored in any reflection on the subject.

In psychoanalysis it seems that, rather than attempting to carry its articulation further, people have deliberately avoided providing any explanation of it. Which is why this great Samson-like body has been reduced to providing grist for the mill of the Philistines of general psychology.

Certainly there is a bone(r) [*os*] here. Since it is precisely what I am claiming—namely, what structures the subject—it essentially constitutes in the subject the gap that all thought has avoided, skipped over, circumvented, or stopped up whenever thought apparently succeeds in sustaining itself circularly, whether the thought be dialectical or mathematical.

This is why I am given to guiding my students to the places where logic is disconcerted by the disjunction that breaks through from the imaginary to the symbolic, not in order to indulge in the paradoxes that are thus generated, or in some supposed crisis in thought, but, on the contrary, to redirect their fake shine to the gap they designate—which I always find quite simply edifying—and above all to try to create a method from a sort of calculus whose very inappropriateness would flush out the secret.

821 Such is the phantom known as the cause, which I have pursued in the purest symbolization of the imaginary through the alternation from the similar to the dissimilar.[9]

Let us observe carefully, therefore, what it is that objects to conferring on my signifier S(Ⱥ) the meaning of mana or of any such term. It is the fact that we cannot be satisfied to explain it on the basis of the poverty of the social fact, even if the latter were traced back to some supposedly total fact.

Claude Lévi-Strauss, commenting on Mauss' work, no doubt wished to see in mana the effect of a zero symbol. But it seems that what we are dealing with in our case is rather the signifier of the lack of this zero symbol. This is why, at the risk of incurring a certain amount of opprobrium, I have indicated how far I have gone in distorting mathematical algorithms in my own use of them: for example, my use of the symbol, $\sqrt{-1}$, also written i in the theory of complex numbers, can obviously be justified only if I give up any claim to its being able to be used automatically in subsequent operations.

We must keep in mind that jouissance is prohibited [*interdite*] to whomever speaks, as such—or, put differently, it can only be said [*dite*] between the lines by whomever is a subject of the Law, since the Law is founded on that very prohibition.

Indeed, were the Law to give the order, "*Jouis!*" ["Enjoy!" or "Come!"], the subject could only reply "*J'ouïs*" ["I hear"], in which the jouissance would no longer be anything but understood [*sous-entendue*].

But it is not the Law itself that bars the subject's access to jouissance—it simply makes a barred subject out of an almost natural barrier. For it is pleasure that sets limits to jouissance, pleasure as what binds incoherent life together, until another prohibition—this one being unchallengeable—arises from the regulation that Freud discovered as the primary process and relevant law of pleasure.

It has been said that in this discovery Freud merely followed the course already being pursued by the science of his time—nay, a long-standing tradition. To appreciate the true audacity of his step, we have only to consider his reward, which was not long in coming: the stalemate regarding the heteroclite nature of the castration complex.

822 The latter is the sole indication of this jouissance in its infinitude, which brings with it the mark of its prohibition, and which requires a sacrifice in

order to constitute this mark: the sacrifice implied in the same act as that of chosing its symbol, the phallus.

This choice is allowed because the phallus—that is, the image of the penis—is negativized where it is situated in the specular image. That is what predestines the phallus to give body to jouissance in the dialectic of desire.

We must distinguish, therefore, between the principle of sacrifice, which is symbolic, and the imaginary function which is devoted to it, but which veils the principle at the same time that it gives it its instrument.

The imaginary function is the one Freud formulated as governing object cathexis as narcissistic. I came back to this myself when I showed that the specular image is the channel taken by the transfusion of the body's libido toward the object. But insofar as a part remains preserved from this immersion, concentrating in itself the most intimate aspect of autoeroticism, its position as a "pointy extremity" in the form predisposes it to the fantasy of it falling off—in which its exclusion from the specular image is completed as is the prototype it constitutes for the world of objects.

It is thus that the erectile organ—not as itself, or even as an image, but as a part that is missing in the desired image—comes to symbolize the place of jouissance; this is why the erectile organ can be equated with the $\sqrt{-1}$, the symbol of the signification produced above, of the jouissance it restores—by the coefficient of its statement—to the function of a missing signifier: (-1).

If it serves to tie together in this way the prohibition of jouissance, it is nevertheless not for reasons of form, but because the supersession of these reasons signifies what reduces all coveted jouissance to the brevity of autoeroticism. The pathways that are altogether traced out by the anatomical conformation of speaking beings—namely, the further perfected hand of the monkey—have not, in effect, been disdained in a certain philosophical ascesis as pathways of a wisdom that has incorrectly been termed cynical. Certain individuals[10] in our times, obsessed no doubt by this memory, have suggested to me that Freud himself belongs to the tradition of "bodily techniques," as Mauss calls it. The fact remains that analytic experience demonstrates the original character of the guilt generated by such practices.   823

Guilt that is related to the reminder of the jouissance that is not found in the service rendered to the real organ, and consecration of the signifier's imaginary function of prohibiting objects.

Indeed, this is the radical function for which a wilder analytic era found more accidental causes (due to education), just as it reinterpreted the other forms—in which it took an interest, to its credit—of sanctification of the organ (circumcision) as traumas.

The shift of $(-\varphi)$ (lowercase phi) as phallic image from one side to the other of the equation between the imaginary and the symbolic renders it positive in any case, even if it fills a lack. Although it props up (-1), it becomes Φ (capital phi) there, the symbolic phallus that cannot be negativized, the signifier of jouissance. And it is this characteristic of Φ that explains both the particularities of women's approach to sexuality, and what makes the male sex the weaker sex with regard to perversion.

I will not take up perversion here, inasmuch as it barely accentuates the function of desire in man, insofar as desire institutes the dominance—in the privileged place of jouissance—of object a in fantasy, which desire substitutes for $\mathcal{A}$. Perversion adds to that a recuperation of φ that would scarcely seem original if it did not concern the Other as such in a very particular way. Only my formula for fantasy allows us to bring out the fact that the subject here makes himself the instrument of the Other's jouissance.

It is of more concern to philosophers to grasp the relevance of this formula in the case of the neurotic, precisely because the neurotic skews it.

Indeed, the neurotic, whether hysteric, obsessive, or, more radically, phobic, is the one who identifies the Other's lack with the Other's demand, Φ with D.

Consequently, the Other's demand takes on the function of the object in the neurotic's fantasy—that is, his fantasy (my formulas make it possible to realize this immediately) is reduced to the drive: $(\$\lozenge D)$. This is why it was possible to catalog all the neurotic's drives.

But the prevalence given by the neurotic to demand—which, in an analytic movement opting for facility, shifted the whole treatment toward the handling of frustration—hides the anxiety induced in him by the Other's desire, anxiety that cannot be misrecognized when it is covered over by the phobic object alone, but which is more difficult to understand in the case of the other two neuroses when one is not in possession of the thread that makes it possible to posit fantasy as the Other's desire. Once we posit this, we find fantasy's two terms split apart, as it were: the first, in the case of the obsessive, inasmuch as he negates the Other's desire, forming his fantasy in such a way as to accentuate the impossibility of the subject vanishing, the second, in the case of the hysteric, inasmuch as desire is sustained in fantasy only by the lack of satisfaction the hysteric brings desire by slipping away as its object.

These features are confirmed by the obsessive's fundamental need to be the Other's guarantor, and by the Faithlessness of hysterical intrigue.

In fact, the image of the ideal Father is a neurotic's fantasy. Beyond the

Mother—demand's real Other, whose desire (that is, her desire) we wish she would tone down—stands out the image of a father who would turn a blind eye to desires. This marks—more than it reveals—the true function of the Father, which is fundamentally to unite (and not to oppose) a desire to the Law.

The Father the neurotic wishes for is clearly the dead Father—that is plain to see. But he is also a Father who would be the perfect master of his desire—which would be just as good, as far as the subject is concerned.

This is one of the stumbling blocks the analyst must avoid, and the crux of the interminable aspect of transference.

It is why a calculated vacillation of the analyst's "neutrality" may be more valuable to a hysteric than any number of interpretations—provided, of course, that the fright this risks bringing about in the patient does not lead to a breaking off of the analysis, and that the analysand is convinced by what follows that the analyst's desire was in no way involved in the matter. This, of course, is not a recommendation regarding technique, but a perspective on the question of the analyst's desire for those who could not otherwise have any notion of it: how the analyst must safeguard the imaginary dimension of his nonmastery and necessary imperfection for the other, is as important a matter to deal with as the deliberate reinforcement in the analyst of his nescience regarding each subject who comes to him for analysis, of an ever renewed ignorance so that no one is considered a typical case.

To return to fantasy, let us say that the pervert imagines he is the Other in order to ensure his own jouissance, and that this is what the neurotic reveals when he imagines he is a pervert—in his case, to ensure control over the Other.

825

This explains the supposed perversion at the crux of neurosis. Perversion is in the neurotic's unconscious in the guise of the Other's fantasy. But this does not mean that the pervert's unconscious is right out in the open. He, too, defends himself in his desire in his own way. For desire is a defense, a defense against going beyond a limit in jouissance.

In its structure as I have defined it, fantasy contains $(-\varphi)$, the imaginary function of castration, in a hidden form that can switch from one of its terms to the other. That is to say, like a complex number, it alternatively imaginarizes (if you will allow me this term) one of these terms in relation to the other.

Included in object *a* is *agalma*, the inestimable treasure that Alcibiades declares is contained in the rustic box the figure of Socrates is to him. But let us note that a minus sign $(-)$ is attributed to it. It is because Alcibiades has not seen Socrates' prick—permit me to follow Plato here, who does not spare us the details—that Alcibiades the seducer exalts in Socrates the *agalma*, the marvel that he would have liked Socrates to cede to him by avowing his desire. Alcibiades' subjective division, which he carries within him, shines through quite clearly on this occasion.

Such is woman concealed behind her veil: it is the absence of the penis that makes her the phallus, the object of desire. Evoke this absence in a more precise way by having her wear a cute fake one under a fancy dress, and you, or rather she, will have plenty to tell us about: the effect is 100 percent guaranteed, for men who don't beat around the bush, that is.

Thus by exhibiting his own object as castrated, Alcibiades flaunts the fact that he is imbued with desire—a fact that does not escape Socrates' attention—for someone else who is present, Agathon. Socrates, as the precursor of psychoanalysis, and confident of his position at this fashionable gathering, does not hesitate to name Agathon as the transference object, bringing to light through an interpretation a fact that many analysts are still unaware of: that the love-hate effect in the psychoanalytic situation is found outside of it.

But Alcibiades is by no means a neurotic. In fact, it is because he is the epitome of desirousness, and a man who pursues jouissance as far as possible, that he can thus (though with the help of an instrumental drunkenness) produce before everyone's eyes the central articulation of the transference, when in the presence of the object adorned with its sparkle.

The fact remains that he projected onto Socrates the ideal of the perfect Master—that he completely imaginarized Socrates through the action of $(-\varphi)$.

In the case of the neurotic, $(-\varphi)$ slips under the $\$$ in fantasy, favoring the imagination that is characteristic of him, that of the ego. For the neurotic underwent imaginary castration at the outset; it sustains the strong ego that is his, so strong, one might say, that his proper name bothers him, so strong that deep down the neurotic is Nameless.

Yes, it is behind this ego, which certain analysts choose to strengthen still more, that the neurotic hides the castration he denies.

But, contrary to appearances, he cleaves to this castration.

What the neurotic does not want, and what he strenuously refuses to do until the end of his analysis, is to sacrifice his castration to the Other's jouissance, by allowing it to serve the Other.

And, of course, he is not wrong, for—although, deep down, he feels he is the most vain thing in existence, a Want-To-Be or a One-Too-Many—why would he sacrifice his difference (anything but that) to the

826

jouissance of an Other, which, let us not forget, does not exist. Yes, but if by chance it was to exist [*existait*], it would enjoy it [*il en jouirait*]. And that is what the neurotic does not want. For he figures that the Other demands his castration.

What analytic experience attests to is that castration is what regulates desire, in both normal and abnormal cases.

Providing it oscillates by alternating between $ and *a* in fantasy, castration makes of fantasy a chain that is both supple and inextensible by which the fixation of object cathexis, which can hardly go beyond certain natural limits, takes on the transcendental function of ensuring the jouissance of the Other that passes this chain on to me in the Law.

Anyone who really wants to come to terms with this Other has open to him the path of experiencing not the Other's demand, but its will. And then: to either realize himself as an object, turning himself into the mummy of some Buddhist initiation, or satisfy the will to castrate inscribed in the Other, which leads to the supreme narcissism of the Lost Cause (the latter being the path of Greek tragedy, which Claudel rediscovers in a Christianity of despair).   827

Castration means that jouissance has to be refused in order to be attained on the inverse scale of the Law of desire.

I won't go any further here.

[Endnote]

This article is coming out here for the first time: an unexpected shortage of the funds that are usually provided in ample quantity to publish the complete proceedings of such colloquia having left it in abeyance, along with all the fine things that adorned it.

I should mention, for the record, that the "Copernican" discussion was added later, and that the end of the article on castration was not delivered at the colloquium due to lack of time, and was in fact replaced by a few words on the machine, in the modern sense of the word, by which the subject's relation to the signifier can be materialized.

From the fellow feeling natural in any discussion, let us not exclude the fellow feeling aroused in me by a particular disagreement. The term "a-human," which someone wanted to attribute to what I had said, did not bother me in the least; I was flattered, rather, as I had helped occasion the birth of the new element it brings to the category. I noted with no less interest the sizzling, that followed soon afterward, of the word "hell," since the voice that pronounced it gave it a certain distinctive piquancy owing to the speaker's declared allegiance to Marxism. I must admit that I appreciate humanism when it comes from a camp where, although employed with no less cunning than elsewhere, it at least has a certain candor about it: "When the miner comes home, his wife rubs him down . . ." That leaves me defenseless.

In a private conversation, someone close to me asked me (this was the form his question took) whether talking to a brick wall implied faith in an eternal scribe. Such faith is not necessary, was the reply, to whoever knows that every discourse derives its effects from the unconscious.

Notes

1. (Added in 1966:) Even in attempting to interest people in telepathy, under the heading of psychological phenomena—or in the whole Gothic psychology that can be resuscitated on the basis of Myers' work—the crudest adventurer will be unable to break out of the field in which Freud has already confined him, by presenting what he accepts of these phenomena as requiring translation, in the strict sense of the term, in the corroborative effects of contemporary discourses.

Even when prostituted, psychoanalytic theory remains sanctimonious (a well-known characteristic of the brothel). As we say since Sartre, she's a respectable girl: she won't walk the street on just any side.

2. *GW* VIII, 237–38.

3. I am referring here to the friend who invited me to this conference, after having, some months before, revealed in print his reservations—based on his personal ontology—about "psychoanalysts" who were too "Hegelian" for his liking, as if anyone in this group but me could even be associated with Hegel.

This in the hodgepodge text of pages from his diary cast to the four winds (of chance, no doubt), from which a journal (*La Nouvelle Revue française*) had nevertheless benefited.

Regarding which I pointed out to him that in the, even entertaining, terms in which he dressed up this ontology of his in his informal notes, I found its "certainly not, but perhaps" procedure designed to mislead.

4. I have left this paragraph in the text only as a monument to an outdated battle (added in 1962: What was I thinking? {1966. 1957. 1968 . . . ha, ha!}).

5. (Added in 1962:) The words in parentheses here have been added with a view to pinpointing later developments regarding identification.

6. This, too, is a reference to what I proffered in my seminar, *L'Éthique de la psychanalyse* (1959-60, forthcoming), on the second death. I agree with Dylan Thomas that there aren't two. But is the absolute Master, then, the only one that remains?

7. [Added in 1966:] The very fact that I said this at the time at this point in my paper, even if I didn't put it more forcefully, suggests an appointment with fate since, three years later, it was precisely regarding the theme of the Name-of-the-Father that I adopted the sanction of laying to rest the theses I had promised in my seminar, due to the permanence of this situation.

8. (Added in 1962:) I have since justified this by means of a topological model borrowed from surface theory in an *analysis situs*.

9. (Added in 1962:) More recently, in the opposite direction, in the attempt to correlate topologically defined surfaces with the terms I employ here in the subjective articulation. Not to mention in the simple refutation of the supposed paradox, "I am lying."

10. (Added in 1971:) This plural covers an eminent contemporary philosopher.

Translator's Endnotes

General Notes

Many of the terms used in this translation could be explained at length, but I will limit myself here to some that may be particularly confusing.

Assumer
Assumer corresponds to the English "to assume" in the sense of to take on (as in "to assume a responsibility"), but also implies taking in, adopting, incorporating, owning, dealing with, and coming to terms with. I generally translate *assumer* as "to assume" and *assomption* as "assumption," and include the French in brackets when the usage seems somewhat foreign (e.g., "the subject assumes an image" and "the subject's assumption of his own sex").

De
This is, in my experience, the most difficult word to translate in *Écrits*. Among its meanings: of, from, with, by, because of, thanks to, based on, by means of, about, and as. Lacan's use of *de* seems to me to be highly unusual among French authors, especially in "Subversion of the Subject."

Certain uses of *de* are particularly open to multiple interpretations, due to its function as either a subjective genitive or an objective genitive (or intentionally designed by Lacan to suggest both). Consider, in particular, formulations like *le désir de l'Autre* (see below) and *la jouissance de l'Autre* (is it the jouissance the Other has or the subject's jouissance of the Other?).

Demande
The French term here can be as strong as the English "demand" or as weak as "request." I have translated it as both, depending on the context, but provide the French in brackets when I render it as the latter.

Le désir de l'Autre
Apart from the usual meanings, "desire for the Other" and "the Other's desire" (only the latter of which is captured by the formula "the desire of the Other," since we say "desire for" not "desire of" something), it should be kept in mind that Lacan often uses the French here as a shorthand for saying "what the Other desires" or "the object of the Other's desire." For example, in the sentence, *Le désir de l'homme, c'est le désir de l'Autre*, one of the obvious meanings is that man desires what the Other desires. It is also implied that, as a man, I want the Other to desire me.

Duel or Duelle (for example, *relation duelle*)
I have avoided the obvious translation "dual" here because, in contemporary American psychology, "dual relations" are when a patient's therapist is also his or her teacher, for example, the therapist playing two different roles in relation to the patient. In Lacan's usage, *la relation duelle* is the imaginary relation between ego (*a'*) and alter ego (*a*), as opposed to the symbolic relation. I have systematically translated the adjective as "dyadic."

Expérience
The French term here is often used by itself, without any predicate (e.g., *dans l'expérience*). Psychoanalytic experience is usually what is at issue, but not always. The term also means experiment, as in a scientific experiment, and it is not always clear which is intended.

Instance
Lacan's *instance*, like Freud's *Instanz*, is often translated here as "agency," especially when Lacan is talking about the various Freudian agencies (id, ego, and superego). However, *instance* also implies a power or authority (as when we speak of a Court of the First Instance), and an *insistent*, urgent force, activity, or intervention. "Agency" in no way conveys the *insistence* so

important to Lacan's use of the term in such contexts. *Instance* also means a particular example or case of something (cf. *enstasis*, the obstacle one raises to an adversary's argument or the exception to a universal predicate, hence an instance or counterinstance that refutes a general claim), as Lacan indicates in Seminar XX, 65.

Jouissance

I have assumed that the kind of enjoyment beyond the pleasure principle (including orgasm) denoted by the French *jouissance* is well enough known by now to the English-reading public to require no translation.

Langue and *Langage*

Given the linguistic backdrop of so much of Lacan's work, I have consistently translated *langage* as "language" and, when I translate *langue* as "language," I always include the French in brackets.

Manque à être

Lacan himself apparently selected the English translation "want-to-be," no doubt at least in part due to its polyvalence. I have generally adopted that translation, though in certain instances I have preferred other renderings, such as "lack of being" and "failure to be."

Méconnaissance

This term is very common in French, and in certain contexts is best translated as "ignorance," "neglect," or "oversight"; similarly, the verb form, *méconnaître*, is often best translated as "to overlook," "to misunderstand," "to be unaware of," "to omit," "to ignore," "to neglect," or "to disregard." Lacan sometimes uses this term to refer to an almost deliberate misrecognition or misunderstanding of something (e.g., an idea or a wish), a knowledge (or knowing) that is missed or botched almost on purpose; in those cases, I render it as "misrecognition" or "misrecognize."

Négation and *Dénégation*

The importance of negation and the different forms it can take is at least as crucial to Lacan's work as it is to Freud's. Many of the terms Lacan uses to talk about it are either accepted translations or his own translations of Freud's terms, each of which has certain technical and/or idiomatic uses in German, which do not necessarily coincide with idiomatic uses in French— all of which is compounded in translating these terms into English.

The rarest, *Verwerfung*, is the easiest from a translator's standpoint; Lacan translates it first as *rejet* (rejection) and *retranchement* (suppression, subtraction, deduction, retrenchment, or entrenchment; see *Écrits* 1966, 386), and then more consistently as *forclusion* (foreclosure). The verb form in French is *forclore*, translated here as "to foreclose."

Verneinung (negation) is rendered in French in two different ways: *négation* and *dénégation*. I render both as either "negation" or "denial," depending on the context. I translate the corresponding French verb, *nier*, as either "to negate" or "to deny," depending on the context.

Verleugnung (disavowal) is rendered in French in two different ways: *déni* and *désaveu*. *Dénier* (the verb form) is very close in French usage to *nier*, but I always translate the former as "to disavow" (except when I include the French in brackets).

Objectivation

The French here means objectification, in the two related senses of the term: turning something into an object and, perhaps more usually, rendering something objective (not necessarily in the absolute sense, but in the sense of putting something "outside" in such a way that others can observe or study it).

Oblativité

A supposed tendency to give to others selflessly or disinterestedly, discussed in French analytic texts of the 1950s, translated here as "oblativity." The term was introduced by Laforgue in 1926 and was rendered as "self-sacrifice" in Lacan's "Some Reflections on the Ego," *IJP* XXXIV, 1 (1953): 17.

Réel

This term is often used by French authors as an alternate term for *réalité* (reality), without any reference whatsoever to the Lacanian category of the real. Lacan himself often uses the term in this way, and always does so *prior* to developing his formulation of the real in juxtaposition to the imaginary and the symbolic in the early 1950s. It is not always obvious whether it should be translated as "real" or "reality" after that time, and so I provide the French in brackets whenever I translate it as "reality."

Savoir and Connaissance

French generally distinguishes between *savoir*, as a factual, explicit, articulated kind of knowledge (e.g., knowing the date of a particular historical event), and *connaissance* as a more experiential kind of knowing (e.g., knowing a person or how to speak a language), though there are numerous exceptions to this rough and ready categorization. See, in particular, Lacan's discussion in "Subversion of the Subject" (*Écrits* 1966, 803). I have translated both *savoir* and *connaissance* as "knowledge," though I provide the French in brackets when the original reads *connaissance* (except in "The Mirror Stage," "Aggressiveness in Psychoanalysis," "The Freudian Thing," "The Instance of the Letter," and "On a Question," where "knowledge" always translates *connaissance* except when followed by *savoir* in brackets). Note that *connaissance* can also mean consciousness and is thus rendered accordingly when the context seems to call for it.

Semblable
This term is often translated as "fellow man" or "counterpart," but in Lacan's usage it refers specifically to the mirroring of two imaginary others (*a* and *a′*) who *resemble* each other (or at least see themselves in each other). "Fellow man" corresponds well to the French *prochain*, points to man (not woman), the adult (not the child), and suggests fellowship, whereas in Lacan's work *semblable* evokes rivalry and jealousy first and foremost. "Counterpart" suggests parallel hierarchical structures within which the two people take on similar roles, that is, symbolic roles, as in "The Chief Financial Officer's counterpart in his company's foreign acquisition target was Mr. Juppé, the *Directeur financier*." Jacques-Alain Miller has suggested that we translate *semblable* as "alter ego," but since "alter ego" is also occasionally used independently by Lacan and since it has a number of inapposite connotations in English ("a trusted friend" and "the opposite side of one's personality"), I have preferred to revive the obsolete English "semblable" found, for example, in *Hamlet*, Act V, Scene II, line 124: "his semblable is his mirror; and who else would trace him, his umbrage, nothing more."

Sens and *Signification*
These two terms are often synonymous and are translated as "meaning" in most contexts. In linguistics, however, a distinction is generally made between *signification* as a psychological process and *sens* as a static term for the mental image resulting from that psychological process. Given the linguistic horizon of so much of Lacan's work, I have translated *sens* as "meaning" and *signification* as "signification," except when indicated. *Sens*, of course, also means direction and sense. See Lacan's later comments on *sens* and *signification* in "L'étourdit" in *Autres écrits* (Paris: Seuil, 2001), 479–80.

Signifiance

This French term, which I generally translate as "signifierness," might also be translated as "significance," "signifyingness," or "meaningfulness." According to André Lalande's *Vocabulaire technique et critique de la philosophie* (Paris: Presses Universitaires de France, 1976), the term was introduced into French linguistics in the 1960s, deriving from the English "significance," and is related to the English "connotation." According to the *Dictionnaire historique de la langue française* (Paris: Robert, 1994), "the word, which until recently was no longer in use, was taken up anew in the vocabulary of semiology and semiotics, designating (probably modeled on the English "significance") the fact of having meaning, opposed to *non signifiance*." Lacan uses it to translate the *deutung* of Freud's *Traumdeutung* (*Écrits* 1966, 623), which Strachey renders as "interpretation." In the course of Lacan's work, it takes on the meaning of "signifierness" or the "signifying nature" of signifiers— in other words, the sense in which the signifier dominates the signified. See, in particular, Lacan's "Instance of the Letter" (1957) where he equates it with *l'effet signifiant*, the signifying effect or signifier effect (*Écrits* 1966, 515, fn2).

Le signifiant

The French here, generally translated as "the signifier," is subject to the same translation headaches as many other singular French nouns: the French tend to use singulars where in American English we would be more likely to use plurals. (In speaking of women, for example, the French would be likely to talk about *la femme* not *les femmes*.) In certain contexts, I have preferred to translate *le signifiant* as "signifiers" (providing the French in brackets), but it should be kept in mind that Lacan also conceives of "the signifier" as forming a system and as collectivizable and unquantifiable in certain respects (see, for example, Seminar XX on this point).

Sujet

Like *réel*, *sujet* (subject) is often used by French authors, and by Lacan himself—at all periods of his work—to refer simply to the subject of a study or experiment, to a patient, or to a person without any reference whatsoever to the Lacanian distinction between the ego and the subject (however the Lacanian subject is conceived of). While I always translate *sujet* as "subject," it should be kept in mind that the technical Lacanian sense often is not intended (indeed, sometimes the meaning of "the topic at hand" is primary). Grammatically, *sujet* is masculine, but it can obviously refer to a man or a woman.

Subjectivation

The French here means either subjectification—turning someone (or something) into a subject—or the fact of rendering something subjective, which I have translated here as "subjectivization." Similarly, *subjectiver* (the verb form) can mean either to subjectify or to subjectivize. It is often unclear which term should be used.

Notes on Texts

In these notes, the numbers in parentheses refer first to the page numbers of the original French edition, *Écrits* 1966—which are provided in the margins of the present translation   and then, after a comma, to the paragraph number (partial and short paragraphs are counted, as well as section titles and epigraphs) or footnote number (abbreviated "fn"). References to Lacan's Seminars are to the volume number and the original French pagination, and then (after a slash) to that of the published English edition, when available (in the case of Seminars III and XX, I provide only the French pagination since it is included in the margins of the English editions). In these notes, words found in parentheses after French text indicate the corresponding text in the English translation.

NOTES TO "THE MIRROR STAGE"

(93,1) *La fonction du Je* (*I* function) could also be rendered as "the function of the *I*" throughout this article.

(93,4) See Wolfgang Köhler, *The Mentality of Apes*, trans. Ella Winter (London: Routledge & Kegan Paul, 1927); the first German edition was published in 1917, the first English edition in 1925.

(93,6) A reference to the work of James Mark Baldwin (1861–1934), the American philosopher and psychologist.

(94,1) *Le fixer* (fix it in his mind) can mean a number of things, including to stare at it, pin it down, and fix it in the sense in which a photographer uses fixer to develop a picture.

(94,3) See general note above on *assumer* and *assomption*.

(95,1) In gestalt theory, *prégnance* refers to the power forms have to impose themselves upon perception or force themselves upon us.

(95,2) *Disposition en miroir* (mirrored disposition) implies the right-left reversal characteristic of mirror images.

(95,3) On the sexual maturation of pigeons, see L. Harrison Matthews, "Visual Stimulation and Ovulation in Pigeons" in the *Proceedings of the Royal Society*, Series B, 126 (1939): 557–60. On the development of the migratory locust, see R. Chauvin's work in *Annales de la Société entomologique de France* (1941, third quarter): 133, 272. These and other references are provided in Lacan's paper "Some Reflections on the Ego," *IJP* XXXIV, 1 (1953): 11–17, and in "Remarks on Psychical Causality" in *Écrits* 1966.

(95,fn1) In English, see "The Effectiveness of Symbols" in *Structural Anthropology*, trans. Claire Jacobson and Brooke Grundfest Schoepf (New York: Basic Books, 1963).

(96,3) *Détermine* (limits) could also be

translated as "specifies," "defines," "decides," or "fixes." André Breton introduced the term *peu de réalité* (scant reality) in his 1924 "Introduction au discours sur le peu de réalité"; see *Point du Jour* (Paris: Gallimard, 1970); in English, see "Introduction to the Discourse on the Paucity of Reality" in *Break of Day*, trans. Mark Polizzotti and Mary Ann Caws (Lincoln: University of Nebraska Press, 1999).

(97,1) The term "fetalization" (also spelled "foetalization") was introduced by Louis Bolk.

(97,2) *Poussée* (pressure) is the usual translation of Freud's *Drang*, one of the components of the drive; see *SE* XIV, 122. *Quadrature* (squaring) is the French term for what is referred to in English as "the squaring of the circle" (*la quadrature du cercle*). *Récolement* (audit) is a legal term designating the operation of reading a witness' deposition back to him or her to see if he or she approves of it. In financial contexts it can also be translated as "audit," "checking," "reexamination," or "verification" (of accounts or inventory); this could lead to the following possible translation: "the inexhaustible squaring (or settling) of the ego's accounts."

(97,3) *Corps morcelé* (fragmented body) is sometimes rendered as "body in pieces."

(98,1) *Annulation* (undoing what has been done) might ordinarily be translated as cancellation, rendering null and void, or invalidation. Here, however, it seems that Lacan is directly referring to the mechanism of "undoing" (something that has been done) found in obsessive neurosis. See, in particular, *SE* X, 235–36 and 243, and *SE* XX, 119–20; in the latter, Strachey indicates that he is translating Freud's *ungeschehenmachen*, which literally means "making unhappened."

(98,6) The French term, *primaire* (rendered in the standard English translation of *narcissisme primaire* by "primary"), also has the connotation of primal or primordial.

(99,1) See Jean-Paul Sartre's *Being and Nothingness*.

(99,2) Lacan's creation here, *self-suffisance* (self*-sufficiency), also suggests a note of self-complacency and smugness.

(99,3) *Concentrationnaire* (concentration-camp) is an adjective that was coined after World War II to describe life in concentration camps. In the hands of certain writers it became, by extension, applicable to many aspects of life. In "Paris Alive: The Republic of Silence" Sartre wrote "Never were we [the French] freer than under the German occupation" (*Atlantic Monthly* [December 1944]: 39–40).

NOTES TO "AGGRESSIVENESS IN PSYCHOANALYSIS"

(103,2) Lacan's use of "bipolar" here is *not* a reference to the contemporary psychiatric label.

(105,3) *Angustiae:* anguishes or narrow straits (of birth).

(106,3) *The Republic*, Book I, 336 ff.

(107,2) *Amour-propre:* self-love, self-regard, self-esteem, vanity, or pride.

(108,3) *Le redan et la chicane* (stepping and staggering technique) was a technique employed in military fortifications at the time of Louis XIV. *Fortifications à la Vauban* (military fortification) were unassailable fortifications designed by Sébastien le Prestre de Vauban, 1633–1707.

(109,1) *Préjudicielle* (prior) is a legal term,

describing questions and costs associated with a legal judgment that must be handed down *prior* to the principal suit. It could also be translated as "preliminary" or "prerequisite." See Freud, "Negation" (*Die Verneinung*), *SE* XIX, 235.

(109,2) *Complaisance* (self-indulgence) could also be translated as "complacency."

(109,6) *Une surface sans accidents* (a smooth surface) has no topographical relief or accidental attributes.

(110,6) See Lacan's 1932 doctoral dissertation published as *De la psychose paranoïaque dans ses rapports avec la personnalité* (Paris: Seuil, 1980).

(110,7) *Kakon:* "bad (object)" in Greek.

(112,2) The French original of this text and *Écrits* 1966 both read *spectaculaire* (spectacular) instead of *spéculaire* three times in this article, whereas Lacan's other texts always read *spéculaire* (specular); *spectaculaire* should probably be understood here in the sense of "relating to or constituting a spectacle."

(112,3) See H. Wallon, *Les origines du caractère chez l'enfant: Les Préludes du sentiment de personnalité* (Paris: PUF, [1934] 1954).

(113,3) *Einfühlung* is usually rendered as "empathy," "understanding," or "sensitivity."

(113,4) *Se fixe à* (fixates on) could also be translated as "latches onto," "attaches himself to," or "freezes himself in."

(114,4) See Freud's discussion of the three possible contradictions of the single proposition, "I love him" (*SE* XII, 63–64). The three principal forms of paranoia Freud discusses there are jealousy, erotomania, and persecution. See Lacan's discussion of this in his "Discours de Rome" in *Autres écrits* (Paris: Seuil, 2001), 156–57. *Désordre* (disorder) can also be rendered as "chaos" or "mess"; it is not a reference to the eponymous psychiatric notion.

(114,5) *The Confessions of St. Augustine*, trans. J. G. Pilkington (New York: The Heritage Press, 1963), 7. To translate the French rendition of the Latin Lacan provides (perhaps taken from a published French translation): "I saw with my own eyes and knew very well an infant in the grip of jealousy: he could not yet speak, and already he observed his foster brother, pale and with an envenomed look."

(116,2) *Désarroi* here means distress, confusion, helplessness, complete disorganization, and disarray.

(116,3) Lacan here uses *répression* (usually reserved in French for "repression" in the political sense) instead of the more usual *refoulement* (reserved in French for "repression" in the psychoanalytic sense).

(117,2) See, in particular, *SE* XIII, 141–43.

(118,1) On identity, cf. *Écrits* 1966, 213; in English, see "Logical Time and the Assertion of Anticipated Certainty," trans. Bruce Fink and Marc Silver, *Newsletter of the Freudian Field* 2 (1988). "Je est un autre" ("I is an

other") is from Rimbaud's letter to Georges Izambard dated May 13, 1871. See Arthur Rimbaud, *Oeuvres complètes* (Paris: Gallimard, 1954), 268.

(118,5) On *oblativité* (oblativity), see general note above.

(119,1) *En libérer l'altruisme* (free altruism from it) could also be translated as "free up its altruism" or "free up the altruism therein." See Maxim 113, "Il y a de bons mariages, mais il n'y en a point de délicieux," in La Rochefoucauld, *Maximes* (Paris: Garnier Frères, 1967).

(119,3) Cf. Seminar III, 287, and Seminar XX, 70, where Lacan refers to Pierre Rousselot, *Pour l'histoire du problème de l'amour au moyen âge* (Münster: Aschendorffsche Buchhandlung, 1907). Rousselot explains that "physical love" was not understood in the Middle Ages as corporal or bodily, but rather as natural love—the kind of love one finds in nature between mother bear and cub, for example (see page 3). In the translation of Saint Thomas Aquinas' *Summa Theologica* prepared by the Fathers of the English Dominican Province, it is rendered as "natural love" (Chicago: Encyclopedia Britannica, 1952) (Question 60).

(119,5) On the climacteric, see *SE* XII, 46.

(120,3) Note that *Malaise dans la civilisation* is the standard French title of Freud's *Das Unbehagen in der Kultur*, known in English as *Civilization and its Discontents*.

(121,2) I have assumed that where the French text reads *ces* (these), it should, in fact, read *ses* (its): "revealing in its crises . . ."

(121,4) Spartacism: the views adopted by the Spartacists in the Spartacus League, which took its inspiration from the revolt of the Roman gladiators.

(122,1) The "winged hornet" might possibly refer to the Orpheus myth; see Offenbach's *Orphée aux Enfers* (*Orpheus in the Underworld*).

(123,5) The two philosophies Lacan just mentioned are those of Darwin and Hegel.

(124,2) The French term, *irresponsable*, is often used like the English "irresponsible" (qualifying, for example, someone who does not think before he or she acts), but the longer-standing meaning of the French term qualifies someone who does not have to answer for his or her acts (for example, the King in certain monarchies is answerable to no one); hence my translation here: "innocent." *En rupture du ban qui voue l'homme moderne* (who has thrown off the shackles that condemn modern man) is quite ambiguous, since being *en rupture de ban* means two rather different things—being someone who

has "illegally returned to a country from which he or she has been exiled" (that is, a certain kind of outlaw) and someone who has been "emancipated from the constraints of his or her condition or state"—and since it could be the *rupture* or the *ban* that "condemns modern man to the most formidable social hell."

NOTES TO "THE FUNCTION AND FIELD"

(239,5) *Soutenance* (claims) literally means a thesis defense; it could, perhaps, also be translated here by "justifications."

(241,9) "Them" (*les*) at the end of the sentence presumably refers to "the side" and "the disorder."

(242,5) A probable reference to Michael Balint's "Changing Therapeutic Aims and Techniques in Psycho-Analysis" (1949) in *Primary Love and Psychoanalytic Technique* (London: Hogarth Press, 1952).

(243,2) On the analyst's being, see "Direction of the Treatment."

(243,3) *Pédagogie maternelle* (child's education by its mother) may be a reference to Anna Freud's "maternal education."

(244,2) *Égarement* (confusion) here could also be translated as "madness."

(244,5) See "Obsessive Actions and Religious Practices," *SE* IX, 117.

(245,1) Lacan presumably means that it is futile "to explain a symptom" to a patient "by its meaning as long as the latter is not recognized" by the patient, and that "in the absence of such recognition, analytic action can only be experienced as aggressive" by the patient.

(245,2) *Annulation* (undoing what has been done) might ordinarily be translated as cancellation, rendering null and void, or invalidation. Here, however, it seems that Lacan is directly referring to the mechanism of "undoing" (something that has been done) found in obsessive neurosis. See, in particular, *SE* X, 235–36 and 243, and *SE* XX, 119–20; in the latter, Strachey indicates that he is translating Freud's *ungeschehenmachen*,

which literally means "making unhappened."

(245,4) See Lacan's "Intervention au Premier Congrès mondial de psychiatrie," republished in *Ornicar?* 30 (1984): 7–10 and in Jacques Lacan, *Autres écrits* (Paris: Seuil, 2001), 127–30.

(246,4) A *magistère* is a grand master of a military order, such as the Order of Malta, or a doctrinal, moral, or intellectual authority that is imposed in an absolute fashion.

(246,5) The "frontier fields" are those enumerated in *Écrits* 1966, 242–43.

(247,1) The reference here is to Rimbaud's "Les chercheuses de poux." See, for example, Arthur Rimbaud, *Oeuvres complètes* (Paris: Gallimard, 1972), 65–66; in English, see "The Ladies Who Look for Lice," in *Arthur Rimbaud: Complete Works*, trans. Paul Schmidt (New York and London: Harper and Row, 1967), 76–77. The "author" in question in the passage is the French analyst, Maurice Benassy.

(247,3) "Donne en ma bouche parole vraie et estable et fay de moy langue caulte." *L'Internele Consolacion*, chapter XLV: "Qu'on ne doit pas chascun croire et du legier trebuchement de paroles." See *L'Internele Consolacion: Texte du manuscrit d'Amiens* (Paris: Éditions d'art Édouard Pelletan, 1926).

(247,4) *Cause toujours* usually implies that the person who says it couldn't care less about or doesn't believe what the other person is saying, and might in fact prefer the latter shut up. *Causer* means to talk or chat, and *cause toujours* could be literally rendered as "keep talking," "talk anyway," or "go on," even though the context indicates that the speaker means the opposite of what he or she is saying (as when we say "go on" ironically or in exasperation). Agrammatically it might be construed to mean "Always a cause." *Causalisme* is the doctrine that science seeks causes and not merely regular antecedents.

(247,5) Note that *réponse* (response) can also be translated as "answer" or "reply."

(248,1) *Appel* means call, appeal, or summons, and is related to *appeler*, which I translate variously as "to call (for)," "to (make an) appeal," or "to summon." *Le vide* (emptiness) can also be translated as "the void," "vacuum" ("nature abhors a vacuum" is, in French, *la nature a horreur du vide*), or "vacuousness"; the latter would be a particularly appropriate alternative in this sentence and again two paragraphs further on. *Parole vide* is translated here as "empty speech."

(248,2) It is not entirely clear from the grammar who begins speaking here, but I have assumed that, since it was the analyst who responded to the patient's speech with silence (two paragraphs back), it is the analyst who now speaks up.

(248,3) It is not clear here if the subject manifests self-indulgence (*complaisance*) or indulgence toward the analyst.

(248,4) A *prud'homme* (bombastic, smug fellow) is a legal magistrate—an elected member of a council or tribunal—whose job it is to rule on employer/employee disputes. However, the term has also come to refer to "a mediocre, conceited bourgeois who likes making emphatic and empty declarations."

(249,2) Boileau, "L'Art Poétique," chant I: "Hâtez-vous lentement, et sans perdre courage,/ Vingt fois sur le métier remettez votre ouvrage" (Paris: Gallimard, 1966), 161. In Pope's translation: "Gently make haste, of labour not afraid/ A hundred times consider what you've said." Somewhat more literally translated: "Hurry slowly, and without lapsing into gloom/ Rework what you've made twenty times on the loom." Cf. *Boileau: Selected Criticism*, trans. E. Dilworth (New York: Bobbs-Merrill, 1965), 16.

(250,2) *La frustration de son travail* (being

frustrated in his labor) could also be translated as "his work being frustrated" or "his work being frustrating." *Désir de mort* could also be rendered as "desire for death."

(251,7) A tessera is a small tablet or die used by the ancient Romans as a ticket, tally, voucher, means of identification, or password. The tessera was used in the early mystery religions, where fitting together again the two halves of a broken piece of pottery was used as a means of recognition by the initiates, and in Greece the tessera was called the *sum bolon*. A central concept involved in the symbol is that of a link. The reference to Mallarmé is to a passage in his preface to René Ghil's *Traité du Verbe* (1866); see Stéphane Mallarmé, *Oeuvres complètes* (Paris: Gallimard, 1945), 368 and 857.

(252,2) A *partie du discours* is a part of speech; here Lacan writes *"partie" de ce discours* ("part" of this discourse). A *soupir* is a sigh, but is also a rest in music—hence "rest of a silence."

(252,4) Regarding *trébuchements si légers* (stumblings so slight), see the epigraph to this section.

(252,5) Molière uses *tarte à la crème* (vacuous buzzword) to qualify a meaningless and pretentious formulation by means of which one claims to have an answer for everything.

(253,5) Reference is made here to the Biblical phrase, "for they have ears in order not to hear," but the French *pour ne point entendre* means both in order not to hear and in order not to understand. I have assumed that Lacan is playing off the two meanings, but their order could be reversed to read as follows: "having ears *in order not to understand*, in other words, in order to detect what is to be heard." The next reference is to Reik's *Listening with the Third Ear*.

(254,3) It should be noted that *anamnèse* (anamnesis) means the history (or story) the *patient* provides of his or her life and illness; "anamnesis" in English does not necessarily imply that it is the patient who recounts the (hi)story, but I use it throughout this article as if it did.

(255,1) The Latin *flatus vocis* means a mere name, word, or sound without a corresponding objective reality, and was used by nominalists to qualify universals.

(255,2) *Verbaliser* (verbalize), in its legal sense, means to book (or report) someone, but it also means to talk too much or too long. *Pandore* (Pandora), in addition to referring to the woman of Greek mythology, is a somewhat old slang term for a policeman. Like "the Word," *le Verbe* is a translation for the Greek "Logos." Hereafter, *le verbe* is always translated as "the Word." The Greek *epos* means word, speech, tale, song, promise, saying, message, or, in the plural, epic poetry or lines of verse.

(256,fn1) See *SE* XVII, 44. The French translation by Marie Bonaparte and Rudolph M. Loewenstein renders it as *après-coup*.

(256,fn2) See *SE* XVII, 45, fn1.

(257,fn2) See *SE* III, 143–56.

(258,1) The order or instruction Lacan usually refers to as a *consigne* is to "say whatever comes to mind" or "say anything and everything that comes to mind" (*tout dire*).

(258,4) The unconscious here is "a third term" between speaker and addressee.

(259,1) *Sit venia verbo*, which might be rendered "if you will pardon the expression," is found in *GW* XII on page 116, where Freud uses it to qualify his syntagma *einen unbewussten Begriff*, rendered by Strachey as "unconscious concept" (*SE* XVII, 84), but which Lacan renders here by *pensée inconsciente* (unconscious thought). *Verbo* literally means word.

Court comme le furet (darts) is a reference to a game in which a group of people sit in a circle and quickly pass a small object— referred to as *le furet*, though a *furet* is literally a ferret—from hand to hand, while a player standing in the middle of the circle tries to guess which hand holds the *furet*.

(259,2) The Italian here is Galileo's famous "And yet it moves!" (referring to the earth's movement around the sun). The Latin could be rendered as a "thought experiment."

(260,2) Cf. *Écrits* 1966, 511, where Lacan associates metaphor with condensation and metonymy with displacement.

(261,3) *Elles* (they) after the dash presumably refers to two different riots (or "riot" as understood at two different moments in time); it could also possibly refer to "victory" and "defeat."

(262,1) *Annuler* (undoes) also means to void, invalidate, annul, and cancel out.

(262,5–263,1) *Aucun ne répugne plus à l'esprit de notre discipline* (No course is more repugnant to the spirit of our discipline) could also be translated as "No one finds the spirit of our discipline more repugnant."

(263,3) *Non liquet:* it is not clear. Cf. *SE* XVII, 57–60 and *SE* XXII, 54.

(263,4) Matthew, 23.4; I have provided this and other translations of the New Testament from *The New Oxford Annotated Bible* (Oxford: Oxford University Press, 1973).

(263,fn1) Pascal's wager is discussed in Pensée 233 of the Brunschvicg edition, 451 of the Pléiade edition. Lacan discussed Pascal's wager at length in Seminars XIII and XVI.

(264,2) "Il y a des gens qui n'auraient jamais été amoureux s'ils n'avaient jamais entendu parler de l'amour" (Maxim 136), in La Rochefoucauld, *Maximes* (Paris: Garnier Frères, 1967), 36. In English, see *The Maxims of La Rochefoucauld* (New York: Random House, 1959), 57.

(264,3) On the Wolf Man, see *SE* XVII, 106–19, especially 110–11.

(264,5) "Une vérité de La Palice" is a self-evident truth, a truism.

(265,1) "No need to close your eyes" may be a reference to one of Freud's dreams, recounted in *The Interpretation of Dreams*, that includes the line "You are requested to close the eyes" (*SE* IV, 317–18).

Rollet (script) is an old term for a small role (a "bit part") or a small scroll or sheet of paper on which words were written.

(265,2) See, in particular, Freud's discussion in *SE* XXII, 47–56; on page 56 of that text, Freud mentions an example from Dorothy Burlingham's "Child Analysis and the Mother," *PQ* IV (1935): 69.

(266,2) There are several extant translations of Jesus' reply to the question "Who are you?": "Even what I have told you from the beginning," "What I have told you all along," "What I have told you from the outset," "Why do I talk to you at all."

(266,6) *Des points faibles de sa chaire*, rendered in context here as "which parts of his body are sensitive," might also suggest "weaknesses of the flesh."

(267,1) See Plato, *The Sophist*, 246. *Dignus est intrare* is the phrase used by the chorus in the macaronic Latin of the burlesque ceremony with which Molière's *Le Malade imaginaire* ends. See, for example, *Molière: Le Malade imaginaire* (Oxford: Oxford University Press, 1965), 145, and *The Would-Be Invalid*, trans. Morris Bishop (New York: Appleton-Century-Crofts, 1950), 75. On being smelled by one's analysand, see Seminar IV, 79.

(267,4) See *SE* XIII, 177.

(268,1) *Version* (version) can also mean translation. *Élaboration* (telling) also means revision, as in "secondary revision."

(268,5) See *The Psychopathology of Everyday Life*, *SE* VI (1901).

(269,1) On numbers, see *SE* VI, chapter 12, 239–79. The next reference seems to be to *GW* IV, 276; in Strachey's rendition, "the existence of highly composite thought processes which are yet quite unknown to consciousness" (*SE* VI, 247).

(269,4) See, above all, *SE* VI, 243–48.

(270,3) See *SE* VIII (1905). Regarding the problems translating important terms found in that book from German into English, see the "Editor's Preface," pages 7–8. Similar problems present themselves here since, while *esprit* translates Freud's *Witz* quite nicely, neither corresponds very well to "wit" or "jokes" in English.

(270,5) See *SE* VIII, 55, 61–65, and 105–8. In Strachey's translation (*SE* VIII, 106): "Anyone who has allowed the truth to slip out in an unguarded moment is in fact glad to be free of pretence."

(271,1) In Strachey's translation (*SE* VIII, 105): "Thus jokes can also have a subjective determinant of this kind . . . It declares that only what I allow to be a joke *is* a joke."

(271,2) The third person is the person who

hears the joke (the first person being the one who tells the joke, the second the one the joke is about). See *SE* VIII, 100, 148–58, and elsewhere. An amboceptor is something that brings things together with its two receptors.

(271,5) The reference here is to I. A. Richards and C. K. Ogden's book, *The Meaning of Meaning* (New York: Harcourt, Brace, 1945 [1923]).

(272,1) The French here, *Argonautes pacifiques*, suggests the title of Malinowski's book, *Argonauts of the Western Pacific* (New York: E. P. Dutton, 1953).

(273,5) See C. V. Hudgkins, "Conditioning and the Voluntary Control of the Pupillary Light Reflex," *Journal of General Psychology* 8 (1933): 3. Hudgkins' work was based on preliminary work by H. Cason, "The Conditioned Eyelid Reaction," *Journal of Experimental Psychology* 5 (1933): 153.

(274,2) *Contre-épreuve* (control test) could also be translated by "countertest" or "test of the contrary hypothesis." Reducing "contract" to its first syllable, con, and pronouncing it *à la française*, evokes the meanings idiot, stupid, and asshole, among others.

(275,3) Jacques Prévert, "Inventaire," *Oeuvres Complètes*, I (Paris: Gallimard, 1966), 131.

(276,1) Anatole France, *L'île des pingouins* (Paris: Calmann-Lévy, 1908); *Penguin Island*, trans. A. W. Evans (New York: Dodd, Mead & Co., 1925).

(276,3) The reference here is to the Fort! Da! game discussed in *Beyond the Pleasure Principle* (1920), *SE* XVIII, 14-7.

(276,5) The Greek here can be rendered as "A possession for all time." Thucydides, *The Peloponnesian War*, I, xxiii. In Crawley's translation: "I have written my work, not as an essay which is to win the applause of the moment, but as a possession for all time"; see, for example, *The Complete Writings of Thucydides* (New York: Modern Library, 1951), 14–15. *Place partout* (ubiquity) is similar in structure and sound to the more usual *passe partout* (skeleton key or master key).

(276,6) This SiRonga proverb is the epigraph to Claude Lévi-Strauss, *Elementary*

Structures of Kinship (Boston: Beacon Press, 1969), found on page 1. I have followed the published translation, which—perhaps erroneously—translates *cuisse* (thigh, or leg when it comes to food) here as "hip."

(278,3) The phrase including *inadéquates* (fail to correspond to) could alternatively be rendered as "that are always more or less incommensurate with."

(278,5) Rabelais' Panurge says that he's always believed debts to be "a sort of connecting-link between Heaven and earth, a unique interrelationship of the human race— I mean without which all humans would soon perish—peradventure to be that great soul of the universe, which, according to the Academics, gives life to all things"; if we imagine a world without debts, "There, among the stars, there will be no regular course whatever. All will be in disarray. Jupiter, not thinking himself a debtor to Saturn, will dispossess him of his sphere . . . The moon will remain bloody and dark: on what ground will the sun impart his light to her? He was in no way bound to. The sun will not shine on their earth, the stars will exert no good influence there, for the earth was desisting from lending them nourishment by vapors and exhalations, by which (. . .) the stars were fed." See *The Complete Works of François Rabelais*, trans. Donald M. Frame (Berkeley: University of California Press, 1991), 267–73 (*Tiers livre*, chapters 3 and 4).

(279,1) On "substantific," cf. Rabelais' *substantifique moëlle* (the very substance, "the real stuff").

(279,2) See, for example, Lévi-Strauss' *Introduction à l'oeuvre de Marcel Mauss* (Paris: PUF, 1950), where he compares the notion of mana to the concept of the zero-phoneme introduced into phonology by Roman Jakobson. In English, see *Introduction to the Work of Marcel Mauss*, trans. Felicity Baker (London: Routledge & Kegan Paul, 1987), 63–64 and 72.

(279,3) "By bone and flesh" is an allusion to an opposition brought out by Claude Lévi-Strauss in *The Elementary Structures of Kinship* (Boston: Beacon, 1969), especially in chapter 24.

(279,6) *Se fait reconnaître* (gains recognition) literally means gets itself recognized; less literally, it means to achieve, garner, or gain recognition (and even to be recognized as a legitimate child, not a bastard).

(280,5) *Qui fait de la maladie l'introduction du vivant à l'existence du sujet* (which makes illness what institutes the existence of the subject in the living being) could also be translated as "which makes illness that which thrusts the living being into existence as a subject."

(281,2) *Chiffre* (cipher) also means number.

(281,4) A palimpsest is a piece of parchment or other writing material from which the writing has been erased to make way for a new text. See Freud's discussion of recollection and memory in "A Note on the Mystic Writing Pad" (1925), *SE* XIX, 227–32.

(281,7) *Désordre* (disorder) can also be rendered as "chaos" or "mess"; it is not a reference to the eponymous psychiatric notion.

(282,4) *L'aire des circonvolutions* (the region of the brain) literally means the area (the language) is wound or coiled around. But *circonvolutions cérébrales* refer to the folds of the brain, gyrus, or circumvolutio. Cf. Seminar I (303/274), where Lacan uses *circonvolutions* alone to refer to gray matter, translated there as "circumvolutions" (convolutions of the surface of the brain). Metaphorically, *circonvolutions* can mean circumlocutions.

(282,5) From T. S. Eliot, *The Hollow Men* (1925); see *T. S. Eliot: Collected Poems 1909–1962* (New York: Harcourt, Brace & World, 1970), 77–82.

(283,1) On "the philosophy of the skull," see Hegel's *Phenomenology of Spirit*, trans. A. V. Miller (Oxford: Oxford University Press, 1977), sections 327–40. Pascal: "Les hommes sont si nécessairement fous, que ce serait être fou, par un autre tour de folie, de n'être pas fou," *Pensées* (Brunschvicg ed. 414, Pléiade ed. 184).

(283,3) On the Church and the army, see in particular chapter V of *Group Psychology and the Analysis of the Ego* (1921), *SE* XVIII.

(283,4) "Direction," that is, "guidance," as in the religious sense of *direction de consciences*.

(284,8) Cf., for example, Claude Lévi-Strauss, *Structural Anthropology*, trans. C. Jacobson and B. G. Schoepf (New York: Basic Books, 1963), 31 ff.

(285,fn1) An English translation of a later version of the article can be found in Claude Lévi-Strauss, *Structural Anthropology*, 55–66.

(286,1) *Front d'airain* (brazen face) seems to be an allusion to Lassalle's *loi d'airain*, the "iron law of wages."

(286,2) This is discussed by Lacan at length in Seminar II.

(286,5) ". . . that [August] Voice / Who knows itself when it sings / To be no longer the voice of anyone / As much as [the voice] of the waves and woods." Paul Valéry, "La Pythie," in *Poésies* (Paris: Gallimard, 1942).

(287,3) See Lacan's "Logical Time and the Assertion of Anticipated Certainty" in *Écrits* 1966; trans. B. Fink and M. Silver, *Newsletter of the Freudian Field* 2 (1988).

(288,1) *Relève* (continuation) can also be translated as "sublation."

(288,2) See Lacan's "The Neurotic's Individual Myth," trans. M. N. Evans, *PQ* XLVIII, 3 (1979): 405–25, originally published in French in 1953.

(288,3) See "The Question of Lay Analysis" (1926), *SE* XX, 246; Strachey renders the last two items in the list as "the science of literature."

(288,4) The "triangle" may be that composed of history, mathematics (or ethnology), and linguistics.

(289,5) See Lacan's later comments on this poem in Seminar XIX, January 6, 1972.

(289,6) "For I have seen with my own eyes the Cumean Sibyll hanging inside a jar, and whenever boys would ask her: 'What do you wish, O Sibyll,' she would reply: 'I wish to die.'" This is the epigraph to T. S. Eliot's *The Waste Land* (1922); see *T. S. Eliot: Collected Poems 1909–1962* (New York: Harcourt, Brace & World, 1970), 51–76.

(290,6) See *SE* X, 166–67. In Strachey's translation, the passage reads as follows: "his face took on a very strange, composite expression I could only interpret as one of *horror at pleasure of his own of which he himself was unaware*."

(291,4) For Freud's first definition of resistance, see "The Psychotherapy of Hysteria" (1895), *SE* II, 290 ff.

(293,2) *Scopie* (vision) comes from the Greek, *skopia*, the act of observing. Socrates and his desire were discussed at length by Lacan in Seminar VIII; Kierkegaard on repetition was taken up in Seminar XI.

(293,3) *Fasse justice de leur puissance* (turns their power into justice) could alternatively mean refutes or challenges their power. *Maîtres-mots* (magic words) refers to words imbued with special powers or with a specific energy or efficacy. On Humpty Dumpty, see Lewis Carroll, *Through the Looking Glass* in *The Annotated Alice*, ed. Martin Gardner (New York: Clarkson N. Potter, 1960), 269.

(295,3) See "Analysis Terminable and Interminable" (1937), *SE* XXIII, 219.

(295,5) See *Shakespear's dramatische Werke*, trans. Ludwig Tieck and August Wilhelm von Schlegel (Berlin: Reimer, 1843).

(296,2) The French rendered here as "*summoning*" reads "intimation" in italics, which could be either the English term or the French (meaning summoning) with emphasis added.

(296,fn1) Kris' article is reprinted in *Selected Papers of Ernst Kris* (New Haven: Yale University Press, 1975), 237–51; see especially 250–51.

(297,4) See, for example, Karl von Frisch, *Bees: Their Vision, Chemical Senses, and Language* (Ithaca: Cornell University Press, 1950 and 1971), chapter 3, above all, pages 89 ff. See also Frisch, *The Dancing Bees: An Account of the Life and Senses of the Honey Bee* (London: Methuen & Co., 1954), especially chapter 11.

(298,4) Pascal: "Tu ne me chercherais pas, si tu ne m'avais trouvé," the words of Christ in "Le mystère de Jesus," *Pensées* (Brunschvicg ed. 553, Pléiade ed. 736).

(298,5) *Vous vous rencontrez avec lui* (you

encounter each other) can also mean you share the same views or you meet.

(298,fn1) See Emile Littré, *Dictionnaire de la langue française*, 7 volumes (Paris: Hachette, 1885), under *parabole*: "action de mettre à côté."

(300,fn1) Lacan discusses this paper again in "Direction of the Treatment."

(301,2) *Corps subtil* (subtle body) is a reference to the matter ("aether" or "ether") formerly believed to surround the earth.

(301,3) See *SE* XVII, 89–97, 107–8, 112–13 (and note); the *Wespe* incident is reported on page 94.

(301,4) See *SE* X, 225, 260, 280–81, 294–95.

(302,1) *Mettre à l'index* (exclude) can also be translated as "to boycott," "to condemn," "to exclude," and "to put on a list of prohibited books." I translate it again as "exclude" a few pages further on.

(302,5) See *SE* X, 198.

(303,3) This is a possible reference to *SE* X, 199–200. Strachey translates Freud as follows here: "He dreamt that *he saw my daughter in front of him; she had two patches of dung instead of eyes.*" Nevertheless, the exact reference is not clear, even in the "Original Record of the Case" (see SE X, 293) and the more complete French edition: *L'homme aux rats: Journal d'une analyse* (Paris: PUF, 1974).

(303,4) In Strachey's rendition (*SE* X, 249): "Like so many other young men of value and promise, he perished in the Great War."

(304,1) *Mortelles* (deadly) can be translated as "mortal," "lethal," "fatal," or "deadly boring." *Se voir* could also be translated as "see himself."

(304,2) The Latin here could be rendered as "To each his own jouissance" or "Everyone is led by his own pleasure (or passion)."

(304,3) Cf. Seminar IV, 27 and *Écrits* 1966, 630.

(305,3) See R. Sterba, "The Fate of the Ego in Analytic Therapy," *IJP* XV, 2–3 (1934): 117–26.

(305,5) "Fragment of an Analysis of a Case of Hysteria" (1905), *SE* VII, 7–122. See Lacan's extensive discussion of the Dora case in "Presentation on Transference" (1951), *Écrits* 1966, 215–26.

(306,1) See *SE* VII, 120–22.

(306,2) *SE* VII, 120, fn1. The account itself was published four years after the breaking off of the analysis in 1901.

(306,3) See Pierre Janet, *The Mental State of Hystericals*, trans. C. R. Corson (Washington, D.C.: University Publications of America, 1977), originally published in French in 1892 and in English in 1901.

(307,6) *Mettre bille-en-tête* (jumping to conclusions) means to run headlong or headfirst. "Shuttling back and forth": presumably from one side of the wall to the other, from the unsaid to the said. I have been unable to determine the meaning of *donne la marque* (starts the ball rolling); it may have to do with starting a race, "pointing the finger," or setting the rhythm. *Aller au trou* (going to prison) also has other slang meanings and it is not entirely clear to me what Lacan is getting at here.

(308,3) "Indication of reality" (*indice de réalité*) here seems to refer to Freud's *Realitätszeichen*; see "Project for a Scientific Psychology" (1895), *SE* I, 325–28 and elsewhere.

(308,4) This may be a reference to "Observations on Transference Love" (1915), *SE* XII, 167–68.

(308,fn1) See Lacan's discussion of bundling in Seminar IV, 87 ff.

(309,1) *Contre-effet* (counter) could alternatively be translated as "side effect."

(310,2) "Lay" in the sense of a simple narrative poem, ballad, or song.

(310,8) *Échéance* (due date) can be translated as "deadline," "maturity date," "payment date," "expiration date," "term," and so on.

(311,2) In the case of the Wolf Man (*SE* XVII, 11); the Latin here could be translated as "out of modesty."

(311,fn1) The usual French translation of "*Die endliche und die unendliche Analyse*" (1937) is "*Analyse terminée et analyse inter-*

minable"; the usual English is "Analysis Terminable and Interminable" (*SE* XXIII, 216–53). Lacan renders it here by *"analyse finie ou indéfinie."*

(311,fn2) Here is the Loeb Classical Library translation, prepared by John C. Rolfe (New York: Putnam, 1927): "When inquiry is made about the choice of a prosecutor, and judgement is rendered on the question to which of two or more persons the prosecution of a defendant, or a share in the prosecution, is to be entrusted, this process and examination by jurors is called *divinatio* . . . But some others think that the *divinatio* is so called because, while prosecutor and defendant are two things that are, as it were, related and connected, so that neither can exist without the other, yet in this form of trial, while there is already a defendant, there is as yet no prosecutor, and therefore the factor which is still lacking and unknown— namely, what man is to be the prosecutor— must be supplied by divination" (131–33).

('312,2) *Un prytanée* (analytic academy) is a kind of educational establishment in France that is free for the sons of military personnel.

(312,3) See Ruth Mack Brunswick, "A Supplement to Freud's 'History of an Infantile Neurosis,'" *IJP* IX (1928), republished in *The Wolf-Man* (New York: Basic Books, 1971), 263–307. For further details and references, see Ernest Jones, *The Life and Work of Sigmund Freud* (New York: Basic Books, 1953), vol. 2, 306–12.

(312,4) Lacan discussed the Wolf Man case at length in his early 1952 seminar at which no stenographer was present.

(313,1) On "the fall of heavy bodies," see Charles François, "La théorie de la chute des graves. Évolution historique du problème," *Ciel et Terre* 34 (1913): 135–37, 167–69, 261–73. See *Lichtenberg: Aphorisms & Letters*, trans. Franz Mautner and Henry Hatfield (London: Jonathan Cape, 1969), 49.

(313,4) See Leenhardt, "La parole qui dure" (Tradition, mythe, statut), *Do Kamo* (1947): 173 ff.

(314,2) The French here, *"la coupure du timing,"* literally means "cutting [the session]

based on timing." Given the context, it seems clear that Lacan is referring to the "standard" practice of timing sessions, that is, ending them based on a specified clock time. Hence: "after a fixed number of minutes has elapsed."

(315,8) Note that *défendre* means both to defend and to prohibit.

(316,7) Wilhelm Reich, *Character Analysis* (New York: Simon & Schuster, 1972), trans. V. R. Carfagno. The schema Lacan refers to here seems to be that found on page 392, "the most general form of this movement of sexual superimposition."

(317,3) See *Beyond the Pleasure Principle*, *SE* XVIII.

(317,5) See Ernest Jones, *The Life and Work of Sigmund Freud* (New York: Basic Books, 1953), vol. 1, 27–29.

(318,1) See *SE* XXIII, 244–47.

(318,2) *SE* XVIII, 57–58.

(318,3) Martin Heidegger, *Being and Time*, trans. John Macquarrie and Edward Robinson (Oxford: Basil Blackwell, 1962): 294. I have followed the translation Lacan gives in the text; the English translation cited here reads: "that possibility which is one's ownmost, which is non-relational, and which is not to be outstripped."

(318,5) *Le mort* (the dead person) can also be translated as "the dummy" in the context of bridge (the card game). Cf. "Direction of the Treatment," *Écrits* 1966, 551.

(319,1) See *SE* XVIII, 14–17.

(319,2) *Son action* (his action) could also possibly be translated as "language's action" or "his desire's action." *Elle* (His action) at the beginning of the next sentence would then be "Language's action" or "Desire's action."

(319,4) The French at the end of the paragraph, *intimation bannissante*, could also be rendered as "formal notification of banishment." "His" in this paragraph seems always to refer back to the child, except the last instance, which seems to refer to the partner.

(319,6) *Truchement* (means) has a number of older meanings, including interpreter, spokesperson, and representative, and newer meanings, including mediation, intermediary, and medium (that which expresses or conveys ideas or feelings, for example, music). Here Lacan seems to be suggesting that death serves as a *means* to an end for the subject (the paragraphs that follow illustrate this).

Vient à la vie de son histoire (is born into the life of his history) could alternatively be rendered as "comes to life through his history."

(320,4) *Jeu de furet* (darting game): see earlier note on *le furet* (corresponding to *Écrits* 1966, 259). It could perhaps be translated here as "guessing game," "shifting game," or "musical chairs."

(320,6) Leenhardt, for example, uses this spatial representation in his *Do Kamo* to represent the native's existence as a locus of relationships with others.

(321,3) *Souci* (care-ridden) is the usual French translation of Heidegger's *Sorge*, and *savoir* (knowledge) of Hegel's *Wissen*.

(321,4) There is a possible reference to *Numbers*, 21.9, at the end of this paragraph.

(321,fn1) See, above all, Seminar IX, "Identification" (1961–62).

(322,8) *"Soumission, don, grâce."* The three Sanskrit nouns (*damah, danam, daya'*) are also rendered "self-control," "giving," "compassion" (*Rhadhakrishnan*); the three verbs, "control," "give," "sympathize" (T. S. Eliot, *The Waste Land*, Part V; "What the thunder said"). For a more recent translation, see *The Brihadaranyaka Upanishad*, trans. Swami Sivanada (India: Divine Life Society, 1985), 487–88.

(322,fn2) In his *Pour un Malherbe*. "Resound" is *résonner* in French; *réson* is a homonym of *raison* (reason). See Lacan's later comments on Ponge's *réson* in Seminar XIX, January 6, 1972.

NOTES TO "THE FREUDIAN THING"

(401,6) *Il se consommait* (it occurred) can also be rendered as "it came to an end" or "it was at its height."

(402,2) It should be kept in mind throughout this article that *sens* (meaning) also means both direction and sense.

(406,2) Lacan makes a pun here on the French pronunciation of *Bondy* and *bandits*. The Bondy Forest, to the north of Paris, was long famous as a haunt of bandits.

(406,3) *Gros sabots* (big clodhoppers) figuratively means all-too-obvious allusions or intentions visible from a mile away.

(407,1) The *Pays du Tendre* was an allegorical country in which love was the sole preoccupation. It was the creation of Mademoiselle de Scudéry and other novelists of the seventeenth century, described in *La carte du tendre* (map of Tendre).

(407,2) *Cornes-au-cul* (all that other crap) is an expression found in Alfred Jarry's "La Chanson du Décervelage," in *Ubu Roi ou les Polonais* (Paris: Eugène Fasquelle, 1922), 183–86. It is an exclamation (like "wow," "damn," or "shiver me timbers"), which literally means horns on (or in) the ass (it is

found, in the singular, with this meaning in Rabelais' *Gargantua*, chapter 16); here it seems to suggest something like "etcetera" or "and all the rest." *Cornes* (horns) by itself commonly refers to cuckoldry.

(407,3) *Mic-mac* (mess) can, alternatively, be rendered as "intrigue." *New-look* ("new-look") was a term introduced by Christian Dior in 1947 to describe a new style in clothing; it was later applied to politics as well.

(408,3) The unusual *s'il faut dire* (if it must be said) may be a play on the homophony between *faut* (must) and *faux* (false). The *écrin* (jewelry box) at the end of the paragraph may be a reference to the "jewel-case" in Dora's dream, which Freud associates with the female genitals (*SE* VII, 64 and 69–70). In old French, *écrin* is occasionally used to refer to a box for precious items of any kind, including the bones of a king, which would perhaps allow it to be rendered as "casket."

(408,4) *La chose parle d'elle-même* (The Thing Speaks of Itself) is an idiomatic expression meaning it is self-explanatory; it could also be translated as "The Thing Speaks All by Itself."

(409,1) *Moi la vérité, je parle* (I, truth, speak) could also be rendered as "I, truth, am speaking." Later on, *je parle* (I speak) could be translated as "I am speaking."

(409,2) *Pigeon-vole* (certain games) refers to a children's game in which one player pronounces the name of an object followed by "vole" (flies), and the other players must raise their hands *only if* the object can, in fact, fly.

(410,1) *Caute* (cunning) is an old French term with a number of different meanings, running the gamut from crafty, subtle, wily, cunning, and sly to circumspect, cautious, prudent, and wary. Cf. Pascal's "Cleopatra's nose: had it been shorter, the whole face of the earth would have changed," *Pensées* (Brunschvicg ed. 162).

(410,2) *SE* IV, 277–78.

(411,1) *Égarement* (deviation) has a number of meanings, including going astray, deviating from the straight and narrow (of a religious or other doctrine), mental distraction, and error (of one's ways).

(411,2) *Flair* (smell) could also be translated as "sixth sense" or "intuition." Cf. Carl Jung, "On the Psychology of the Trickster-Figure" (1954), *Collected Works*, vol. 9. *Je me défends* (I am being defensive) could also be rendered as "I am defending myself" or "I defend myself."

(411,3) *Parade* (parade) is a fencing term that can be translated as "parry" or "parade"; it also means (ceremonial) display.

(411,4) *Les bijoux indiscrets* (*The Indiscrete Jewels*) is a book by Denis Diderot, written in 1748.

(412,1) A golem, in Jewish folklore, is a man-made figure constructed in the form of a human being and endowed with life, an automaton.

(412,3) *Boursouflure* (budding) could also be rendered as "swelling."

(412,4) See Giordano Bruno, *De gli eroici furori* in *Opere italiane* (Bari: Gius, Laterza & Figli, 1923-27), translated by Paul Eugene Memmo, Jr., as *The Heroic Frenzies* (Chapel Hill: University of North Carolina Press, 1966). In the myth, Actaeon, coming upon Diana during her bath, is turned by her into a stag and then chased and killed by his own dogs.

(413,1) *Aigle* (eagle) is also slang for "genius." Lacan seems to be making fun here of those who would situate the role of language at this level (where the fact that an airplane in the sky looks like the analyst—or like the eagle that represents the analyst's "genius"—is considered to be an articulate response from the gods).

(413,2) *Fonds ni forme* (content nor form): *le fond et la forme* is usually translated as "content and form" or "substance and form"; note, however, that Lacan uses *fonds* here, which has certain meanings that differ from those of *fond* (such as fund, collection, land, business, assets, reserve, ground, and even constitution, as in *fonds mental*). Note, too, that *fond* and *fonds* overlap in meaning so much in certain cases that many authors use them interchangeably; Littré suggests they should be considered the same word.

(414,1) On Stalin's pronouncement, see *Écrits* 1966, 496, fn1.

(414,3) *Ordre de la chose* (The Thing's Order) could also be understood as "How the Thing is Ordered (or Organized)."

(414,6) *Unité* (unity) can also be rendered as "unit."

(414,7) *S'assure ordinairement de* (usually secures) can also be rendered as "usually ensures" or "is usually ensured by."

(415,2) *Désordre* (disorder) can also be rendered as "chaos" or "mess"; it is not a reference to the eponymous psychiatric notion.

(415,8) Regarding the "total social fact," see Marcel Mauss, *The Gift*.

(416,1) *Conscience commune* (collective consciousness) seems to be a sociological term introduced by Durkheim.

(416,4) "They will never know anything about it, even in the way implied by repression": This seems to be a paraphrase of Freud's comment about the Wolf Man's *Verwerfung* of castration (*SE* XVII, 84).

(416,6) The German is from *GW* XV, 86; see *SE* XXII, 80.

(416,fn1) See Lacan's "Science and Truth"

in *Écrits* 1966; trans. B. Fink, *Newsletter of the Freudian Field* 3 (1989).

(417,1) Actually, there seems to be no such published English translation. The early translation of the *New Introductory Lectures on Psycho-Analysis* by W. J. H. Sprott (New York: Norton, 1933) provides "Where id was, there shall ego be"; the *Standard Edition* provides "Where id was, there ego shall be" (1964). The fact remains that both translations take *Es* and *Ich* here to be the Freudian agencies, id and ego.

(417,fn1) In the *Standard Edition*, the following translation is provided: "It is a work of culture—not unlike the draining of the Zuider Zee" (*SE* XXII, 80).

(418,fn1) Marie Bonaparte was the author of that translation.

(419,3) See Lacan's "Variations on the Standard Treatment" (1955) in *Écrits* 1966, written as a counterweight to an article that appeared in the same *Encyclopédie médico-chirurgicale, Psychiatrie* describing the "standard treatment."

(420,1) *Retourner* (re-turn) means to turn around, turn over, turn upside down, invert, reverse, return, and send back.

(420,2) The Latin here refers to the correspondence theory of truth whereby truth lies in the correspondence (*adæquatio*) between a thing (*rei*) and our conception of it (*intellectus*). French uses the term *adéquation* where English uses "correspondence." In the next sentence, Points reads *qui nous parle, voire qui parle à nous* (instead of *en nous*), which might be translated as "that speaks us, nay, that speaks to us."

(420,5) *Chosisme* (literally "thingism") here is likely a reference to the *nouveau roman* (or antinovel), characterized by the novelist's concern with things in themselves, not things as human symbols or metaphors. It simultaneously refers to a philosophical doctrine in which concepts are taken as concrete things. Note that Lacan refers to Anna Freud's language in *The Ego and the Mechanisms of Defense* as "*chosiste*" (Seminar I, 76/63).

(421,2) Heinz Hartmann's "The Development of the Ego Concept in Freud's Work," *IJP* XXVII, 6 (1956): 425–38, includes much of this terminology about the ego being autonomous. Later in the paragraph we find another reference to Heinz Hartmann who, in his "Technical Implications of Ego Psychology," writes that "analysis is gradually and unavoidably, though hesitantly, becoming a general psychology . . ." (*PQ* XX, 3 [1949]: 35), and who, in "The Development of the Ego Concept in Freud's Work," writes that "the trend toward a general psychology has been inherent in psychoanalysis from its inception" (*IJP* XXVII, 6 [1956]: 434). In Seminar I (33/25) Lacan seems to suggest that Kris also refers to it in that way. Cf. R. M. Loewenstein's "Conflict and Autonomous Ego Development During the Phallic Phase" in *The Psychoanalytic Study of the Child*, V (New York: International Universities Press, 1950).

(421,4) Lacan here and in the next sentence shortens the usual *opération* (operation) to *o-pé*, leaving out *ration*; pronounced in a certain way, *c't o-pé* sounds like *stopper* (to stop).

(421,6) Regarding the "pulpit of quarrelsome memory," see Nicolas Boileau's poem, "Le lutrin." A *table à la Tronchin* is a writing table whose top can be raised and tilted as much as one likes. Introduced in the fifteenth century, it was popularized in the eighteenth century by Théodore Tronchin, a Swiss doctor (1709–1781).

(422,2) Speculation, faulty banking policy, and political intrigue (in which John Law played an important role) centering around the rue Quincampoix in Paris led to the bankruptcy of the French financial system in 1720. A well-known hunchback in that street let people sign agreements on his hump as if it were a desk or lectern, a service for which he is reported to have received 150,000 pounds (the "hefty rent"). *Cote* (standing) also happens to mean furniture tax!

(422,3) *Intersigne* (index) is a mark or index, or the mysterious relationship that appears (by telepathy or second sight) between two facts.

(423,2) A *motion nègre-blanc* (ambiguous

mollifying motion) is a (parliamentary) motion written in ambiguous terms designed to appease a number of different parties.

(423,3) Cf. Pascal's reference to man as "un roseau pensant" ("a thinking reed"), *Pensées* (Brunschvicg ed. 347–48).

(424,2) Or "some supposedly internal progress . . . as sporadic as the purely external arrangements that condition it." This is a possible reference to the mirrors placed on opposite walls in the entrance halls of thousands of Parisian apartment buildings.

(424,5) *Elles* (they) seems to refer back to "technical analyses" here.

(425,3) *À sa mesure* (measured against) suggests that reality is considered to correspond to the ego, fit the ego, or be proportionate to the ego (as when we say "on a human scale"). But it also evokes the saying that "man is the measure of all things," evoked again a few lines down.

(426,2) *Moi* also means ego. Giving a "t" to *doit* makes it a third person singular.

(426,5) The pleonasm seems to be the addition of the "personally" to the "you" in "interest you personally" (in the French, "you" and "personally" are separated by the clause between the dashes in the English).

(428,2) In France, a notary has considerable legal training and exercises many of the functions of a lawyer. *Attelage* (team) evokes a team of oxen or horses, or the harness or yoke that keeps them working as a team. It can also mean coupling or attachment. In military parlance, *Rassemblement!* (Regroup!) would normally be translated as "Fall in!" But it literally means assembling, gathering, union, rallying, and rounding up.

(429,1) "So are you": or "Takes one to know one" (said when someone accuses you of being a pig, for example); cf. *SE* XII, 52.

(429,2) Although I have been unable to find the adjective *recollectif* (recollective) anywhere, it seems to be related to *rassemblement* (regroup). The series of three here (intuitive illumination, recollective command, and the retorting aggressiveness of verbal echo) thus corresponds to the three sit-

uations Lacan described above: the "Aha!" moment, "Regroup!" and the "So are you" of the transitivist quarrel. On "retorting aggressiveness," cf. *Écrits* 1966, 199 where we find the expression "aggressive retortions."

(429,4) See John Rickman, *Selected Contributions to Psycho-Analysis* (New York: Basic Books, 1957 and Glasgow: The University Press, 1957), above all chapters 19, 21, and 22. *Insoutenable* (untenable) also means unbearable.

(429,6 430,1 and 3) Note that, while in the text I translate *l'Autre* as the Other with a capital O, and *l'autre* as the other with a lowercase o, in Lacan's schemas and mathemes the former is designated by A and the latter by *a* and *a'*. *Réunion* (union) is a term used in set theory and is an early reference to the different "vels" Lacan discusses in Seminar XI.

(430,2) *Dégager*, in *qui dégage formellement la mort* (which formally brings out death), has many different meanings, including to redeem, release, radiate, separate out, isolate, set off, highlight, define, elucidate, relieve, and liberate.

(430,7) Points erroneously reads *contraires* (contraries) instead of *contraintes* (constraints) in the first sentence.

(431,1) *Ajustées à* (worked out at) could alternatively be translated as "adjusted to" or "adapted to."

(432,1) See Lacan's discussion of the plus/minus (+/-) series in Seminar II and his development of the 1,2,3, and α,β,γ,δ series in the "Suite" to the "Seminar on 'The Purloined Letter'" in *Écrits* 1966.

The last sentence of the paragraph is Lacan's way of saying that the nth term in the series is determined by the several terms that precede it in the series; the nth term can be *any* of the possible letters (α,β,γ,δ) only if the n-1st, n-2nd, and n-3rd terms are not fixed in advance (i.e., the "compensations demanded by" the n-4th term are satisfied by the nth term).

(432,2) *Motifs* (motives) can also be rendered as "themes" or "leitmotivs."

(432,3) Points erroneously reads *conversation*

(conversation) here instead of *conservation* (preservation).

(433,6) *L'invité de pierre* (the stone guest) evokes the statue of the dead commander in the Don Juan story; see, for example, Molière's version entitled *Dom Juan ou le festin de pierre*, known in English as *Don Juan or the Stone Guest*.

(433,7) The use of *raisin* (grape) at the beginning of the sentence and *grappe de la colère* (literally, bunch or bundle of anger) evoke the French title of John Steinbeck's *The Grapes of Wrath* (borrowed from "The Battle Hymn of the Republic"): *Les raisins de la colère*.

(434,5) *Quiproquo* (case of mistaken identity) also means misunderstanding.

(436,3) On Freud's three challenges or "'impossible' professions," see, for example, *SE* XXIII, 248. On certain points made in "The Freudian Thing," see Lacan's later comments in Seminar XIX, March 8, 1972.

NOTES TO "THE INSTANCE OF THE LETTER"

(493,1) *Instance* (Instance) can take on virtually all of the meanings of "instance" in English (urgent or earnest solicitation, entreaty or instigation, insistence, lawsuit or prosecution, argument, example or case, and exception); in addition, it can mean authority as well as agency (it is used, for example, to refer to Freud's agencies, *Instanzen*, the ego, id, and superego).

(493,3) *Commandait* (commissioned) can also mean commanded, obliged, imposed, forced, necessitated, ordered, exacted, required, called for, and enjoined. The first two occurrences of "writing" in this text translate *l'écrit* and the third occurrence *un écrit*, not *écriture*; the first two could also be translated as "the written" and the third as "a written text."

(493,4) It should be kept in mind throughout this essay that *sens* (rendered in this instance as "sense") can also be translated as "meaning" or "direction." *Facteur* (factor) can also mean postman, mailman, or purveyor.

(493,5) The exceptional class may be an allusion to Seminar III, chapter 19, "Freud in the Century."

(493,fn1) See *The Notebooks of Leonardo Da Vinci* II, trans. Edward MacCurdy (New York: Reynal & Hitchcock, 1938), 499. Cf. Seminar IV, 337.

(494,7) *Le véridique* (veracity) could, perhaps, also be rendered as "the veridical." See, in particular, the December 1956 issue of the *IJP*, mentioned in Seminar IV, 188.

(494,fn2) See "The Question of Lay Analysis," *SE* XX, 245–48.

(495,fn1) In English, see "Two Aspects of Language and Two Types of Aphasic Disturbances," in *Selected Writings*, vol. II (The Hague: Mouton, 1971), 239–59.

(496,1) *Le drame historique* (the drama of history) could, alternatively, be rendered as "historical drama."

(497,2) As J.-A. Miller points out (in his 1993–94 seminar entitled "Donc," May 11, 1994), the French here should read *étages* ("floors" or "levels," as it is rendered here), as in the originally published version of the paper, instead of *étapes* (stages).

(497,3) Saussure's text was originally published in French in 1915; a critical edition was prepared by Tullio de Mauro (Paris: Payot, 1972). In English, see Saussure, *Course in General Linguistics*, trans. Wade Baskin (New York: McGraw-Hill, 1959) and, more recently, trans. Roy Harris (Chicago: Open Court, 1983). Page references here to Saussure are first to the critical French edition and then to Baskin's translation.

(498,2) *Nom* (noun) could alternatively be translated as "name." *Rayon* (ray) also means beam, radius, spoke, shelf, and department.

(498,fn1) June 23, 1954, corresponds to chapter 20 of Seminar I.

(498,fn2) The first book mentioned here is Ivor Armstrong Richards and C. K. Ogden, *The Meaning of Meaning* (New York: Harcourt, Brace, [1923] 1945). The full reference for the second book is *Mencius on the Mind: Experiments in Multiple Definition* (London: Kegan Paul, Trench, Trubner & Co., 1932).

(500,1) *Isoloir* (private stall) literally means polling or voting booth; in the nineteenth century, it was used to refer to a place where one is off by oneself, isolated, apart from others.

(500,2) The last few words of the paragraph could, alternatively, be rendered as "in two lines down the main aisle."

(500,5) *Il faudrait n'avoir pas les yeux en face des trous* (one would have to be half blind) literally means one must not have one's eyes in front of holes or lined up with the holes (sockets); figuratively it means one must be half-asleep, half-blind, or not seeing clearly. Lacan adds here that "it is a fitting image."

(501,2) See Swift's *Gulliver's Travels* (part I, chapter 4), in which the prolonged war between the two kingdoms of Lilliput and Blefuscu originated in a dispute over whether eggs should be broken at the large or small end.

(501,3) The S is not, unfortunately, visible in the English here, the plural of "gentleman" being indicated otherwise than by the addition of an "s." *Coudes* (curves) also means elbow joints and bends. Cf. *Écrits* 1966, 518.

(501,4) The "access" in question here is presumably from one side to the other, that is, from the outside of the train to the inside.

(501,7) Didot and Garamond are names of different typefaces.

(502,1) *Anneaux* (links) is often translated as "rings," but in the context of a *chain*, it means links. The term translated here by "necklace," *collier*, can also be translated as "chain." Saussure introduces the term "chain" in his *Course in General Linguistics*, 103/70.

(502,2) *Locution verbale* (verbal locution) could, alternatively, be translated as "verb phrase."

(502,6) The allusions are to the "I am very dark, but comely" of the Song of Solomon 1.5, and to the nineteenth-century cliché of the "poor, but honest" woman.

(502,fn1) The reference here is to Seminar III, *The Psychoses*. See also *Écrits* 1966, 539–40.

(503,1) See Saussure, *Course in General Linguistics*, 156/112.

(503,2) A "button tie" is a stitch used by an upholsterer to secure a button to fabric and stuffing, for example, to prevent the stuffing from moving; it is, I think, the closest English term to the upholsterer's term Lacan uses: *point de capiton*. Russell Grigg, in his translation of Lacan's Seminar, Book III, *The Psychoses* (New York: Norton, 1993), renders *capitonnage* as "quilting" and *point de capiton* as "quilting point"; see 293–305.

(503,3) As in "Paul is hit by Peter." Cf. Seminar III, 256. *Temps* (time) also means tense, in the grammatical sense.

(503,fn1) See Seminar III, 297–304 and 326; see also *The New Statesman and Nation*, May 19, 1956.

(504,1) In French, *arbre de la croix*, "tree of the cross," refers to the cross to which Jesus was attached (see the second sentence in the paragraph). I have forged a verb, "to historiate," from the adjective "historiated," meaning decorated with figures of people, animals, or flowers, as illuminated or ornamental initial letters, for example.

On Heraclitus' Ἕν Πάντα, see Lacan's translation of Heidegger's "Logos" in *La Psychanalyse* 1 (1956): 59–79.

The verses, in French, are "Non! dit l'Arbre, il dit: Non! dans l'étincellement / De sa tête superbe / Que la tempête traite universellement / Comme elle fait une herbe." This is the last stanza of Paul Valéry's, "Au Platane" in *Charmes* (Paris: Gallimard, 1952), 43; note that according to the edition cited here, the first line reads: "—Non! dit l'Arbre. Il dit: Non! par l'étincellement."

(504,5) I have assumed that the original version, reading *sache* (know) should be preferred here to *cache* (hide) found in *Écrits* 1966.

(504,7) *Étage* (level) also means floor; cf. *Écrits* 1966, 497.

(505,1) A probable reference to Stendhal's "La parole a été donnée à l'homme pour cacher sa pensée" ("Speech was given to man to disguise his thought").

(505,2) *Grimper à l'arbre* literally means to climb the tree, but figuratively means to be fooled, to be a dupe, to be taken in. *Arborer*, meaning to raise (a flag or banner, for example), has come to mean to display or wear ostentatiously.

(505,4) According to Bloch and Von Wartburg, *trouver* probably comes from *tropare*, a derivative of *tropus*, meaning figure of rhetoric.

(505,5) *Bateau* can also take on the figurative sense of an old saw or hackneyed theme.

(506,3) The verse here, "Sa gerbe n'était point avare ni haineuse," is from the poem "Booz endormi." In French and English, see *The Penguin Book of French Verse*, 3 (Baltimore: Penguin Books, 1957), 69–73; the prose translation given there is: "His sheaves of corn were not mean or hateful." Note that *Écrits* 1966 erroneously reads *pas* instead of *point*. On metaphor, see Seminar III, chapters 17 and 18.

(506,fn1) Rudolf M. Loewenstein, the author of the paper mentioned in the third paragraph, refers in it to a "personal communication" with Roman Jakobson.

On Jeannot, see Voltaire's short story, "Jeannot and Colin" (1764), in *Voltaire: Candide, Zadig and Selected Stories*, trans. D. M. Frame (New York: New American Library, 1961), 243–51.

The passage by Goethe can be found in English in *Wilhelm Meister's Apprenticeship*, trans. Eric A. Blackall (New York: Suhrkamp, 1989), 180: "The creepiness, the bowing and scraping, the approving, flattering and insinuating, their adroitness and strutting, wholeness and emptiness, their utter roguery, their ineptness—how could all this be portrayed by one person? There should be at least a dozen of them, if that were feasible. For they are not just something in society, they are society."

(507,4) See Tardieu's play, *Un mot pour un autre* ("One Word for Another"), in *Le professeur Froeppel: nouvelle édition revue et augmentée de Un mot pour un autre* (Paris: Gallimard, 1978). Cf. Seminar III, 257–58.

(508,1) *Aune* (standards) also means alder (a type of tree).

(508,2) First sentence, alternate rendering: "But if, in this profusion, the giver disappears with the giving of the gift . . ."

(508,4) See Seminar III, 257.

(508,5) *Mot* has a number of different meanings, including word, solution, and witticism. In the latter context, *esprit* means wit, though a few paragraphs down, Lacan plays off the fact that *esprit* also means spirit and mind. See Strachey's remarks on *Witz* in his preface to *Der Witz und seine Beziehung zum Unbewussten*, known in English as *Jokes and their Relation to the Unconscious*, *SE* VIII, 6–8.

(509,3) The "noble victim" may well be Loewenstein, whose letter ("personal communication" with Jakobson) is alluded to in Lacan's footnote on page 506.

(509,fn2) See Sigmund Freud, *The Origins of Psychoanalysis: Letters to Wilhelm Fliess* (New York: Basic Books, 1954).

(510,1) The term "rebus" seems to initially appear on the first page of chapter 6, "The Dream-Work" (*SE* IV, 277). Lacan seems to have coined a new adjective here, *littérant* ("literating"), in order to avoid saying "literal." See the general note above on *signifiance* (signifierness).

(510,2) The French *déterminatif* is a bit narrower in meaning than "determinative," and refers to "a sign that is not pronounced, which is placed before an ideogram to complete its meaning" (J.-F. Phelizon, *Vocabulaire de la linguistique* [Paris: Roudil, 1976]).

(510,4) Jean-François Champollion (1790–1832), the first scholar to decipher the Egyptian hieroglyphics. *Stations* (journey) recalls the "stations of the cross."

(511,3) *Entstellung* is usually translated into French as *déformation* and into English as "distortion."

(511,7) *Rücksicht auf Darstellbarkeit* is translated as "Considerations of representability" in *SE* V, 339. The "parlor game" here is known in English as "charades."

(512,1) On the dream-work, see *SE* IV, 326 ff.

(512,2) *Von unserem wachen Denken nicht*

zu unterscheiden is from *GW* II/III, 493, and is translated as a psychical function "which is indistinguishable from our waking thoughts" in *SE* V, 489.

(514,5) Cf. "Position of the Unconscious" in *Écrits* 1966; trans. B. Fink, *Reading Seminar XI: Lacan's Four Fundamental Concepts of Psychoanalysis*, eds. R. Feldstein, B. Fink, and M. Jaanus (Albany: SUNY Press, 1995), 259–82.

(515,2) *Le manque de l'être* could alternatively be translated as "being's lack."

(516,1) See *Écrits* 1966, 504.

(516,4) *Sous la forme de son actualité* (in the form of its actuality) might, alternatively, be rendered "in its instantaneousness" or "instantaneously." *"Cogito ergo sum" ubi cogito, ibi sum* can be rendered as "Where I am thinking 'I am thinking, therefore I am,' there I am."

(516,fn1) See *Pourquoi des philosophes* (1957), the title of a book by Jean-François Revel; it can be found in a recent edition of his works, *Jean-François Revel* (Paris: Robert Laffont, 1997).

(517,6) *Tour* (trick) has many meanings, including turn, tour, trip, twist, and trick.

(517,8) *Ambiguïté de furet* (elusive ambiguity) literally means "ferret-like ambiguity" and is one of Lacan's many references to the game involving the *furet*.

(518,1) *Double coude* (double elbow) also means double curve, bend, elbow joint, or knee. It harks back to the *coudes* (curves) the S of the signifier impresses upon the ducts (*Écrits* 1966, 501).

(518,3) *Décevante* (deceptive) could alternatively be rendered as "disappointing." *Kern unseres Wesen* (the core of our being) is found in *SE* V, 603, and *SE* XXIII, 197.

(518,4) *Mécanisme à double détente* (two-stage mechanism) could also be translated as two-cycle, double-trigger, or double-reduction mechanism. *Fixe* (fixes) does not mean repairs, but rather freezes or renders fixed in place.

(518,6) The French *composition* (in the phrase "signifying composition") could also be translated as "structure," "configuration," or "combination."

(519,3) See Holderlin's poem "Home-

coming/To the Kinsmen." The end of the paragraph could alternatively read: "that led him from the royal principle of the Logos to rethink the deadly Empedoclean antinomies."

(519,4) Regarding the "other scene," see *SE* IV, 48, and *SE* V, 536.

(520,1) In Strachey's rendition, Freud's passage reads as follows: "Long before he was in the world, I went on, I had known that a little Hans would come who would be so fond of his mother that he would be bound to feel afraid of his father because of it" (*SE* X, 42).

(520,2) Alternate for "being raises it *in* the subject's *place*": "being raises it *in* the subject's *stead*." The original version of the French text read "Aristotle's man" instead of "antiquity's man."

(521,1) See Otto Fenichel, *Problems of Psychoanalytic Technique* (New York: The Psychoanalytic Quarterly, 1941).

(521,4) The *Fliegende Blätter* was a comic weekly of the late nineteenth and early twentieth centuries. *Fanfreluches antidotés* (antidoted fanfreluches) is from Rabelais' *Gargantua*, chapter 2; it literally means something like "remedied frills," but constitutes here a consummately obscure literary reference. There could also be a play here on *métier* (career), which also means loom (*métier à tisser*); thus "Must we serve as a loom for 'antidoted fanfreluches?'"

(522,3) *Transfert* (transference) also means transfer, conveyance, and even translation, in certain contexts. Cf. *SE* IV, 277, where *Übertragung* is rendered as "transcript."

(522,5) Alternate for "with which to close [*sceller*] these remarks": "with which to put a stamp of approval on." Alternate for "that attached him [*l'attachait*] to": "that made him attached to."

(522,fn1) See *SE* XXI, 152.

(523,3) Cf. Seminar III, 258.

(524,1) *Wo Es war, soll Ich werden* is from *GW* XV, 86, and corresponds to *SE* XXII, 80.

(524,3) See, for example, *SE* XXII, 15 and 222.

(524,8) See, for example, "Direction of the Treatment," *Écrits* 1966, 623–24.

(525,4) *Parole* (speech) can also be understood here as word, in the sense in which one says, "I give you my word (i.e., I promise) that I'll do it."

(525,5) See *SE* VIII, 115. Strachey renders the joke as follows: "Two Jews met in a railway carriage at a station in Galicia.

" 'Where are you going?' asked one.

" 'To Cracow,' was the answer.

" 'What a liar you are!' broke out the other. 'If you say you're going to Cracow, you want me to believe you're going to Lemberg. But I know that in fact you're going to Cracow. So why are you lying to me?' "

(525,7) On Midas, cf. *Écrits* 1966, 547.

(526,4) Alternate for "confusion": "embarrassment."

(526,5) *Reviser* (reconsider) is an alternate spelling of *réviser*.

(526,6) *Fait mon être* (constitutes my being) could also be translated as "creates my being" or "plays the part of my being."

(527,4) A reference to the collective publication, *La psychanalyse d'aujourd'hui*

("Contemporary Psychoanalysis") (Paris: PUF, 1956), discussed in "Direction of the Treatment."

(528,2) See Lacan's aforementioned translation of Heidegger's "Logos."

(528,5) End of paragraph, presumably, "against the collateral of his intentions."

(528,6) This obscure abbreviation was explained by Lacan (in a note to his Spanish translator, Tomás Segovia, dated October 15, 1970) as "*Tu t'y es mis un peu tard*," loosely translated as "You got down to it a bit late." The "e." for "*es*" is missing in all editions.

(528,7) The text, *La nouvelle rhétorique: Traité de l'argumentation* (Paris: PUF, 1958), is by Charles Perelman and Lucie Olbrechts-Tyteca; in English see *The New Rhetoric: A Treatise on Argumentation* (Notre Dame and London: University of Notre Dame Press, 1969). *Écrits* 1966 here erroneously reads *Théorie* instead of *Traité*, and on page 889 provides the date of Lacan's presentation as June 23, 1960.

NOTES TO "ON A QUESTION"

(531,2) *La Psychanalyse* 4 (1959): 1–50.

(532,2) *Percipiens:* one that perceives. *Perceptum:* object perceived, sense-datum. *Sensoriums:* senses, sensory apparatuses, seats or organs of sensation.

(533,1) *Renvoi* has a large number of meanings, including referral, deferment, suspension, discharge, sending back, return, and cross-reference.

(534,1) See Seminar III, chapter 4.

(535,3) *Intention de rejet* (rejecting intention) includes Lacan's first translation (*rejet*) of Freud's *Verwerfung*, which he renders further on as "foreclosure."

In French, a dash is often provided in a written text before a quoted reply. Lacan provides dashes before *Chou!* and *Rat!*

(535,fn1) See Roman Jakobson, *Selected Writings*, vol. 2 (The Hague: Mouton, 1971), 130–47.

(535,fn2) February 8, 1956, corresponds to chapter 10 in Seminar III.

(536,fn2) The translation has been reissued with an introduction by Samuel M. Weber (Cambridge, Mass.: Harvard University Press, 1988).

(536,fn3) In English, see Jacques Lacan, "The Case of Aimée," in eds. John Cutting and M. Shepherd, *The Clinical Roots of the Schizophrenia Concept* (Cambridge: Cambridge University Press, 1987).

(537,5) For passages from the *Memoirs* quoted by Freud in his commentary, I provide Strachey's translation; otherwise I use the previously referenced English version, changing the text at times to better render Lacan's own translation. Here that version reads, "In contrast the genuine basic language . . . excelled in form also by its dignity and simplicity."

(538,1) Strachey translates *Nervenanhang* as "nerve-connection" (SE XII, 39fn1) and Macalpine and Hunter as "nerve-contact" (S. 82).

(539,2) *Erinnerungsgedanken* is translated by Macalpine and Hunter as "human-thoughts-of-recollection" (S. 165).

(541,5) *Increvable* (inexhaustible) also means tireless and unburstable.

(541,7) See *SE* XII, 63–64.

(542,6) This seems to be a reference to the last paragraph of Freud's paper, "prop room" corresponding to what Strachey renders as "store-house" (*SE* XIX, 187).

(543,4) This might seem to be blatantly contradicted in the Schreber case itself, where the word "frustration" is found in Freud's discussion of the Schreber case (*SE* XII, 57 and 62). But the German reads *Versagung* in both cases (*GW* VIII, 293 and 298), which Lacan says implies renunciation, not frustration (*Écrits* 1966, 460–61).

(544,4) The English reads "rather pleasant" (S. 36) where Lacan reads *beau* (beautiful).

(544,6) Strachey tends to translate this as the "negative" Oedipus complex, but occasionally renders it as "inverted" (e.g., *SE* XVII, 6), the translation used systematically in *Memoirs*.

(545,2) Cf. *Écrits* 1966, 315.

(545,4) Reading *ailleurs* (as in the original version of the text, rendered here as "elsewhere") instead of *d'ailleurs* (moreover).

(545,fn1) See Seminar III, 347.

(546,1) See *Memoirs*, 23 and 410–11.

(546,fn1) See *SE* XVII, 89–91.

(547,2) On Midas, cf. *Écrits* 1966, 525.

(547,5) *Pensant à la dépense* (thinking of the expense) is borrowed from Paul-Jean Toulet's (*Contrerimes* (Paris: Gallimard, [1921] 1999).

(547,6) *Le pense-sans-rire* (deadpan thinkers) is a pun on *pince-sans-rire*, "deadpan."

(547,fn2) See *SE* XII, 54 and *Thus Spoke Zarathustra* in *The Portable Nietzsche*, trans. Walter Kaufmann (New York: Viking, 1968).

(548,1) *Le pense-à-penser le plus pensable* (the most thinkable one who thinks-about-thinking) would seem to be a reference to the ego.

(548,2) Cf. Lichtenberg's comment: "We should say *it thinks*, just as we say *it lightens*. To say *cogito* is already to say too much as soon as we translate it *I think*. To assume, to postulate the *I* is a practical requirement." G. C. Lichtenberg, *Aphorisms*, trans. R. J. Hollingdale (London: Penguin, 1990).

(548,3) A pun on "Baudelaire" and the oath *bordel de Dieu*. Cf. Baudelaire's phrase, "le vert paradis des amours enfantines."

(548,4) The original version and *Écrits* 1966 both read *le réaliste* (the realist), whereas Points reads *l'organiciste* (the organicist). On the *anderer Schauplatz*, see, for example, *SE* IV, 48, and *SE* V, 536.

(548,6) The complete L schema was introduced on page 53 of *Écrits* 1966 in a text not included in this Selection: the "Suite" to the "Seminar on 'The Purloined Letter.' "

(549,1) For a different gloss on *discours de l'Autre*, see *Écrits* 1966, 814, where it is translated as "discourse about the Other."

(550,4) *Intra-mondaine* (within-the-world) seems to be a translation of Heidegger's *innerweltlich*

(550,8) *Verbe* (Word): like "the Word," *le Verbe* is a translation for the Greek "Logos." Hereafter, *le verbe* is always translated as "the Word."

(551,5) *Où peut s'identifier l'Autre* (where the Other may be identified) could possibly—assuming an unusual use of *où*—be rendered as "with which the Other may be identified."

(551,6) *Jeu* (play) can also be translated as "game" and is so translated below. *Le mort* can be translated as "the dead person" or "the dummy" as in bridge. Cf. *Écrits* 1966, 589.

(552,1) *En tant que mort* (as the dummy) could also be rendered by "as dead," and *comme vivant* (as a living being) by "as alive."

Il lui faut prendre la couleur qu'il annonce (he must play the suit he calls trump) evokes the expression *annoncer la couleur*, meaning to lay one's cards on the table or say where one stands; literally, it means to propose, in a card game (such as bridge), what suit will be trump.

(552,2) Instead of "it proves appropriate

for providing," one could read "it finds itself appropriated to provide."

(552,4) *Où le sujet s'identifie . . . avec* (where the subject is identified . . . with) could possibly—assuming an unusual use of *où*—be rendered as "where the subject identifies . . . with."

(553,3) Instead of "where the ego identifies itself," one could read "with which the ego is identical" or "where the ego is identified."

(554,fn1) *Représentant de la représentation* (representation's representative) is Lacan's translation for Freud's *Vorstellungsrepräsentanz*, rendered in the *Standard Edition* by "ideational representative," and generally designates that which stands in for (or represents) the drive at the "ideational" level (i.e., at the level of representation); it could also be translated as "the representative of representation." In Seminar VII, Lacan equates Freud's *Vorstellungsrepräsentanz* with the signifier (page 75–76/61).

(555,2) Raymond Queneau employs the slang term *phalle* (dick) in a passage from *Les Enfants du limon* (Paris: Gallimard, [1938] 1987): "détailler les phalles de messieurs et les mottes de dames, qui ni d'Adam ni d'Ève elle ne connaissait."

(557,6) Instead of "Mother's Desire," one could read "Desire for the Mother." Note that the formula "Desire of the Mother" does not, in fact, capture both of these meanings, but only the former.

(557,7) *Carence* (lack) also means deficiency.

(558,2) See *SE* XIX, 235–39. *Aveu* (owning) means avowal, confession, owning up, and admission.

(558,4) Or "At the point to which the Name-of-the-Father is summoned." An alternative reading for the first part of the sentence: "A pure and simple hole in the Other may thus correspond to the point to which the Name-of-the-Father is called upon [to come]—we shall see how."

(558,6) *Désordre* (disturbance) can also be rendered as "disorder," "chaos," or "mess"; it is not a reference to the eponymous psychi-

atric notion. I translate it again as "disturbance" on *Écrits* 1966, 563.

(558,fn1) The English translation reads as follows: "I want to say by way of introduction that the leading roles in the genesis of the development, the first beginnings of which go back perhaps as far as the eighteenth century, were played on the one hand by the names of Flechsig and Schreber (probably not specifying any individual member of these families), and on the other by the concept of *soul murder.*"

(559,1) Lacan uses a very uncommon, if not invented, term here, *apophanies* (manifestations). It may possibly be related to the English "apophany," which is a kind of rhyme in which two single-syllable words share opening and closing consonants but not the intervening vowel; in that case, Ahriman would be one of the rhyming forms of the name of God in Schreber's delusion.

(560,3) Strachey translates *Denkzwang* as "enforced thinking" (*SE* XII, 25), and Macalpine and Hunter render it as "compulsive thinking." *Liegen lassen* is translated in *Memoirs* as "forsakes him" and "forsaken," depending on the context (S. 56 and 94, and *Memoirs*, 362).

(561,1) *Météores* (meteors) could also be rendered here as "flashes."

(561,4) For the first part of the first sentence here, Macalpine and Hunter provide "Many in One or One in Many" (S. 196n).

(562,4) This seems to be a reference to *Memoirs*, 379n.

(563,4) *De Malebranche ou de Locke / Plus malin le plus loufoque . . .*

(564,1) Strachey translates *Verfluchter Kerl* as "The deuce of a fellow," *SE* XII, 36.

(564,5) "Conscientious objection" would seem to refer here to male impotence. Cf. Lacan's comment: "Analytic discourse demonstrates—allow me to put it this way—that the phallus is the conscientious objection made by one of the two sexed beings to the service to be rendered to the other" (Seminar XX, 13).

(564,fn1) See also *Memoirs*, 24, 27, and 361; note that Strachey did not change "emasculation" to "unmanning" in the *Standard Edition*.

(565,2) "Real castration": castration of the biological organ, as opposed to symbolic castration.

(565,5) *Manque-à-être*: see general note above.

(566,1) *Manque à* (is missing) means both does not have (lacks) and pines for.

(566,4) *Du rififi chez les hommes* (brawling among men) is a book by Auguste Le Breton (Paris: Gallimard, [1953] 1992) that was made into a film by Dassin. See *SE* X, 13, where we find Hans' addition to the giraffe drawn by his father; see also Seminar IV, 264.

(566,fn1) Strachey translates this as "cursorily improvised men" and Macalpine as "fleeting-improvised-men." Pichon's translation, *ombres d'hommes bâclés à la six-quatre-deux* (shadows of men thrown together 1, 2, 3), may also contain a reference to a technique for very quickly sketching a human profile by drawing the numbers 6, 4, and 2 in a certain arrangement.

(567,5) *La personne du sujet* (him) literally means the person of the subject, and less literally means the subject's personality or the subject as a person.

(568,8) "Radical rectifications": presumably, sex-change operations.

(569,1) "Psycho-Analytic Notes on an Autobiographical Account of a Case of Paranoia," *SE* XII, 30, fn2.

(571,1) In "the symbolization of the Mother insofar as she . . .," *elle* (she) could alternatively be translated as "it," referring back to symbolization.

(572,fn1) See *SE* XII, 48.

(573,2) Niederland does not claim that "lewd" means whore, nor does it seem to be borne out etymologically.

(573,4) *Décalage* (skew) could also be translated as "gap" or "discrepancy."

(575,3) See the "Suite" to the "Seminar on 'The Purloined Letter,' " especially *Écrits* 1966, 42, 52, and 56. *L'être de l'étant* (the being of entities) could also be translated as "the Being of beings."

(575,7) *Isole . . . de* (distinguish . . . on the

basis of) could, alternatively, be rendered "distinguish . . . from." Further on, I read *montrent* (show, after the second dash) for *montre* (shows). Note that all three French editions of this text read *pour* ("for" or "because of") instead of *par* found in the usual expression "appeler les choses par leur nom" (to call things by their rightful names).

(576,3) On Pascal, see *Écrits* 1966, 283.

(577,7) *Un-père* could alternatively be rendered as "A-father."

(578,3) *Redouble* (redoubles) could also be translated as "relines," "increases," "intensifies," "duplicates," or "reduplicates."

(578,4) Hide-the-thimble is the "hot and cold" game in which one player hides an object and another player searches for it, the first player giving clues like "cold" (when the second is not at all close to the object), "warm" (when closer), and "hot," "boiling," or "burning" (when right in front of it).

(578,5) On "Whom do you love more, daddy or mommy?" see *SE* X, 238.

(579,4) *Pires* (lowest of the low) could also be translated as "worst elements."

(581,1) In Ancient Rome, the members of the Senate were referred to as *patres conscripti*, *pères conscrits*, conscripted (or conscribed) fathers.

(581,4) The usual expression, *de part en part* (through and through), has been changed here, at the end of the paragraph, to *de père en part*. The latter might even evoke *de père en fils*, "from father to son." *Trame* means plot, web, or warp.

(581,fn1) Macalpine renders it as "How to Achieve Happiness and Bliss by Physical Culture."

(582,3) *Jaculation* (jaculation), which literally means pitching, throwing, or hurling, has in French taken on the figurative sense of *élan d'enthousiasme*, passionate impulse or enthusiastic surge.

(582,4) *Comput* (computation) refers to the set of rules allowing one to determine the date of a holiday, for example, in the context of the establishment of a calendar.

(582,fn1) In the English translation, we find the following: "The phrase 'O damn' in particular was a remnant of the basic language, in which the words 'O damn, that is hard to say' were used whenever the souls became aware of a happening inconsistent with the Order of the World, for instance

'Oh damn, it is extremely hard to say that God allows himself to be f......' " (179).

(583,fn1) I have followed the slightly modified Points text here.

NOTES TO "THE DIRECTION OF THE TREATMENT"

(585,3) *La personne de l'analysé* (the analysand as a person) and *la personne de l'analyste* (the analyst as a person) could alternatively be translated as "the analysand's (or analyst's) person" or "the analysand's (or analyst's) personality."

(585,fn3) See Anne Berman's translation, *Nouvelles conférences sur la psychanalyse* (Paris: Gallimard, 1936).

(586,7) It should be kept in mind that *paroles* (words) can also be translated as "speech."

(589,2) *Malheur de la conscience* (troubled conscience) seems to be a reference to *conscience malheureuse* (unhappy consciousness), the usual French translation of Hegel's *unglückliches Bewusstsein*. See Jean Wahl, *Le Malheur de la conscience dans la philosophie de Hegel* (Paris: PUF, 1951).

(589,3) *Le mort* (the dummy) also means the dead man. *Lien* (restraint) also means link, bond, tie, and shackle.

(590,6) This is a reference to Heinz Hartmann who, in his "Technical Implications of Ego Psychology," writes that "analysis is gradually and unavoidably, though hesitantly, becoming a general psychology . . ." (*PQ* XX, 3 [1949]: 35), and who, in "The Development of the Ego Concept in Freud's Work," writes that "the trend toward a general psychology has been inherent in psycho-analysis from its inception" (*IJP* XXVII, 6 [1956]: 434). In Seminar I (33/25), Lacan suggests that Kris also refers to analysis as a "general psychology." The idea of a "nonconflictual sphere" was first introduced by Hartmann in "Ich-Psychologie und Anpassungsproblem," *Internationale Zeitschrift für Psychoanalyse und Imago* XXIV (1939), published in English as *Ego Psychology and the Problem of Adaptation*,

trans. D. Rapaport (New York: International Universities Press, 1958).

(590,7) The French pronunciations of *égaux* (equal) and *egos* are usually identical.

(590,fn1) "The doctrinaire of being" is Sacha Nacht.

(592,3) *Moi* means both me and ego.

(593,2) *Elle* (the last "thought" in the first sentence) could, alternatively, refer back to "the transmutation" and *passer au fait* could, alternatively, be understood as "gets to the point" or "gets down to brass tacks." Alternate reading for the end of the paragraph: "where the subject is subordinated (or subordinate) to the signifier to so great an extent that he is seduced by it."

(593,3) *Recel* (possession) also means receiving or harboring (usually of stolen goods).

(593,6) See Jakob Böhme's *De Signatura Rerum* (1651); in English see *The Signature of All Things and Other Writings* (Cambridge and London: James Clarke, 1969).

(593,7) *Être à l'heure de Freud* (to keep time with Freud) literally means to be at the same time or hour as Freud (to be in the same time zone or register, to keep in step with him, or to synchronize watches with him).

(594,1) Alternate reading for end of paragraph: "through being inscribed there, can produce anything new."

(594,4) Regarding "repetition automatism": Lacan does not employ here the more usual French translation of Freud's *Wiederholungszwang* (usually translated into English as "repetition compulsion"), which is *compulsion de répétition*. But he does employ it later in this article.

(596,3) Lacan provides here his own translation, *travail du transfert* (work of transference), of Freud's *Durcharbeitung*, which is usually translated into French as *perlaboration*. Later in the text he provides *travail de transfert*.

(596,5) *Désordre* (disorder) can also be rendered as "havoc," "chaos" or "mess"; it is not a reference to the eponymous psychiatric notion.

(596,6) See "Presentation on Transference" (1951) in *Écrits* 1966.

(597,2) *Principe* (crux) also means principle and recalls the title of the present article. "Crux" always translates *principe* in this article.

(597,4) Lacan uses *tendance* (tendency) instead of *pulsion* (drive) almost exclusively in this paper.

(597,5) Presumably "prescribed" in the legal sense of a debt not paid off in the stipulated time frame and that is no longer claimable by the creditor.

(598,4) Regarding "what an opportunity for contempt I would be offering to those who wish to find fault": the French, *que n'offrirais-je à honnir à ceux qui mal y pensent*, is based on François I's "honni soit qui mal y pense" (evil be to him who evil thinks).

(598,5) Regarding "rectification of the subject's relations with reality": this is a probable reference to Freud's remarks to the Rat Man in their very first sessions (*SE* X, 169 and 173) regarding the "errors of memory" and "displacements" involved in the pince-nez matter, and to Freud's remarks to Dora, mentioned earlier in the text (*SE* VII, 35–36).

(598,7) See Lacan's commentary on this case in Seminar I, 71–72/59–61; Seminar III, 92–93; and *Écrits* 1966, 393–99.

(599,2) The French here reads *infantile*, instead of "adolescent," but the case history (see reference 15) twice mentions "puberty," as does Lacan himself elsewhere (*Écrits* 1966, 394 and 396).

(599,3) On "analyzing the defense before the drive," see H. Hartmann and E. Kris, "The Genetic Approach in Psychoanalysis," *The Psychoanalytic Study of the Child*, vol. 1 (New York: International Universities Press, 1945), 15: "interpretation should start as close as possible to the experience of the patient—

'from the higher layers'—and elucidate the structure of the 'defenses' before they proceed to what stems from the id."

(600,2) *Moutarde après dîner* (post-session condiment) is most often seen in the expression "c'est (comme) de la moutarde après dîner" (literally, "it's like an after-dinner mustard"), meaning it's something that came too late, only after it was no longer of any use (presumably, one would have wanted to have the mustard as a condiment *during* dinner).

(600,5) The original text plays on the two-part negation in French: "Ce n'est pas que votre patient ne vole pas, qui ici importe. C'est qu'il ne . . . Pas de ne: c'est qu'il vole *rien*."

(601,2) "The mental realm" as opposed to the realm of food.

(601,3) *Rien à frire* (nothing doing) literally means nothing to fry, and is preferred here to the more usual *rien à faire*, due to the reference to fish in the previous sentence.

(602,1) *Carte* (map) also evokes the menus Kris' patient studied (thus: "To take desire off the menu . . .").

(602,4) Cf. Lacan's comments on the distinction between the need for repetition and the repetition of need in Seminar VIII, 207.

(602,5) See, above all, *Écrits* 1966, 647–84.

(603,5) *Écrits* 1966 reads *particularités* (particularities), but the earlier version in *La Psychanalyse* 6 reads *partialités* (partialities), which makes more sense here.

(604,2) See "The Genetic Approach in Psychoanalysis," 24.

(604,4) On such patterns, see "The Genetic Approach in Psychoanalysis," 12.

(605,3) *Objectalité* (objectality) might also be rendered as "object relatedness," but its contrast with "objectivity" would then be diminished.

(605,5) "Negative" here in the sense of the photographic negative of an image. This quote and a number of those that follow are from Maurice Bouvet, "La clinique psychanalytique. La relation d'objet," in *La psychanalyse d'aujourd'hui* (Paris: PUF, 1956); Lacan also discusses Bouvet's article in Seminar IV, chapters 1 and 2.

(606,7) The antinomy: pregenital versus genital.

(607,1) See, for example, "On the Universal Tendency to Debasement in the Sphere of Love," *SE* XI, 179–90.

(607,4) See Matthew, 23.4, and *Écrits* 1966, 263.

(607,6) The French *hérésie* (heretical) is a quasi-homonym of R.S.I. (the title of Lacan's Seminar XXII, 1974–75), which stands for real, symbolic, imaginary, and may be an early play on that homophony. The three sides here are the three theories: geneticism, object relations, and intersubjective introjection.

(608,2) See, for example, Bouvet, "La clinique psychanalytique," 102–3.

(609,6) On this "case of pure obsession in a man," cf. Seminar V, 447.

(609,8) Cf. "Function and Field," 267.

(610,2) *Pif* means nose, and to do something *au pif* or *au pif(f)omètre* (following one's nose) is to do it by guesswork, without calculating, "to play it by ear." Lacan discusses the case mentioned here at length in Seminar IV, 88–92.

(611,1) See André Breton's 1924 "Introduction au discours sur le peu de réalité" in *Point du Jour* (Paris: Gallimard, 1970); in English, see "Introduction to the Discourse on the Paucity of Reality" in *Break of Day* (Lincoln: University of Nebraska Press, 1999).

(611,9) A probable reference to Virgil's *labor improbus* in *Georgica* 1, 146, translated as "remorseless toil" by James Rhoades in *Great Books of the Western World*, XIII (Chicago: Britannica, 1952), 41.

(612,3) Lacan discussed object-relation themes in Seminar IV, 1956–1957.

(612,6) *Pataquès* (linguistic error) most commonly means a mistake in pronunciation, but can also mean any big linguistic error.

(613,1) The second topography is that of the id, ego, and superego.

(614,3) *Heurter* (affront) also means to hurt, offend, clash, oppose, and even buck the trend.

(614,4) "Won or lost": see *Écrits* 1966, 853;

in English see "On Freud's '*Trieb*' and the Psychoanalyst's Desire," trans. B. Fink, in *Reading Seminars I and II: Lacan's Return to Freud*, eds. R. Feldstein, B. Fink, and M. Jaanus (Albany: SUNY Press, 1996).

(615,2) This is a reference to a story about a rich man who is told he can become happy by wearing a happy man's shirt; he searches far and wide until he finds a happy man, but the latter is so poor he has no shirt to give the rich man. "Happy shade" is a reference to Chateaubriand's *Mémoires d'Outre-tombe*.

(615,4) *Malheurs de l'être* (misfortunes of being): cf. *Écrits* 1966, 589 (where *malheur* is translated as "troubled") and 636.

(616,1) *Essai de l'action* could also be rendered as "experimental action." Cf. *SE* XII, 221, and *SE* V, 599–600.

(618,1) *Prescription* (statute of limitations) is a legal term implying a certain time limit; the idea thus seems to be that signifiers used in the demands in question are not supposed to be used beyond a certain age, that they are out of date.

(618,8) See Seminar IV, 69. On defiles, cf. Freud's "defile of consciousness" in *SE* II, 291.

(619,1) *S'il ne remplit certes pas tout* (while it does not fulfill all functions) could also be translated as "even if it doesn't fill everything."

(620,4) *Fusent* (fizzle out) could also be translated as "sizzle" or "burn out," since in the context of pyrotechnics, *fuser* means to burn without exploding.

(620,fn1) In English, see *The Origins of Psychoanalysis* (New York: Basic Books, 1954), 296–97, and *The Complete Letters of Sigmund Freud to Wilhelm Fliess*, 1887–1904 (Cambridge, Mass.: Harvard University Press, 1985), 370–71.

(621,4) *Glissement* (sliding) can be translated as sliding, slippage, or shifting and is used here by Lacan to translate Freud's *Verschiebung*, usually translated as "displacement" (*déplacement* in French). See, in particular, "Instance of the Letter," *Écrits* 1966, 511.

(621,fn1) Strachey provides the following

translation of the dream recounted by the "butcher's witty wife" (*SE* IV, 147): "I wanted to give a supper-party, but I had nothing in the house but a little smoked salmon. I thought I would go out and buy something, but remembered then that it was Sunday afternoon and all the shops would be shut. Next I tried to ring up some caterers, but the telephone was out of order. So I had to abandon my wish to give a supper-party." The dream is also discussed by Lacan in Seminar V, chapter 20, and Seminar XVII, 84–85.

(622,3) On metaphor as a positive meaning effect, see *Écrits* 1966, 515. The French at the end of the sentence, *un certain passage du sujet au sens du désir*, allows for a number of other possible readings: "a certain movement of the subject in terms of desire," "a certain movement of the subject toward the meaning of desire," "a certain movement of the subject in the direction of desire," "a certain shift by the subject in relation to desire," "a certain shift by the subject as regards her desire," and "a certain shift of the subject as desiring subject."

(622,4) Regarding "the desire to have an unsatisfied desire," see Freud's various formulations in *GW* IV, 153, and *SE* IV, 148–49.

(622,5) On the "royal road," see *SE* V, 608. The French translation is *voie royale; voie* is used again in Lacan's text, *Écrits* 1966, 624 and 626.

(622,7) Regarding *peu de sens* (scant meaning), cf. Breton's expression "peu de réalité" (scant reality) from "Introduction au discours sur le peu de réalité . . ."

(623,2) *Signifiance*, rendered in this translation as "signifierness," might also be translated here as "significance" or "meaningfulness."

(623,4) The dream's "elaboration" is probably the "first revision" of the dream by displacement and condensation, prior to the secondary revision (known in French as *l'élaboration secondaire*); it could also possibly be the recounting of the dream by the dreamer. On "linguistic structure," see Saussure's *Course in General Linguistics* (New York: McGraw-Hill, 1959).

(623,5) Desire is associated with metonymy, while the subject is associated

with metaphor; see *Écrits* 1966, Appendix II, "Metaphor of the Subject" (in English, trans. B. Fink, *Newsletter of the Freudian Field* 5 [1991]). Lacan is surely referring in this passage to his "Graph of Desire" (*Écrits* 1966, 805 and 817). *Dérivation* (branch line) could also be translated as "branch circuit." Cf. *SE* VII, 72.

(623,6) *Le désir ne fait qu'assujettir ce que l'analyse subjective.* *Assujettir* could also be translated as "to subject" (e.g., to subject someone to something); *subjective* could also be translated as "renders subjective," "renders subject," or "subjectifies." Desire subjugates the drives (the id) whereas analysis brings the subject into being there; see, for example, *Écrits* 1966, 524: "Where it (or id) was, it is necessary for me to come into being" (*"Là où fut ça, il me faut advenir"*). Cf. "On Freud's '*Trieb*' and the Psychoanalyst's Desire," *Écrits* 1966, 851–54; in English, see *Reading Seminars I and II: Lacan's Return to Freud*, eds. R. Feldstein, B. Fink, and M. Jaanus (Albany: SUNY Press, 1996), 417–21.

(623,8) In the next paragraph, Lacan plays on the "fire" (*feu*) in the expression *faire long feu* (falters) in this paragraph: it was extinguished or went out (*s'éteignait*) and cast light. The expression itself derives from early firearms terminology; when the fuse on a gun cartridge burned too slowly, the gun would go off at the wrong time and *one would miss one's mark*. The expression is more often used nowadays in its negative form (*ne pas faire long feu*) to indicate that something has not lasted very long. In the present context, one could also translate the phrase as, "but my voice drawls interminably before finishing."

(624,1) In the preceding paragraph, Lacan mentioned that dreams are designed for the "recognition of desire"; here it is the "desire for recognition" that is at stake.

(624,5) This entire paragraph seems to be ironic, Lacan clearly agreeing with Freud that one gets better because one remembers.

(625,2) In Strachey's rendition of Freud's account, the husband is said to have replied that "he was sure the painter would prefer a piece of a pretty young girl's behind to the whole of his face." In Lacan's account, he is characterized as replying, "une tranche du train de derrière d'une belle garce, voilà ce qu'il vous faut," literally, "a slice of a pretty bitch's rear end is what you need" (*garce* can also mean "prostitute," and *une belle garce* can mean "hot stuff").

(625,6) Jean-Gabriel de Tarde, the French sociologist (1843–1904), believed that social phenomena were based on the repetition of individual psychical processes (such as invention and creation, on the one hand, and imitation, diffusion, and tradition, on the other). See, in particular, his book, *Les Lois de l'imitation*, published in 1890; in English, *The Laws of Imitation*, trans. E. C. Parsons (Gloucester, Mass.: P. Smith, 1962).

(626,3) The French at the end of the paragraph, *qui va du désir de son amie faire l'échec de sa demande*, is quite vague, and could also be rendered as "makes use of her friend's desire to thwart her own demand." The only request (*demande*) in question thus far in Lacan's discussion seems to be the friend's request "to come dine at the patient's house," but in the next sentence Lacan characterizes the patient's phone calls to caterers in her dream as a request as well. The desire most recently mentioned is the husband's presumed desire for his wife's friend, but the way it is expressed it could also be understood as the friend's desire for the patient's husband. Thus the patient "thwarts her own request due to her friend's desire for the husband or her husband's desire for her friend." Thanks to her "hysterical identification" with her friend, however, by thwarting her own request she also thwarts her friend's request to dine at the patient's home. *Sa demande* can thus imply "her own request" as well as "her friend's request," just as *le désir de son amie* can imply "her husband's desire for her friend," "her friend's desire for her husband," and even "her own desire for her friend," for (as we shall see) her husband's desire becomes her own.

(626,6) Recall that *le désir de l'Autre* (the Other's desire) is also a shorthand, at times, for "the object of the Other's desire" or "what the Other desires."

(627,1) What was revealed in the mysteries is a matter of much debate. Part of the Orphic ritual is thought to have involved the mimed or actual dismemberment of an individual representing the god Dionysus. Cf. Lacan's reference to the pound of flesh and the lost phallus of Osiris embalmed two pages further on, his reference to Freud's unveiling of the phallus at the end of this article, and his further reference to the mysteries in *Écrits* 1966, 555 and 688. As Jacques-Alain Miller has pointed out, here as elsewhere in *Écrits* the fish seems to have to do with a kind of ultimate meaning or truth: a phallic signification. See, in particular, *Écrits* 1966, 805.

(627,3) Figuratively speaking, *logogriphe* (obscure discourse) can mean an obscure, unintelligible discourse or language; literally, it means a word game or enigma in which one must guess the word whose letters allow one to form several other words—given "sire" and "deer," for example, one has to find "desire." On Freud's later considerations on the castration complex and penis envy, see *SE* XXIII, 252–53.

(627,9) Alternate reading for "limbo realm": "purgatory." Regarding the "it" that speaks in him: there are too many masculine nouns in this passage (need, being, love, and lure) to be absolutely sure which one Lacan has in mind, though "need" seems quite likely. In the next sentence, *à sa place* (in its place) could refer to being's place, need's place, nonbeing's place, or even desire in its place or desire where it is situated.

(628,7) Reading *un* (an), as in the original version of the text, instead of *en*.

(628,8) Regarding *ein anderer Schauplatz*, see *SE* IV, 48, and *SE* V, 536. *Écrits* 1966 erroneously reads *eine* instead of *ein* and *andere* instead of *anderer*.

(629,1) See *Écrits* 1966, 623.

(629,2) *Accompli* is a synonym of *perfectif* (perfective) in this context. See J.-F. Phelizon, *Vocabulaire de la linguistique* (Paris: Roudil, 1976).

(629,4) The grammar of the second sentence allows of a different reading: "demand evokes the want-to-be in the following three figures: the nothing that constitutes the heritage of the demand for love, the hatred that goes so far as to negate the other's being, and the unspeakable in what is not known in its request." *Fonds* (ground) could also be rendered as "fund" or "reserve" here. *Corps subtil* (subtle body) is a reference to the matter ("aether" or "ether") formerly believed to surround the earth.

(629,5) *Insignifiante* could, alternatively, be rendered as "insignificant" or "nonsignifying."

(630,2) Alternative for "in desire's quest": "in the quest for desire."

(630,3) *Colin-tampon* (pounding away) is a name given to a former battery of drummers in Swiss regiments. The more usual expression, *se soucier de quelque chose comme de colin-tampon*, means to not make anything of something, not concern oneself with it. The grammar at the end of this paragraph also allows us to read "thus surmising his desire itself insofar as it was the Other's desire."

(630,4) *Arranger* (arrange) can mean to organize or even stage something, "stage" in the sense of fixing the outcome of a match in advance. Note that, while in the text I translate *l'Autre* as the Other with a capital O, and *l'autre* as the other with a lowercase o, in Lacan's schemas and mathemes the former is designated by A and the latter by *a* and *a'*.

(630,5) Alternate term for "traffic circle": "roundabout."

(631,3) *D'âge mûr* (of mature years) probably strikes Lacan as comical because it contains the word *mûr* (ripe), which English only includes in the contraindicated "ripe old age."

(631,4) *Inamovible* (permanent) also means fixed (in place).

(631,9) *Commère* (shrewd paramour) formerly meant godmother, but has taken on several more recent meanings: gossip; cunning woman; bold and energetic woman; and a music hall emcee.

(632,4) Cf. Rabelais' "science without conscience is but the demise of the soul."

(632,8) *Le cède au sien* (yields to his desire) could also be rendered as "is inferior to," but my sense is that that is not the intended meaning.

(633,2) *Le mépris de sa mère acariâtre à décrier* (his ill-tempered mother's contempt for) could also be translated as "his contempt for his ill-tempered mother for disparaging."

(633,4) *Mettre à gauche* (tuck it away) is usually used in reference to money: "to put money aside," "to tuck (or sock) some money away." Alternative reading for "his desire is for difficulty": "his desire is based on difficulty."

(633,6) *S'imprimer* (rendered here as "(im)printed") could also be translated as "etched," "stamped," "published," "communicated," or "transferred." Cf. Lacan's discussion of the sign and the phallus in Seminar VIII, chapter 18 (April 26, 1961).

(633,7) The "mark of origin" may be an allusion to Freud's "Negation," *SE* XIX, 236.

(634,1) On *coïtus normalis dosim repetatur*, cf. *SE* XIV, 14–15.

(634,4) *Foi* (word) literally means faith. *Tu es* (you are) is similar in pronunciation to *tuez* (kill).

(634,8) This is a heraldic reference to the slanted bar one finds on certain coats of arms, said in a number of works of fiction (in error, apparently) to represent the fact that their bearers are bastards of noble birth.

(635,6) The "object of the demand for love" would seem to be the person to whom one's demand for love is addressed.

(635,7) *Scandent* (punctuate) comes from *scander*, to scan verse; cf. "scansion."

(636,8) A *palotin* (foolish acolyte) is an acolyte, associate, or henchman of Father Ubu's in Alfred Jarry's play *Ubu Roi ou les polonais* (Paris: Eugène Fasquelle, 1922 [1888]); in English see *King Turd*, trans. B. Keith and G. Legman (New York: Boar's Head Books, 1953). Alternate reading for "Is that all you've got?": "What else is new?"

(637,6) *Mise en fonction* (set to work) could, alternatively, be rendered as "put into operation."

(638,3) This is, once again, a commentary on the Graph of Desire.

(638,4) The French here evokes the *chanson de geste*, a set of medieval French epic poems relating the deeds of one and the same hero. *Passage à l'acte* is the French translation of the German *Agieren* (translated into English as "acting out") that was usual in the 1950s. Lacan confirms that here; see also Daniel Lagache's translation of Melitta Schmideberg's "Note sur le transfert" ("Note on Transference") in *RFP* XVI, 1–2 (1952): 263–67, especially page 265, and the *Robert* dictionary under "acte." Nevertheless, Lacan begins to distinguish *passage à l'acte* from acting out later (see, for example, Seminar XIV, February 22, 1967).

(639,3) *Hostie* (Host) is the eucharistic wafer; between the fourteenth and seventeenth centuries it meant a victim offered up in sacrifice. Alternative reading for "idiotic desire": "dulled desire."

(639,6) On the young homosexual woman and Dora, see, in particular, Seminar IV, chapters 7 and 8.

(639,7) See *SE* XVIII, 107.

(640,1) *Oblat* (sacrificial object) has a number of meanings: a child given to the Church and dedicated to God, a member of a religious order who gives up his or her possessions but takes no vows, a person who sacrifices him- or herself, or the eucharistic wafer.

(640,4) *Ils n'en ont cure* (they couldn't care less) is a play on words here, for it literally means "they have no cure for it."

(640,8) Cf. Seminar IV, 246.

(641,6 and 7) *Aveu* (owning) means avowal, confession, owning up, and admission.

(641,10) The French here contains a *ne pas* (not) before "attributing" that I have left out, believing that it was included in error.

(641,11) The "tunic of Nessus" is the poisoned tunic that caused Hercules' death.

(642,3) See Mauriac's *Le Fleuve de feu* (Paris: Bernard Grasset, 1923); in English, *The River of Fire*, trans. G. Hopkins (London: Eyre & Spottiswoode, 1954).

(642,4) The *jeu du furet* (swiftly shifting game) is a game in which a group of people sit in a circle and quickly pass a small object—referred to as *le furet*, though a *furet* is literally a ferret—from hand to hand, while a player standing in the middle of the circle tries to guess which hand holds the *furet*. Cf. *Écrits* 1966, 259.

(642,8) *S'articule au* (linked to) could also be translated as "is articulated in (or with)" or "links up with." See Lacan's comments on Freud's "Splitting of the Ego in the Defensive Process" in chapter 22 of Seminar VII.

(644,ref.18) A sample of Lagache's work on transference can be found in English in "Some Aspects of Transference," *IJP* XXXIV, 1 (1953): 1–10.

NOTES TO "THE SIGNIFICATION OF THE PHALLUS"

(685,1) The title of this article, *La signification du phallus*, could also be translated as "The Phallus' Signification," "What the Phallus Signifies," "The Phallus as Signification," or "The Signification That the Phallus Is." See Lacan's discussion of the title as involving a subjective genitive or an objective genitive in Seminar XIX (January 19, 1972).

(685,8) See Freud's article, "Analysis Terminable and Interminable" (1937), *SE* XXIII, 209–54. In "Variations on the Standard Treatment," Lacan translates the

title of this article as "L'analyse finie et l'analyse sans fin," "Finite (or Finished) Analysis and Endless Analysis."

(686,4) Presumably, a "transference" from the mother to the father.

(687,2) Cf. "Guiding Remarks," *Écrits* 1966, 730. For another example of such ignorance, consider the wedding night of Louis the Sixteenth as told by Alexandre Dumas senior in *Joseph Balsamo*, chapter 64.

(687,3) The person who "sometimes . . . says both" seems to be Ernest Jones; see "Guiding Remarks," *Écrits* 1966, 732. On transmutations of the object see, for example, R. von Krafft-Ebing's *Psychopathia Sexualis* (New York: Physicians and Surgeons Book Company, [1900] 1935).

(687,6) Jones used the Greek term "aphanisis" to refer to the "total, and of course permanent, extinction of the capacity (including opportunity) for sexual enjoyment"; see "Early Development of Female Sexuality" (1927), in *Papers on Psycho-Analysis*, 5th edition (Boston: Beacon, 1961), 440. According to Jones, the fear of aphanisis is more fundamental than that of castration in both sexes, castration being only a "special case" of aphanisis in boys. The other two articles in the series Lacan mentions are "The Phallic Phase" and "Early Female Sexuality," both of which are included in *Papers on Psycho-Analysis*. The key mentioned at the end of the paragraph would seem to be the term "signifier."

(688,2) Lacan plays, at the very beginning of the paragraph, on the expression *noyer le poisson* (to throw someone off track, create confusion, or mix things up, in order to dodge a question), saying "le poisson ne se laisse pas noyer." The phallus is often associated by Lacan with a fish; see, for example, *Écrits* 1966, 626–27 and 805. "Male and female created He them" is found on page 484 of Jones' paper, "The Phallic Phase."

(689,4) Regarding *ein anderer Schauplatz*, see *SE* IV, 48, and *SE* V, 536. *Écrits* 1966 erroneously reads *eine* here instead of *ein* and *andere* instead of *anderer*; this is corrected in Points. *Versants* (axes) is Lacan's translation into French of Jakobson's term, "aspects," in his article "Two Aspects of Language and Two Types of Aphasic Disturbances," in *Selected Writings*, vol. II (The Hague: Mouton, 1971), 239–59.

(689,5) Or "The discovery of what he articulates . . ."

(690,5) This might seem to be contradicted in Freud's discussion of the Schreber case (*SE* XII, 57 and 62), for example, but the German there reads *Versagung* (*GW* VIII, 293 and 298), which Lacan says implies renunciation, not frustration (see *Écrits* 1966, 460–61).

(691,1) Love as "giving what you don't have" is a major theme in Seminar VIII (see, for example, pages 46 and 157), but was introduced by him a number of years earlier.

(691,2) *Aufhebt* is a verb form of *Aufhebung*, an Hegelian term now often translated into English as "sublation," the infinitive verb form being "to sublate." Alternate reading for "the crushing brought on by the demand for love": "the crushing (or annihilation) of the demand for love."

(691,4) Note that *signifier* (signifying) also means to legally notify or serve a notice.

(692,2) A reference to Franz Alexander's *The Psychoanalysis of the Total Personality: The Application of Freud's Theory of the Ego to the Neuroses* (New York: Nervous and Mental Disease Publishing Company, [1927] 1930).

(692,4) *Attraper* (grasped) could also be rendered here as "grabbed."

(692,fn1) Note that *Pudeur* (Shame) is better translated as "modesty" in most contexts.

(693,1) *Raison du désir* also means the "reason for desire" and "desire's reason."

(693,9) *L'épreuve du désir* (the test constituted by desire) can be understood as "the test (or testing) of desire," "desire as a test," "desire's acid-test," or "the ordeal, trial, or test (the subject undergoes) due to desire." *L'épreuve du désir de l'Autre* (the test constituted by the Other's desire) two paragraphs further on can be understood along the same lines.

(694,1) *Manque à avoir* could also be translated as "want-to-have" or "lack-in-having."

(694,5) *Paraître* could also be translated as "appearing." There seems to be a problem in the French here, given the parallel structure Lacan sets up here: ". . . in one case, . . . in the other" (the French reads *dans l'autre* instead of *de l'autre*). In any case, it seems clear that the protecting has to do with men and the masking with women.

(695,1) See Freud's article, "On the Universal Tendency to Debasement in the Sphere of Love" (1912), *SE* XI, 177–90.

(695,3) *L'Autre de l'Amour* (Loving Other)

could also be rendered as "the Other of Love," "the Other who gives Love," or "the Other involved in Love." *Recul* (backcourt) can also mean recoil, backward movement, stepping back, distance, distancing, and background.

Notes to "The Subversion of the Subject"

(793,3) The proceedings of the Bonneval Colloquium, published six years after the Colloquium was held as *"L'Inconscient". VIe Colloque de Bonneval, 1960* (Paris: Desclée de Brouwer, 1966), did not come out until after *Écrits* was published in 1966.

(793,4) See Jacques Lacan, *Le Séminaire, Livre V, Les Formations de l'inconscient, 1957–1958* (Paris: Seuil, 1998), edited by Jacques-Alain Miller.

(795,4) *Doubler* (doubling) also means to line (as when one lines a coat with another layer of fabric).

(796,fn2) *Respectueuse* (respectable girl) is a reference to Sartre's play, *La putain respectueuse* (Paris: Nagel, 1946).

(797,1) *L'écliptique* could refer to eclipses or to the ecliptic, the plane of the earth's path around the sun; the earth's axis forms an angle of about 23 degrees 27 minutes with respect to the ecliptic, which may be the way in which the earth "bows assent."

(797,3) "Ellipse" derives from the Greek *elleipsis* meaning lack. Regarding "celestial revolutions," cf. the title of Copernicus' work, *De revolutionibus orbium coelestium.*

(797,5) Copernicus seems to come up with a model in which the sun is at the center of the universe *in order to simplify computation* of the positions of the heavenly bodies, and seems to divorce the model from Truth as revealed in Scripture.

(797,8) The French at the end of the first sentence, *ce qui manque à la réalisation du savoir*, could also be translated as follows: "what is missing when knowledge is realized."

(798,1) *Principielle* (principial) means relative to a principle as the first cause of a thing.

(798,3) *À se donner voix fort confuse dans les grandes consciences* (confusedly given voice to by the great minds) could also be translated as "confusing the great minds."

(799,2) "Skew" is included by Lacan in the original as a translation for *de travers* (skewed).

(799,3) "Protopathic" to be understood in the etymological sense of the term: originally feeling, experiencing, or suffering.

(799,4) The parenthetical reference is to the phrase *ein anderer Schauplatz* found in *SE* V, 536, and *SE* VIII, 176.

(799,5) In particular, the mechanisms of condensation and displacement belong to the primary process. See "The Instance of the Letter," above all *Écrits* 1966, 511.

(800,3) I have adopted the following convention in this article: I have rendered je as I, Je as *I*, and *Je* as *I*. *Le sujet de l'énoncé* has been rendered here as "the subject of the statement," while *le sujet de l'énonciation* has been rendered as "the enunciating subject." The latter could also be rendered as "subject of (the) enunciation."

(800,5) Under the assumption that "but" or "not but" in English serves a function similar to that of the so-called expletive *ne* in French, I have attempted to provide English sentences here that illustrate the same point as Lacan's French.

(800,6) *Tue* is the first and third person singular of *tuer*, to kill, in the present and present subjunctive tenses, as well as the imperative, "kill." *Ils m'assomment* (they are killing me) also means they are boring me to death or overwhelming me. *Tu* is the informal form of "you," and *toise* also contains *toi* (you).

(800,9) *Interdit* (without the dash) means prohibited, interdicted, or forbidden; *inter-dit* may be a French translation of the Greek μη όν (another translation being *dit-que-non*), a kind of no-saying or nay-saying. Cf. Seminar IX, *Identification*. The French text in this paragraph is immensely complicated and my impression is that the third to last *la* should be deleted.

(801,2) See Mallarmé's preface to René Ghil's *Traité du Verbe* (1866) in Stéphane Mallarmé, *Oeuvres complètes* (Paris: Gallimard, 1945), 368 and 857.

(801,3) The first few words of the paragraph, *Cette coupure de la chaîne signifiante*, could also be translated as "The cut [the analyst makes] in the signifying chain," "The signifying chain as cut," or "The signifying chain's cut."

(801,4) The German text is found in *GW* XV, 86; in English, see *SE* XXII, 80.

(801,5) *Fut* (was) is a *passé simple* or historical past tense. *Eût été* (might have been) is a pluperfect subjunctive.

(801,6) The French imperfect *était* allows for at least two different translations: "was" or "was to be" (in the sense of was supposed to be or designed to be, it not being specified if it actually came to be); Lacan refers, in Seminar XV (January 10, 1968), to the French linguist Gustave Guillaume (1883–1960) on this point. *Là où c'était pour un peu* (where it was for a short while) can also be rendered as "where it would have been if not for [something that happened]" or "where it would only have taken a little bit more for it to be." Note that *peut* is the third person singular form of the present verb, *pouvoir*, not the first. *Écrits* 1966 mistakenly reads *peux*; the Points edition corrects this.

(801,7) The reflexive verbs here could be translated differently: "An enunciation that is denounced, a statement that is renounced, an ignorance that is dissipated, an opportunity that is missed . . ."

(802,1) In the English translation, the sentence reads as follows: "his father had really died, only without knowing it" (*SE* XII, 225–26). In *The Interpretation of Dreams*, the same dream is recounted in the following terms: "he had really died, only he did not know it" (*SE* V, 430).

(802,4) The French imperfect in the second sentence, *il savait*, allows for two different translations: "A bit later he knew" and "He was supposed to find out a bit later." I try to suggest a similar ambiguity with the wording I provide here.

(803,3) *En position de signifiant* (in signifying position) could also be translated as "in the position of a signifier." The French at the end of the paragraph, *cet objet est le prototype de la signifiance du corps comme enjeu de l'être*, can be translated in a number of other ways: "this object is the prototype of the body qua signifierness as being's stakes" or "of the body's significance as what is at stake for being (or for human beings)."

(803,6) *Du peu de physiologie que l'inconscient intéresse*, could also be translated as "how little physiology the unconscious involves (or brings into play)."

(804,1) In the first sentence, *le réel du corps et de l'imaginaire de son schéma mental*, is somewhat ambiguous; if the first *de* is simply an error, which seems likely to me, and is removed we could translate as follows: "psychoanalysis concerns the reality (or real) of the body and the imaginary of its mental schema (or its mental schema as imaginary)."

(804,3) *D'aujourd'hui* (contemporary) is a probable reference to the collection entitled *La Psychanalyse d'aujourd'hui* ("Contemporary Psychoanalysis") discussed by Lacan in "Direction of the Treatment."

(805,2) A "button tie" is a stitch used by an upholsterer to secure a button to fabric and stuffing, for example, to prevent the stuffing from moving; it is, I think, the closest English term to the upholsterer's term Lacan uses: *point de capiton*. Russell Grigg, in his translation of Lacan's Seminar, Book III, *The Psychoses* (New York: Norton, 1993), renders *capitonnage* as "quilting" and *point de capiton* as "quilting point"; see 293–305. *Rétrograde*, apart from its usual meaning (retrograde), takes on the specific mathematical meaning of "negatively oriented" in relation to vectors. In the last sentence of the paragraph, Lacan is playing on the French expression, *noyer le poisson*, literally "to drown the fish," figuratively, to bury the subject being discussed or sidestep the issue.

(805,4) *Le chien fait miaou, le chat fait oua oua* (the dog goes meow, the cat goes woof-woof) is a nursery rhyme or song in which various animals are attributed the wrong sound. The French at the end of the paragraph, *ouvre la diversité des objectiva-*

tions à vérifier, de la même chose (makes necessary the verification of multiple objectifications of the same thing), is somewhat obscurely phrased but seems to imply that the child's contempt for verisimilitude is such that the same thing (e.g., an animal) can be characterized or objectified in multiple manners (e.g., by different cries), and we have to look to experience to verify which of them is correct.

(806,1) The *jeu des quatre coins* (four-corners game) is a sort of musical chairs game with five players; four players begin in the four corners of a quadrilateral, and have to try to change corners while the fifth player tries to claim one of the corners for him- or herself. The four corners may be a reference to the quadripartite structure of metaphor adumbrated by Lacan in June of 1960 and written up in "Metaphor of the Subject," *Écrits* 1966, 889–92.

(806,2) I have translated *connoté* here, and in the next sentence, by "labeled," as it does not seem to me that Lacan is referring to the connotation/denotation distinction. Saussure uses the term *trésor* (treasure or treasure trove) to describe language (*langue*) in *Cours de linguistique générale*, ed. Tullio de Mauro (Paris: Payot, [1915] 1972), 30. It is translated as "fund" in *Course in General Linguistics*, trans. Roy Harris (Chicago: Open Court, 1983), 13.

(806,5) This passage clearly evokes Lacan's early paper, "Logical Time and the Assertion of Anticipated Certainty," trans. B. Fink and M. Silver, *Newsletter of the Freudian Field* 2 (1988). *Insignifiante* (meaningless) could, alternatively, be rendered as "insignificant" or "nonsignifying."

(806,6) Presumably "making his own calculations" regarding the Other's strategy.

(807,2) See *Hegel's Phenomenology of Spirit*, trans. A. V. Miller (Oxford: Oxford University Press, 1977), 117. *Préalable* (preliminary) can also be rendered as "prerequisite" or "prior."

(807,4) *Parade* (display) is also a fencing term (as are *feinte*, feint, and *rupture*, retreat) that can be translated as "parry" or "parade"; it also means (ceremonial) display.

(808,2) "The first words spoken": *Le dit premier.*

(808,3) See *SE* XIX, 31.

(809,3) *Trait unaire de l'idéal du moi* (the ego-ideal as unary trait) could also be translated as "the ego-ideal's unary trait."

(809,4) *Écrits* 1966 mistakenly reads $\overrightarrow{s(A).A}$; this is corrected in Points. See Damourette and Pichon, *Des mots à la pensée: Essai de grammaire de la langue française*, 7 vols. (Paris: Bibliothèque du français moderne, 1932–51). Note that *étoffée* (filled out) can also mean stuffed or enriched, and that *subtile* (ethereal) can also mean subtle or rarefied.

(809,fn2) See, in particular, Seminar IX (1961–62), *L'identification* (unpublished).

(810,2) *Fléau* (balance arm) also means scourge, curse, bane, or plague. Cf. *Écrits* 1966, 99.

(810,fn1) The seminar referred to here was edited by Jacques-Alain Miller and published by Seuil in 1986. It was translated into English by Dennis Porter as *The Seminar of Jacques Lacan, Book VII: The Ethics of Psychoanalysis* (New York: Norton, 1992).

(811,2) See Lacan's 1953 paper, "Le mythe individuel du névrosé ou poésie et vérité dans la névrose," published in *Ornicar?* 17/18 (1979): 289–307. In English, see "The Neurotic's Individual Myth," *PQ* XLVIII (1979): 405–25. *L'histoire* (the story) could also be translated as "history."

(811,5) Taking *relever* (redeemed) differently here, *que ne relèvent même plus ses mollesses* could also be translated as "that is no longer even highlighted by its lack of verve (or lifelessness)."

(811,8) *Saugrenu* (ludicrousness) means bizarre, unexpected, and somewhat ridiculous.

(812,2) *Fêlure* (flaw) also means crack, fissure, fracture, and split.

(812,3) *Guignol* (puppet) also means someone who is funny or ridiculous without trying to be.

(812,fn1) Lacan had initially entitled the seminar to be held in 1963–1964, "The Names-of-the-Father"; owing to Lacan's exclusion from the Société Française de Psychanalyse, only one class of the intended seminar was given, an English translation of which can be found in *Television: A Challenge to the Psychoanalytic Establishment*, ed. Joan Copjec (New York: Norton, 1990). The seminar that was given instead was the *Four Fundamental Concepts of Psychoanalysis* (Seminar XI), given under the auspices of the École Normale Supérieure at the invitation of Louis Althusser. I have assumed that there is a negation missing at the beginning of the note, for the French reads *fût-ce en termes plus vigoureux* (even if in stronger terms) instead of *ne fût-ce en termes plus vigoureux*.

(813,3) See Seminar VIII, 121–22.

(813,4) *Le*, which I have translated here as "it" (in "to seek it") would seem to refer back to "guarantee," but in that case it would have to be *la*. The only masculine nouns it could refer to are "the Other" or "locus."

(813,7) Lacan is playing on the expression *ébats amoureux*, which can mean lovemaking, making out, petting, and so on. He splits the expression such that *l'amour* (love) appears before the dash and *d'ébat* (which is usually plural, not singular as it is here) appears after it in a context where *débat* (debate) would usually go. *Ébat* alone also means frolicking.

(813,9) Here as elsewhere, *désir de l'Autre* (the Other's desire) could also be translated as "desire for the Other" or "desire for what the Other desires."

(814,1) *Vertige* is more polyvalent than "vertigo," connoting not only giddiness, but also intoxication, madness, temptation, and confusion.

(814,3) The "shred of blanket" is often referred to as a tickle blanket, blankey, or nappy. On the transitional object, see D. W. Winnicott, "Transitional Objects and Transitional Phenomena," in *IJP* XXXIV (1953), reprinted in D. W. Winnicott, *Through Pediatrics to Psycho-Analysis* (New York: Brunner/Mazel, 1992), 229–42.

(814,4) *Représentant de la représentation* (representation's representative) is Lacan's translation for Freud's *Vorstellungsrepräsentanz*, rendered in the *Standard Edition* by "ideational representative," and generally concerns something that stands in for (or represents) the drive at the "ideational" level

(i.e., at the level of representation); it could also be translated as "the representative of representation." In Seminar VII, Lacan equates Freud's *Vorstellungsrepräsentanz* with the signifier (pages 75–76/61).

(814,6) The French here could also be translated as "discourse on (or concerning) the Other." The deliberately incorrect (forced) Latin, *de Alio in oratione*, could be translated as "concerning the Other in discourse (or the Other who is speaking)," and *tua res agitur* as "it concerns you" or "your interest is at stake. "*Tua res agitur* comes from Horace's *Epistles*, Book 1, Epistle 18, where we find "Nam tua res agitur, paries cum proximus ardet, et neglecta solent incendia sumere vires." This has been translated as " 'Tis your own safety that's at stake when your neighbor's wall is in flames, and fires neglected are wont to gather strength." Freud modifies the phrase in *SE* V (441) as does Lacan in *Écrits* 1966 (574); cf. "Father, don't you see I'm burning," *SE* V, 509.

(815,1) Lacan borrows this "*Chè vuoi?*" from Jacques Cazotte's *Le diable amoureux* (1772); see, in particular, the annotated French edition by Annalisa Bottacin (Milan: Cisalpino-La Goliardica, 1983), pages 56–57. In English, see *The Devil in Love* (New York: Houghton Mifflin, 1925).

(815,3) *Clé universelle* (master key) is also the technical term for a specific tool, known in English as an adjustable spanner, monkey wrench, or pipe wrench, that resembles Graph 3 in certain respects. Lacan makes it clear in Seminar XV (January 17, 1968) that what he has in mind here is "the key that opens all boxes," that is, a "skeleton key" or a "master key."

(816,4) *Se règle sur* (adjusts to) can also be translated as "models itself on," "adapts itself to," or even "targets." Note that while (on Graph 3) desire (*d*) is on the right and fantasy ($S\Diamond a$) is on the left, the ego (*m*) is on the left and the body image, *i(a)*, is on the right. This is, I believe, the "inversion" Lacan is referring to here. The French at the end of the paragraph, *là où s'était l'inconscient*, provides a reflexive where Lacan's more usual translation of Freud's *Wo Es war, soll Ich werden* reads *là où c'était. S'était* and *c'était* are homonyms. Cf. "The Freudian Thing."

(816,5) *Étoffe* (stuff) also means fabric, cloth, and material. I translate it in the same way throughout this article.

(816,7) *Repérage* (pinpointing) means position finding, getting one's bearings, finding landmarks helping one get oriented, identification, registration, marking out, and locating. It is sometimes translated as "mapping."

(817,1) See, in particular, "Instincts and Their Vicissitudes," *SE* XIV, 126–35. For early commentary on the Graph, see Seminar V; for later commentary on the Graph, see Seminar XVI, December 11, 1968, and January 8, 1969.

(818,1) See *Écrits* 1966, 54–55, where Lacan uses the same term, *doublure* (lining).

(818,2) In French, *proie* (translated here as "substance") is usually "prey," but is also used in the phrase *lacher la proie pour l'ombre* ("to drop the substance for the shadow" or "to give up what one already has for some uncertain alternative").

(819,2) *Un trait qui se trace de son cercle* (a line that is drawn from its circle) seems to be a direct commentary on the Complete Graph; a few pages back, Lacan tells us that the drive ($\$\lozenge D$) is the treasure trove of signifiers, and S(A) is found at the end of a line drawn from the circle that contains ($\$\lozenge D$). Elsewhere, I have translated *trait* as "characteristic." The verb *tracer* could also be interpreted in the sense of "to blaze (a trail)" or "to outline" here.

(819,4) See, for example, *Écrits* 1966, 515.

(819,5) *Ce qu'il est d'impensable* (what is unthinkable about him) literally means "what he is that is unthinkable," i.e., his "unthinkableness." *En défaut* (missing) can take on a number of different meanings: in error, at fault, in the wrong, or failing to fulfill one's commitments.

(819,6) Earlier (*Écrits* 1966, 802) Lacan mentioned the father, in a dream Freud recounts, who "did not know he was dead."

(820,1) *Inconsistant* (inconsistent) can also mean insubstantial or weak.

(820,3) *Avec sa dialectique* (by means of its

dialectic) could alternatively be translated as "along with its (or his, i.e., Freud's) dialectic."

(820,5) *Os* (literally "bone") would normally be translated as "hitch" in this context, but given that Lacan is discussing the castration complex here, the slang meaning, "hard-on," should probably be kept in mind.

(820,6) See Edmund Husserl, *The Crisis in the European Sciences and Transcendental Phenomenology*, trans. David Carr (Evanston: Northwestern University Press, 1970).

(821,1) On the alternation from the similar (*semblable*) to the dissimilar, see the "Presentation of the Suite" to the "Seminar on 'The Purloined Letter,' " *Écrits* 1966, 41–61.

(821,3) See Lévi-Strauss' comments on the "zero-phoneme" in *Introduction à l'oeuvre de Marcel Mauss* (Paris: PUF, 1950); in English, see *Introduction to the Work of Marcel Mauss*, trans. Felicity Baker (London: Routledge & Kegan Paul, 1987). "Used automatically": that is, as mathematicians use it.

(821,5) *Sous-entendue* (understood) means the jouissance is implied or hinted at.

(822,4) *Caducité* (falling off) comes from the Latin *caducus* and *cadere*, meaning to fall. Ordinary modern meanings include out-of-date, null and void, and dépassé; in botany, *organes caducs* are parts of a plant that are designed to detach themselves from the plant and fall off. Assuming there were no mistake in the French at the end of the sentence, *où vient s'achever l'exclusion où elle se trouve de l'image spéculaire et du prototype qu'elle constitue pour le monde des objets*, would be translated as follows: "in which is completed its exclusion from the specular image and from the prototype it constitutes for the world of objects." Since the phallus here seems to constitute the prototype of the world of objects, I have assumed that the last *du* in the sentence should in fact be *le*; Lacan could, however, be saying that it constitutes the prototype and yet is excluded therefrom.

(822,6) *Pour ces raisons de forme* (for reasons of form) could also be translated as "for these formal reasons" or "for these reasons of shape," or possibly even "for form's sake."

(823,2) In *la fonction du signifiant imaginaire* (the signifier's imaginary function), the adjective "imaginary" could grammatically qualify either "function" or "signifier," but there doesn't seem to me to be any such thing in Lacan's work as an "imaginary signifier."

(823,4) *D'un côté à l'autre de l'équation de l'imaginaire au symbolique* (from one side to the other of the equation between the imaginary and the symbolic) could alternatively be translated as "from one side of the equation to the other, from the imaginary to the symbolic." The equation in question is, I suspect, the one found on page 819, with $(-\varphi)$ equated with s, as indicated on page 822.

(824,1) Alternate for "to posit fantasy as the Other's desire": "to posit fantasy as what the Other desires."

(824,2) *Se porter caution de l'Autre* (to be the Other's guarantor) could also be translated as "to stand security for the Other" or "to be surety for the Other," both financial metaphors.

(824,3) The parenthetical clarification Lacan provides here, "that is, her desire," remains ambiguous since he says *son désir* (one's desire) instead of *son désir à elle* (her desire). An alternate translation for the text between the dashes, *Autre réel de la demande dont on voudrait qu'elle calme le désir (c'est-à-dire son désir)*, would be: "the real Other of the demand with which we wish she would calm desire (that is, our desire)." *Fermerait les yeux* (would turn a blind eye) may be a reference to one of Freud's dreams, recounted in *The Interpretation of Dreams*, that includes the line "You are requested to close the eyes" (*SE* IV, 317–18).

(824,4) The French at the end of the paragraph, *ce qui vaudrait autant pour le sujet*, could also be translated as "which would amount to the same thing (or more) for the subject."

(825,1) *S'assurer de* (ensure control over) can mean to verify or become sure of, but when it is used in reference to a person it means to maintain control over or keep in one's possession. In reference to God, it could mean to verify or assure oneself of God's existence.

(825,2) *En tant que* (in the guise of) could also be translated as "qua." *À ciel ouvert* (right out in the open) is the expression Lacan uses to describe the unconscious in psychosis. An alternate translation for the sentence would be: "But this does not mean that the pervert wears his unconscious on his sleeve."

(825,4) See Plato's *Symposium* and Lacan's detailed commentary on it in Seminar VIII.

(826,3) *Imagination* (imagination) can also mean chimera, dream, or imagining.

(827,7) *Parler pour le tableau noir* (talking to a brick wall) literally means speaking for the blackboard.

Clarification

1. The reader will find in this index, prepared according to an order that I have established, the major concepts of Lacan's theory, keyed to the contexts here that provide their essential definitions, functions, and principal properties.

2. On the pages listed after each term in the index, it is the concept that must be looked for, not the word. I have chosen to designate what is subsumed by the expression that seemed to me most adequate and most comprehensive, usually proceeding retroactively from the latest stage of the theory.

3. It did not escape me that, with such an articulation, I was offering an interpretation. It thus seemed opportune to me to explain it briefly, so that one might, after following my reasoning, deduct it from the sum of the index.

4. I have opted to isolate the concepts which, touching on the theory of the subject, concern the human sciences as a whole, if only by denying them their name, with the effect of punctuating the specificity of analytic experience (in its Lacanian definition: the bringing into play of the reality of the unconscious, the introduction of the subject to the language of his desire).

5. If the signifier is constitutive for the subject (I, A), we may follow, through its defiles, the process of transformation (mutilation) that makes a subject of man by means of narcissism (I, B). The properties of symbolic overdetermination explain why the logical time of this history is not linear (I, C).

6. We must next consider in their simultaneity the elements successively presented (II, A, B, C). We will note that the topology of the subject finds its status only by being related to the geometry of the ego (II, B, 4 and II, C, 3). Then we will be able to grasp the functioning of communication: all the pieces of the game fall into place in its structure (II, D).

7. From the structure of communication, we will deduce the power of the treatment, with what ear to listen to the unconscious, and what training to give analysts (III, A, B). The last part (III, C) is centered on the eminent signifier of desire. The following section (IV) is clinical (its inventory is succinct).

8. As for Lacanian epistemology, it marks, in my sense, psychoanalysis' position *in* the epistemological break, insofar as the subject foreclosed from science returns in the *impossible* of his discourse through the Freudian field. There is, therefore, but one ideology Lacan theorizes: that of the "modern ego," that is, the paranoiac subject of scientific civilization, whose imaginary is theorized by a warped psychology in the service of free enterprise.

9. The density of certain texts makes it pointless to break them down in the index. This includes the "Introduction to the Seminar on 'The Purloined Letter' " (the theory of the chain), "Kant with Sade" (desire and the Law, the structure of fantasy), "Subversion of the Subject and Dialectic of Desire" (the subject and the signifier), and "Position of the Unconscious" (desire and fantasy, alienation and splitting).

10. Let me add here that it is clear that Lacanian discourse is closed to enthusiasm, having recognized in what is known as its "openness" the progress of a systematization whose coherence was definitively established by the Rome Paper ["Function and Field"], and whose closure was assured. This is why, according to my conception of these *Écrits*, it is to our benefit to study them as forming a system, despite the elliptical style, necessary, Lacan says, to the training of analysts. For my own part, not needing to concern myself with the theory's efficacy in that field, I will encourage the reader by proposing that there is no outer limit (that is, not produced by the functioning of thought under the

constraint of its structure) to the expansion of formalization in the field of discourse, in that there is no locus where its power fails whose circumference it cannot discern—and eliminate the hole by changing syntax. We must be prepared to see its negative reform elsewhere. I am referring to Boole, to Carnap, and to Guéroult's studies on Berkeley.

Jacques-Alain Miller

[N.B.: Page numbers correspond to the French pagination in the margins. Italicized page numbers reference the most important passages.]

I. The Symbolic Order

A. THE SUPREMACY OF THE SIGNIFIER

B. THE DEFILES OF THE SIGNIFIER

C. THE SIGNIFYING CHAIN

1. Repetition (repetition automatism, the insistence of the chain): 318, 502–503, 557 (see: *Regression*).

2. Overdetermination and logical time (anticipation and retroaction; chance, encounter, and fate): 256–57, 287, 552, 554, 808.

3. Recalling, remembering: 431–32 (contrasted with imaginary reminiscence), *518–19.*

4. Death, the second death, the death drive, the real as impossible, the being of entities: 101, *123–24, 316–21, 430, 520, 552, 573, 810–11.*

897

II. *The Ego, the Subject*

A. THE BODY, THE EGO, THE SUBJECT
(THE ORGANISM, ONE'S OWN BODY, THE FRAGMENTED BODY)

(see: *The mirror stage, The subject of the chain*)

94, 97, *104–105, 262–63, 280, 301,* 415, 513, *552,* 610, *803–4, 817–18.*

B. THE FUNCTION OF THE EGO

(see: *The genesis of the ego, The theory of ideology*)

1. The illusion of autonomy.
a. Misrecognition: 99, *109–14,* 249–50, *428.*
b. The paranoiac structure of the ego (and of human knowledge): *96, 111, 428.*
c. Staging: *512–13, 637* (see: *Desire and Fantasy*).
d. Defense: 98, 103 (see: *"Frustration," Resistance*).
e. Love and hate: 100, 264, 605, 618 (see: *Primordial symbolization, Narcissism, Object* a).

2. Projection.
a. Identification with the other, transitivism, projection, the dyadic relation: 102, 109, *423–24.*

b. The animal (animal psychology): *95–96,* 300, *496, 551, 807.*
c^1. Hegelian categories: the struggle to the death, recognition, prestige, the absolute Master: 120–23, 250, *314, 432–33, 809–10.*
c^2. Self-consciousness, infatuation, the beautiful soul, the law of the heart, the cunning of Reason, absolute knowledge: *292–93,* 409, *415, 797–99.*

3. "Group psychology": 639–40 (see: *Ego-ideal, Unary trait*).

4. Geometry of the ego (imaginary space): 96, *122–23,* 310, *423–24* (see: *Topology of the subject*).

C. THE STRUCTURE OF THE SUBJECT

1. The true subject.
a. The subject of the chain: *285–86, 531–33, 551.*
b^1. The subject of science: *281–83,* 576,

793–94 (see: *Psychoanalysis and science*).
b^2. *"Wo Es war, soll Ich werden": 416–18, 524, 801–2,* 816.
b^3. *"Cogito, (ergo) sum": 516–17, 809.*

898

C. THE PHALLUS

IV. Clinical Practice

A. Freud's Cases

B. PSYCHIATRY'S CLINICAL CATEGORIES

V. Epistemology and Theory of Ideology

A. Epistemology

1. The epistemological break (the example of physics): 103, *284*, 401, 531, 796–97.

2. Truth
a. Truth as fiction, as secret, as symptom: *255–56, 286, 313* (opposed to exactness), 411, *807–8.*

b. Psychoanalysis and science: *266, 284, 288–89, 513, 527.*

3. Conjecture   902
a. The conjectural ("human") sciences: *277, 284 89*, 496–98.
b. Psychology as science; its object: *419.*

B. The Theory of Ideology

1. The ideology of freedom: theory of the autonomous ego, humanism, human rights, responsibility, anthropomorphism, ideals, instinctual maturation, etc.: 121 22, 262 64, 421, *517, 576, 590–91,* 808.

2. The ideology of free enterprise: the American way of life, human relations, human engineering, brain trust, success, happiness, happy ending, basic personality, pattern, etc.: 245–46, 402–3, 416, 591, *604.*

Commentary on the Graphs

If it is true that perception eclipses structure, a schema will infallibly lead the subject "to forget, because of an intuitive image, the analysis on which this image is based" (*Écrits* 1966, 574).

It is the task of symbolism to prohibit imaginary capture—by which its difficulty follows from the theory.

While reading some clarifications about Lacan's schemas, this warning should not be forgotten.

The fact remains that such a precaution reveals the a priori lack of correspondence between a graphic representation and its object (the *object* of psychoanalysis) *in the space of intuition* (defined, if you will, by Kant's aesthetic). Thus all the constructions gathered together here (with the exception of the networks of overdetermination which function in the signifier's order) have only a didactic role: their relation to the structure is one of analogy.

On the other hand, *there is no longer any occultation of the symbolic* in the topology that Lacan establishes, because this space is the very space in which the subject's logical relations are schematized.

The inadequacy of analogies is unequivocally pointed out by Lacan in the optical model of the ideals of the person, precisely in the absence of the symbolic object *a*. From the note added to the **R** schema (*Écrits* 1966,

553–54), one may learn the rules by which to transform intuitive geometry into the topology of the subject.

J.-A. M.

I. The Schema of the Intersubjective Dialectic   904
("L Schema," 548)

The schema shows that the dyadic relation between the ego and its projection *a a′* (indifferently its image and that of the other) constitutes an obstacle to the advent of the subject, S, in the locus of its signifying determination, A. The quaternary is fundamental: "A quadripartite structure can always be required—from the standpoint of the unconscious—in the construction of a subjective ordering" (*Écrits* 1966, 774). Why? Because to restore the imaginary relation in the structure that stages it leads to a duplication of its terms: the other with a lowercase o [designated as *a* on the schema] being raised to the power of the Other with a capital O [designated as A on the schema], the cancellation of the subject of the signifying chain doubling the ego. Symmetry or reciprocity belongs to the imaginary register, and the position of the Third Party implies that of the fourth, who is given, depending on the levels of analysis, the name of "barred subject" or dummy (*mort*). (See 589, analytic bridge).

II. The Structure of the Subject   905
(The R Schema, 553; Schreber's Schema (I), 571)

1. Composition of the symbolic, the imaginary, and the real ("R Schema").

The **R** schema is made up of the union of two triangles, the symbolic ternary and the imaginary ternary, by the quadrangle of the real, delimited in a square by the base of each triangle. If the triangle of the symbolic occupies half of the square all by itself, the other two figures sharing the other half, it is because, in structuring them, it must overlap them in the drawing.   906
The dotted line stands for the imaginary.

This construction requires a twofold reading:

1. It may be read as a representation of the statics of the subject. One can thus distinguish: (a) the triangle **I** resting on the dyadic relation between the Ego and the Other (narcissism, projection, capture), with, as its apex, φ, the

phallus, the imaginary object, "the one where the subject is identified, on the contrary, with his living being" (552), that is, the form in which the subject represents himself to himself; (b) the field **S**, with the three functions of the Ego-ideal, I, in which the subject situates himself in the register of the symbolic (see the optical model), of the signifier of the object, M, of the Name-of-the-Father, P [for *père*], and in the locus of the Other, A. The line I M may be regarded as doubling the relation between the subject and the object of desire through the mediation of the signifying chain, a relation that Lacan's algebra later wrote as $\$ \lozenge a$ (but the line immediately proves to be an inadequate representation); (c) the field **R**, framed and maintained by the imaginary relation and the symbolic relation.

2. But it is also the subject's history that is noted here: along the segment *i* M are situated the figures of the imaginary other, which culminate in the figure of the mother, the real Other, inscribed in the symbolic under the signifier of the primordial object, the subject's first outside, which bears in Freud's work the name *das Ding* (cf. *Écrits* 1966, 656); along the segment *m* I follow the imaginary identifications that form the child's ego until he receives his status in the real from symbolic identification. One thus finds a specified synchrony of the ternary, **S**: the child in I is linked to the mother in M, as desire for her desire; in the tertiary position is the Father, conveyed by the mother's speech.

In his note added in 1966, Lacan shows how to translate this square into his topology. The surface **R** is to be taken as the flattening out of the figure that would be obtained by joining *i* to I and *m* to M, that is, by the twist that characterizes the Möbius strip in complete space: the presentation of the schema in two dimensions is thus related to the cut that spreads the strip out. This explains why the straight line I M cannot refer to the relation between the subject and the object of desire: the subject is merely the cut of the strip, and what falls from it is called object *a*. This verifies and complements Jean-Claude Milner's formulation regarding "$\$ \lozenge a$": "the terms are heterogeneous, although there is homogeneity attached to the places" (*Cahiers pour l'analyse* 3 [1966]: 96). Therein lies the power of the symbol.

2. Schreber's schema.
"Schema of the subject's structure at the end of the psychotic process."

This schema is a variation of the preceding one: the foreclosure of the Name-of-the-Father (here P_0), which leads to the absence of representation of the subject, S, by the phallic image (Φ_0 here), skews the relation among the three fields: the divergence of the imaginary and the symbolic, the reduction of the real to the slippage between them. The point *i* of the delusional ego is substituted for the subject, while the ego-ideal, I, takes the place of the Other. The trajectory S *a a*′A is transformed into the trajectory *i a a*′I.

907

III. The Graphs of Desire
(Graph 1, 805; Graph 2, 808; Graph 3, 815; Graph 4, 817)

On Graph 1, one may read the inversion that constitutes the subject in his traversing of the signifying chain. This inversion takes place by *anticipation*, whose law imposes at the first intersection (on the vector $\overrightarrow{S.S'}$) the last word (also to be understood as the solution [*fin mot*], that is, punctuation), and *retroaction*, enunciated in the formulation of intersubjective communication, which necessitates a second intersection, in which the receiver and his battery are to be situated. Graph 2 combines, starting from the elementary cell, imaginary identification and symbolic identification in subjective synchrony; the signifying chain here receives its specification as speech. It becomes the vector of the drive, between desire and fantasy, in the complete graph—the intermediary graph simply punctuating the subject's question to the Other: "What does he want from me?" which is to be inverted in its return, "What do you want from me?"

908

Index of Freud's German Terms

[N.B.: Page numbers correspond to the French pagination in the margins.]

Index of Proper Names

[N.B.: Page numbers correspond to the French pagination in the margins.]